E/2008/50/Rev.1
ST/ESA/317

Department of Economic and Social Affairs

World Economic and Social Survey 2008

Overcoming Economic Insecurity

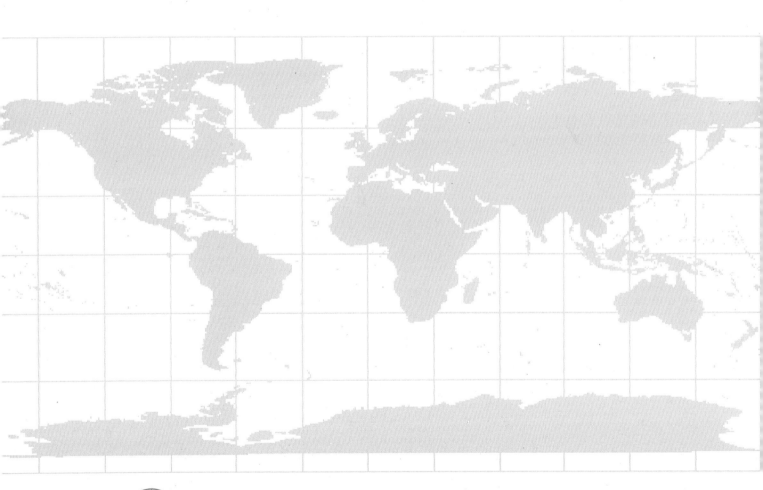

United Nations
New York, 2008

DESA

The Department of Economic and Social Affairs of the United Nations Secretariat is a vital interface between global policies in the economic, social and environmental spheres and national action. The Department works in three main interlinked areas: (i) it compiles, generates and analyses a wide range of economic, social and environmental data and information on which States Members of the United Nations draw to review common problems and to take stock of policy options; (ii) it facilitates the negotiations of Member States in many intergovernmental bodies on joint courses of action to address ongoing or emerging global challenges; and (iii) it advises interested Governments on the ways and means of translating policy frameworks developed in United Nations conferences and summits into programmes at the country level and, through technical assistance, helps build national capacities.

Note

Symbols of United Nations documents are composed of capital letters combined with figures.

E/2008/50/Rev.1
ST/ESA/317
ISBN 978-92-1-109157-1

United Nations publication
Sales No. E.08.II.C.1
Printed by the United Nations
Publishing Section
New York

Preface

In rich and poor countries alike, economic security is under threat. Sixty years ago, the Universal Declaration of Human Rights affirmed that everyone should have access to a standard of living adequate for their health and well-being, "…including food, clothing, housing and medical care and necessary social services, and the right to security in the event of unemployment, sickness, disability, widowhood, old age or other lack of livelihood in circumstances beyond his control" (article 25). Yet, despite considerable progress since then at all levels, heightened risks and new threats jeopardize a more secure future and the goal of achieving development for all.

Climate change and the damage to economic livelihoods caused by natural disasters, whether droughts in Australia or floods in Bangladesh, are stark warnings of the consequences of complacency. Health pandemics, such as that of HIV/AIDS, raise similar concerns. Further, it is the world's poorest and most vulnerable communities that are on the front line of exposure to these truly global threats. In 2008, rising food prices have triggered serious political unrest in a number of countries and led to renewed support for putting food security back in the international agenda. The recent financial turmoil in the world economy still threatens a sharp growth slowdown which will endanger livelihoods in rich and poor countries alike.

The *World Economic and Social Survey 2008* argues that unregulated markets have contributed to increased economic insecurity without providing adequate social protection. The *Survey* calls for a different approach—one that utilizes more proactive and coherent policy responses, at both national and international levels, to help communities better manage economic risks, cope with economic insecurity and secure their livelihoods. It promises to make for stimulating reading for policymaker, practitioner and concerned citizen alike.

BAN KI-MOON
Secretary-General

Overview

Insecurity spreads

When the Berlin Wall collapsed in 1989, the talk was of an emerging era—an era of widespread peace, prosperity and stability, thanks to the spread of democratic values and market forces. Bank runs, plummeting house prices, gyrating currencies, food riots, election violence, ethnic carnage—to name just some of the phenomena that have dominated the international news media over the past 12 months—were certainly not to be a part of its future.

In a poll undertaken earlier this year in 34 countries for the BBC World Service, the unchecked pace of globalization and the unfair distribution of its benefits and damages emerged as widely shared concerns. Similar findings have been reported by the Pew Foundation and the German Marshall Fund, among others. Survey evidence is no substitute for careful analysis. Still, it does highlight a growing sense of unease over the economic course that has been charted in recent years.

This unease has emerged strongly in advanced countries where increased economic insecurity has been associated with rising inequality and the squeezing of social provisioning. In middle-income countries, economic shocks, accelerated trade liberalization and premature deindustrialization have constrained economic diversification and formal job creation. In still other places, intractable poverty has fed a vicious circle of economic insecurity and political instability and, on occasion, ferocious communal violence.

These concerns have been compounded by new global threats. Climate change has become the defining generational challenge for the international community. Several increasingly destructive natural disasters have provided tangible evidence of the threat that this poses for economic livelihoods in rich and poor countries alike. Unstable financial markets and volatile capital flows are currently threatening economic livelihoods across the world economy owing to their adverse impact on productive investment, economic growth and job creation. Since early 2008, a growing mismatch between the supply of and demand for agricultural products has triggered serious political unrest in a number of countries and put the issue of food security back in the international agenda.

The attention brought to the presence of these heightened economic risks and compounded threats has often been met with the response that the forces behind them are autonomous and irresistible, and beyond our collective political control. The call invariably has been to cast aside old institutions and loyalties and embrace the new and efficient market practices of a borderless world. The *World Economic and Social Survey 2008* argues that this is the wrong response to increasing levels of economic insecurity. It calls instead for more active policy responses to help communities better manage these new risks, increased investment in preventing threatening events from emerging and more concerted efforts to strengthen the underlying social contracts which are, in the end, the real basis of a more secure, stable and just future.

The myth of the self-regulating market

The self-regulating market was the idée fixe of the late twentieth century. Freeing markets promised to unleash the wealth-creating forces of unrestricted competition and risk-taking, as well as to ensure that the resulting prosperity would be inclusive and the outcome stable. A more flexible workforce, greater asset ownership and easier access to financial markets would help households better respond to market signals and smooth incomes as well as consumption over time. Greater security would naturally follow.

Pushing this idea was always a gamble. At least since Adam Smith, careful observers have understood that markets do not regulate themselves, but depend on an array of institutions, rules, regulations and norms which help moderate their more destructive impulses, mediate possible tensions and conflicts which normally arise and facilitate peaceful bargaining over how the gains and losses from risk-taking activities are to be distributed.

The pioneers of the post-1945 mixed economy had been persuaded by the experience of the interwar years that unregulated markets were more prone to self-destruction than to self-regulation. Idle tools, wasted wealth, wretchedness and, ultimately, political strife proved too high a price to pay for stable money and flexible markets. Their stated goal was a "new deal" which would satisfy the "craving for security" without extinguishing the creative impulses generated by the market economy. Full employment would be achieved through active macroeconomic management, public goods would be provided through a larger fiscal base and markets would become a more dependable source of wealth creation through an appropriate mixture of incentives and regulation. Moreover, given the close economic ties among countries, the new consensus would have an international dimension to ensure that trade and capital flows complemented these objectives.

Dismantling the checks and balances that emerged with this consensus has proceeded at an uneven pace among the advanced countries and has often been more enthusiastically embraced in the developing world and in transition economies, where "shock therapies" promised rapid and positive effects. As part of a global trend, many of the stresses and burdens of unregulated markets have been unloaded onto individuals and households, and with diminished or only limited offsetting government responses. This has been described, with reference to the United States of America, as the "great risk shift".

Security matters

It is not easy to give a precise meaning to the term economic insecurity. Partly because it often draws on comparisons with past experiences and practices, which have a tendency to be viewed through rose-tinted lenses, and also because security has a large subjective or psychological component linked to feelings of anxiety and safety, which draw heavily on personal circumstances. Still, in general terms, economic insecurity arises from the exposure of individuals, communities and countries to adverse events, and from their inability to cope with and recover from the costly consequences of those events.

Sixty years ago, the Universal Declaration of Human Rights[1] declared:

- Everyone has the right to a standard of living adequate for the health and well-being of himself and of his family, including food, clothing,

---

1   General Assembly resolution 217A (iii).

housing and medical care and necessary social services, and the right
to security in the event of unemployment, sickness, disability, widowhood, old age or other lack of livelihood in circumstances beyond his
control.[2]

In trying to gauge the possible damage from these sources of insecurity, economists have
distinguished between *idiosyncratic risks*, generated by individual and isolated events such
as an illness, an accident or a crime, and *covariant risks*, which are attached to events that
hit a large number of people simultaneously, such as an economic shock or climatic hazard, and often involve multiple and compounding costs.

Finding the right mix of informal, market and social measures to help citizens
cope with and recover from these events, which has been a long-standing policy challenge,
has essentially meant weighing up the advantages of pooling the risks against the offsetting administrative and behavioural costs (moral hazard) that this can produce. Such
an approach is easier when the threat is small and reasonably predictable: Precautionary
savings, or spreading the risk through insurance contracts, can often suffice, particularly
in response to idiosyncratic threats. The fact that covariant risks, which carry significant
negative spillovers, are more difficult to manage in this way has led to various forms of
social insurance and assistance.

In most advanced countries, a mixture of public and private mechanisms has
been used to ensure maximum coverage and protection. In poorer countries, the mix of
options is much more limited, with greater reliance on informal mechanisms such as family support or moneylenders. Expanding those options of risk management has received
greater attention from the policy community in recent years.

However, managing risk does not exhaust the insecurity challenge, owing to
the fact that, for many of the events that threaten downside losses, the causes are more
systemic in nature, and the outcomes can be catastrophic. Such events are much more difficult to predict and to cope with. For example, this is true of economic crises but much
the same can be said of natural disasters and political conflicts. Such threats are the topic
of this year's *World Economic and Social Survey*.

It is primarily the responsibility of national Governments to address these
threats by removing underlying vulnerabilities, greatly reducing the exposure of households and communities, and supporting their recovery if disaster does strike. Such an
effort requires not only undertaking significant investment in prevention, preparation
and mitigation measures but also filling the public domain with a dense network of institutions—arising from a social contract—that can secure spaces in which individuals,
households, firms and communities are able to pursue their day-to-day activities with a
reasonable degree of predictability and stability, and with due regard for the aims and interests of others. This is particularly vital in societies with an increasingly complex division
of labour, where high levels of trust, long-term investments in physical, human and social
capital and openness to innovation and change are key ingredients of long-term prosperity
and stability. In this respect, providing economic security is a complementary component
of any virtuous circle involving creative markets and inclusive political structures.

Establishing such positive interaction appears to have become much more difficult in recent years and in some cases has even gone into reverse.

---

2   Ibid., article 25, para. 1.

Globalization and economic insecurity

Trade shocks

Few dispute that increased international trade can be a means to achieve greater national wealth. However, for some of those required to adjust to a more open economy, it can also be a source of insecurity. Policymakers in advanced countries have long recognized that increased trade has two faces and have long debated what to do about this, especially in terms of compensating the losers.

Recently, the debate has focused on "offshoring" manufacturing and service activities to lower-cost locations, leaving only core competencies at home. The process has its roots in the early 1970s, but its acceleration in recent years has coincided with the coming on tap of vast new sources of labour in the developing world, particularly in China and India, and with the proliferation of trade and investment agreements involving developed and developing countries.

The evidence does suggest that this wave of globalization has raised worker vulnerability in the industrialized countries, heightening inequality between high- and low-skill workers, dampening employment growth and lowering the overall share of wages in national income. However, these trends pre-date the recent rise in offshoring and point to other, more significant sources of rising labour-market insecurity. Just as important is the fact that increased vulnerability does not translate directly into greater economic insecurity, which depends on whether or not effective institutional supports and national policies are available to reduce and absorb the risk of sudden employment loss and provide alternative sources of income.

Managing trade pressures, however, is not the sole problem of policymakers in advanced countries. Indeed, the flip side of the offshoring of jobs by multinational companies is often low value added and unstable assembly jobs in emerging markets. Many of these countries have been trading much more in recent years, but earning less from doing so, thanks to a combination of greater capital mobility, heightened competition in labour-intensive activities and flexible markets. The fact that, all too often, such production still takes place in enclaves with the shallowest of linkages with the surrounding economy can leave them exposed to unexpected shocks if firms decide to run down or shift the activity.

Trade shocks are an even bigger challenge in countries reliant on more traditional export sectors. The contrast between East Asia and other regions is striking. The share of primary products and resource-based and low-technology manufacturing in the total exports of East Asia declined from 76 per cent in 1980 to 35 per cent in 2005. China alone reduced its share from 93 per cent in 1985 to 44 per cent in 2005. Other regions have been less successful in transforming the structure of their production for exports. South America and Central America still rely on primary products and simple manufactures (about 78 per cent of exports in 2005, down from about 90 per cent in 1983). In Africa, the concentration of exports in low value added products is even greater (83 per cent in 2005).

For many countries in Latin America and Africa, the overall impact of terms-of-trade shocks over the period 1980-2005 was negative, with a brief reversal in the second half of the 1990s, when some countries benefited from favourable movements, and again since 2003. International trade, in that sense, continues to be a major source of instability in countries with weakly diversified economies. Moreover, in some of these regions, notably Latin America, capital-account liberalization has greatly amplified trade shocks by attracting pro-cyclical capital flows. The vulnerability that this can generate was clearly demonstrated in the abrupt reversal of the net transfer of resources following the East Asian financial crisis of the late 1990s.

Policymakers have long sought ways to manage international trade in order to maximize the benefits and limit the costs. Success cases have never relied solely on trade liberalization. Offshoring in the advanced countries and trade shocks in the developing world point to a worrying shift in underlying macroeconomic conditions which has made success all the more difficult, though recent terms-of-trade gains have obscured these problems.

Unleashing global finance

Significant underlying changes in the operation of market economies have been occurring in recent years in all countries. In particular, the weight and influence of financial markets, financial actors and financial institutions have grown dramatically. This has been accompanied by a massive accumulation of financial assets and by a variety of institutional innovations that have supported growing levels of debt in the household, corporate and public sectors. In some countries, domestic financial debt as a share of gross domestic product (GDP) has risen four- or fivefold since the early 1980s. This process of "financialization" has, in turn, helped to entrench a singular macroeconomic policy focus on fighting inflationary threats.

In the decades following 1945, the business cycle was mainly driven by investment and export demand and underpinned by strong wage growth which fed into high levels of consumer spending. This was not always a stable process. Levels of volatility were often quite high, and wages, profits and tax revenues would often outpace productivity growth, leading to inflationary pressures, current-account deficits and rising indebtedness. These trends signalled to policymakers that action needed to be taken, oftentimes ending in cyclical downturn.

This pattern has been changing as debt, leverage, collateral value and expected asset prices have become dominant drivers of the cycle. The growing tendency of the financial system, including international capital flows, to assume a strongly pro-cyclical stance is a reflection of the fact that asset prices are driven not so much by improved prospects of income gains or losses as by expectations of price changes. This development derives mainly from the pro-cyclical risk attitudes of lenders and investors, underestimated in the upswing and overestimated in the downturn—attitudes encouraged by financial innovations that promise security against downside risks.

Financial booms often give rise to lopsided investments, which often involve little more than rearranging existing assets through leveraged buyouts, stock buy-backs and mergers and acquisitions, or are carried out in sectors susceptible to speculative influences, such as property markets. Unlike earlier cycles, these booms have delivered few benefits in terms of rising wages and employment. However, increased access of households to credit has meant that consumer spending can increase, even with stagnant incomes, as (rising) levels of indebtedness substitute for (falling) household savings. But as balance sheets adopt smaller margins of safety, the system becomes more and more fragile.

The shift from an income-constrained to an asset-backed economy has been supported by the liberalization of international capital markets. Indeed, the links between domestic financial markets and capital flows are much stronger in developing countries, many of which opened their capital accounts prematurely in the 1990s.

These flows have been strongly pro-cyclical. Their effects are often transmitted through public sector accounts, especially through the effects of available financing on government spending, and of interest rates on the public debt service; but the stronger effects typically run through private spending and balance sheets. During booms, private sector deficits and borrowing tend to rise and risky balance sheets to accumulate, riding on perceived "success", as typically reflected in low risk premiums and spreads. Reversals in such perceptions lead to a cut-off from external financing and provoke sudden increases in the cost of borrowing, inducing downward adjustment.

The shift towards export-led strategies in the developing world has actually accentuated this pattern in many countries. The growing influence of financial calculation has meant that commodity price volatility operates in an even more exaggerated procyclical manner, further amplified by pro-cyclical policies, among others, which expand fiscal expenditures during the boom and reduce spending when prices are down. Cutting expenditure in the downturn is reinforced by the conditionality linked to international financial assistance during crises, which involves orthodox macroeconomic stabilization policy packages.

These financial dynamics have far-reaching implications for the real economy. Episodes of exceptionally rapid economic expansion driven by financial bubbles can bring about periods of growing prosperity, but they can end very suddenly, leading to deep recessions or even longer periods of stagnation. Vulnerability to a sharp reversal of flows varies, but in many emerging markets, it is often triggered by factors beyond the control of recipient countries, including shifts in monetary and financial policies in the major industrialized countries.

The evidence suggests that, since the 1990s, the instability of investment has increased relative to GDP in both developed and developing countries. Investment cycles have become more pronounced than income cycles, a trend that is particularly acute in middle-income countries (see figure O.1). With the exception of South Asia, and despite a recent worldwide recovery, this heightened volatility has resulted in average rates of capital formation that are still well below those enjoyed in the 1970s. Infrastructure investment and additional manufacturing capacity, both critical to improving the resilience of countries against external shocks, appear to have been hardest hit.

Moreover, losses of investment, employment and income incurred during recessions are not fully recovered when the economy turns up, pulling down the longer-term average. The rise of the financial sector has, in many countries, also gone hand in hand with more flexible hiring practices. All of these factors spell considerable income and job insecurity, even under conditions of relatively strong expansion, clear sign of which has been the failure in the majority of advanced industrialized countries of the growth of labour compensation to keep pace with labour productivity, although the same trend has been apparent in emerging markets as well.

This can frequently lead to countries' appearing successful, even when the majority of their citizens are not seeing rising standards of living. Oftentimes, the flip side of this development is rising levels of income inequality. The combination of rising insecurity and inequality is one facet of what some have described as "a new gilded age".

Figure O.1
Volatility of output and fixed investment growth, developed countries, Latin America and the Caribbean, Africa and East and South Asia, 1971-2006 *(standard deviation of growth rates)*

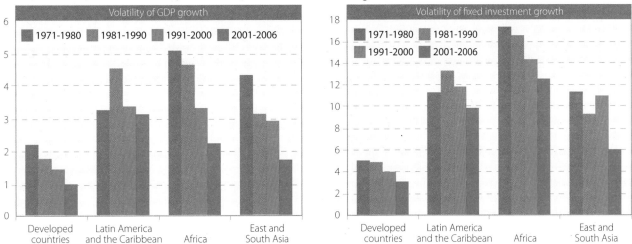

Source: UN/DESA, based on United Nations Statistics Division, National Accounts Main Aggregates database.

Managing the business cycle

Adverse external shocks transmitted through the trade and capital accounts have direct impacts on economic security and the fight against poverty, whether through wasted resources or lost output. During the 1980s and 1990s, many developing countries tried to mitigate the impacts of these shocks with policies that emphasized controlling inflation and restoring fiscal balance. This not only delayed the recovery, but has, in many cases, made it weaker and more vulnerable to future shocks. A different approach is required.

The need for counter-cyclical macroeconomic policies

Governments can enhance the scope for counter-cyclical policies by improving the institutional framework for macroeconomic policymaking. Setting fiscal targets that are independent of short-term fluctuations in economic growth (so-called structural budget rules) can be effective in forcing a counter-cyclical policy stance. Some developing countries, such as Chile, have been able to manage such fiscal rules successfully.

The establishment of commodity and fiscal stabilization funds could also help smooth out fiscal revenues, such as those based on primary export production. They are by no means a panacea, however, and careful management of such funds is required. One complication is the difficulty of distinguishing cyclical price patterns from long-term trends, in part because of the increased influence of speculative financial investments in commodity markets. This has made it more difficult for Governments to determine the adequate size of stabilization funds. It is therefore important that developing countries also be able to rely on an adequate multilateral system of compensatory financing facilities to protect them against the larger commodity price shocks (see below).

Integrated macroeconomic and development policies

Macroeconomic policies should be supportive of sustaining economic growth and employment-generation. This requires that macroeconomic policies be embedded in a broader development strategy, which was the case for the fast-growing East Asian economies. Fiscal policies would give priority to development spending, including investment in education, health and infrastructure, as well as subsidies and credit guarantees for infant industries. As with the experience of East Asia, monetary policy would be coordinated with financial sector and industrial policies, including directed and subsidized credit schemes and managed interest rates, to directly influence investment and savings. Maintaining competitive exchange rates is considered essential for encouraging export growth and diversification. In contrast, macroeconomic policies in many Latin American and African countries since the 1980s have been focused on much more narrowly defined short-term price stabilization objectives and this has often resulted in exchange-rate overvaluation and unbalanced growth.

Foreign reserve management: reducing the need for "self-insurance"

A common response in many developing countries to the vulnerability associated with sudden stops and reversals of capital flows has been a rapid build-up of reserves. Foreign reserves held by developing countries have climbed, on average, to no less than about 30 per cent of their GDP (with or without China in the sample). Even low-income countries, including the least developed countries, have increased their reserve positions to reduce their debt vulnerability. Reserves went up from 2-3 per cent of GDP in the 1980s to about 5 per cent in the 1990s and to about 12 per cent in the current decade. This has given developing countries a greater buffer or "self-insurance" to cope with external shocks; after the Asian crisis, following speculative attacks on currency-exposed countries, this appeared to be a sensible counter-cyclical strategy.

However, such a strategy carries a high price tag, both directly in terms of the high carry cost of reserves, amounting to as much as $100 billion and representing a net transfer to reserve-currency countries well above what they provide in terms of official development assistance (ODA), and in terms of forgone domestic consumption or investment. The alternative will require a strengthening of regional and global forms of financial cooperation and of macroeconomic policy coordination.

Moreover, for countries that have accumulated large amounts of resources in official reserves holdings and in sovereign wealth funds (SWFs), a small proportion of these could be set aside for development lending. Developing countries own over $4.5 trillion in official reserves and the estimated size of existing SWF assets is at least $3 trillion. Allocating just 1 per cent of those assets (or the equivalent from the asset returns) on an annual basis would amount to about $75 billion, which is triple the size of gross annual lending by the World Bank. Possibly double that development lending capacity could be created if those resources were to be allocated as paid-in capital of development banks.

Multilateral responses

A major challenge for the multilateral financial institutions is to help developing countries mitigate the damaging effects of volatile capital flows and commodity prices and provide counter-cyclical financing mechanisms to compensate for the inherently pro-cyclical movement of private capital flows. A number of options are available to dampen the pro-cyclicality of capital flows, and provide counter-cyclical finance, and thus help create a better environment for sustainable growth.

A first set of measures would include improved international financial regulation to stem capital flow volatility and provision of advice in designing appropriate capital controls, including on a counter-cyclical basis.

At the same time, there is a need for enhanced provision of emergency financing in response to external shocks, whether to the current or to the capital accounts, so as to ease the burdens of adjustment and reduce the costs of holding large reserve balances. Current mechanisms are limited in coverage, too narrowly defined, or subject to unduly strict conditionality. International Monetary Fund (IMF) facilities should be significantly simplified and should include more automatic and quicker disbursements proportionate to the scale of the external shocks. Lending on more concessional terms is highly desirable, especially for heavily indebted low-income countries. A new issuance of special drawing rights (SDRs) could be one option for financing a significant increase in the availability of compensatory financing.

Natural disasters and economic insecurity

The recent threat to global financial stability has provoked endless parallels with the impact of natural disasters. Nature can certainly be a destructive force. More than 7,000 major disasters have been recorded since 1970, causing at least $2 trillion in damage, killing at least 2.5 million people and adversely affecting the lives of countless others.

Fewer lives lost, more livelihoods threatened

Events such as the December 2004 Indian Ocean tsunami are a reminder of the deadly threat of natural forces. Yet, the number of deaths linked to such disasters has been declining, which reflects improved warning systems and more effective food and emergency aid. Other signs, however, are less encouraging: Disasters occur more than four times as frequently today than in the 1970s, displacing many more people and costing, on average, almost seven times as much (see figure O.2). As disasters have become less life-threatening, they have become much more threatening to the economic well-being of the countries and communities hit.

Precisely what role climate change has played in this trend is difficult to say, though the scientific community has no doubt that the link does exist. The business community is certainly listening. Insurance companies anticipate significant rises in climate-related losses over the next decade, which could top the one trillion dollar mark in a bad year.

Death rates from natural disasters are 20 to 30 times higher in developing than in developed countries and the recovery from disasters is much slower in the former. This uneven threat to economic security from natural hazards reflects the difficulties experienced by households, communities and Governments in preparing for them, mitigating their impact and coping with the aftermath.

High rates of poverty, high levels of indebtedness, inadequate public infrastructure, lack of economic diversification, and the like create the structural backdrop for developing countries as they face the threat of natural disaster. Moreover, poor infor-

Figure O.2
Natural disasters are claiming fewer lives, but are affecting the livelihoods of more people

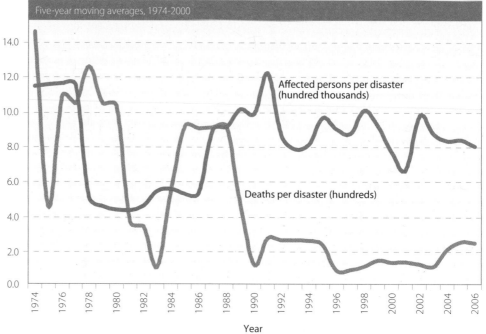

Source: UN/DESA, based on data from the OFDA/ CRED International Disaster Database (EM-DAT) (available at www.emdat.net), Université Catholique de Louvain, Brussels.

mation, inadequate access to finance, ineffective institutions and poor social networks adversely affect resilience, exacerbate impacts and reduce the quality and effectiveness of policy responses. Together, these factors expose poor countries and communities, not just to potentially catastrophic large-scale disasters, but also to frequent smaller-scale disasters which occur seasonally, such as flooding in Bangladesh and windstorms in the Caribbean and Pacific regions.

Under these conditions, families quickly exhaust coping mechanisms such as use of savings and credit, sales of assets and migration, and can be forced into more risk-bearing survival strategies such as the taking out of high-cost loans, which only further perpetuate vulnerability. At the aggregate level, the public response is compromised by an already low level of public investment, often squeezed by ongoing adjustment programmes. It is only further exacerbated by falling incomes and worsening trade and fiscal balances in the wake of the disaster. The risk is of countries' being locked in vicious circles, as economic insecurity is ratcheted up through fragile food, health and employment conditions which slow recovery and increase exposure to the next hazard.

Dealing with natural disasters

An integrated national policy response

To manage these shocks, households and Governments need better coping strategies. Much attention, particularly by the donor community, has been given in recent years to strategies for pooling and transferring disaster risk and smoothing incomes through market-based financial instruments, such as crop and livestock insurance and catastrophe bonds. At the regional level, some innovative efforts, such as the Caribbean Catastrophe Risk Insurance Facility, have also explored this option.

Such initiatives merit further investigation. However, their impact should not be overstated. Market-based strategies are really a serious option only at higher levels of development where they complement a broad set of mitigation instruments. Insurance is less relevant to countries with underdeveloped financial sectors and within the context of widespread income insecurity. Moreover, the covariant nature of large-scale disasters and their resulting widespread impact can threaten even well-capitalized insurance markets, making these costly options.

The highest priority in managing disasters must be increased investment in preparation and adaptation so as to reduce the risk of natural hazards' turning into disasters. Only 2 per cent of disaster management funds are spent by bilateral and multilateral donors on proactive disaster risk reduction, despite the estimate of the United States Geological Survey that economic losses worldwide from disasters in the 1990s could have been cut by some \$280 billion through investing \$40 billion in disaster risk reduction.

Because disasters may increase food insecurity, preventive measures designed to deal with food vulnerability are likely to be a crucial part of disaster preparedness in many poorer countries. This will require early warning systems, including at the international level, mapping of food-insecure households classified by degree of malnutrition and deficiencies in food consumption, and active support to small and medium-scale crop agriculture (for example, subsidies to agricultural inputs), as well as cash transfers.

Another effective approach to reducing vulnerability is to link medium-term development strategies to relief activities. A ubiquitous finding from empirical research is that more diversified economies suffer smaller losses from natural hazards and recover more quickly than less diversified economies. For many developing countries, diversification of production is greatly constrained by geographical factors. Still, tailored development strategies will need to move in this direction. A combination of public investment and cheap credit will be an element critical to making progress; but the space within which to implement appropriate industrial policies in support of diversification will also be important.

International insurance and coping mechanisms

For some countries, particularly smaller and poorer rural economies, disasters are often too big to handle. Although the international community is often quick to respond to emergency calls following large-scale disasters, there has been a persistent tendency for delivery to fall short of pledges: funds requested by the United Nations for disasters have consistently failed to reach the desired level.

Multilateral loan facilities, such as the Exogenous Shocks Facility for low-income countries managed by IMF, have been designed to provide assistance for addressing temporary balance-of-payments needs arising from shocks such as natural disasters. However, high levels of conditionality limit their effectiveness. One action that could be quickly implemented to better assist countries affected by disasters would entail introducing a simple mechanism for extending a moratorium on debt servicing through, for example, improvements made to the Paris Club process.

The international community has been moving towards a more integrated strategy for increasing the resilience of vulnerable populations and countries. However, the process has been a slow one. In part, this reflects a wider problem with the aid architecture, including the influence of economic and geopolitical interests.

A global disaster mechanism to mobilize the resources for an integrated risk management approach needs to be established. Initially, such a mechanism could serve as a better means of providing disaster relief, but it should quickly gear up to assume a wider set of responsibilities linked to disaster management. This mechanism could eventually absorb the various facilities that are already in place, but fragmented, with the aim of evolving into a well-funded facility that could not only provide sufficient financing quickly and automatically to countries hit by disaster, but also begin to perform the much more demanding task of investing in disaster reduction for the longer term. Taking the figures from the United States Geological Survey cited earlier as a guide, a $10 billion dollar facility would seem to represent the kind of target that the international community should be aiming for if real progress in reducing this threat is to be achieved.

Things fall apart: civil wars and post-conflict recovery

In some States, increased economic insecurity has become part of a compounding process of deepening social divisions and increasing political instability. Their fragile societies are vulnerable to a multiplicity of threats ranging from natural disasters and food shortages to financial shocks, rising inequality, and badly handled elections, any of which could tip them into widespread, and even genocidal, levels of violence. Under these conditions, the threat exists of the State's losing control, not only of its ability to deliver basic services, but also of its traditional monopoly over the forces of law and order, and ultimately, its hold on political legitimacy.

This possibility has changed the face of contemporary warfare over the last three decades. Armed conflicts between States have given way to civil wars fought principally within national borders. These are much more likely to reinforce deep and cumulative divisions that undermine social cohesion, threaten State norms and institutions, and create a deep sense of fear and distrust among citizens.

Longer and more disruptive conflicts

While each conflict has its own distinct characteristics, the larger picture is one of increasingly protracted and disruptive conflicts concentrated in countries with an annual per capita income of under $3,000; on average, conflicts can last between seven and nine years today, compared with just two or three years in the 1960s and 1970s (see figure O.3). At the same time (with the pattern being very much like that for natural disasters), there has been a declining number of battle-related deaths accompanied by a larger impact in terms of displaced persons and disrupted economic livelihoods. Serious damage has often been done to the environment, while health crises and hunger are endemic.

Many of these costs are borne directly at the household and community levels; and along with the destruction and theft of productive assets, they make the recovery of economic and social positions all the more difficult once the fighting has stopped. At the same time, falling incomes, the informalization of economic activity, sharp declines in investment levels and declining fiscal revenues, as well as a shift in the composition of spending towards military activities, make it increasingly difficult for the State (or what remains of it) to offset these rising costs of the conflict.

As these costs mount, insecurity, capital flight, and the erosion of "social capital" can undermine State institutions and result in conflict traps. The deeply fragile societies that remain after the fighting has ended lack the institutional infrastructure needed to build a new social contract and ensure a rapid and lasting recovery. Not surprisingly, the threat of renewed violence is never very far away: a country with a history of conflict is from two to four times more likely to experience a subsequent war than one without such a history. This possibility adds a distinct dimension to the policy challenge in such countries.

Figure O.3
Conflicts worldwide became more prolonged over the period 1946-2005

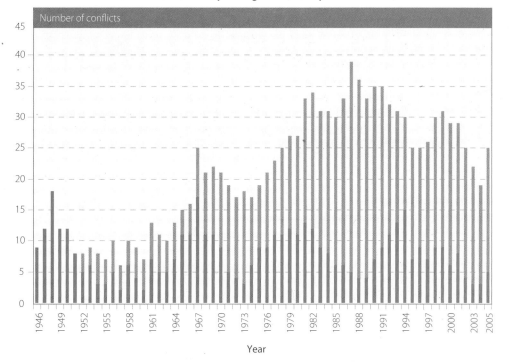

Conflict types:

▓▓▓ Ongoing conflicts having lasted more than five years

▬▬▬ Ongoing conflicts having lasted from one to five years

▬▬ Onsets of new conflicts

Source: UN/DESA, based on UCDP/PRIO Armed Conflict Dataset (2007). Abbreviations: UCDP, Uppsala Conflict Data Programme at the Department of Peace and Conflict Research, Uppsala University, Uppsala, Sweden; PRIO, International Peace Research Institute, Oslo (Centre for the Study of Civil War).

Economic insecurity and post-conflict reconstruction

Closing the institutional gap

Such societies do not have the luxury of meeting the goals of security, reconciliation and development in a measured or sequenced manner, but must begin the recovery process on all fronts. This is made difficult by the large institutional gap in post-conflict countries. Filling it requires a strategic and integrated approach through which to gradually repair trust in public institutions and develop a mixture of political and economic mechanisms that can help create a unifying national identity, establish an effective central authority to manage interregional transfers and resources and begin to outline social and economic priorities as well as create the policy space needed to achieve them.

From an early date, the State will be required not only to establish the institutions and rules that allow markets to function, but also choose reforms and adopt policies that do not increase insecurity or aggravate socio-economic inequalities. Accordingly, building a durable peace will require active economic policies, including unconventional macroeconomic measures. In this respect, a key idea to be kept in mind when thinking about the links between State-building and economic recovery in post-conflict countries is that of adaptive efficiency—the capacity to develop institutions that provide a stable framework for economic activity but are at the same time flexible enough to provide maximum leeway for policy choices in any given situation.

A different approach to official development assistance

Building State capacities to mobilize domestic revenue and provide sustainable funding needed to close the institutional gap will be a crucial issue from the outset of recovery. In many cases, reliance on external support is unavoidable, and managing international aid flows will be among the first economic policy tests for both the national authorities and the donor community. However, aid to post-conflict countries often tapers off prematurely and, often, at the very moment when countries have rebuilt institutions and are in a better position to absorb aid and spend it effectively. Steps are being taken by the international community within the context of the Development Assistance Committee (DAC) of the Organization for Economic Cooperation and Development (OECD) and the Peacebuilding Commission to ensure stable and adequate aid flows for sufficiently long periods of time.

Traditionally, donors have preferred to finance specific projects, but particularly in light of the legitimacy deficit faced by States, resources should be channelled through their budgets as far as possible, and every effort should be taken to avoid setting up competing points of authority. In this regard, dual-signature systems designed to approve spending decisions have been found to be effective in addressing both corruption and accountability concerns. Another aspect of the challenge will be the rebuilding of credit and financial markets including through innovative sources of financing.

More equitable public spending

While priorities have to be set by local authorities, both donors and national Governments will need to pay particularly close attention to the links between public expenditure decisions and the grievances that drive the conflicts. Two sets of distributional issues are particularly relevant concerning: (a) how to incorporate equity concerns into spending decisions and (b) how to allocate expenditures across the political landscape so as to bolster incentives for the implementation of accords and the consolidation of peace. Taxation of luxury consumption deserves much more attention from the government side. Conflict impact assessments and peace conditionalities, which seek to calibrate the flow of support to specific peacebuilding steps, could constitute useful means of addressing both sets of issues from the donor side.

As sustained peace is the most important goal that foreign aid can help achieve, it is particularly important that instead of imposing their own institutional models and policy priorities on the receiving countries, donors work to mobilize local knowledge and capacities in respect of addressing the needs of the affected populations and to restore the legitimacy of those local institutions that are crucial to repairing the social contract.

Poverty, insecurity and the development agenda

That economic liberalization and deregulation have created new sources of economic insecurity, even as they have increased exposure to long-standing vulnerabilities and failed to generate appropriate policy responses, can be seen in countries at all levels of development. It is the poorest communities, however, that are often most at risk from financial crises, natural disasters and civil conflicts. Indeed, more often than not, poverty acts to compound these threats, while for poorer people, there is a dearth of effective mitigation, coping and recovery mechanisms. The food riots that broke out in a number of countries in early 2008 have laid bare the fragility of economic livelihoods for those at the bottom of the development ladder.

Successful developing countries have not turned to the self-regulating market for ideas on how to design their development strategies. Instead, a mixture of market incentives and strong State interventions, often running counter to orthodox economic wisdom, has provided the formula for rapid growth. Various economic measures aimed at socializing the risks arising from the undertaking of large-scale investments and adopting unfamiliar technologies have helped nurture a domestic entrepreneurial class. Such support was often guided by a more encompassing development vision which judged policy interventions in terms of their contribution to diversifying economic activity, creating jobs and reducing poverty.

However, growth is a necessary but not a sufficient condition for tackling poverty (see figure O.4). What is needed is a package of universal social policies and some targeted economic policies tailored to individual country conditions and based on a strong "social contract" designed to secure the spaces within which individuals, households and communities can pursue their interests and make the most effective use of the creative impulses generated by market forces. This requires taking a more integrated approach to economic and social policies and demonstrating a much greater degree of pragmatism in their design and implementation.

Figure O.4
Increasing growth and reducing volatility help reduce poverty, but they are not sufficient

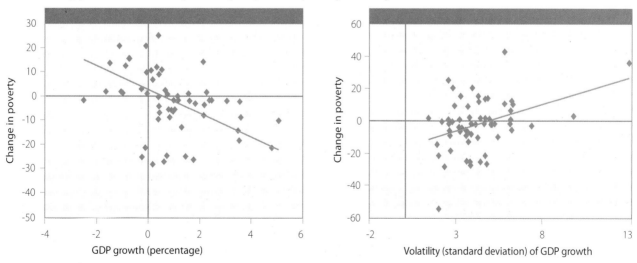

Sources: UN/DESA, based on United Nations Statistics Division, National Accounts Main Aggregates database, for GDP growth; and World Bank, PovcalNet, available at http://iresearch.worldbank.org/PovcalNet/jsp/index.jsp.

Note: Change in poverty is measured as a percentage point change in the incidence of poverty for the $1 per day poverty line, over the period 1981-2004.

Dealing with household economic insecurity

Pro-poor macroeconomic and growth policies

For most developing countries, poverty and the insecure livelihoods that it breeds can be tackled only through sustained rapid growth and expansion of formal employment. In many cases where rural growth is likely to reduce poverty faster than urban growth, agriculture—neglected in policy advice in recent decades—needs to be the focus of increased support, including for small farmers. However, with the general pace of urbanization accelerating, labour-intensive manufacturing and a more sophisticated service sector will also need to be encouraged if poverty is truly to become history. As seen in the cases of natural disasters and civil conflict, economic diversification remains among the most successful means to insure against insecurity.

Pro-poor macroeconomic policies certainly need to be included in the mix for tackling chronic levels of insecurity. In many developing countries where agriculture is still a principal source of income and export earnings, policies will be aimed at managing "commodity cycles", as these tend to hit the poorest particularly hard on the downside. Stabilization funds will have a role to play in this task.

Competitive and stable exchange rates along with low and stable real interest rates will also be part of the mix, often requiring delayed capital-account liberalization and the measured use of capital controls. Stable fiscal revenues are also essential, particularly for filling the infrastructural gaps which are a major constraint on growth in most poor countries.

Finance and insurance for the poor

Innovative sources of finance have a role to play in tackling the poverty-insecurity nexus. In recent years, microfinance has become the policy of choice, particularly among the donor community, for encouraging enterprise and tackling poverty. An initial interest in microcredit has expanded to include microsavings and microinsurance. This has produced some positive social outcomes, particularly in alleviating poverty among women. However, these activities still constitute a very small part of the financial sector in most countries, and often fail to generate significant productive employment. The poorest communities therefore remain vulnerable to systemic shocks. In this regard, Governments must examine the situation closely to determine whether the subsidies used to support these schemes are the best means of tackling poverty or whether other mitigation and coping strategies might provide a more suitable response.

Welfare programmes and social protection

Such strategies come in various forms. These range from workfare programmes, which have been in place in many countries for a long time, to cash transfer programmes, which have become popular recently. While most of these programmes were originally launched and used as ex post measures to help affected people cope with economic downturns, in more recent years they have been increasingly used as ex ante measures to reduce the exposure of the poor to insecurity. For example, India has recently adopted a workfare scheme that guarantees 100 days of employment in a year to all those who wish to participate—an example of workfare's being transformed from a post-shock temporary arrangement into a semi-formal permanent employment scheme.

A similar transformation of arrangements from ex post to ex ante is exemplified by cash transfer programmes used to promote specific development objectives, such as school attendance by children and use of health services. Just as budgetary support has become a more popular form of providing aid at the macrolevel, so has provision of cash become a more popular form of social protection at the household level.

A perennial issue with respect to the design and implementation of such measures is whether they are best pitched as universal policies or as policies specifically targeted at the poor. Although the trend in recent years has been towards the latter approach, this has not achieved the right balance. The fact that, in general, universal systems have a better track record in eliminating poverty reflects the combination of a better income distribution (with potentially stronger growth dynamics), a broader political appeal, particularly with support from the middle classes, and some clear administrative and cost advantages.

Back to the multilateral drawing board

The simple message conveyed by this year's *Survey* is that markets cannot be left to their own devices in respect of delivering appropriate and desired levels of economic security. This should not, however, be taken as promoting an agenda for the abandoning of market forces; in this case, the agenda is rather one of making security and cohesion the basis for the unleashing of the creative impulses generated by those forces. Just what combination of regulation, mitigation, protection and relief is required will depend on the kind of threats being faced, and on the local capacities and resources that can be mobilized, as well as on local preferences and choices. However, when dealing with the kind of systemic shocks under discussion, there is likely to be a particularly prominent role for the international community.

Strengthening that role is a matter less of inventing new modalities than of returning to the principles of multilateralism that were prematurely abandoned through a misplaced faith in self-regulating market forces. Those principles had been fashioned at a time when the threats to security arising from operating in an interdependent world economy were more firmly grasped by policymakers than has recently been the case. The international community should consider:

- **A renewed Bretton Woods**. Much as in the interwar years, leaving the management of cycles to flexible labour markets and independent central banks has not proved successful. A singular focus on price stability has not contained asset-centric boom-bust cycles, even as it has pushed employment objectives and a healthy balance between wages and productivity growth off the policy agenda. Counter-cyclical macroeconomic measures and financial regulation need to be revived. Achieving this means that the international financial architecture can no longer continue to be organized around the principle of laissez-faire, which has extended the global reach of financial markets without establishing matching global rules, resources and regulations. Filling that gap is an urgent priority.

  The process should begin with a reconsideration of the level and terms of access of developing countries to IMF resources, especially compensatory financing mechanisms designed to assist in coping with external shocks. It is also important to eliminate the tendency to impose pro-cyclical macroeconomic conditionality at higher access levels. Improved multilateral surveillance will also need to take account of all possible international spillovers of national economic policies.

- **Revisiting the Marshall Plan principles**. A more effective aid architecture is needed, especially for countries vulnerable to natural disasters and those recovering from conflict. Meeting the long-standing target for ODA of 0.7 per cent of the gross national income of DAC members is important, but it will not be sufficient. Current arrangements lack a proper framework of organizing principles through which to encourage and complement domestic efforts at resource mobilization, one that is consistent with local priorities and capacities, and supports the recipient Government's own development priorities and strategy.

  The benchmark for aid effectiveness was set over 60 years ago by the Marshall Plan, and while the times and the challenges have changed, the principles for coordinating national development plans with international assistance remain germane. These include, in particular, front-loaded and generous support for national development priorities that is unburdened by excessive conditionality and donor demands, and attuned to national constraints and sensibilities.

- **A global New Deal**. Much like focusing on the Marshall Plan, invoking a "new deal" has become part of today's development policy debates. The recent food security crisis has led the World Bank to plead for a new deal on global food policy. The operation of market forces should, on this account, be extended through further agricultural trade liberalization, and, at the same time, compensatory financing mechanisms and social safety nets should be designed to help food importers. However, these recommendations underemphasize some of the key elements of President Roosevelt's original New Deal developed in response to the Great Depression, in particular the mechanisms that were created to expand and better manage markets, along with redistributional measures aimed at better distributing the burden of shocks. Just how far the redistribution agenda can be pushed towards rebalancing globalization and preventing a potentially damaging backlash is a subject open to debate. One suggestion entails a minimum basic income in the form of a cash grant to all households, which picks up and extends the idea of a basic pension as proposed in the 2007 *World Economic and Social Survey*. Such measures are, of course, fraught with complications and difficulties. And asking at what level and with what resources this could be pursued as part of a wider security agenda remains an abstract policy point. Still, there are interesting precedents: the State of Alaska has been implementing such a measure since the early 1980s and there are similar initiatives elsewhere. More recently, United Nations organizations have begun examining the concept of a "global social floor" designed to provide a minimum level of security in line with the principles of the Universal Declaration of Human Rights. This serves as a reminder that in an interdependent world, social cohesion is not a luxury, but rather a necessary component of a healthy and vibrant system.

Against the growing backdrop of increasing economic and political insecurity in interwar Europe, John Maynard Keynes called for "new policies and new instruments to adapt and control the workings of economic forces, so that they do not intolerably interfere with contemporary ideas as to what is fit and proper in the interests of social stability and social justice". Those words resonate just as strongly today. The responsibility for the choice and mix of policies required to guarantee prosperity, stability and justice, remains, of course, with national institutions and constituencies, but in an increasingly interdependent world and on a fragile planet, building a more secure home is a truly international endeavour.

Sha Zukang
Under-Secretary-General
* for Economic and Social Affairs*
May 2008

Contents

Boxes

Figures

Tables

Explanatory notes

The following symbols have been used in the tables throughout the report:

..   **Two dots** indicate that data are not available or are not separately reported.

–   **A dash** indicates that the amount is nil or negligible.

-    **A hyphen (-)** indicates that the item is not applicable.

-    **A minus sign (-)** indicates deficit or decrease, except as indicated.

.   **A full stop (.)** is used to indicate decimals.

/   **A slash (/)** between years indicates a crop year or financial year, for example, 1990/91.

-    **Use of a hyphen (-)** between years, for example, 1990-1991, signifies the full period involved, including the beginning and end years.

Reference to "dollars" ($) indicates United States dollars, unless otherwise stated.

Reference to "billions" indicates one thousand million.

Reference to "tons" indicates metric tons, unless otherwise stated.

Annual rates of growth or change, unless otherwise stated, refer to annual compound rates.

Details and percentages in tables do not necessarily add to totals, because of rounding.

The following abbreviations have been used:

ASEAN	Association of Southeast Asian Nations
BIS	Bank for International Settlements
CARICOM	Caribbean Community
CGAP	Consultative Group to Assist the Poor
CIS	Commonwealth of Independent States
CRED	Centre for Research on the Epidemiology of Disasters (Université Catholique de Louvrain (Brussels))
DAC	Development Assistance Committee (OECD)
ESCAP	Economic and Social Commission for Asia and the Pacific
EU	European Union
FAO	Food and Agriculture Organization of the United Nations
FDI	foreign direct investment
FIVIMS	Food Insecurity and Vulnerability Information and Mapping Systems (FAO)
GDP	gross domestic product
GIEWS	Global Information and Early Warning System on Food and Agriculture (FAO)
GNI	gross national income
GNP	gross national product
HiCN	Households in Conflict Network (University of Sussex, United Kingdom)
ILO	International Labour Organization
IMF	International Monetary Fund
LIBOR	London Interbank Offered Rate
NAFTA	North American Free Trade Agreement
NBER	National Bureau of Economic Research (Cambridge, Massachusetts)
NFIP	National Flood Insurance Program (United States)
ODA	official development assistance
OECD	Organization for Economic Cooperation and Development
PPP	purchasing power parity
R & D	research and development
ROSCA	Rotating Savings and Credit Association
SDRs	special drawing rights
SWF	sovereign wealth fund
UNCTAD	United Nations Conference on Trade and Development
UN/DESA	Department of Economic and Social Affairs of the United Nations
UNDP	United Nations Development Programme
UNHCR	Office of the United Nations High Commissioner for Refugees
WHO	World Health Organization
WMO	World Meteorological Organization

The designations employed and the presentation of the material in this publication do not imply the expression of any opinion whatsoever on the part of the United Nations Secretariat concerning the legal status of any country, territory, city or area or of its authorities, or concerning the delimitation of its frontiers or boundaries.

The term "country" as used in the text of this report also refers, as appropriate, to territories or areas.

For analytical purposes, unless otherwise specified, the following country groupings and subgroupings have been used:

Developed economies (developed market economies):

European Union, Iceland, Norway, Switzerland, Japan, United States of America, Canada, Australia, New Zealand.

Subgroupings of developed economies:

Europe:

European Union (EU):

Austria, Belgium, Bulgaria, Cyprus, Czech Republic, Denmark, Estonia, Finland, France, Germany, Greece, Hungary, Ireland, Italy, Latvia, Lithuania, Luxembourg, Malta, Netherlands, Poland, Portugal, Romania, Slovakia, Slovenia, Spain, Sweden, United Kingdom of Great Britain and Northern Ireland.

EU-25:

EU excluding Bulgaria and Romania.

EU-15:

EU-12 plus Denmark, Sweden and the United Kingdom of Great Britain and Northern Ireland.

EU-12 (euro area):

Austria, Belgium, Finland, France, Germany, Greece, Ireland, Italy, Luxembourg, Netherlands, Portugal, Spain.

EU-10:

EU-25 minus EU-15.

Other Europe:

Iceland, Norway, Switzerland.

Economies in transition:

South-eastern Europe:

Albania, Bosnia and Herzegovina, Croatia, Montenegro, Romania, Serbia, the former Yugoslav Republic of Macedonia.

Commonwealth of Independent States (CIS):

Armenia, Azerbaijan, Belarus, Georgia, Kazakhstan, Kyrgyzstan, Moldova, Russian Federation, Tajikistan, Turkmenistan, Ukraine, Uzbekistan.

Developing economies:

Latin America and the Caribbean, Africa, Asia and the Pacific (excluding Japan, Australia, New Zealand and the member States of CIS in Asia).

Subgroupings of Latin America and the Caribbean:

South America and Mexico:

Argentina, Brazil, Chile, Colombia, Ecuador, Guyana, Mexico, Paraguay, Peru, Uruguay, Venezuela (Bolivarian Republic of).

Central America and the Caribbean:

All other countries in Latin America and the Caribbean.

Subgroupings of Africa:

Northern Africa:

Algeria, Egypt, Libyan Arab Jamahiriya, Morocco, Tunisia.

Sub-Saharan Africa:

All other African countries.

Subgroupings of Asia and the Pacific:

Western Asia:

Bahrain, Iraq, Israel, Jordan, Kuwait, Lebanon, Occupied Palestinian Territory, Oman, Qatar, Saudi Arabia, Syrian Arab Republic, Turkey, United Arab Emirates, Yemen.

East and South Asia:

All other developing economies in Asia and the Pacific (including China, unless stated otherwise). This group is further subdivided into:

South Asia:

Bangladesh, Bhutan, India, Iran (Islamic Republic of), Maldives, Nepal, Pakistan, Sri Lanka.

East Asia and the Pacific:

East Asia:

China

Newly industrialized economies:

Hong Kong Special Administrative Region of China, Republic of Korea, Singapore, Taiwan Province of China.

Other East Asia:

Democratic People's Republic of Korea, Mongolia.

South-East Asia:

Brunei Darussalam, Cambodia, Timor-Leste, Indonesia, Lao People's Democratic Republic, Malaysia, Myanmar, Philippines, Singapore, Thailand, Viet Nam.

Oceania:

Fiji, Kiribati, Marshall Islands, Micronesia (Federated States of), Papua New Guinea, Samoa, Solomon Islands, Tonga, Tuvalu, Vanuatu.

Least developed economies:

Afghanistan, Angola, Bangladesh, Benin, Bhutan, Burkina Faso, Burundi, Cambodia, Cape Verde, Central African Republic, Chad, Comoros, Democratic Republic of the Congo, Djibouti, Equatorial Guinea, Eritrea, Ethiopia, Gambia, Guinea, Guinea-Bissau, Haiti, Kiribati, Lao People's Democratic Republic, Lesotho, Liberia, Madagascar, Malawi, Maldives, Mali, Mauritania, Mozambique, Myanmar, Nepal, Niger, Rwanda, Samoa, Sao Tome and Principe, Senegal, Sierra Leone, Solomon Islands, Somalia, Sudan, Timor-Leste, Togo, Tuvalu, Uganda, United Republic of Tanzania, Vanuatu, Yemen, Zambia.

Chapter I
Overcoming economic insecurity: issues at stake

At the end of the cold war, the easing of long-standing political tensions coupled with a rapidly integrating world economy held out high hopes for a new era of peace, prosperity and stability. This became the moment when getting prices right would guarantee big efficiency gains and unleash the dynamic forces of competition and risk-taking. Armed with a ready set of explanations of how unfettered markets lift all boats, trigger converging incomes and put an end to stop-go cycles, conventional economists helped fashion a policy consensus for the new era.

Gains have certainly been made: inflation has been contained, international trade has expanded and capital has flowed across borders on an unprecedented scale. Still, the growth record has been uneven and the macroeconomic environment increasingly unbalanced. The one ubiquitous trend has been sharply rising inequalities.

Yet, perhaps more than any single issue, it is a growing sense of economic insecurity that has come back to haunt the advocates of unfettered markets. In 2008, rising food prices and a growing incidence of hunger have provided a deadly demonstration of the mismatch between market forces and socio-economic well-being. For many of the countries facing severe food insecurity, the problem is often one of multiple threats from poverty, natural disasters and civil violence (see table I.1); but the outbreak of food riots in rapidly urbanizing middle-income countries, some with a solid growth record, suggests more serious structural deficiencies within these markets. The problem has been compounded by energy insecurity as fuel prices hit new highs and future supplies become entangled in a complex web of geopolitical calculations.

Increasingly flexible labour markets have also undermined employment security. In many developing countries, the void left by stagnant or declining public sector jobs and industrial downsizing has been filled by more precarious or poorly paid jobs in the informal economy or the expanding service sector. In advanced countries, middle-class lifestyles have been hollowed out, leaving policymakers scrambling to avoid a populist backlash against cheap imports, the offshoring of jobs and the presence of immigrant workers. Instead of providing shelter against the upsurge of these increasingly turbulent economic waters, money markets have added greatly to the sense of expanding insecurity. Volatile international financial flows, boom-bust cycles, collapsing currencies and speculative panics have put jobs, homes and pensions at risk for many in the advanced countries.

Still, heightened insecurity cannot be put down simply to the destructive impulses of markets. Creative destruction is after all their modus operandi. Rather, it has much to do with the eagerness with which policymakers have ceded economic responsibility to independent central bankers, footloose corporations and managers of unregulated hedge funds, on the promise that they would deliver a healthy investment climate and help secure large economic gains for all. As discussed in chapter II, while the macroeconomic climate has become less volatile, productive investment has not picked up. At the same time, more and more households, communities and countries are being exposed to adverse shocks and downside risks, while their ability to cope with and recover from the consequences is sharply diminished.

Despite greater price stability and increased openness, the growth record has been uneven and the macroeconomic environment unbalanced

Food, fuel and financial markets are not delivering economic security

Volatile international financial flows, boom-bust cycles, collapsing currencies and speculative panics have put jobs, homes and pensions at risk

Table I.1
Countries facing a food crisis that are in need of external assistance

Country	Food insecurity	Vulnerability to natural hazards	Socio-political factors	Economic vulnerability, 1996-2006	
				Number of years in negative growth	Average annual per capita growth
Iraq	Exceptional	Drought, floods	Conflict, insecurity	5	1.0
Zimbabwe	Exceptional	Drought, windstorms	Potential civil strife	9	-3.7
Swaziland	Exceptional	Drought, windstorms, floods		2	0.6
Somalia	Exceptional	Drought, wave surges	Conflict	6	-0.3
Lesotho	Exceptional	Drought, windstorms		3	1.5
Burundi	Severe	Floods, windstorms, drought, earthquakes	Civil strife, internally displaced persons, returnees	7	-1.5
Central African Republic	Severe	Windstorms, floods	Refugees, localized insecurity	6	-1.3
Chad	Severe	Drought, floods	Refugees, conflict spillovers	4	4.4
Côte d'Ivoire	Severe		Civil strife	5	0.1
Ghana	Severe	Floods		0	2.4
Guinea	Severe	Windstorms, floods	Refugees	2	1.7
Guinea-Bissau	Severe	Drought, floods	Localized insecurity	5	-2.7
Kenya	Severe	Landslides, drought, wave surges, floods	Civil strife	4	0.4
Nepal	Severe	Floods, landslides, drought	Conflict	2	1.4
Timor-Leste	Severe		Internally displaced persons, post-conflict	5	-1.7
Ethiopia	Severe	Drought, floods	Insecurity in parts	3	2.8
Democratic People's Republic of the Congo	Severe	Windstorms, floods, volcanic eruptions	Internally displaced persons	6	-2.1
Sudan	Severe	Drought, windstorms, floods	Civil strife	0	5.3
Uganda	Severe	Drought, windstorms, floods	Civil strife in the north.	0	2.9
Sri Lanka	Severe	Floods, wave surges, windstorms, drought	Civil conflict	1	4.2
Bolivia	Severe	Floods, drought, windstorms, landslides		2	1.2
Haiti	Severe	Floods, windstorms, drought		6	-0.8
Bangladesh	Severe	Floods, windstorms, waves, earthquakes		0	3.6
China	Severe	Floods, windstorms, earthquakes, landslides, drought		0	8.4
Dominican Republic	Severe	Windstorms, earthquakes		1	4.4
Ecuador	Severe	Floods, volcanic eruptions, landslides		1	1.8

Table I.1 (cont'd)				Economic vulnerability, 1996-2006	
Country	Food insecurity	Vulnerability to natural hazards	Socio-political factors	Number of years in negative growth	Average annual per capita growth
Nicaragua	Severe	Windstorms, drought, floods, landslides		1	2.4
Tajikistan	Severe	Floods, earthquakes, landslides, drought		1	3.6
Viet Nam	Severe	Floods, windstorms, drought		0	5.7
Eritrea	Widespread	Drought, floods	Post-conflict, internally displaced persons	7	-1.1
Liberia	Widespread		Post-conflict	2	7.7
Mauritania	Widespread	Drought, floods		5	1.3
Sierra Leone	Widespread	Floods	Post-conflict	4	-1.6
Afghanistan	Widespread	Landslides, drought, earthquakes, floods	Conflict, insecurity	..	..
Democratic People's Republic of Korea	Widespread	Windstorms, floods		4	-0.2

Sources: Food and Agriculture Organization of the United Nations and UN/DESA secretariat.

The politics of economic insecurity

The fact that no social or economic order will be secure if it fails to benefit the majority of those who live under it demands nothing less than what European political philosophers in the seventeenth and eighteenth centuries called a "social contract": an implicit understanding among members of a community to cooperate for mutual benefit, along with formal rules and institutional mechanisms to help build trust, balance competing interests, manage disputes and provide a fair distribution of the rewards that are generated. A modern State cannot advance to high levels of economic and social development, internal order and peace without such cooperation and rules. Moreover, the higher the level of development, the more complex must be the collaborative effort needed to safeguard past achievements and utilize them as a springboard for further progress.

A modern State cannot advance to high levels of economic and social development, internal order and peace without cooperation forged through a strong social contract

In the modern era, that contract has been forged out of the challenges and risks generated by expanding markets and a more intricate division of labour. In response to those challenges and risks, there emerged new mechanisms of social protection against work-related accidents, illness and disability, as well as social support for the unemployed, those rearing children and those entering old age. However, the right balance of interests was difficult to secure, all the more so as democratic institutions amplified the demands of those most vulnerable to downside risks. During the interwar years, the fragile consensus had broken down under the impact of waste, despair and violence which had attained unprecedented levels.

The new deal that emerged after 1945 was built around a "craving for security". New policies and institutions were developed to adapt and control the workings of economic forces and to guarantee social protection. Policies to stimulate domestic investment and growth not only helped prevent a return to the economic chaos of the interwar years, but ushered in an era of full employment, rising wages and freer trade. Strong growth made it easier to fund social protection and to extend the reach of the welfare State. Social stability in turn helped underpin long-term investment planning and facilitate technological progress. A virtuous circle emerged.

Positive leadership was also extended at the international level, backed by resources and willingness to compromise on national self-interest. Newly independent developing countries saw an opportunity to break with the legacy of economic exploitation, backwardness and insecurity which had been the hallmarks of colonial rule. With encouragement and support from their more advanced country partners, the new economic policy wisdom was oriented towards orchestrating an industrial take-off, managing a big push, and moving catch-up countries to higher rungs of the development ladder. Social policy lagged behind, but steady investments in human capital and infrastructure helped many countries break out of a vicious poverty trap.

This period of unprecedented socio-economic progress and security lasted until the early 1970s, when, beginning in the more advanced economies, a combination of internal tensions and external shocks began to threaten the existing consensus. At the end of the decade, an abrupt tightening of macroeconomic policy in these countries signalled a break with past practice, and a willingness to rethink the social contract. Citizenship, cooperation and social protection slipped down the agenda and, in some cases, dropped off altogether; in their place, consumer choice, competition and risk-taking moved to centre stage.

The trend has often been restrained in the advanced countries by practical and social constraints on policymaking. Resistance has proved much weaker in many developing countries, leaving them more vulnerable to downside risks. Indeed, as discussed throughout the present *Survey*, restoring more effective State institutions is an urgent challenge within the context of creating and preserving more secure spaces within which individuals, communities and ultimately countries can pursue their activities with a reasonable degree of predictability and stability, and with due regard for the aims and interests of others.

The economics of insecurity: risk, vulnerability and uncertainty

A rising level of economic insecurity is obviously damaging to the well-being of the affected households and individuals. It can also threaten socio-economic progress by stifling innovation, shortening investment horizons, narrowing choices and generating opportunistic and undesirable behaviour. On the other hand, economic insecurity is an unavoidable fact of economic life and—to the extent that it challenges sclerotic behaviour and opens up new investment opportunities—is to some degree healthy.

Economists have tried to make sense of this duality by identifying insecurity with risk, whose upside is the spurring of entrepreneurial behaviour but whose downside is income and welfare losses. If these alternative outcomes can be calculated with some reasonable level of precision, then individuals can make preparations in advance, by organizing family support, building up savings or hedging through some kind of insurance policy. These are essentially all different types of private strategies for coping with the consequences of risk.

Of course, individuals have little or no influence over many of the events that generate insecurity. In trying to gauge the possible damage from these events, economists

Since the late 1970s, a new social contract has replaced citizenship, cooperation and social protection with consumer choice, competition and risk-taking

Economic insecurity can threaten socio-economic progress by stifling innovation, shortening investment horizons and generating undesirable behaviour

have distinguished between *idiosyncratic risks*, generated by individual and isolated events such as an illness, an accident or a crime, and *covariant risks*, which are associated with events that hit a large number of people simultaneously, such as an economic shock or a climatic hazard, and often involve multiple and compounding costs.

Both types of risk can, in principle, be privately insured or can be covered through various forms of social protection paid for from taxation. Economists and policy-makers have long debated the merits of these options, both of which are available in most societies. Assessing the desirable mix is in part a matter of weighing up the potentially negative spillover effects (externalities) that are generated by risky events and often make them difficult to price, against the costs of moral hazard associated with collective response.

In general, private coping mechanisms work best for idiosyncratic risks which carry small potential damages. However, these are often unavailable to the most vulnerable populations. The exclusionary nature of these private strategies and the potentially large size of losses associated with illness, unemployment or destitution in old age provide the rationale for social protection through the welfare State, and make all the more urgent the affirmation by the United Nations that economic security is a basic human right.

To recognize the above is also to accept the implication that risk is not the same as insecurity. Insecurity, which is less clear-cut, has been described as lying at the intersection of perceived and actual downside risk (Jacobs, 2007). Economists have generated a vast and highly specialized literature on the subjective dimension of risk (Osberg, 1998). Perceptions of insecurity are linked, however, to very concrete differences in the degree of exposure to a shared threat and to differences in the ability to control and recover from unforeseen events.

In this regard, vulnerability points to a source of insecurity that is more structural than subjective, which is obviously the case for many poorer countries lacking the resources to cope with threats, particularly those of a more compounded nature. On some counts, this makes poverty the real source of insecurity. Yet, such an argument can be misleading. Vulnerability to significant downside losses may occur at different levels of development with deeply damaging social and economic repercussions. This is obviously true with respect to systemic or catastrophic risks which carry large and widespread damage and are difficult to predict in advance. Indeed, in a world of structural vulnerabilities and endemic uncertainty, insurance is unlikely to create the requisite degree of economic security for individuals, households and countries. Rather, it is investing in preparation, planning and prevention mechanisms before the threat generates real and lasting damage that in fact constitutes the real challenge.

Certainly, then, economic insecurity is a development challenge, but it is also linked to the role of the State in forging a strong social contract.

The rise and fall of the self-regulating market

The concept of a self-regulating market was not new to the late twentieth century. Economists had been tinkering with it since the late nineteenth century, and it had made a brief (albeit disastrous) appearance on the policy stage in the years immediately after the First World War. What was new was the belief that, thanks to a series of technological, organizational and political developments, this concept could now be given a truly global run.

The political checks and balances that had previously determined how markets could best serve the objectives of growth and stability were rolled back. According to

Dealing with downside risks requires a mixture of public and private strategies

Overcoming structural vulnerabilities and endemic uncertainty requires investing in preparation, planning and prevention mechanisms

some, markets could do without a social contract altogether. On other counts, the market would spontaneously forge its own social contract, one centred around strong property rights, the rule of law and low transaction costs. In a world of flexible labour markets, complete and competitive insurance markets, where individuals could purchase protection against any risk at a fair price, and perfect capital markets through which individuals could smooth out their income and consumption decisions, there would be no real insecurity to speak of.

There are growing concerns about the impact of unregulated financial markets

Most recently, unregulated financial markets have received most attention from the adherents of market parthenogenesis, thanks to their attributed informational efficiency (the "efficient market hypothesis") and their ability to conquer risk ("securitization"), which together promise stable growth and a smooth consumption path into the distant future.

How these developments have played out in the real world, particularly among developing countries, is discussed in greater detail in chapter II. Advanced industrialized economies, for their part, are already wondering whether "financialization" has gone too far. Moreover, the worry is not just that these markets have, in the words of *Financial Times* commentator Martin Wolf (2007), a tendency to "go crazy", but that by heightening social divisions, underinvesting in social capital and undermining the bonds of community, they might actually threaten the very survival of the market system itself.

Not surprisingly, the theorists of the self-destructive market have begun to make something of a comeback: Karl Polanyi's *The Great Transformation* (Polanyi, 1944) is required reading again; market analysts have rediscovered Hyman Minsky's financial instability hypothesis; George Soros has warned about "market fundamentalism"; and Gunnar Myrdal's notion of vicious circles is liberally quoted. More surprising still, the greatest adversary of the "casino economy", John Maynard Keynes, until recently persona non grata in policy circles, is once again the "defunct economist" to consult.

Overcoming economic insecurity

The simple truth is that most people in most places want much the same thing; a decent job, a secure home, a safe environment, and a better future for their children. Markets are central to these goals, but they cannot be left alone to achieve them. Various alternative approaches for guaranteeing a more secure economic future have stepped into the breach. For some, the challenge is essentially one of extending the agenda set out in the Universal Declaration of Human Rights.[1] This approach insists that the economic, social and political dimensions of security need to be pursued simultaneously. More recently, "human security" has been closely tied to guaranteeing the "capabilities" that all people need to live a full and free life (United Nations Development Programme, 1994).

For others, insecurity involves more the challenge of providing the world's poorest communities with effective mechanisms to help them better manage risk by mitigating the impact of shocks through targeted policy measures and strengthening their ability to cope with the consequences through insurance measures and safety nets and by strengthening civil society groups (World Bank, 2001).

For still others, the challenge is principally one of building social solidarity, centred around secure jobs and decent employment conditions, by strengthening the collective representation and voice of working people (International Labour Organization, 2004a).

---

1   General Assembly resolution 217 A (III).

These perspectives shed light on the insecurity challenge. They confirm its multidimensional nature and indicate that security and growth need not necessarily be opposing objectives. They do not, however, unite so as to yield a more integrated perspective. This is, in part, because they tend to depict the origins of insecurity as lying in its omission from an otherwise sound economic policy agenda and, in part, because they tend to be infused with the belief in a ubiquitous process of rising insecurity, when the reality is that some—including intellectual property owners, international bankers and transnational corporations—have enjoyed rising levels of protection in recent years, while others—the landless and working poor, small farmers, industrial workers, and those in the informal sector—have seen their levels of protection fall; but in largest part, the lack of integration is due to the fact that these perspectives all tend to reflect a somewhat hostile view of the State and understate the pivotal role of policy measures in creating and addressing economic insecurity.

Arguably, the security of its citizens, in all its dimensions, is the defining responsibility of the State, even when this involves some delegation of responsibility to non-State actors. Guaranteeing that security also requires an integrated policy approach which mixes regulation, redistribution and risk management.

This year's *Survey* builds on a number of interlocking themes which point towards a new deal on economic security:

- Systemic risk, in particular as linked to unregulated financial markets, has become the most serious threat to economic security (chap. II): volatile capital flows, asset bubbles and rising levels of debt have failed to establish a strong investment climate or to create an inclusive and stable pattern of growth. Moreover, this has often come at the cost of diminished policy space which makes it all the more difficult for countries to manage their integration into the world economy in a balanced manner.

- In many developing countries, economic insecurity is compounded by their vulnerability to repeated and catastrophic shocks associated with natural disasters (chap. III) and civil conflict (chap. IV), which can lead to vicious circles of chronic poverty and perpetuate exposure to future shocks. Safety nets, insurance schemes, and risk management techniques can help countries respond to idiosyncratic shocks and to smooth income and consumption, but these are not in themselves enough to address the insecurity challenge or to build sustainable and inclusive recoveries.

- A basic challenge facing policymakers is one of investing ex ante in various mechanisms needed to plan for shocks and prevent them from turning into disasters. This requires effective State capacity to implement public policy responses and deliver public goods. In the case of post-conflict countries, this challenge is inseparable from that of rebuilding an effective State which can prevent the return of violence (chap. IV).

- The fact that, for most developing countries, economic insecurity is first and foremost a development challenge calls for economic diversification and policies that foster productive investment (chap. II and III). However, bringing the State back into focus in the security agenda also requires a better marriage of economic and social agendas (chap. V), which can strengthen efficiency gains and create a stronger growth environment. Doing this will probably necessitate a shift from an approach comprising targeted social policies and universal economic rules to one characterized by a more universal social agenda and targeted economic policies.

Guaranteeing economic security requires an integrated policy approach which mixes regulation, redistribution and risk management

A global new deal

Developing an alternative economic security agenda will, of course, require plenty of inge-
nuity if the new forms of solidarity and political mobilization appropriate to today's more
integrated world economy are to be established. The chapters in this *Survey* offer policy
options at both the national and the international level for dealing with the different dimensions of economic insecurity that are discussed.

In an interdependent
world, economic security
cannot be guaranteed by
countries acting alone

Each country will need to experiment and find the configuration of institutions and conventions that will work best within its national conditions and that will
meet the expectations of its population. However, in an interdependent world, economic
security cannot be guaranteed by countries acting alone. In the world of the first three
decades of the post-war period, this was achieved by establishing a multilateral trade and
payments system that would facilitate rapid growth and development. In addition to a
formal mechanism of multilateral negotiation needed to establish a more open trading
system, this system also required additional safeguards to ensure its efficient operation
and preservation; and it was backed up by a an orderly system of multilateral payments
at stable, but multilaterally negotiated adjustable exchange rates, in conditions of strictly
limited private international capital flows. While it is recognized that the growth in global
interdependence poses greater problems today, the mechanisms and institutions put in
place over the past three decades have not been up to the challenge regarding the coher-
ence, complementarity and coordination of global economic policymaking. Strengthening
multilateral arrangements based on full participation and open dialogue across the international community is the best hope for providing a secure economic future for all.

Chapter II
Dealing with macroeconomic insecurity

The stop-go cycle associated with periodic balance-of-payments crises was a major constraint on long-term growth in many developing countries during the 1960s and 1970s. A radical change in policy advice in the late 1970s should have put an end to that cycle, by switching to a market-driven outward-oriented development strategy. This promised a return to macroeconomic stability along with a stronger, more inclusive and more secure economic growth path by removing State-induced distortions and unleashing the forces of global competition. In recent years, there has been a clear improvement in the macroeconomic performance of most countries in terms of lower volatility of key variables and a moderation in price inflation. However, this has not led to the expected economic dynamism, nor has it had the expected impact in reducing the vulnerability of people to downside economic risks, whether income declines or employment losses. Major regions of the world are still highly vulnerable to external shocks and in most countries, greater economic stability, narrowly defined, appears to have occurred at the cost of weaker growth of gross domestic product (GDP) and lower investment rates, at least when the situation is compared with that of the 1960s and 1970s. In the absence of effective countervailing measures, both national and multilateral, increasing instability in commodity prices and capital flows has, in particular, forced Governments to build excess international reserves at a further cost in terms of forgone investment and consumption. Thus, while the new policy regime has upended the old cycle, it has not replaced it with a vigorous alternative.

> There is improved macroeconomic stability in most countries …

The present chapter will examine the way changes in the business cycle in both developed and developing countries have impacted on economic insecurity.

> … but it has not translated into dynamic growth and economic security

Growth and macroeconomic instability

By many macroeconomic measures, we seem to be living in an economically more secure world. Macroeconomic volatility has decreased worldwide over the past decades as compared with the 1970s and 1980s. Fluctuations in output growth and inflation rates have fallen across all regions (see table II.1), though volatility remains much higher in developing than in developed countries. The standard deviation of output growth fell to less than 1 per cent in the developed countries during the present decade, compared with more than 2 per cent during the 1970s. In developing countries, the fluctuation around the average economic growth rate has come down to 2.4 percentage points, less than half the degree of volatility in the 1970s or 1980s. Output volatility is generally lower in developing Asia than in other parts of the developing world. Inflation rates have fallen worldwide and with them, also aggregate price volatility. In Latin America and the Caribbean, average inflation volatility dropped significantly in the 1990s and further in the present decade, in a clear break with the hyperinflation episodes of the 1980s. In other developing-country regions, gains in terms of greater price stability are more recent.

> Output and price volatility are still high in developing countries

In Africa, output volatility declined sharply in the early 1990s and this has persisted even with the acceleration of growth in the present decade. However, both private consumption and investment growth are more volatile than elsewhere, and volatility in

Table II.1

Macroeconomic volatility, developed economies and selected regions, 1971-2006

Standard deviation as percentage				
	1971-1980	*1981-1990*	*1991-2000*	*2001-2006*
Developed economies				
GDP growth	2.43	1.88	1.55	0.98
Gross fixed capital formation	5.99	5.42	4.44	3.44
Private consumption	7.17	5.60	4.93	5.59
Inflation[a]	9.20	6.09	2.39	2.00
Latin America and the Caribbean				
GDP growth	3.30	4.60	3.38	3.11
Gross fixed capital formation	11.26	13.26	11.79	9.83
Private consumption	6.19	5.16	5.64	3.36
Inflation[b]	63.31	310.26	23.36	7.61
Africa				
GDP growth	5.17	4.74	3.24	2.22
Gross fixed capital formation	17.34	16.52	14.34	12.53
Private consumption	7.46	9.53	7.98	8.75
Inflation[c]	12.97	16.01	103.87	13.73
East and South Asia				
GDP growth	4.62	3.42	3.05	1.63
Gross fixed capital formation	11.33	9.26	10.96	6.00
Private consumption	4.91	3.94	3.70	1.56
Inflation[d]	9.92	8.98	9.36	5.39
Western Asia				
GDP growth	8.23	6.54	5.00	4.57
Gross fixed capital formation	25.27	13.82	12.87	16.44
Private consumption	16.79	10.08	6.56	10.34
Inflation[e]	19.23	33.79	33.58	10.85

Sources: UN/DESA, based on United Nations Statistics Division, National Accounts Main Aggregates database; inflation estimates based on World Bank World Development Indicators Online database, available at http://ddp-ext.worldbank.org/ext/DDPQQ/member.do?method=getMembers; Series Code is FP.CPI.TOTL.ZG, (accessed 8 May 2008).

Note: Volatility of GDP growth, investment and consumption is measured by the standard deviation of these variables at constant prices of 2000. Regional averages are weighted by the relative share of countries' GDP at the beginning of the period. Inflation is defined as the weighted average change of annual consumer prices It was calculated for the subset of countries with available data.

a   Inflation figures for developed countries do not include economies in transition.
b   Inflation rates for 16 Latin American countries and Barbados which represent about 55 per cent of regional GDP.
c   Inflation rates for 28 African countries which represent almost 90 per cent of regional GDP.
d   Inflation rates for East and South Asia include 10 countries that represent about 60 per cent of regional GDP.
e   Inflation rates for Western Asia include 7 countries that represent almost 90 per cent of regional GDP.

private consumption growth remains as high in Africa as in preceding decades, suggesting that lower aggregate output volatility is not translating into greater economic security for households.

Table II.1 also shows that, while investment growth has fallen somewhat in most regions, it remains highly volatile in all developing-country regions. During the present decade, there has been a significant fall in investment volatility in East and South

Investment growth has remained volatile in all developing-country regions

Asia, but much of it is explained by the fast economic growth context in China and India. In other developing-country regions, investment volatility has remained high (see figure II.1).

Figure II.1
Growth of GDP and investment volatility, 1971-2000

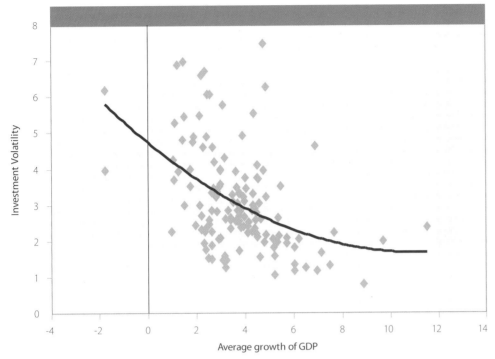

Source: UN/DESA based on United Nations Statistics Division, National Accounts Main Aggregates database.
Notes: At constant prices of 2000 for the period 1971-2006.
Coefficient of variation (CV) of the annual growth rate of gross capital formation at 2000 prices in 1971-2006. The coefficient of variation is defined as the standard deviation divided by the mean for the period.

The continued high investment volatility in developing countries results from a combination of factors. The frequency and depth of economic recessions have remained high since the 1970s (see table II.2). While their intensity seems to have tapered off somewhat during the present decade, this remains a major source of business uncertainty, holding off long term productive investment. Accelerated trade and capital market opening during the 1990s have been related sources of volatility and investment uncertainty. This has been reinforced by the mostly pro-cyclical macroeconomic policy stance in many countries in response to downturns and recessions. As discussed further below, the emerging phenomenon described as "financialization" possibly has also tilted incentives against productive investment and job creation and has presented itself as a new source of economic insecurity.

Reduced macroeconomic volatility has, by and large, come at the cost of lower average growth rates. In developed countries, growth of GDP per capita has been on a declining trend since the 1970s (see figure II.2a). For developing countries, trend growth has been up since the 1990s, but this is largely explained by fast growth in China and India. When these are left out, the trend level of per capita output growth over the past three decades (as well as during the recovery in the current decade) is well below that of the 1970s (figures II.2b and II.2c).

The correlation of this pattern with macroeconomic volatility is shown in figures II.3a and II.3b. The graphs compare the pattern of growth and volatility for individual countries in the period 2001-2006 in relation to the 1970s. Countries that grew

Improved stability has come with lower economic growth owing to persistent investment volatility

Table II.2
Incidence of recessions, selected country groups and regions, 1971-2006

	1971-1980			1981-1990			1991-2000			2001-2006		
	Number of recessions	Average length in years	Average GDP shortfall	Number of recessions	Average length in years	Average GDP shortfall	Number of recessions	Average length in years	Average GDP shortfall	Number of recessions	Average length in years	Average GDP shortfall
Developed economies[a]	44	1.22	-2.52	44	1.38	-1.90	66	2.44	-8.78	17	1.46	-1.36
Developing economies	122	1.79	-4.18	134	2.36	-4.89	121	1.72	-3.77	47	1.54	-2.75
Latin America and the Caribbean	27	2.26	-2.74	50	2.52	-4.37	40	1.48	-2.79	19	1.25	-2.57
South and East Asia	22	1.44	-3.76	13	2.02	-3.90	19	1.95	-4.83	8	1.25	-1.75
East Asia	12	1.29	-3.07	10	2.02	-3.82	14	2.10	-5.77	7	1.29	-1.72
South Asia	10	1.65	-4.72	3	2.00	-4.18	5	1.44	-1.70	1	1.00	-1.93
Western Asia	30	1.63	-7.29	30	2.35	-8.00	28	1.48	-4.84	10	1.83	-4.36
Africa	43	1.68	-3.83	41	2.34	-4.00	34	2.09	-3.45	10	2.06	-2.31
Least developed countries	85	2.24	-4.39	75	2.74	-4.13	70	2.47	-4.75	33	1.59	-3.37

Source: UN/DESA, based on United Nations Statistics Division, National Accounts Main Aggregates database.
Note: A recession refers to episodes of negative growth. Average length is the average number of years of negative GDP growth. Average shortfall is the average decrease in GDP growth during a recession.
a   Including countries belonging to the European Union (EU), non-EU and Commonwealth of Independent States (CIS), and economies in transition.

Figure II.2a
Growth of GDP per capita, developed countries, 1971-2006

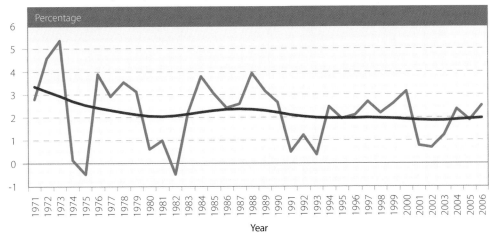

HP-filtered growth
Observed growth

Source: UN/DESA, based
on United Nations Statistics
Division, National Accounts
Main Aggregates database.

Figure II.2b
Growth of GDP per capita, developing countries, 1971-2006

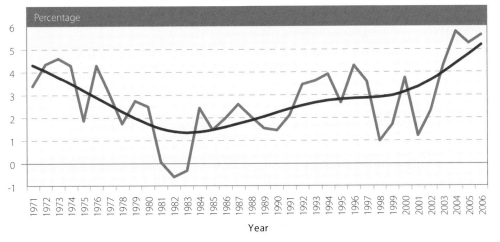

Note:

The red line is a smooth
trend on the rate of growth
of GDP per capita calculated
with a Hodrick-Prescott Filter
(HP). It removes short-term
fluctuations from longer-
term trends. Following the
literature, the long-term trend
in the figure was calculated
with a lag of 1 and μ = 100, as
suggested for yearly data.

Figure II.2c
Growth of GDP per capita, developing countries, excluding China and India, 1971-2006

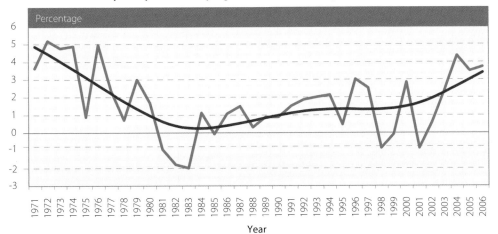

Figure II.3a
Growth of GDP per capita and volatility, 2001-2006, compared with 1971-1980, selected regions

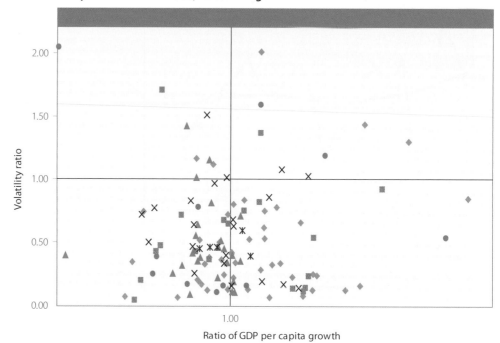

Africa ◆
East and South Asia ▣
Europe ▲
Latin America ✕
Non-EU ✴
Western Asia ●

Source: UN/DESA, based on United Nations Statistics Division, National Accounts Main Aggregates database.

Note: The measure of volatility is the coefficient of variation of GDP per capita growth. The four quadrants are built around the ratio of average GDP per capita growth and the measure of volatitity.

Figure II.3b
Growth of GDP per capita and volatility, 2001-2006, compared with 1971-1980, selected regions, excluding Africa

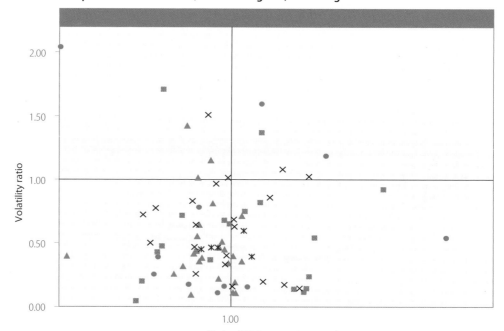

faster in the 2000s compared with the 1970s are to the right of the vertical line. Countries with lower volatility, as measured by the coefficient of variation of per capita GDP growth, are below the horizontal line. Most countries in the world were able to reduce volatility at the cost of lower growth rates, excluding sub-Saharan Africa. The strong recent growth performance of most countries in sub-Saharan Africa comes after two decades of low (or negative) growth and high volatility and has been buoyed by rising commodity prices and recovery from civil strife and conflict. Other countries that did better in 2001-2006 compared with the 1970s are concentrated in East and South Asia. A few Latin American countries (like Argentina, Chile, Jamaica and Costa Rica) also did better, in part because of crises suffered during the 1970s. In the vast majority of developed and developing countries in Europe, Western Asia, most of Latin America and the Caribbean, and parts of East and South Asia, greater stability has been achieved at the cost of lower rates of growth.

A predictable macroeconomic environment is an essential element of a strong investment climate. A volatile business climate can increase uncertainty, making investors reluctant to expand capacity, which in turn can slow productivity growth, increasing the potential for further uncertainty. In the absence of automatic stabilizers and because of the heavier reliance of investment on external financing and imported capital goods, the business cycle is expected to be more volatile in developing than in developed countries. This can make it all the more difficult to establish a long-term development path in some countries, given that the minimum scale of investment required to launch and sustain an industrialization drive has been steadily rising (United Nations Conference on Trade and Development, 2003; United Nations, 2006).

Lower growth performance of the past decade may further be explained by the strong deceleration of growth in public consumption and public investment in a majority of countries. Governments in many developing countries have cut back public spending as part of orthodox stabilization programmes and as pro-cyclical responses to economic downturns and external shocks. Especially during the 1980s and 1990s, fiscal austerity forced many Governments to sacrifice important infrastructure investment projects as well as social programmes in order to meet these goals. This trend was especially noticeable in Latin America and sub-Saharan Africa (United Nations, 2006).

Slow growth of productive investment in recent decades is perhaps the clearest indication of the failure of the predominant approach to macroeconomic policies to stimulate creative innovation and growth. The narrow approach to macroeconomic policymaking based on low-inflation targeting and fiscal balance failed to sustain higher growth rates because it did not pay enough attention to the factors that determine capital formation, productivity and the full and efficient utilization of productive capacity.[1]

Macroeconomic policies failed to stimulate creative innovation and growth

External shocks and volatility

Few dispute that increased international trade and capital mobility can be a means of achieving greater national wealth. However, they can also be a source of insecurity.

Policymakers in advanced countries have long recognized this dual face of increased trade and have debated what to do about it, especially in terms of compensating the losers. Trade shocks are an even bigger challenge in countries reliant on more tradi-

High volatility of commodity prices remains a source of instability

1   See, for further analysis and discussion, Ffrench-Davis (2006); Easterly, Islam and Stiglitz (2001); and Ocampo and Vos (2008).

tional export sectors. Most developing countries are producers and exporters of primary products or commodities and their economic activity heavily relies on these sectors. The recent increase in commodity prices associated with the strong demand from China and India has helped exporting countries, mainly in Africa and Latin America, to improve growth. High volatility of commodity prices, however, continues to be a source of instability. Managing commodity booms proved particularly difficult in the past; and downturns, particularly when these have been sharp, have left a significantly damaged economy which it has been difficult to turn around. Moreover, the recent surge in fuel and food prices is putting pressure on inflation and may lead to a rapid deterioration of income among households, reversing much of the gains made by countries in the area of poverty reduction (see box II.1). The lack of control over these variables, especially by smaller economies that cannot influence the external environment, has created greater and harder-to-manage economic insecurity.

Box II.1

The macroeconomics of food security

According to the Food and Agriculture Organization of the United Nations (FAO), "food security exists when all people, at all times, have access to sufficient, safe and nutritious food to meet their dietary needs and food preferences for an active and healthy life". An acute food crisis has erupted in 2008. Strongly rising world food prices are making it more difficult to provide emergency food aid and to buy food on the world market, increasing the sense that food security is under threat. This is on top of the chronic malnutrition from which close to 1 billion people are estimated to suffer (see figure).

The present situation has its roots in a long period of neglect of agricultural production, especially in developing countries; but there is also a more conjunctural macroeconomic dimension to the crisis.

Figure
Undernourished world population, selected regions, 1990-1992 and 2001-2003

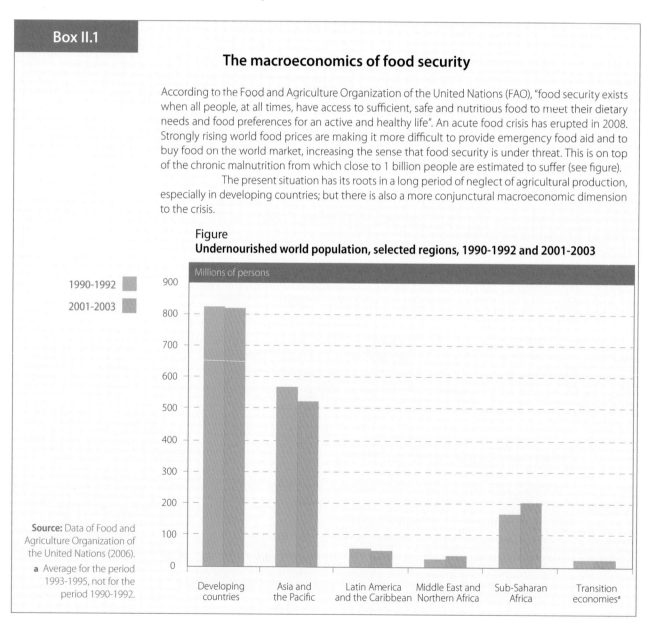

Source: Data of Food and Agriculture Organization of the United Nations (2006).

a Average for the period 1993-1995, not for the period 1990-1992.

Box II.1 (cont'd)

Food insecurity and poverty

In early 2008, there were 37 countries requiring immediate food assistance, of which one third were in sub-Saharan Africa and most of the others in Asia (Food and Agriculture Organization of the United Nations, 2008). According to one estimate, another 109 million people may have fallen below the $1 per day poverty line because of the rise in food prices since 2006 (see table). Other things being equal, in sub-Saharan Africa, the incidence of extreme poverty may have risen by almost 8 percentage points, implying that the recent food price increases have more than wiped out the poverty reduction achieved in the region between 1990 and 2004.

Impact on global poverty of the surge in agricultural commodity prices

	Simulated pass-through to consumer food prices of 69 per cent increase in world agricutural food prices, 2006-2008 (percentage)	Poverty incidence (percentage) ($1 PPP per day poverty line)			Number of poor (millions)			Total population covered in simulation (millions)
		Base (2004)	Food price simulation	Increase in poverty incidence	Base	Food price simulation	Increase in poor	
East Asia	5	9.6	10.8	1.2	150.5	169.9	19.5	1 570.7
South Asia	5	31.2	34.7	3.5	433.8	481.8	48.0	1 390.4
Latin America and the Caribbean	6	8.7	9.6	0.9	45.5	50.3	4.8	524.2
Sub-Saharan Africa	19	36.9	44.6	7.8	175.9	212.9	37.0	476.9
Total		**20.3**	**23.1**	**2.8**	**805.7**	**914.9**	**109.2**	**3 962.2**

Source: UN/DESA, based on household survey data using the PovcalNet of the World Bank. See Vos (2008) for estimation methodology.

Macroeconomic causes of food insecurity

Much of the recent surge in food prices is related to a series of compounding short- and long-term factors which have combined to create this unprecedented situation. After a slump during the first half of the 1980s in the developing countries, agricultural investment recovered somewhat, but did not return to the levels seen in the 1970s (Food and Agriculture Organization of the United Nations, 1999). In addition, growth rates of yields for major cereals (wheat, maize and rice) have slowed since 1960 in the developing countries (World Bank, 2007). Although the average yield for coarse grains increased from 1.4 millions to 3.2 millions of tons per hectare from the 1960s to the present, productivity growth decelerated from 2.6 per cent per year in the 1960s to 1.6 per cent per annum over the past decade.[a]

A series of structural and macroeconomic factors are now exposing these long-term shortcomings. First, the persistent weak dollar has increased the international trading prices of all food products, along with those of other commodities. Although changes in global food prices are not as readily transmitted to the consumer, studies have shown that these are significant, especially in developing countries. At least half of the basket of consumer goods in developing countries consists of food products; hence, increases in the global food prices have a significant effect on inflation. This has ended the downward trend of inflation and has added another element of economic insecurity to the present conjuncture. Second, the high economic growth of some large developing countries and an accelerated pace of urbanization have shifted consumption patterns towards higher-value food products, such as meat. This has increased the demand for animal feed, including grains, which are also the main ingredients for staple food. Third, the sharp increase in the price of oil has increased the cost of transportation of food commodities and the production costs of fertilizers. Fourth, concerns about energy security have increased the demand for biofuels, which has required greater production of corn and sugar cane. Estimates suggest that, in 2006 and 2007, almost half the

[a] Calculations based on Commodity Research Bureau, *The CRB Commodity Yearbook 2007* (Hoboken, New Jersey, John Wiley and Sons, 2007).

Box II.1 (cont'd)

increase in the demand for major food crops in the United States was for corn-based ethanol production (International Monetary Fund, 2008), while almost all of the increase in global maize production between 2004 and 2007 was used for biofuel production in the United States (World Bank, 2008a).

Financial speculation has also played a role in the recent surge in food prices. Prices in the futures market of wheat and grains have risen recently and are much higher than in the spot or cash market; and since 2006, there has been no convergence between these two sets of prices, as would have been expected. Traders seem to expect shortages in these markets; but since the futures price has been higher than the cash price on the delivery date, hedgers buy at the cash price, store the produce and sell a futures contract in order to make a profit. This phenomenon has not only added a premium on the traded commodity but also increased volatility in the market. It has furthermore created uncertainty for producers who rely on these instruments to ensure an adequate price for long-term investment and production planning. Additional uncertainty originates from the increased demand which has driven inventories to record lows, especially for cereals. This makes the world price more sensitive to any news about supply problems, thus adding to price volatility.

Development policy implications

In the short run, the humanitarian and food emergency needs have been clearly spelled out by the designated United Nations organizations. Additional food and monetary aid is necessary to alleviate severe starvation. The most vulnerable parts of the population during the present food crisis are those who were already dependent on food assistance and have seen their rations decreased or depleted. Also affected have been subsistence farmers who lost their harvest for various reasons and net-buying poor farmers who had to assimilate higher costs of production and higher prices of food to complement consumption.

Several countries have imposed export controls, ranging from quotas and tariffs to complete export bans, in order to maintain their national food security. Although each country has the right to pursue its own food security, such "beggar-thy-neighbour" type measures may be counterproductive. In many cases, food exporters have protested against these measures as regards their interrupting even the domestic supply of food and further increasing prices. At the same time, these non-cooperative measures have decreased the supply of food at the regional and global levels, thereby exacerbating the problem.

In order to discourage such measures, countries in crisis, especially low-income food-deficit countries, are in need of immediate assistance. During the present crisis, the weakness of short-term food assistance was exposed as rising prices reduced the volume of aid. Hence, a price indexation mechanism or the assurance that contributions are defined in food quantities (rather than values) should be put in place for pledges to aid agencies made by donor countries. The situation has not been helped by the shift in the composition of official development assistance (ODA) in recent years away from productive sectors such as agriculture, which has seen its share drop to only 3.1 per cent of these flows. In addition, the (reduced) aid to agriculture has been focused in a few countries, leading to much duplication and contradiction among donor interventions (World Bank, 2007). Thus, greater coordination to improve aid effectiveness is required.

Although complete global food security will be difficult to achieve, in the long run, agrarian development and reform programmes are needed to raise investment and stimulate productivity of food production. These programmes should focus on small poor farmers since they constitute the most vulnerable group in the rural areas, through providing investment in rural infrastructure and access to credits, to affordable modern farm inputs and to land through land redistribution. South Asia and sub-Saharan Africa (and some countries in Latin America and the Caribbean) should be the priority focus of these programmes, since they are the most vulnerable in terms of food security. A recent report of the Economic and Social Commission for Asia and the Pacific (United Nations, Economic and Social Commission for Asia and the Pacific, 2008) has shown that, in Asia, raising agricultural productivity in all countries in the region to the level of that of Thailand could lift more than 200 million people out of poverty. Land and labour productivity of cereal production in Africa has been lower than in Asia and Latin America (World Bank 2007).

Box II.1 (cont'd)

Increased public spending on research and development to improve agricultural technology and raise productivity is essential. In the 1980s, Governments reduced research and development spending for agricultural development because it was thought that the food security problem had been resolved. This trend has been detrimental for agricultural productivity, especially for small farmers in developing countries.

Subsidies of agriculture in Europe and the United States of America have made it difficult for many developing-country producers to compete in world markets and have been a factor in the slowdown of productivity growth. Although agricultural support in Organization for Economic Cooperation and Development (OECD) countries dropped between the mid-1980s and the period between 2004 and 2006, it is still high, reaching to a level of 60 per cent of farm receipts in some countries (Organization for Economic Cooperation and Development, 2007a). In addition, most of the support is still targeted to single commodities, which raises specific prices. Further reduction or elimination of farm subsidies in Europe and North America should be part of a medium-term strategy. Initially such a measure will likely lead to a further increase in international food prices. Preventing an adverse impact of agricultural trade liberalization on the food security in low-income countries would be a further justification of the much needed reform of international compensatory financing mechanisms as discussed in this report.

At the same time, the weight and influence of financial markets, financial actors and financial institutions have grown dramatically in recent decades (see below). This could have provided a stimulus to growth, but the volatile and pro-cyclical nature of capital flows has at the same time turned the financial growth into a source of economic insecurity. Their effects are often transmitted by way of public sector accounts, especially through the effects of available financing on government spending and of interest rates on the public debt service. However, the stronger effects typically run through private spending and balance sheets.

The shift towards export-led strategies in the developing world has actually accentuated this pattern in many countries. The growing influence of financial calculation has increased commodity price volatility, the impact of which on the business cycle is further amplified by pro-cyclical policies, among others, by expanding fiscal expenditures during the boom and reducing spending when prices are down. The latter is reinforced by the conditionality linked to international financial assistance during crises, which involves orthodox macroeconomic stabilization policy packages.

These financial dynamics have far-reaching implications for the real economy. Episodes of exceptionally rapid economic expansion driven by financial bubbles can bring periods of growing prosperity, but they can end very suddenly, leading to deep recessions or even longer periods of stagnation. Vulnerability to a sharp reversal of flows varies, but in many emerging markets, it is often triggered by factors beyond the control of recipient countries, including shifts in monetary and financial policies in the major industrialized countries.

The growing influence of financial markets adds to economic insecurity

Trade and current-account shocks

Trade volumes and terms-of-trade fluctuations have historically played a major role in the business cycles in developing countries, particularly in commodity-dependent economies. This still may well be the case and with the widespread shift towards export-led strategies in the developing world, this role has likely been accentuated.

Vulnerability of countries to trade shocks is associated with their degree of export diversification

A decomposition analysis of current-account shocks and domestic adjustment gives an idea of the changing nature and intensity of external shocks across countries over the past few decades.[2] Trade shocks (in terms of both prices and volumes) still pretty much dominate current-account adjustment and became more predominant again after much of the external debt overhang of developing countries, accumulated with commercial banks, had been restructured in the late 1980s, in particular in Latin America. The vulnerability to trade shocks is closely associated with the nature and degree of export diversification.

Table II.3

Decomposition analysis of the current account of the balance of payments, Asia, East Asia, Latin America and the Caribbean and sub-Saharan Africa, 1981-2005

Percentage of GNP								
From:	1981-1985	1986-1990	1991-1995	1996-2000	1981-1985	1986-1990	1991-1995	1996-2000
To:	1986-1990	1991-1995	1996-2000	2001-2005	1986-1990	1991-1995	1996-2000	2001-2005
	Asia				East Asia			
Observed deficit increase	-0.95	0.45	-2.22	-0.93	-1.14	0.51	-3.41	-1.06
External shocks	-1.13	-0.11	-2.28	0.60	-1.82	-0.02	-2.43	2.44
Terms-of-trade deterioration	-1.96	-0.92	-0.38	2.25	-3.34	-2.30	-1.28	3.05
Imports price effect	2.23	-0.74	0.43	0.19	4.15	-1.83	0.95	0.47
Exports price effect	-4.19	-0.18	-0.81	2.06	-7.49	-0.46	-2.22	2.58
Interest-rate shock	-0.29	-0.18	-0.17	-0.40	-0.37	-0.25	-0.17	-0.33
World trade retardation	1.12	0.99	-1.73	-1.26	1.89	2.52	-0.99	-0.29
Other external variables	1.05	0.43	0.36	-0.13	0.89	0.41	0.98	-0.71
Debt accumulation burden	0.60	0.14	0.27	0.08	0.72	0.10	0.37	-0.24
Change in direct investment income	0.16	0.26	0.32	-0.04	0.11	0.28	0.65	-0.22
Change in remittances	0.28	0.04	-0.22	-0.14	0.08	0.04	-0.02	-0.18
Change in official transfers	0.02	-0.01	-0.01	-0.04	-0.01	-0.01	-0.02	-0.06
Domestic adjustment	-1.66	-0.18	-0.04	-3.30	-1.63	-0.68	-1.52	-6.27
Domestic spending	-0.72	0.63	-1.12	-0.99	-1.04	1.23	-1.65	-1.25
Consumption contraction	-0.54	-0.41	-0.76	-0.55	-0.74	-0.38	-1.05	-0.64
Private consumption	-0.40	-0.43	-0.62	-0.61	-0.47	-0.48	-0.81	-0.76
Public consumption	-0.14	0.02	-0.15	0.06	-0.28	0.11	-0.24	0.12
Investment reduction	-0.18	1.04	-0.36	-0.44	-0.30	1.61	-0.60	-0.61
Trade ratios	-0.95	-0.81	1.08	-2.31	-0.59	-1.91	0.13	-5.02
Import replacement	1.63	4.38	3.57	7.52	2.41	5.07	3.25	10.04
Export penetration	-2.57	-5.19	-2.49	-9.83	-3.00	-6.98	-3.12	-15.07
Interaction effects	0.79	0.32	-0.26	1.91	1.42	0.81	-0.43	3.49

Table II.3 (cont'd)								
From	1981-1985	1986-1990	1991-1995	1996-2000	1981-1985	1986-1990	1991-1995	1996-2000
To	1986-1990	1991-1995	1996-2000	2001-2005	1986-1990	1991-1995	1996-2000	2001-2005
	Latin America and the Caribbean				Sub-Saharan Africa			
Observed deficit increase	0.51	2.42	-0.07	-3.77	-6.42	0.80	1.17	1.44
External shocks	3.60	-2.51	-5.30	-5.97	-0.55	-13.25	-13.19	-9.23
Terms-of-trade deterioration	4.48	0.85	-0.53	-0.56	3.78	-0.54	-0.82	-0.58
Imports price effect	1.48	-2.12	-1.95	0.68	4.08	0.16	-0.23	0.01
Exports price effect	3.00	2.98	1.41	-1.24	-0.30	-0.70	-0.60	-0.59
Interest-rate shock	0.41	-0.91	-0.18	-0.65	-1.10	-2.01	-0.21	-0.64
World trade retardation	-1.30	-2.45	-4.59	-4.76	-3.23	-10.70	-12.15	-8.01
Other external variables	-0.88	3.28	0.49	1.30	0.21	1.26	-0.04	-0.24
Debt accumulation burden	-1.49	4.21	1.02	0.76	0.73	0.32	-0.06	0.06
Change in direct investment income	0.82	-0.63	-0.35	1.19	0.79	0.90	-0.21	1.66
Change in remittances	-0.18	-0.31	-0.20	-0.66	-1.44	0.12	0.03	-2.04
Change in official transfers	-0.03	0.01	0.01	-0.01	0.13	-0.08	0.21	0.08
Domestic adjustment	-1.04	6.12	5.41	2.55	-5.61	9.75	10.76	10.22
Domestic spending	-0.78	0.15	-0.06	0.01	-2.62	3.70	-1.42	0.20
Consumption contraction	-0.51	-0.03	-0.21	0.14	-1.88	5.04	-1.63	-0.55
Private consumption	-0.50	0.17	-0.05	0.22	-0.52	5.51	-1.24	0.12
Public consumption	0.00	-0.20	-0.15	-0.08	-1.36	-0.47	-0.39	-0.66
Investment reduction	-0.28	0.18	0.15	-0.13	-0.73	-1.33	0.22	0.75
Trade ratios	-0.26	5.96	5.47	2.54	-2.99	6.05	12.17	10.01
Import replacement	0.59	6.62	6.48	1.61	-3.47	-4.91	3.29	6.22
Export penetration	-0.85	-0.66	-1.01	0.93	0.48	10.96	8.88	3.80
Interaction effects	-1.16	-4.47	-0.66	-1.66	-0.47	3.04	3.63	0.69

Source: UN/DESA calculations, based on United Nations Statistics Division, World Bank Global Development Finance (GDF) and International Monetary Fund International Financial Statistics online databases.

Note: See appendix, section A, for methodology. Regions are also defined in section A of the appendix. Regional averages are weighted by GNP. A positive (negative) sign refers to an increase (decrease) in the deficit and thus to an adverse (favourable) external shock.

Despite the greater emphasis on export-led growth strategies, the size of terms-of-trade shocks relative to the gross national product (GNP) of developing countries has been reduced, on average, in comparison with those witnessed during the 1980s (see tables II.3 and II.4).[3] Primary commodity exporters, most of which are concentrated in sub-Saharan Africa and Latin America, had seen strongly adverse terms-of-trade shocks during the 1980s, especially because of a collapse in export prices. Commodity price volatility remained high during the 1990s (see figure A.9) but—again on average—terms-of-trade shocks were positive for commodity-exporting regions, especially during the present decade. In contrast, net commodity importers, especially in Asia, have suffered adverse terms-of-trade effects because of the recent surge in commodity prices. Most least developed countries, on the other hand, especially those in Africa, have suffered continued adverse terms-of-trade effects throughout the 1980s, the 1990s and the present decade.

Global trade has grown consistently faster than output since 1945 and significantly so for the last 25 years. Over this same period, the share of developing countries has risen steadily, including in the export of manufactures. A more outward-oriented growth

Most developing countries have failed to diversify their exporting sectors and remain vulnerable to external shocks

3   Please note that the decomposition methodology describes changes in the current-account *deficit*. This means that in the tables, values with a negative sign refer to positive shocks and those with a positive sign, to adverse shocks.

Table II.4
Terms-of-trade shocks, selected regions, 1981-2005

Regions[a]		1981-1985 / 1986-1990	1986-1990 / 1991-1995	1991-1995 / 1996-2000	1996-2000 / 2001-2005
Latin America and the Caribbean	Terms-of-trade deterioration	4.48	0.85	-0.53	-0.56
	Imports price effect	1.48	-2.12	-1.95	0.68
	Exports price effect	3.00	2.98	1.41	-1.24
South America	Terms-of-trade deterioration	3.43	2.10	-0.98	-0.34
	Imports price effect	0.75	-0.96	-2.07	3.97
	Exports price effect	2.68	3.06	1.09	-4.30
Central America, without Mexico	Terms-of-trade deterioration	-1.14	-1.74	-1.13	1.58
	Imports price effect	-0.70	-0.95	0.45	-0.11
	Exports price effect	-0.45	-0.79	-1.58	1.70
Mexico	Terms-of-trade deterioration	8.60	-2.15	0.92	-1.55
	Imports price effect	4.42	-5.81	-2.00	-8.21
	Exports price effect	4.18	3.66	2.92	6.66
Caribbean	Terms-of-trade deterioration	-0.83	-1.07	-2.55	-0.51
	Imports price effect	-6.46	-5.32	2.15	3.13
	Exports price effect	5.62	4.25	-4.69	-3.64
Asia	Terms-of-trade deterioration	-1.96	-0.92	-0.38	2.25
	Imports price effect	2.23	-0.74	0.43	0.19
	Exports price effect	-4.19	-0.18	-0.81	2.06
East Asia, without China	Terms-of-trade deterioration	0.67	-0.61	-1.70	2.75
	Imports price effect	-0.28	-3.60	4.91	3.12
	Exports price effect	0.96	2.98	-6.61	-0.37
South Asia, without India	Terms-of-trade deterioration	0.35	0.47	-0.89	3.37
	Imports price effect	0.38	0.13	0.58	2.29
	Exports price effect	-0.03	0.34	-1.48	1.08
China	Terms-of-trade deterioration	-4.53	-2.80	-1.16	3.14
	Imports price effect	5.47	-1.31	-0.23	-0.32
	Exports price effect	-10.00	-1.49	-0.92	3.46
India	Terms-of-trade deterioration	0.01	-0.01	0.49	1.92
	Imports price effect	0.10	-0.37	-0.54	1.08
	Exports price effect	-0.10	0.35	1.04	0.84
Western Asia	Terms-of-trade deterioration	-0.29	2.38	2.10	-0.80
	Imports price effect	-1.40	2.40	-0.38	-2.87
	Exports price effect	1.11	-0.03	2.48	2.07
Africa	Terms-of-trade deterioration	3.14	-0.42	-0.67	-0.48
	Imports price effect	3.35	0.12	-0.18	0.03
	Exports price effect	-0.21	-0.53	-0.49	-0.51
Africa, excluding Nigeria	Terms-of-trade deterioration	3.25	-1.03	-0.23	-0.09
	Imports price effect	3.11	0.52	-0.44	0.43
	Exports price effect	0.14	-1.55	0.21	-0.52
Nigeria	Terms-of-trade deterioration	1.13	10.42	-8.44	-7.41
	Imports price effect	7.57	-7.10	4.44	-7.01
	Exports price effect	-6.44	17.52	-12.88	-0.40

Table II.4 (cont'd)		1981-1985	1986-1990	1991-1995	1996-2000
Regions[a]		1986-1990	1991-1995	1996-2000	2001-2005
Northern Africa	Terms-of-trade deterioration	0.28	0.14	0.00	-0.04
	Imports price effect	0.11	-0.05	0.02	0.12
	Exports price effect	0.18	0.19	-0.01	-0.15
Least developed countries in sub-Saharan Africa	Terms-of-trade deterioration	4.77	4.20	1.68	1.66
	Imports price effect	4.92	8.68	0.23	2.43
	Exports price effect	-0.15	-4.48	1.45	-0.80
Other countries in sub-Saharan Africa[b]	Terms-of-trade deterioration	9.37	-8.40	-2.55	-1.86
	Imports price effect	8.78	-5.68	-2.13	-0.50
	Exports price effect	0.59	-2.72	-0.42	-1.37

Source: Appendix table A.2.

Note: A positive (negative) sign refers to an increase (decrease) in the deficit and thus to an adverse (favourable) external shock.

a　Regions as defined in section A of the appendix.

b　Excluding Nigeria.

strategy can make for a more stable growth path, particularly where the domestic market is small. However, greater reliance on export markets may increase the vulnerability of countries to sudden changes in the volume of exports or the terms of trade when they are not able to diversify their structure of production and exports. The decomposition analysis shows that the expansion of world trade has significantly helped reduce the current-account deficits of countries in sub-Saharan Africa (since the mid-1980s) and Latin America (since the 1990s, although to a lesser extent) (see table II.3). Its effect in East Asia has not been as large, as shown by the small negative sign for world trade (indicating that world trade growth helped reduce the current-account deficit) since the 1990s. The main difference among these regions arises from the large effort that countries in East Asia (mainly China) have made to diversify their exporting sectors and improve their competitive position in world markets. Results presented in table II.3 show that most countries in Latin America and the Caribbean and Africa and the small island developing States have lost ground in international markets (Vos and Parra, 2008). This lack of export competitiveness (reflected by a positive sign for the export penetration effect) is most severe among the least developed countries (see table A.2). By contrast, the members of the group of Asian countries included in the analysis have been able to increase competitiveness and thus export penetration.

Differences in the performance of these regions in world markets signal more fundamental differences in the capacity of countries to benefit from the expansion of trade. East Asian countries were very successful in achieving a rapid transformation of exporting sectors, away from primary products and resource-based and low-technology manufacturing towards more capital-intensive and high-technology goods. The share of the former type of goods in total exports of the region dropped from 76 per cent in 1980 to 35 per cent in 2005. In China, this share fell from 93 per cent in 1985 to 44 per cent in 2005. Other regions have been less successful in transforming their structure of production for exports. South and Central America still rely on primary products and simple manufactures (about 78 per cent of exports in 2005, though down from about 90 per cent in 1983). In Africa, the concentration of exports in low value added products is greater still (83 per cent in 2005) (see table A.3).

Increasing imports in
Africa and Latin America
reflect greater demand for
consumption goods

The high positive import-replacement ratios (reflecting rising import dependence) across developing countries during the 1990s evidence the impact of trade liberalization, albeit with important regional differences. In East Asia, the rise in import demand has gone hand in hand with export-led industrialization strategies, reflecting higher demand for raw materials and industrial inputs, including through the establishment of international production networks (United Nations, 2006). On average, the rise in import dependence has been outweighed by the increase in export penetration and a shift towards rising trade surpluses. Elsewhere, in most parts of Latin America and Africa, rising import dependence has had little to do with economic diversification, and more with rising imports of consumer goods and/or growth of footloose low value added manufactures.[4]

Greater reliance on primary
exports is associated
with higher output and
investment volatility

The degree of diversification of countries and their insertion into world markets constitute an important factor explaining growth and economic instability. The steady diversification of economic activity has been identified as a common feature of a modern growth path and closely associated with industrial development (Imbs and Wacziarg, 2003). The diversification of exports towards higher value added products increases the resilience of countries to trade shocks and provides a stronger foundation for improving growth and stability over longer periods of time (Rodrik, 2007). Figure II.4a and 4b shows that greater reliance on primary exports is associated with higher output and investment volatility. This effect becomes even stronger with the lowering of the degree of export diversification.

Export diversification
requires sustained
investment...

In the context of increasing integration of the world economy, the gains from globalization depend on the ability of countries to develop dynamic competitive advantages based on innovation and productive diversification. This requires sustained investment

Figure II.4a
Primary export dependence and volatility of GDP per capita

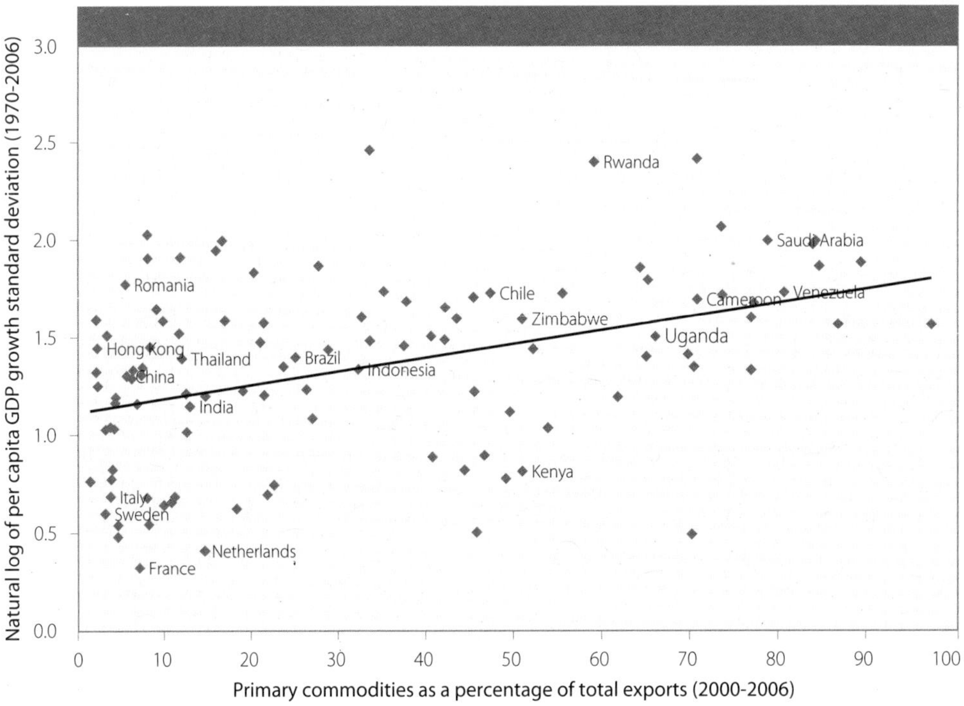

4   The latter effects are important in the rise of import dependence in Mexico and the Central American countries, for instance. See table A2.B.

Figure II.4b
Primary export dependence and investment volatility

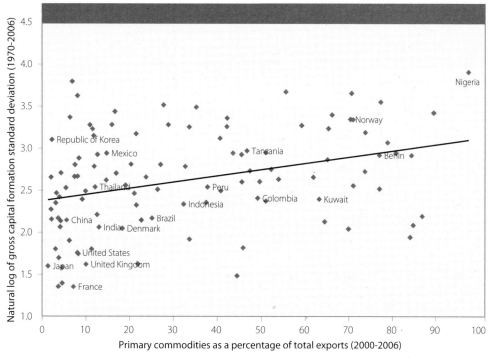

Source: UN/DESA calculations, based on United Nations Statistics Division National Accounts database and United Nations Commodity Trade database.

flows to facilitate the introduction of new technology and the development of infrastructure and workers' skills (United Nations, 2006). International competitiveness based on low wages gives countries an initial advantage in world markets and may be an appropriate employment-generation strategy for countries with a large share of unskilled labour. However, there are limits to the effectiveness of this strategy. Indeed, those limits may have tightened in recent years. In a study of 127 developed and developing countries, Dowrick and Golley (2004) found that, between 1960 and 1980, increased trade had helped accelerate productivity growth twice as much in poorer countries as in richer countries. That gain was reversed, however, in the period between 1980 and 2000 of more open trade, when the marginal impact of trade on productivity growth favoured the richer countries and turned negative for poorer countries. This has been associated with the "fallacy of composition" facing exporters of some manufactured goods and reflects the widespread efforts to replicate the export-led growth strategies of East Asian newly industrializing economies (United Nations Conference on Trade and Development, 2002). This may cause some countries to get stuck on a weak investment-low productivity growth path which is vulnerable to exogenous shocks of one kind or another.

The fact that long-term competitiveness and development are determined by capital-intensive and knowledge-based exports requires an explicit industrial policy designed to give support to infant industries and exporting firms and to introduce local content rules and coordinate large investment in infrastructure and human capital.

It was precisely because macroeconomic policies were well integrated with other policy areas that the transformation of the structure of exports in East Asia was successful. Monetary policy was coordinated with financial sector and industrial policies, including directed and subsidized credit schemes and managed interest rates, to directly influence investment and saving, while competitive exchange rates were considered essential for encouraging exports and export diversification.

… which requires consistent macroeconomic and industrial policies for development

Similarly, East Asia's productive transition towards higher value added products was supported by fiscal policies that gave priority to investment in education, health and infrastructure, as well as subsidies and credit guarantees for export industries. There was also a close link between economic and social policies (see chap. V). Macroeconomic policies in those countries were part of a broader development strategy which contributed to long-run growth. In contrast, macroeconomic policies in many Latin American and African countries since the 1980s have been focused on much more narrowly defined short-term stabilization objectives, often leading to declining public investment and exchange-rate overvaluation which undermine efforts to diversify production and exports (United Nations, 2006).

Capital flows and the changing dynamics of business cycles

Liberalization of capital markets led to an expansion of net financial flows

Parallel to the large expansion of trade, the lifting of capital controls in most countries supported greater financial integration in industrialized and developing countries (Prasad and others, 2003). Net financial transfers to developing countries had increased substantially starting from the early 1990s after a drought in the 1980s.[5] Figure II.5 shows continued strong expansion of net foreign direct investment (FDI) flows. Growth of net transfers related to other portfolio investments were (in the aggregate) rather short-lived and these were reversed after the Asian financial crisis of 1997. The reversal more than offset the growth in net FDI flows. The shift was associated with the sudden stop in private capital flows to emerging market economies in response to the string of financial crises that had occurred in the late 1990s. This stop was followed by a strong shift towards current-account surpluses in many developing countries. The pattern is similar, though it varies in degree, across developing-country regions (see figure II.6)

Strongly rising current-account surpluses were registered in East Asia from 1998 onward thanks to a combination of sharply declining imports (due to an economic slowdown) and rising exports (due to currency depreciation). Many commodity-exporters also started to generate large current-account surpluses, oil-exporters in particular, following the surge in commodity prices from the early 2000s. In Asia, growing external surpluses reflect the desire for greater "self-insurance" against external shocks through the accumulation of official reserves. As the countries in the region witnessed, at the same time, a return of strong capital inflows, part of the reserve accumulation can be seen to have consisted partly of "earned reserves" (that is, reserves generated by current-account surpluses) and partly of "borrowed reserves", a distinction relevant for the policy implications, as discussed further below.

The growing influence of financial markets and institutions on economic growth and development has been described as a process of "financialization". It involves a structural shift in the organization of economic activity with an "increasing role of financial motives, financial markets, financial actors and financial institutions in the operation of the domestic and international economies" (Epstein, 2005, p. 3).

Indeed, the global stock of financial assets has risen 12-fold since 1980, three times as fast as global GDP. The value of daily foreign-exchange transactions, which amounted to just $80 billion in 1980 now stands at close to $2,000 billion, a growth rate six times faster than that of foreign trade. There have been massive two-way flows of funds dominated by short-term capital movements in the form of cross-border bank lend-

---

5   Net transfers are defined as net financial inflows less related investment income payments to abroad.

Figure II.5
Net transfer^a of resources, developing countries, 1975-2005

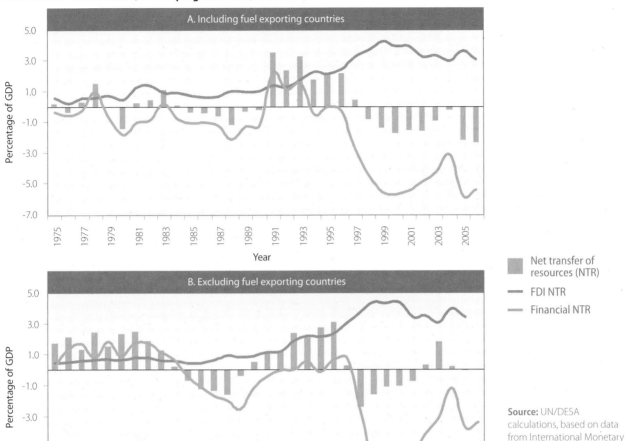

Legend:
Net transfer of resources (NTR)
FDI NTR
Financial NTR

Source: UN/DESA calculations, based on data from International Monetary Fund (IMF) International Financial Statistics (IFS) online database.

a Defined as net financial inflows less investment income payments to abroad.

ing, equities and bonds. The market for corporate control through cross-border mergers and acquisitions has also mushroomed and a good deal of foreign investment has been in banking, insurance and other financial services (Cumming, 2006).

These trends are closely associated with the rapid liberalization of domestic financial markets and the opening up of the external capital accounts, which, together with the increase in cross-border flows, were expected to bring large efficiency gains and faster growth (Mishkin, 2006). These benefits would derive, in part, from a better intertemporal match among a larger pool of savers and investors. Moreover, financial innovation (closely associated with more competitive financial markets) and the greater depth of financial markets would greatly reduce risk as hedging and insurance options became more attractive, and the threat of shocks and crises diminished. Indeed, the term "securitization", coined to describe the plethora of new financial instruments devised to pool and transfer risk, would suggest that the unshackling of finance brings about a safer and more stable world economy.

Larger financial flows were expected to bring efficiency gains and faster growth ...

Figure II.6
Net transfer[a] of financial resources, Latin America, Africa and East Asia, excluding China, 1975-2005

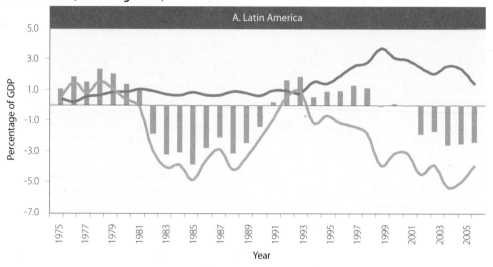

A. Latin America

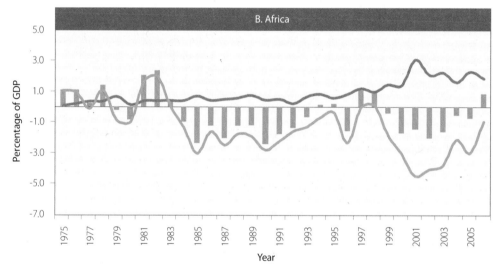

B. Africa

Net transfer of resources (NTR)

FDI NTR

Financial NTR

Source: UN/DESA calculations, based on data from International Monetary Fund (IMF) International Financial Statistics (IFS) online database.

a Defined as net financial inflows less investment income payments to abroad.

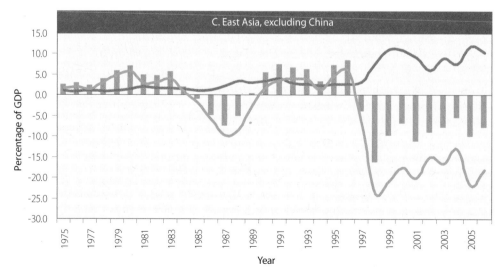

C. East Asia, excluding China

However, in practice, these financial dynamics, with their introduction of heightened risks of strongly pro-cyclical volatility, have had far-reaching implications for the real economy. Episodes of exceptionally rapid economic expansion driven by financial bubbles can bring periods of growing prosperity, but they can end very suddenly in recessions or longer periods of slow growth. Sharp swings in asset prices, exchange rates and aggregate demand cause a fundamental uncertainty regarding the return on capital, shorten planning horizons and promote defensive and speculative strategies in investment which can, in turn, exert a significant adverse influence on the pace and pattern of capital accumulation, economic growth and employment.[6] These problems are particularly serious in developing countries in view of the limited scope therein for pursuing effective counter-cyclical macroeconomic policies.[7] The nature of vulnerability to capital flow reversals varies, but in many emerging markets since the 1970s, a financial crisis has often been triggered by factors beyond the control of recipient countries, including shifts in monetary and financial policies in the major industrialized countries.

The developing world has experienced two full medium-term cycles in capital flows that have had a strong impact on stability and growth in many countries, and the world seems to have entered a third cycle most recently. The first cycle had started with the boom in international bank lending to developing countries in the 1970s and ended in debt crises in the 1980s. Another boom occurred in the 1990s, which was mainly driven by portfolio investment flows and, to a lesser extent, FDI; it came to an end with a sharp decline in net flows after the Asian financial crisis. The recovery from the global slowdown in 2001, an improved international economic environment and strengthened economic conditions in developing countries have provided the basis for a renewed recovery of private capital flows since 2003, indicating the beginning of a third cycle. The pro-cyclical nature of capital movements has been well documented (see, among others, United Nations Conference on Trade and Development, 1991; Vos, 1994; World Bank 1999; United Nations, 2006, chap. IV).

Aside from being characterized by strong pro-cyclical features, boom-bust cycles tend to spill over to other markets (contagion). Mexico's currency crisis led to capital reversals in other emerging market economies. The Asian crisis and the Russian default in 1998 caused a more general withdrawal of funds invested in developing countries. Since a country's loss of access to markets for international banks or bond markets spreads to include other sources of financing (in addition to the fact that it may affect market access of other countries), an across-the-board market closure may follow. Even when countries do not fully lose market access, they tend to be subject to increases in risk premiums. The pro-cyclical downgrades by credit-rating agencies often exacerbate both reduced access to portfolio loans and the higher spreads at which bonds can be issued.

Although FDI flows had also been negatively affected by the Asian crisis, they remained positive and became the dominant source of private capital flows to developing countries. It is worth noting, however, that FDI also moves pro-cyclically, although not to the same extent as do short-term lending and portfolio investment (World Bank, 1999). Therefore, FDI can also increase macroeconomic instability. This is so, in part, because an important share of FDI takes the form of mergers and acquisitions of firms in develop-

… but financial markets increased the vulnerability of countries to factors beyond their control

Foreign direct investment (FDI) is also pro-cyclical, particularly when it is motivated by mergers and acquisitions

6   In the East Asian countries hit by financial crisis in the late 1990s, for example, the boom had been accompanied by a 7 percentage point rise in the average investment ratio and by more than a 16 percentage point decline in the crisis. Investment stagnated in the subsequent recovery, with the result that there was a sharp decline in the investment ratio over the entire cycle (United Nations Conference on Trade and Development, 2000).

7   See Ocampo (2003); United Nations (2006); and Ocampo and Vos (2008).

ing countries, which are pro-cyclical (United Nations, 2006, chap. III). Moreover, to the extent that FDI is geared towards the domestic market, it is also likely to respond to an economic downturn in the same way that domestic investment does.

The pro-cyclical nature of private capital flows limits the space available to Governments in developing countries for conducting counter-cyclical macroeconomic policies. In this respect, capital-account liberalization has added a new and increasingly dominant dimension to financial cycles in developing countries, creating mutually reinforcing interactions among credit, capital and currency markets. The failure to contain the impact of surges in capital inflows can thus lead to large macroeconomic imbalances, which will call for sizeable downward adjustment of the economy when there is a sudden stop in the access to external financing. This reduced capacity to implement counter-cyclical policies implies that access to international financial flows also has an impact on the real economy, although not by smoothing the business cycle, as had been anticipated by economic theory, but rather by magnifying it (Kaminsky, Reinhart and Végh, 2004; Ocampo and Vos, 2008). Under weak regulation, common to most developing countries, surges in capital flows will exacerbate the tendency towards excessive risk-taking and create the conditions for boom-bust cycles.

The volatility and pro-cyclical nature of private capital flows to developing countries explain in part why no evidence can be found indicating that such capital movements in general have resulted in increased investment or higher long-term economic growth during the past three decades (Prasad and others, 2003; Ramey and Ramey, 1995). While capital surges stimulated aggregate demand and investment, a large part of the gains were often more than reversed in cases where the sudden stop triggered a financial crisis. Financial volatility thus translated into increased investment uncertainty and greater output volatility, which were detrimental for long-term economic growth, consistent with the evidence presented in the previous section.

Over the past decade, liquidity expansion and low interest rates have also resulted in a rapid growth of lending in property markets in developed countries, notably the United States of America, where high-risk sub-prime mortgages rapidly became a source of global instability. The impact has been felt beyond the mortgage market by third-party investors, as the rights to mortgage payments had been transferred by original lenders in packages of mortgage-backed securities and collateralized debt obligations. Despite the intervention by central banks in industrialized countries, conditions in credit markets are tight as banks started to reveal major losses. There are strong signals that the exceptionally favourable cyclical conditions prevailing in the world economy since the early years of the decade are coming to an end, creating a growing concern that the financial excesses may not be undone through an orderly correction (United Nations, 2008a).

Financial bubbles almost always give rise to lopsided expansions in some sectors which become unviable with a return to normal conditions. This is particularly true for areas susceptible to speculative investment such as that involving residential and commercial property, although more productive sectors can also experience such a phenomenon, as was the case in South-East Asia in the run-up to the crisis in 1997. Furthermore, with increased access of households to credits, financial booms can also produce sharp increases in consumer spending, reducing household savings and raising indebtedness, as in Latin America during the 1990s. Greater prominence of financial markets in the world economy could thereby divert resources from productive investment. This draining of resources for productive investment may be one of the reasons why the output lost during a negative economic shock is usually not regained during periods of expansion, particularly in countries with liberalized capital accounts.

From economic vulnerability to economic insecurity

The pro-cyclical behaviour of finance and the vulnerability of countries to external shocks result in economic insecurity for individuals and households. Evidence presented above shows that reduced volatility in key macroeconomic variables is not enough to stimulate productive investment and faster growth in many countries. The remaining high investment volatility and consequent lower growth has adversely affected growth of employment and household incomes. Episodes of exceptionally rapid economic expansion driven by financial bubbles can no doubt bring greater prosperity than expansions where finance plays a more passive role. However, there are serious questions about how far that prosperity spreads and whether susceptibility to deeper recessions or longer periods of stagnation do not result in considerable waste of resources of both capital and labour. Economic insecurity is further aggravated by the absence of a social contract that provides minimum protection to citizens against unanticipated income loss (see chap. V).

The problem is particularly serious in many developing countries in view of their limited capacity to pursue effective counter-cyclical macroeconomic policies. Extreme poverty, defined as the lack of resources to meet the daily food intake requirement of individuals, is the most damaging expression of economic insecurity. Economic growth in recent years has, in many cases, failed to generate rising incomes for the poor. Even countries that have been growing faster and showed more stability were not necessarily able to translate growth into poverty reduction. This is one of the reasons only a weak correlation has been observed between per capita income growth and poverty reduction across countries (see figure II.7).[8] Such an outcome reflects, in part, the tenuous links among growth, investment and labour-market performance in the new economic environment.

Concerns about the instability of employment, low pay and lack of protection systematically appear among the top preoccupations of people in developed and developing countries. In Latin America, unemployment is mentioned as the number one problem in 10 out of 18 countries. In 2006, 67 per cent of people in the region were preoccupied (or very preoccupied) by the possibility of losing their job.[9] In Asia, opinion surveys in 34 countries pointed to poverty and unemployment as the issues of most concern.[10] Opinion surveys conducted in 15 African countries in 2002-2003 had revealed a rather pessimistic view about the economy and the personal situation of people and families. While there was no explicit reference to employment, about 50 per cent of people felt their living conditions were "fairly bad" or "very bad".[11] In the 2007 opinion surveys in Europe, unemployment figured prominently as the most important problem: 34 per cent of people said

Increasing vulnerability to external shocks results in economic insecurity for individuals and households

Poor employment conditions are a source of preoccupation for people in all countries

---

8   While most regions of the world show greater economic stability and growth, poverty estimates for 100 countries, which account for 93 per cent of the population in low- and middle-income countries, show little progress in terms of poverty reduction, except for China (Chen and Ravallion, 2007).

9   Results are from Latinobarómetro (Opinion Pública Latinoamericana). They can be consulted at: www.latinobarometro.org (accessed 14 September 2007).

10 A complete list of countries including in these surveys and the country reports may be consulted at: https://www.asiabarometer.org/en/findings/General%20findings (accessed 14 September 2007).

11 Results for Africa are based on survey results reported by AFRO barometer for 15 countries in 2002-2003. Full report and results for these surveys can be found at: http://www.afrobarometer.org/papers/AfropaperNo34.pdf (accessed 14 September 2007).

Figure II.7
Growth, volatility and poverty reduction, 1981 and 2004

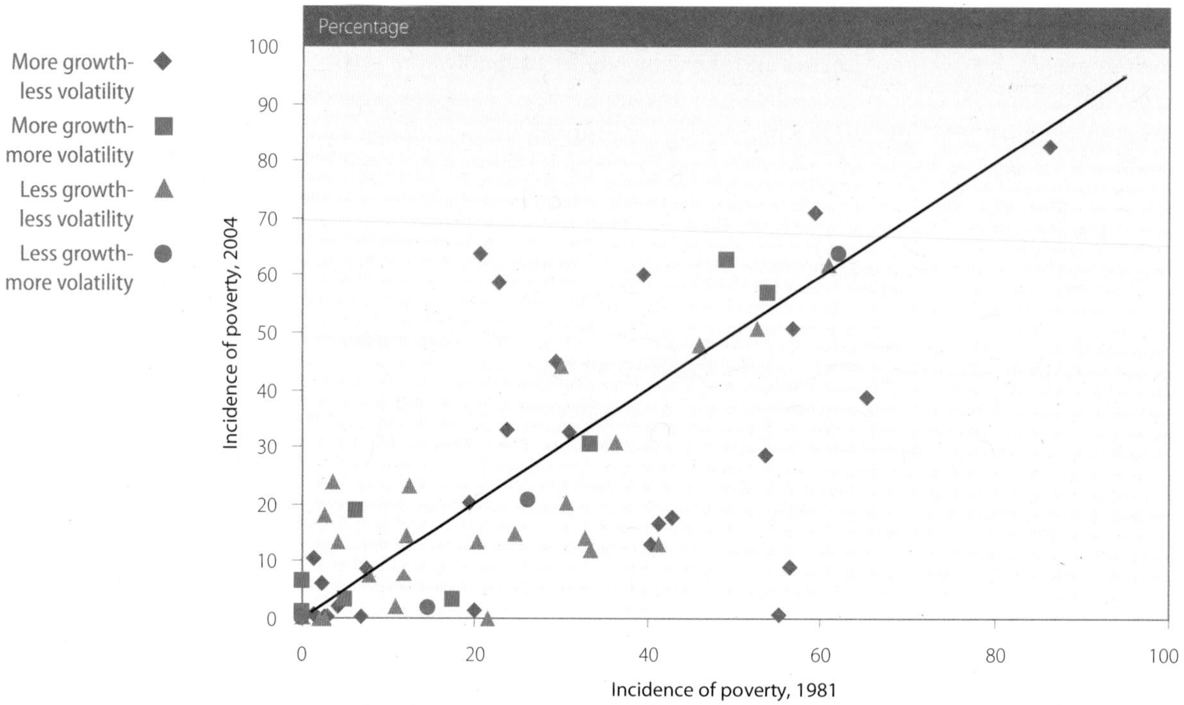

More growth- ◆
less volatility

More growth- ■
more volatility

Less growth- ▲
less volatility

Less growth- ●
more volatility

Source: UN/DESA based on United Nations Statistics Division National Accounts database; and World Bank PovcalNet, for poverty estimates.

Note: The classification of countries was based on the following criteria: More (less) growth refers to countries with faster (lower) rates of growth in GDP per capita in the period 2001-2006 when compared to average growth in 1971-1980. More (less) volatility refers to countries with higher (lower) volatility of GDP per capita growth in 2001-2006 when compared to 1971-1980. Volatility was measured by the coefficient of variation of GDP growth.

it was the issue of most concern to them, followed by crime (24 per cent), the economic situation, inflation and health care.[12]

Such perceptions seem to be at odds with the reference to sound fundamentals and the observed declines in macroeconomic volatility. Hence, it must be the case that, underneath those aggregates, there have been changes in labour markets, affecting the sense of job security, fair remuneration, career perspectives, and minimum income security. The present section will try to identify the changes that have taken place in global labour markets over the past decades in order to assess whether vulnerability has in fact increased.

Increased labour-market vulnerability in developed countries

The sense of insecurity reflected in opinion surveys is likely associated with more fundamental changes in the structure of employment and the system of social protection, particularly in developed countries. As we have seen, macroeconomic instability in previous decades and orthodox policy responses in most countries have produced a more pronounced investment cycle, with investment rising faster than income during expansions and falling

---

12   The survey was carried out in April-May 2007 in 30 European countries. See website of Eurobarometer: http://ec.europa.eu/public_opinion/archives/eb/eb67/eb_67_first_en.pdf (accessed 14 September 2007).

faster during contractions; this higher degree of investment uncertainty has generally been accompanied by a lower average rate of investment growth. A concomitant feature of this cycle has been a rising share of profits in most countries which has not translated into an equally strong increase in the share of investment in GDP, and which has in many cases been accompanied by a declining share (figure II.8).

Ceteris paribus, slower investment growth translates into lower employment-creation and a likely deterioration in the conditions of employment. This would be especially the case if the reduction of investment affects those productive sectors that require large investment in fixed capital over longer periods of time—presumably, the sectors that would normally be able to offer greater job stability and better conditions of employment.

The combination of higher profits and stagnant or lower investment appears to be linked to the prominent role of the financial sector in recent years. Stockhammer (2004) suggests that the advent of new financial instruments and changes in the pay structure of managers (for example, stock options) has changed management priorities in some countries, moving them away from long-term company growth and towards short-term shareholder returns. This change can include large restructuring and an intensive search for cost-cutting strategies even in reasonably good times, leading to the reduction of jobs and productive capacity for the purpose of generating cash to boost share prices and buy-backs. Moreover, the exposure of financial fragility and over-indebtedness during a cyclical downturn can also lead to an increased use of profits to reduce debt rather than

The prominence of the financial markets has resulted in the shift of incentives away from productive investment and employment-creation

Figure II.8
Change in profit share and investment in developed economies, 2000-2006 versus 1980-1990

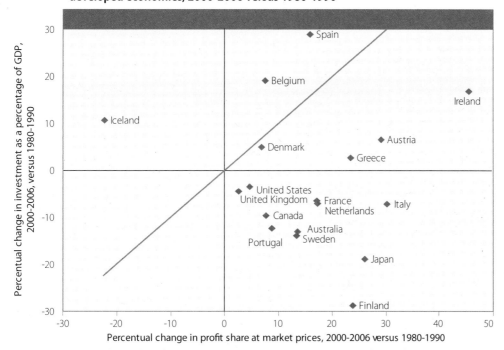

Source: UN/DESA calculations, based on AMECO (annual macro-economic database) of the European Commission Directorate General for Economic and Financial Affairs.

Note: The profit share is defined as a 1-wage share, where the wage share is defined as the compensation per employee as a percentage of GDP at market prices. Investment is defined as private sector gross fixed capital formation as a percentage of GDP at market prices. Presented are the percentual changes between the variables' annual averages for 2000-2006 and 1980-1990.

expand productive capacity as things turn around, resulting in a combination of weak employment with rising productivity and profits, even as economic conditions improve. This is not helped by lingering uncertainties about the strength of the recovery following finance driven recessions, which further discourage firms from making long-term employment commitments. Indeed, one of the consequences of increased financial instability is the growing demand by firms for more flexible hiring-and-firing practices as a buffer against large and unexpected swings in the overall level of economic activity.

One sign of weak or deteriorating labour-market conditions in a number of developed countries is the increasing share of involuntary part-time employment. Some workers in the labour market may consider part-time work to be an attractive option, and this has helped to increase the participation of young people, women with children and older workers in some countries. However, for an increasing number of workers who are unable to find full-time employment, part-time employment has become an "option of last resort", serving as a substitute for full-time work. Although the share of involuntary part-time workers—those who would prefer full-time work but cannot find it—constitutes a small proportion of total employment, this increasing trend in a number of countries is a cause for concern, suggesting either that not enough full-time jobs are being created for the labour force, or that the jobs being created are not suitably matched with the skills of the labour force (see figure II.9).

The growing importance of global supply chains has increased anxiety regarding the possibility of larger job loss

Another factor changing the conditions of global employment is the emergence of export-oriented newly industrializing economies. This trend is part of an ongoing process of closer integration through trade which has steadily modified the structure of production and the patterns of trade across countries. The argument that trade with newly industrializing economies can cause employment adjustments, possibly quite large, in es-

Figure II.9
Incidence of involuntary part-time work, selected regions, 1983-2004

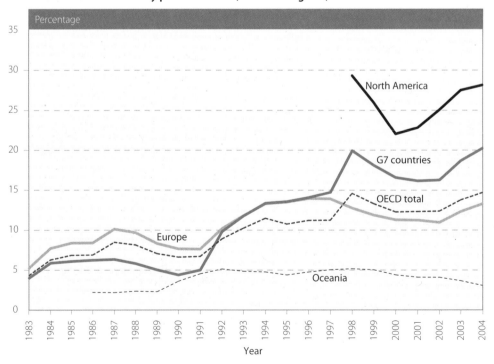

Source: Organization for Economic Cooperation and Development (2007b).

tablished producers is certainly a plausible one; the argument, however, that it has been an *independent* cause of labour-market vulnerability in the advanced countries is much less convincing. Rather, the possibility that the normal adjustments have produced an abnormal sense of insecurity has much more to do with the existence of unfavourable macroeconomic conditions since the late 1970s, even as closer trade integration continued, which has made it more difficult for displaced workers to find comparable or better employment opportunities (United Nations Conference on Trade and Development, 1995).

On some assessments, these adjustments have become greater and more difficult to manage as a result of the intertwining of trade, technological change and increased capital mobility in the form of global supply chains and the possible "offshoring" of economic activities. The resulting expansion of job opportunities among unskilled workers in developing countries has almost certainly led to a displacement of workers in developed countries. The scale of this recent displacement has been much debated and there are clearly variations among countries (Milberg and Scholler, 2008). However, it is not a new phenomenon and offers no more of a convincing explanation, by itself, of the rising levels of anxiety associated with deteriorating labour-market conditions than do previous episodes of rapid trade expansion.[13] Rather, this latest manifestation has, in many countries, taken place against a backdrop of declining social protection, whether measured by the unemployment benefit replacement rate, trade union membership, spending on active labour-market policies, the strength of hiring and firing regulations, or other indicators. Indeed, differences across countries in the coverage of social protection appear to be a strong guide to how workers perceive the threat from international trade (ibid.).

An important measure of economic insecurity is based on the ability of workers displaced by trade to find new work and not suffer a loss in earnings. Kletzer (2001) has carried out the most extensive analysis of the re-employment rate and replacement wage for workers displaced as the result of foreign trade. In a study of the United States from 1979 to 1999, she found that earnings losses from job dislocation had been large and persistent over time. Specifically, she found that 64.8 per cent of manufacturing workers displaced from 1979 to 1999 had been re-employed and one fourth of those re-employed suffered earnings declines of greater than 30 per cent. Workers displaced from non-manufacturing sectors did a little better: 69 per cent were re-employed, and 21 per cent suffered pay cuts of 30 per cent or more. The Organization for Economic Co-operation and Development (2005) conducted a similar study for 14 European countries for 1994-2001 and found that, while re-employment rates in Europe were lower than in the United States, a much lower share had earnings losses of more than 30 per cent upon re-employment and a slightly higher share either had no earnings loss or were earning more than before displacement (table II.5).

Workers displaced from current employment suffer a decline in wages upon re-employment

Labour-market vulnerabilities in developing economies

The impact of globalization on the conditions of employment in developing countries has also brought much controversy in recent years. On the one hand, most employment in the developing world is in non-tradable sectors, including the informal urban areas, and in subsistence agriculture (especially in low-income countries). Thus, the evolution of employment

The large number of workers in the informal economy is a source of economic insecurity in developing countries

---

13 The first offshore assembly plant for transistors, and integrated circuits, had been established in Hong Kong Special Administrative Region of China in 1961 by Fairchild Semiconductor of the United States, but intra-European FDI in the 1960s exhibited some of the same characteristics and the implications with respect to North-South trade were already being discussed in the 1970s (see, for example, Streeten (1973)).

Table II.5
Adjustment costs of trade-displaced workers in Europe and the United States of America, 1979-2001

Industry	Fourteen European countries, 1994-2001[a]			United States, 1979-1999		
	Share re-employed two years later	Share with no earnings loss or earning more	Share with earnings losses > 30 per cent	Share re-employed at survey date	Share with no earnings loss or earning more	Share with earnings losses > 30 per cent
Manufacturing	57.0	45.8	6.5	64.8	35.0	25.0
High international competition	51.8	44.0	5.4	63.4	36.0	25.0
Medium international competition	58.7	45.7	7.0	65.4	34.0	25.0
Low international competition	59.6	47.3	6.8	66.8	38.0	26.0
Services and utilities[b]	57.2	49.6	8.4	69.1	41.0	21.0
All sectors	57.3	47.1	7.5	-	-	-

Sources: Organization for Economic Cooperation and Development (2005, p. 45, table 1.3); and Kletzer (2001, p. 102, table D2).

a   Secretariat estimates based on data from the European Community Household Panel (ECHP) for Austria, Belgium, Denmark, Finland, France, Germany, Greece, Ireland, Italy, Luxembourg, the Netherlands, Portugal, Spain and the United Kingdom of Great Britain and Northern Ireland.

b   Services for Europe.

Economic recoveries do not generate enough employment to compensate for the loss during recessions

conditions has been subject to significant country-specific factors. On the other hand, greater integration in the trade and financial markets has led to important changes in the nature and characteristics of business cycles and a large restructuring of production across countries.

The expansion-recession-recovery cycles driven by international capital flows have been characterized by similar developments in investment and employment in developing and in developed countries. Not only do boom-bust cycles distort the composition of investment, but they tend, as discussed earlier, to lower its average level over the entire cycle. In the labour market, booms generated by capital inflows had often raised real wages, but the behaviour of employment depended on several factors. However, in all countries, real wages fell and unemployment rose sharply during busts, often to levels below those of the previous recession. Moreover, the subsequent recoveries were by and large "jobless": the unemployment rates remained above the rates reached during expansion by between 4 and 6 percentage points even after income losses had recovered. Indeed, evidence suggests that under conditions of increased instability and uncertainty, even longer periods of growth may fail to generate decent jobs.[14] In the case of Turkey, the World Bank, Independent Evaluation Group (2006, p. 4) has noted that "the growth that did occur (during 1993-2004) was relatively jobless as the volatility of the economy made employers less likely to hire new workers than to extend work hours of existing employees".

A more difficult issue entails assessing the impact of trade liberalization and the fast growth of FDI associated with the growing importance of global production chains and outsourcing. On standard theoretical grounds, expected large welfare gains in developing countries from trade liberalization would come from the fuller utilization of their existing resources, through expanded production in either the primary sector or labour-intensive manufactures. However, more sophisticated models in which trade depends on more than just factor endowments suggest more varied welfare possibilities. Empirical results show that the impact of trade on growth and employment is diverse, is generally small and is the

---

14   On the evidence for jobs and wages in these cycles, see United Nations Conference on Trade and Development (2000); International Labour Organization (2004b); and van der Hoeven and Lübker (2006).

result of the complex interaction of supply and demand factors in the economy as well as government policies designed to regulate the macroeconomy and the labour markets.[15]

Evidence presented in *World Economic Situation and Prospects 2008* (United Nations, 2008, chap. I) and reproduced in figure II.10 below shows that the recent recovery of growth in developing countries has not been accompanied by a parallel improvement in the conditions of employment. About one half of the countries that experienced high rates of growth had similar improvements in employment. There were few countries with low rates of economic growth and greater employment-creation. For a large number of countries, high unemployment is the expression of job creation insufficient to accommodate a rapidly growing labour force.

Figure II.10
GDP and employment growth in selected developing countries and areas, 2000-2006

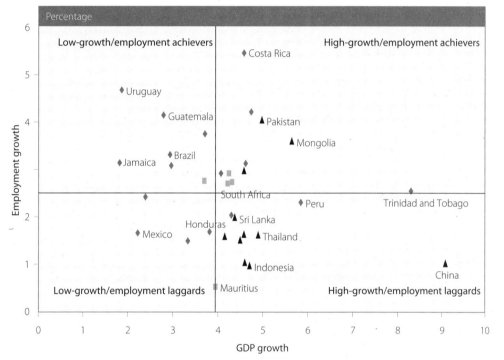

Source: UN/DESA, based on International Labour Organization, *Key Indicators of the Labour Market: Fifth Edition* (Geneva, International Labour Office, 2007); and World Bank, *World Development Indicators* (Washington, D.C., 2007, World Bank).

The lack of adequate systems of social protection increases the economic insecurity of workers

As discussed earlier, countries with less diversified production and export structures tend to show greater investment volatility and are more vulnerable to external shocks. With the lack of adequate social protection systems, such volatility directly translates into more insecure employment conditions in most developing-country contexts. Further, specialization on primary export production and light manufacturing, typical in most offshore production zones, does not, in the absence of other policy measures, create strong employment multiplier effects. Mineral exports and some agricultural export crops tend to involve relatively capital-intensive production processes with low direct employment-creation.[16]

---

15   For a review of this discussion in the literature, see, for example, Vos (2007); International Labour Organization and World Trade Organization (2007); Spiezia (2004); and De Ferranti and others (2000).

16   This is linked to the employment-generating qualities of FDI; a recent study of the impact of FDI on employment found little impact in low-income countries but a stronger impact in high-income countries (Spiezia, 2004).

Much of the production of light manufactures for exports involves assembly operations (maquiladoras), which, while labour-intensive, are also characterized by a low share of value-added generation and limited spinoff effects to the rest of the economy, as production is highly reliant on imported inputs. A recent study of Mexico, for example, estimates that imports for processing constitute as much as one half to two thirds of total sales of affiliates of United States-based transnational corporations in industries such as computers and transport equipment, while the growth in value added has been negligible (Hanson and others, 2002). Even in South-East Asia and, more recently, China, where these sectors have produced very large increases in exports and employment, wages have lagged behind productivity growth and the lack of linkages to the domestic economy and the weakness of upgrading into medium-level technology sectors are raising concerns among policymakers.[17]

For the majority of urban workers in developing countries, the lack of employment-generation in high-productivity activities (and the downsizing of public sector employment) continues to push vast numbers of workers into low-paid informal sector jobs, generally characterized by a high degree of job and income insecurity.[18] In low-income countries, agriculture remains the main employer, but with a growing share of workers engaging in urban informal activities.

The absence of universal social protection for most of these workers leaves them without proper access to health-care services and pensions for old age. In 2005, in Latin America, for example, while 58.9 per cent of the total urban employed had health and/or

Economic security requires decreasing investment instability, higher productivity and universal systems of social protection

Figure II.11
Urban employed population with health and/or pension coverage in selected Latin American countries, 2005

Informal economy

Formal economy

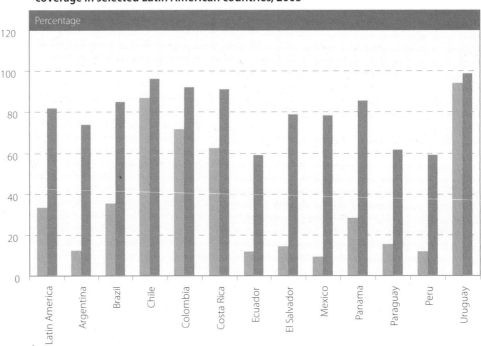

Source: ILO, *2006 Labour Overview: Latin America and the Caribbean* (Lima, International Labour Office, Regional Office for Latin America and the Caribbean, 2006).

17   On the different employment and upgrading patterns in Asia, see United Nations Conference on Trade and Development (1996); and United Nations Industrial Development Organization (2002). A recent study of Chinese exports estimates that two thirds of the value of exports is imported (Institute for International Economics (IIE), 2006).

18   Informal sector activities are characterized by low productivity and earnings. In 2002, the International Labour Organization expanded the concept of the informal sector to extend it to the informal economy so as to account for the existence of precarious employment in the formal sector (Tokman, 2007).

pension coverage, the lowest coverage (33.4 per cent) was in the informal economy, where 48.5 per cent of workers are employed (figure II.11). A large share of informal employment is associated to low levels of development (Figure II.12). Decreasing the vulnerability of workers in the informal sector will require an expansion of social protection programmes and stronger regulatory frameworks (see chap. V); but more than anything, it will require the adoption of policies designed to decrease macroeconomic instability and raise the level of productive investment and, along with explicit industrial policies, to increase the level of employment and productivity in the formal economy.

Figure II.12
Relation between the share of self-employed and contributing family workers to total employment and GDP per capita, 2005

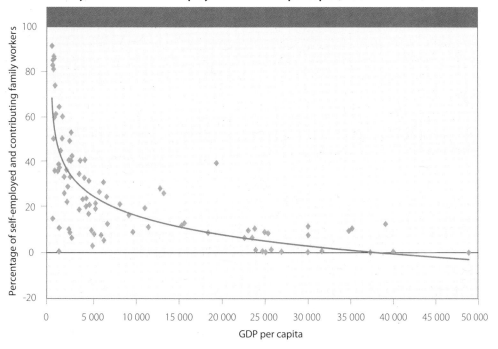

Sources: UN/DESA based on International Labour Office, *Global Employment Trends, 2007* (Geneva, International Labour Office, 2007); and World Bank, World Development Indicators online (2008).

Note: Latest available year is 2003, 2004 or 2005 depending on data availability for 89 countries; years correspond for the two variables.

Managing external shocks and the business cycle

Adverse external shocks transmitted through the trade and capital accounts have direct impacts on economic security and the fight against poverty, whether through repressed investment, wasted resources or lost output. During the 1980s and 1990s, many developing countries had tried to mitigate the impacts of these shocks with measures that emphasized controlling inflation and restoring fiscal balance. This not only delayed the recovery, but has, in many cases, actually made countries weaker and more vulnerable to future shocks. These policies have been detrimental to long-term investments, especially infrastructure and human capital development (United Nations, 2006). They have also intensified boom-bust cycles which have negatively impacted on productive investment. More recently, many developing countries have accumulated vast amounts of international reserves as a self-insurance against commodity price shocks and sudden stops and reversals in capital flows. This insurance strategy comes, in most cases, with rather high costs, however. A different approach is required.

Past policies increased vulnerability to future shocks because they were detrimental to long-term investment

The key elements of an alternative approach are presented in the present section. First of all, macroeconomic stabilization policies should be well coordinated with other areas of economic policies to ensure that the overall policy stance is conducive to preserving stability while promoting economic growth, diversification of production and employment-generation. Second, developing countries need to create more space within which to conduct counter-cyclical macroeconomic policies. This not only would involve avoiding pro-cyclical monetary and fiscal policy stances, but also might include—depending on country conditions—important roles for fiscal stabilization or savings funds and counter-cyclical prudential financial regulation and capital controls. Third, such national policy efforts will need to be supported by regional and multilateral cooperative actions. For many Governments of developing countries, the space for conducting counter-cyclical macroeconomic policies is limited, as the available fiscal and foreign-exchange resources tend to be small relative to the size of the external shocks they face. International action mitigating the impact of private capital flow volatility and providing liquidity that can be quickly disbursed with low policy conditionality can enhance the necessary policy space. This should also involve better reserve pooling mechanisms to reduce the costs of self-insurance.

Integrating macroeconomic and development policies

Economic growth in recent years does not necessarily translate into better incomes and greater economic security for people. For economic growth to be inclusive in the sense of reducing vulnerability, macroeconomic policies must place employment and economic security at the centre of the policy agenda. The Millennium Development Goals were recently expanded to incorporate the objective of achieving full and productive employment and decent work for all as part of the first Goal. Achieving this Goal will require a view of the policy framework that extends beyond price stability and fiscal balance to incorporate employment-creation as a central policy objective.

This requires that macroeconomic policies be embedded in a broader development strategy, as was the case in the fast-growing East Asian economies. Fiscal policies would give priority to development spending, including investment in education, health and infrastructure. It would also mean using fiscal instruments such as tax breaks, accelerated depreciation allowances and subsidies to boost productive investment. As with the East Asian experience, monetary policy would be coordinated with financial sector and industrial policies, including directed and subsidized credit schemes and managed interest rates, so as to directly influence investment and savings. The right mix of these policies can be applied deliberately so as to promote investment in specific industries at specific times, but it should be especially promoted in sectors with the greatest potential for upgrading skills, reaping economies of scale and raising productivity growth, thereby increasing the rates of return on investment.

Such measures can further set the tone for a different kind of competition policy which, instead of promoting competition for its own sake, looks to utilize it to foster diversification and development. Maintaining competitive exchange rates is considered essential for encouraging export growth and diversification. A depreciated real exchange rate lowers labour costs and enhances the competitiveness of labour-intensive exports. The empirical evidence suggests, however, that this does not "condemn" countries to permanent specialization in low-tech exports; rather, with consistent policy direction, export diversification into higher-end products will be promoted (Rodrik, 2005; Ocampo and

Vos, 2008). Macroeconomic policies in many Latin American and African countries since the 1980s, in contrast, have been focused on much more narrowly defined short-term price stabilization objectives and this has often resulted in exchange-rate overvaluation, unbalanced growth and a lack of economic diversification (United Nations Conference on Trade and Development, 2003).

The need for counter-cyclical macroeconomic policies

Governments can enhance the scope for counter-cyclical policies by improving the institutional framework for macroeconomic policymaking. Setting fiscal targets that are independent of short-term fluctuations in economic growth (so-called structural budget rules) as well as commodity stabilization funds can be effective in forcing a counter-cyclical policy stance. In developing countries with open capital accounts, where conducting counter-cyclical monetary policies has become increasingly difficult, there is a need to consider effective measures to control and regulate international capital flows as well as the operations of the domestic financial sector.

Fiscal targets, stabilization funds and regulations placed on capital flows are tools for improving economic stability

A role for counter-cyclical monetary policies?

The role of monetary policy in managing the business cycle is fairly limited. In general, even in developed countries, monetary policy is seen to be more effective in restraining an overheated economy than in stimulating an economy in recession. Monetary policy has proved to be ineffective in stimulating growth in countries experiencing inflation. In the United States, lowering interest rates in 2001-2003 had done little to stimulate private investment; however, it did induce a housing boom which stimulated growth of household consumption, but which also forged a widening of external deficits and the build-up to the financial sector woes that had pushed the United States economy back into recession by 2008.

Monetary policy cannot be an effective tool for achieving stability …

The effectiveness of monetary policies in developing countries tends to be even weaker, particularly during asset price-driven cycles.[19] Monetary policy tends to have its most direct impact through the banking sector. With a more developed financial sector, the impact of monetary policies will be more significant by affecting the cost and availability of investment financing. In countries with open capital accounts, however, the degree of monetary policy autonomy is strongly reduced and fluctuations in economic activity are strongly associated with cycles in capital inflows. In such a context, lowering interest rates can induce capital outflows and a weaker exchange rate. The latter could help promote export diversification, as indicated, but the weakened balance sheets of the financial sector that often result from currency depreciation—especially when there is significant liability dollarization in the system—will limit credit availability and this in turn will weaken the stimulus to aggregate demand. Increasing interest rates could push these ambiguous effects in the opposite direction. Most importantly in the context of volatile capital flows, the uncertainty about

… if it is not used in combination with fiscal policy and greater regulation of the banking system

---

19   The limitations of monetary policy rules with respect to managing asset price-driven booms is discussed by Kindleberger (1995, p. 35), who notes: "When asset and output prices are stable or move in the same direction, or domestic and international goals call for the same policy response, both of which happens much of the time, such rules are supportable. When speculation threatens substantial rises in asset prices, with a possible collapse in asset markets later, and harm to the financial system, or if domestic conditions call for one sort of policy and international goals another, monetary authorities confront a dilemma calling for judgement, not cookbook rules of the game."

their impact can thus easily turn the use of traditional monetary policy instruments into a source of economic insecurity rather than of stability (Akyüz, 2008; Stiglitz and others, 2006). While this does not preclude a role for monetary policy, it should operate in combination with alternative measures, including counter-cyclical fiscal policies and counter-cyclical regulation of the banking system and capital flows, as discussed below.

Counter-cyclical fiscal policies and stabilization funds

Structural budget rules have proved effective in smoothing the business cycle

Countries should avoid existing pro-cyclical biases in fiscal policy. This can be achieved through the establishment of broad fiscal rules that guarantee the long-term sustainability of fiscal balances, including targets for the budget deficit and limits to public indebtedness. However, defining and adhering to such rules may not be an easy task, not even in developed economies, as demonstrated by the debates over the European Stability and Growth Pact. Such targets will work counter-cyclically if they focus on the "structural fiscal deficit", which measures what the budget balance would be without cyclical fluctuations. This would imply, for instance, that if tax revenues declined because of a recession, the "current" fiscal deficit would widen, but the structural (full employment) deficit would remain unaffected and the Government would not be forced to tighten fiscal policy in order to meet the given target. Some developing countries, such as Chile during the current decade, have been able to manage such structural budget rules. The management of this counter-cyclical policy stance has been one ingredient in the much stronger growth performance and macroeconomic stability of Chile compared with other Latin American countries (Fiess, 2002; Ffrench-Davis, 2006).

Stabilization funds also help to smooth out fiscal revenues …

The establishment of stabilization funds could also help smooth out fiscal revenues, especially in countries where commodity prices have a large impact on the economy and the fiscal balance. Commodity exporters face highly uncertain prices. Price volatility is transmitted to the government budget through its impact on tax revenue or on profits of State-owned enterprises in the commodity sector. Two key factors underscore the need for specific measures to smooth government expenditures. First, external financing for commodity exporters tends to be pro-cyclical. It is easily available when commodity prices boom, but that source of financing of fiscal deficits tends to dry up or become more costly when export prices drop. Second, the costs of shutting down lumpy investment projects and other essential public expenditures during downswings tend to be high. Countries facing such constraints will put a high premium on liquidity. A commodity fund, as a form of self-insurance, can help achieve a smoother path of fiscal expenditures and, as such, give Governments an instrument of counter-cyclical management. Also, funds set up as a savings fund to smooth public expenditure over generations (such as Norway's State Petroleum Fund and Kuwait's Reserve Fund for Future Generations) offer an element of short-term security if they also save a share of current revenues (Davis and others, 2001).

With the help of existing or newly created stabilization or savings funds, countries like Algeria, Chile, Colombia, Ecuador, Kuwait and Mexico have been able to reduce both fiscal and overall growth volatility, but this apparently has not been the case in Nigeria and the Bolivarian Republic of Venezuela (Budnevich, 2008).

… but they must be carefully managed

Fiscal stabilization funds are by no means a panacea and careful management of such funds is required. One complication is the difficulty of distinguishing cyclical price patterns from long-term trends, in part because of the increased influence of speculative financial investments in commodity markets. This has made it more difficult for Governments to determine the adequate size of stabilization funds. The usefulness of such funds as a form of self-insurance has been questioned on these grounds, given that pro-longed commodity price booms or collapses risk either endlessly accumulating resources or rapidly exhausting them. Contingent, market-based insurance instruments are some-times seen to be better mechanisms (Davis and others, 2001; Devlin and Titman, 2004). However, such markets for commodity derivatives and insurance are rather shallow and few commodity producers have relied on them.

The effectiveness of commodity stabilization and savings funds will very much depend on the strength of fiscal institutions. Additional rules for fiscal discipline, debt management, and overall expenditure smoothing typically are required. This requirement could be met by embedding fiscal policy in a medium-term budgetary framework, which may include stabilization funds. A preferred approach would be to base annual public expenditures on expected revenue in the medium run based on a conservative projection of the commodity price trend. In this approach, consistent fiscal surpluses would be gen-erated over time so that financial reserves could be built up during years of upward price trends to finance desired levels of expenditures when commodity revenues fell short. It would also ensure that fiscal policy was counter-cyclical in relation to commodity prices. Appropriately designed stabilization funds can help increase transparency and account-ability of fiscal policy by making it possible to track what funds are accumulated, how they are managed, and how much is transferred to be spent through the government budget.

The effectiveness of the fiscal instruments for achieving stabilization depends on institutional strength …

All these conditions may prove to be insufficient in situations of large or pro-longed adverse commodity shocks or because of large asymmetries in a country's export price cycles and other external shocks affecting the fiscal balance and the economy at large. It is therefore important that developing countries be able to also rely on an adequate multilateral system of compensatory financing facilities to protect them against the larger commodity price shocks (see below).

… yet they still may be insufficient to counter large or prolonged shocks

Effectively managing such a system requires prudent and consistent policy-makers and political support to uphold the rules. In general, in the more appropriate institutional setting for macroeconomic policies, a balance should first of all be struck between fiscal and monetary prudence and flexibility in such a way as to ensure both policy credibility and fiscal sustainability. A certain degree of discretionary power should be retained. As the structure of the economy changes over time, so will the vulnerability to external shocks. For instance, financial shocks may become more important than terms-of-trade shocks. In such a changing context, predetermined policy rules likely become less relevant or turn out to be too rigid or the nature of fiscal stabilization funds likely need to be changed. Moreover, as the risks and uncertainties facing an economy never present themselves in exactly the same way or with the same degree of intensity, a certain amount of space for discretionary policies is always needed in order for adjustments to be made that will minimize macroeconomic losses.

An effective multilateral system is necessary to protect countries

Prudential regulation, capital controls and risk management

The limited effectiveness of monetary policies, the pro-cyclical nature of capital flows and the intrinsic imperfections in financial markets justify the prudent use of capital-market interventions. Such interventions may help mitigate volatility in short-term capital flows, discourage long-term capital outflows, reduce the likelihood of financial crises, and stimu-late growth by reducing the volatility in the availability and cost of domestic borrowing.

Prudent interventions in capital markets are needed to mitigate volatility

Prudential regulation and effective supervision of financial institutions should aim at ensuring the solvency of financial institutions by establishing adequate capital requirements, appropriate standards for risk assessment and diversification, sufficient provision for non-performing and questionable portfolios, and adequate levels of liquidity to address maturity mismatches between their assets and liabilities. However, many of the existing risk assessment methods and prudential rules, including Basel I and Basel II, can serve to amplify cyclicality. This is clearly the case for loan-loss provisions based on current rates of loan delinquency. At times of boom, when asset prices and collateral values are rising, loan delinquency falls and results in inadequate provisioning and overexpansion of credit. When the downturn comes, loan delinquency rises rapidly and standard rules on provisions can lead to a credit crunch. Similar difficulties also apply to capital charges. Banks typically lose equity when an economy is hit by a massive exit of capital, hikes in interest rates and declines in the currency. Enforcing capital charges under such conditions would serve only to deepen the credit crunch and recession. This happened in Asia during the 1997-1998 crisis as a result of extensive efforts to strengthen regulatory regimes as part of the International Monetary Fund (IMF) packages of financial support (United Nations Conference on Trade and Development, 1998).

Current financial regulations should be redesigned to improve their effectiveness

Prudential regulation of the financial sector should thus be redesigned in a counter-cyclical fashion to make the regulatory mechanisms act as built-in stabilizers.[20] Forward-looking rules may be applied to capital requirements in order to introduce a degree of counter-cyclicality. This would mean establishing higher capital requirements at times of financial booms, based on the estimation of long-term risks over the entire financial cycle, not just on the actual risk at a particular phase of the cycle. Similarly, not current but future losses can be taken into account in making loan-loss provisions, estimated on the basis of long-run historical loss experience for each type of loan. Again, long-term valuation may be used for collaterals in mortgage lending in order to reduce the risks associated with the ups and downs in property markets.

Maturity mismatches, currency mismatches and exchange-rate risks require improved regulations

While useful in containing the damage that may be inflicted by financial crises, none of these measures could adequately deal with the risks associated with sharp swings in capital flows and exchange rates or prevent crises. Such risks can be restricted by more stringent rules for capital charges, loan-loss provisions, liquidity and reserve requirements for transactions involving foreign currencies or through direct restrictions on foreign borrowing and investment. More generally, bank regulations for the management of risks involving foreign-exchange positions need to address three fundamental sources of fragility: maturity mismatches, currency mismatches and exchange rate-related credit risks.

Policymakers in China, India and Malaysia have successfully applied quantitative capital-account regulations to achieving such objectives. Malaysia, for instance, imposed direct quantitative restrictions on acquisitions of short-term securities by non-residents in 1994; and research suggests that these were effective in improving the external debt profile, preventing asset-price bubbles, and allowing greater space for macroeconomic policy (Epstein, Grabel and Jomo, forthcoming). Chile effectively used a price-based measure, unremunerated reserve requirements, in a counter-cyclical manner, which was applied to all loans at times of strong inflows in the 1990s, but the measure was phased out when capital dried up at the end of the decade.

A permanent system of controls, as opposed to ad hoc regulations, is more effective

Prudent management of capital controls may be more effective with a permanent system in place (Akyüz, 2008). A problem with introducing more ad hoc counter-cyclical capital control measures is that they can trigger an adverse reaction from financial

---

20   This approach is finding considerable support in the Bank for International Settlements (2001, chap. VII); see, also, Borio, Furfine, and Lowe (2001) and White (2006). For further discussion, see Akyüz (2008) and Ocampo, Spiegel and Stiglitz, eds. (forthcoming).

markets, leading to sharp falls in stock prices and causing concern among Governments. This was the case in Thailand when a 30 per cent reserve requirement was imposed at the end of 2006 on capital inflows held less than one year, including portfolio equity flows, in order to check continued appreciation of the currency. This provoked a strong reaction from the stock market, forcing the Government to exempt investment in stocks from reserve requirements. More recently, in October 2007, the proposal by the Securities and Exchange Board in India to restrict foreign buying of shares through offshore derivatives resulted in a plunge in shares and suspension of trade, recovery from which occurred only after a plea for calm from the Government. The adverse market reaction to the introduction of counter-cyclical restrictions could be much more dramatic in countries with large stocks of foreign debt, weak current-account positions and a high degree of dependence on foreign capital. This is why, under such conditions, Governments may be inclined to allow inflows of speculative, short-term capital even when they are aware of their potential risks. For these reasons, a permanent system of controls, with instruments' being adjusted according to cyclical conditions, might make for a more stable environment.

When capital inflows are excessive, it is also possible to adjust the regime for resident outflows so as to relieve the upward pressure on the currency. Chile followed this path in the 1990s for direct investment abroad. More recently, China took a decision to permit investment by its residents in approved overseas markets in order to mitigate the pressure on the exchange rate to appreciate further. Such a policy response is, in fact, an alternative to sterilized intervention, but would do nothing to prevent currency and maturity mismatches in balance sheets. Therefore, prudential management of capital control measures should go hand in hand with the application of counter-cyclical regulation of banks and other financial intermediaries.

Foreign reserve management: reducing the need for "self-insurance"

As discussed earlier, a common response in many developing countries to the vulnerability associated with commodity price shocks and sudden stops and reversals of capital flows has been a rapid build-up of reserves. Official international reserve holdings surged from $1.6 trillion in 1999 to about $6.0 trillion in 2007. Developing countries as a group have accumulated three quarters of world reserves, or $ 4.3 trillion. China alone increased its reserve holdings from $0.1 to $1.3 trillion during that period. Foreign reserves held by developing countries have climbed, on average, to no less than about 30 per cent of their GDP – with or without China in the sample (see figure II.13). Even low-income countries, including the least developed countries, have increased their reserve positions so as to reduce their debt vulnerability. Reserves went up from 2-3 per cent of GDP in the 1980s to about 5 per cent in the 1990s and to about 12 per cent in the 2000s (see figure II.14).

This has given developing countries a greater buffer or "self-insurance" to cope with external shocks. After the Asian crisis, following speculative attacks on currency-exposed countries, this appeared to be a sensible counter-cyclical strategy.

A level of reserves covering about three months of imports had used to be considered adequate, but one of the lessons drawn from the Asian crisis by emerging market economies was that they should also have adequate reserves to cover their short-term external debt. At present, however, developing countries have been accumulating reserves well in excess of that more recent standard. Both low- and middle-income countries have

Countries have responded to shock by building up reserves …

… beyond the level that is considered adequate …

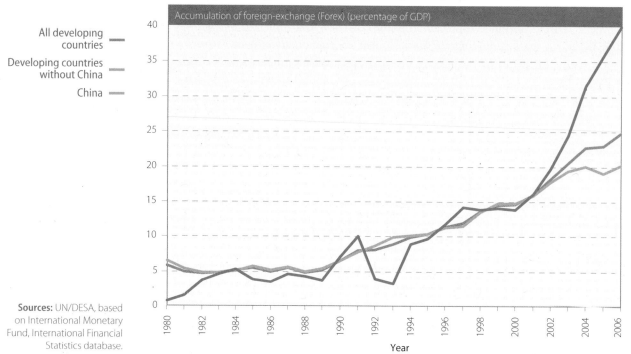

Figure II.13
Foreign-exchange reserve accumulation by developing countries, 1980-2006

Accumulation of foreign-exchange (Forex) (percentage of GDP)

All developing countries
Developing countries without China
China

Year

Sources: UN/DESA, based on International Monetary Fund, International Financial Statistics database.

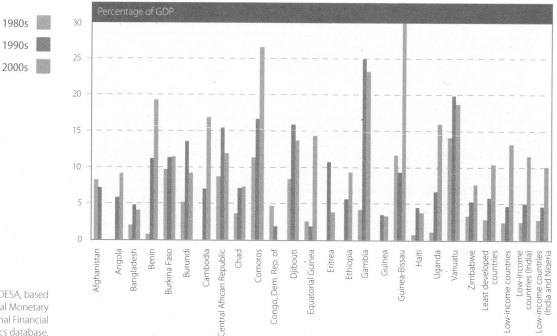

Figure II.14
Foreign-exchange reserve accumulation by low-income countries, 1980s, 1990s and 2000s

Percentage of GDP

1980s
1990s
2000s

Sources: UN/DESA, based on International Monetary Fund, International Financial Statistics database.

reserves that are almost twice as great as the sum of the value of three months of imports and the stock of short-term external debt. China's reserves are three times as great. Reserves of the least developed countries are now close to that target.

The excess reserve build-up by developing countries suggests that this has been motivated by more than "self-insurance". Export-led growth strategies in a context of rapid growth of world trade and buoyant commodity prices have led to increasing developing-country trade surpluses and, in this context, the reserve build-up is part and parcel of the dramatic widening of global imbalances over the past decade or so (United Nations, 2008a).

In addition, the emerging market economies especially have also seen strong private capital inflows; and in this regard, countries have been able to increase reserve levels through both current- and capital-account surpluses or through a combination of current-account deficits and capital-account surpluses.

While providing a buffer and space for counter-cyclical response to adverse external shocks and capital flow reversals, the large build-up of reserves also carries a high price tag. There are a number of significant costs to consider. First, for those countries that borrowed to accumulate reserves (that is, through running capital-account surpluses), there are substantial carry costs. Almost half of reserves accumulated since 2001 have been "borrowed reserves", equivalent to about $ 2 trillion (Akyüz, 2008). The annual carry cost of borrowed reserves is estimated to amount to as much as $100 billion, representing a net transfer to reserve-currency countries well above what they provide in terms of official development assistance (ODA).[21]

... with significant costs for developing countries

Second, there may be important opportunity costs, as foreign-exchange reserves are the financial resources set aside for precautionary needs, which could otherwise be used at the time for domestic consumption or investment. Incurring such costs is justifiable as long as they are smaller than the potential benefits of holding the reserves. These opportunity costs may outweigh the benefits when the accumulation of reserves goes beyond the minimally required level and in cases where resources for long-term investments are scarce. Especially in the low-income countries, such opportunity costs likely will be high.

Third, direct financial costs are also rising along with the accumulation of reserves. For example, monetary authorities may try to sterilize excessive domestic money supply growth associated with increased foreign-exchange reserves. However, the domestic bonds or central bank papers that are issued often carry higher interest rates than those on foreign reserve assets. The higher the interest-rate differential, the larger the costs will be. This fiscal burden can become particularly acute in situations where economies are already under pressure to reduce fiscal deficits and consolidate their public finances. In this sense, accumulation of reserves may become inconsistent with fiscal policy objectives.

Fourth, without sterilizing the monetary effects, large reserve holdings will exert upward pressure on the real exchange rate and domestic prices. This may conflict with other policy objectives, for example, maintaining a competitive exchange rate as part of strategies to achieve diversification of production and export structures, which is critical to long-term growth and employment-generation.

The accumulation of reserves may also conflict with other development objectives

While reserves in developing countries have been rising in recent years for self-insurance, there has been considerable diversity regarding their size and sources, which has implications for the costs and risks of holding reserves. Countries with current-account surpluses are translating most or all of these surpluses into international reserves at relatively high opportunity cost. Those countries, notably in Latin America, with weak

---

21 The estimate is based on Akyüz (2008, p. 34) who assumes a moderate average rate of a 500 basis points margin between the borrowing rate and the return on reserves.

growth and balance of payments are compelled to absorb net capital inflows into low-yielding reserve assets instead of using them for investment. Moreover, some countries still lack self-insurance and are exposed to sudden stops because large amounts of capital received have been absorbed by the current-account deficits that these inflows helped to generate by appreciating the currency.

The high carry cost of official reserves coupled with the risk of exchange-rate losses has encouraged alternative investments in higher-yielding foreign securities primarily through sovereign wealth funds (SWFs). These have recently been acquiring equity in developed-country banks hit by the sub-prime crisis, thereby acting as a force for global stability. However, this also carries high risks. An alternative would be to recycle the resources in the sovereign wealth funds to development financing in support, for example, of infrastructure development. Developing countries own over $4.5 trillion in official reserves and the estimated size of existing sovereign wealth funds assets is at least $3 trillion. An allocation of just 1 per cent of those assets (or the equivalent from the asset returns) on an annual basis would amount to about $75 billion, which is triple the size of annual lending by the World Bank. International development lending capacity could increase probably by more than double that amount if used as laid-in capital for domestic and multilateral development banks, including at the regional level.

Large accumulation of reserves signals the inadequacy of liquidity provisions globally

Crucially, the tendency to accumulate vast amounts of foreign currency reserves in developing countries has its roots in more fundamental deficiencies of the international monetary and reserve system. Improved prudential capital-account regulation, as sketched above, can help reduce the need for and the cost of self-insurance via reserve accumulation. The need for self-insurance can further be reduced with more effective mechanisms for liquidity provisioning and reserve management at the international level, both regionally and multilaterally (see below).

Multilateral responses

Multilateral financial institutions need to create appropriate instruments for reducing vulnerability to financial shocks

In today's world of increased economic and political interdependence, achieving a broad-based, rapid and sustained growth in incomes and employment involves even more complex policy challenges than in the past. Certainly, the external environment of developing countries has undergone a number of fundamental changes that are unlikely to be reversed in the foreseeable future. Despite these challenges and changes, the mechanisms and institutions in place at the multilateral level have not been adequate to strengthen global economic policymaking.

The multilateral arrangements designed at Bretton Woods had not included a global regime for capital movements, given that capital mobility was expected to be limited. However, no such regime has emerged even after the breakdown of these arrangements, and despite the surge in private capital flows. Various codes and standards have been established through international institutions, not just with respect to the financial sector, but also regarding auditing and accounting, data collection, and so on. While these could have benefits over the longer term, they will not necessarily contribute to financial stability, and in many cases they will involve substantial costs.

A major outstanding challenge for the multilateral financial institutions is to help developing countries mitigate the damaging effects of volatile capital flows and commodity prices and provide counter-cyclical financing mechanisms to compensate for the inherently pro-cyclical movement of private capital flows. A number of options are available to dampen the pro-cyclicality of capital flows, provide counter-cyclical finance, and thus help create a better environment for sustainable growth.

Multilateral surveillance

As a first set of measures, multilateral surveillance mechanisms should be improved to increase the scope for counter-cyclical policies. Surveillance remains a key tool responsibility of IMF in crisis prevention and safeguarding macroeconomic stability. The inability of the Fund to convince major economies to alleviate exploding global financial imbalances such as those built up over the past decade has been a stumbling block in discussions about the reform of the surveillance mechanism. With the revision of the system of surveillance of member States adopted in 2007 (the first major revision of the framework in 30 years), the Fund has put external stability and exchange-rate assessment at the centre of surveillance. The balance-of-payments position of a country should not give rise to disruptive adjustments in exchange rates. This requires that the underlying current account be broadly in equilibrium and that the capital-account position be such that it does not entail risks of abrupt shifts in capital flows. This requirement may lead the Fund to exert undue pressure on developing countries pursuing export-led growth strategies, by asking them to allow exchange-rate appreciation (and hence stimulate domestic demand) when successful in export growth or attracting foreign investment, and vice versa. For reasons indicated above, developing countries should try to aim at a long-term stability of competitive real exchange rates and move towards counter- rather than pro-cyclical macroeconomic policies. Furthermore, the revised framework does not differentiate among countries in terms of their influence on systematic stability, that is to say, surveillance is not more rigorous for countries issuing major reserve currencies. This is at variance with the intended "even-handedness" of the new decision.

To soften swings in the global business cycle and address the global financial imbalances, a framework for internationally concerted macroeconomic policies is needed. In the current context, the recession in the United States economy should be met with a global demand stimulus in order to avert a worldwide downswing (United Nations, 2008a). The below-trend growth in the United States would justify further interest-rate cuts to stimulate the economy, but this may not be sufficient in the current context of a fragile financial sector and a weakened dollar as a result of the prolonged accumulation of external deficits. Global rebalancing would thus require stimulus from other parts of the world, especially in surplus countries like China, the major oil exporters, Japan and parts of Europe. However, acting on their own, countries may be more likely to take a "beggar-thy-neighbour" policy stance. IMF has initiated multilateral consultations to deal with the global imbalances through concerted policy actions. The participants in this dialogue, which include the United States, Japan, the euro area, China and Saudi Arabia, seem to agree on the desirability of correcting the global imbalances without jeopardizing sustained growth and on the need for concerted action to achieve this. They have not yet followed through with any concrete policy actions. It is important that the discussions be broadened to involve more parties, developing countries in particular, and that agreement be reached on multi-year policy adjustment schedules that can be monitored so as to make participants accountable and enhance the likelihood of compliance with agreed concerted action. For the multilateral consultations for policy coordination to work, the perceived legitimacy of the mediator (that is to say, IMF) needs to be enhanced and any doubts that may exist about its impartiality in the process need to be removed. This requires a reform

Multilateral surveillance mechanisms should be a first step towards safeguarding stability ...

... followed by a framework for internationally concerted macroeconomic policies ...

of the voting power and governance structure of IMF in favour of a better representation of developing countries that is farther-reaching than the piecemeal change agreed upon at the 2008 spring meetings of the Bretton Woods institutions.

Pooling international reserves

... and the reform of the
current international
reserve system

Second, fundamental reforms of the current international reserve system will be needed to prevent the current constellation of imbalances from re-emerging. The use of the national currency of the United States as the main reserve currency implies that for the rest of the world to accumulate reserve assets, the United States needs to run a current-account deficit. This, as we have seen, has enabled developing countries to meet their demand for "self-insurance" against external shocks by building up vast amounts of dollar-denominated official reserves. Over time, however, such a pattern inevitably erodes the value of the dollar, as has been the case since 2002, enhancing the cost to countries for continuing to hold vast amounts of reserves; and this may well cause a run against the dollar, with probable strong destabilizing consequences that will be felt worldwide (United Nations, 2008a).

Over time, a market solution to this problem may develop. If a number of competing reserve currencies existed, each of which were to account for a significant share of foreign-reserve portfolios, it would be easier for central banks to alter the composition of their reserves continuously over time and avoid situations where serious doubts would arise regarding the value of a specific reserve currency and the sustainability of the obligations of its issuer. Such a market solution is problematic, however, as it would likely not be smooth and, more likely, would involve a collapse of the dollar, which would disrupt financial markets.

A new supranational
currency could be the
optimal long-term
solution ...

The emergence of a new, supranational currency based on the scaling up of special drawing rights (SDRs) is probably the best solution for redesigning the global reserve system in a stable way, but this can only be a long-term option (United Nations, 2005a). Therefore, the more immediate reform would entail promoting an officially backed multi-currency reserve system. This idea should be as compelling as the pursuit of a multilateral trading system. Similar to multilateral trade rules, a well-designed multilateral financial system should create equal conditions for all parties and prevent unfair competition and an asymmetric burden-sharing of exchange-rate adjustments. It should also help to increase stability in the international financial system by reducing the likelihood of a crisis scenario where capital flight out of the major single reserve currency causes potentially far-reaching repercussions throughout the global economy.

... together with the
creation of regional
reserve funds

A case can also be made for the development of regional reserve funds as a complement to multilateral and national mechanisms of macroeconomic insurance against external shocks. The large currency and financial crises in developing countries since the 1990s have been regional in nature. Countries should have an interest in helping put out a fire in neighbouring countries before it spreads to them. Pooling reserves regionally likely will also reduce costs to individual countries, just as a universal health insurance reduces costs to individuals. Yet, experience with such regional reserve mechanisms is limited. The Latin American Reserve Fund (FLAR), though limited in membership (to the Andean countries and Costa Rica), has had a successful experience in supporting member countries during the debt crisis of the 1980s and during the Asian crisis of the late 1990s. After the East Asian crisis, Japan had proposed the creation of an Asian monetary fund, but this proposal—while well received in the region—was not pursued after objections were presented from outside the region. Instead, initiatives have been developed to improve regional surveillance and create collective liquidity-support mechanisms. The collective liquidity support under the Chiang Mai Initiative agreed in May 2000 involves bilateral currency swap arrangement among the Association of Southeast Asian Nations (ASEAN) member countries plus China, Japan and the Republic of Korea. The effectiveness of the Chiang Mai Initiative in dealing with financial crises has as yet to be tested. This regional framework is complementary to the IMF global facilities and does not negate the need for a crisis-prevention framework for IMF itself.

International financial regulation

A third set of measures would include improved international financial regulation to stem capital flow volatility and provide advice in designing appropriate capital controls, including on a counter-cyclical basis. Policymakers in developed countries should pay more attention to preventing harmful effects of financial excesses. Risk assessments by rating agencies are highly pro-cyclical (Persaud, 2000; United Nations, 2005a; International Monetary Fund, 2008) and tend to react to the materialization of risks rather than to their build-up. As indicated above, existing tools are not very effective in addressing the consequences. International regulations on the capital adequacy of banks tend to be pro-cyclical too, requiring lenders to raise more capital only when problems in financial markets have already occurred. The Basel I rules allowed banks to hide risky loans off their balance sheets, eroding effectiveness of regulation even further. The Basel II rules are more sophisticated in treating risk, but rely heavily on risk assessment models developed by banks themselves, which ignore contagion effects and herding behaviour which are intrinsic to the functioning of financial markets.

> Improved international financial regulation would decrease capital volatility …

Both national and international prudential regulatory frameworks need to be modified to focus on the systemic components of risk build-up in financial markets. Furthermore, the improved framework should apply equally to banks and to non-banks in order to be effective. Regulation can be made counter-cyclical by requiring that buffers (capital adequacy) be built up during upswings in order to both restrain excesses and provide a greater cushion against losses in the downswing. Such rules should be international so as to ensure that banks and other financial institutions do not try to evade national requirements by shifting portfolios to offshore holdings.

> … as long as it focused on the systemic components of risk

Enhancing and reforming compensatory financing mechanisms

A fourth set of measures would address the need for enhanced provision of emergency financing in response to external shocks, whether to the current or to the capital accounts, so as to ease the burdens of adjustment and reduce the costs of holding large reserve balances. Current mechanisms are limited in coverage, too narrowly defined, or subject to unduly strict conditionality (Griffith-Jones and Ocampo, 2008; United Nations, 2008b). The Supplemental Reserve Facility, established in 1997, provides some collective insurance to countries hit by capital-account crises, but the Facility does not provide enough protection in the case of a typical sudden reversal in capital flows. The Contingent Credit Line was unused and expired in 2003, and little has been done to revitalize the Compensatory Financing Facility, which provided the liquidity to developing countries needed to manage terms-of-trade shocks. IMF has proposed the establishment of a Reserve Augmentation Line as part of the Supplemental Reserve Facility which would provide emergency liquidity to members that have strong macroeconomic policies, a sustainable debt situation and

> An enhanced provision of emergency financing would reduce the cost of adjustment

proved credibility in policy implementation, but that are still faced with vulnerabilities with respect to capital-account crises. To overcome the potential stigma associated with the facility, there is a need to enhance the reliability of access to financial resources and re-inforce positive signalling to markets. A significant number of emerging market members should qualify, based on the information available from past IMF Article IV consultation reports. Allowing automatic front-loaded drawing of up to 500 per cent of quota, based on simple and transparent guidelines, for eligible members would send a clear signal to private markets that the line is an insurance facility. If such a mechanism could emulate the lender-of-last-resort functions of central banks, it could reduce the demand for high reserve build-up in developing countries. This in turn could create more policy space in developing countries by offloading pressures towards exchange-rate appreciation.

More generally, IMF facilities should be significantly simplified and include more automatic and quicker disbursements proportionate to the scale of the external shocks. Lending on more concessional terms is highly desirable, especially for heavily indebted low-income countries. A new issuance of special drawing rights could be one option for financing a significant increase in the availability of compensatory financing.

Strengthening the multilateral trading system

Despite the general acceptance of the benefits of freer trade, the international division of labour is greatly influenced by commercial policies that favour products and markets in which more advanced countries have a dominant position and a competitive edge. In particular, high tariffs, tariff escalation, and subsidies in agriculture and fisheries are applied extensively to products that offer the greatest potential for export diversification in developing countries (see box II.2). The situation in respect of protectionism is no better for industrial products including footwear, clothing and textiles, sectors where many developing countries have competitive advantages. The trading system is also vulnerable to the increasingly volatile working of the international financial system, reversing the original intentions of the post-war multilateral architects and adversely affecting developing-country prospects. A major concern is the destabilizing and deflationary feedbacks among trade and financial flows. These, as discussed earlier, can create impediments to development, including through unstable and misaligned exchange rates and boom-bust cycles, which lead to excessive expansion of investment, production and trade in particular sectors, and eventually come to an end with the collapse of the bubble, resulting in sharp declines in trade flows and prices.

Reforming the international financial system should be undertaken with the basic objective of easing the integration of developing countries into the international trading system. The interest of developing countries in the stability of the international financial system is underpinned by the wish that it could allow greater participation in international trade to be combined with the full exploitation of their development potential.

It is also to be expected that the internationalization of production will continue, and that the *outsourcing* of jobs will influence employment outcomes as emerging economies tap deeper into global supply chains in attempts to create additional job opportunities for their workers. Indeed, there are reasons to expect that this trend will become even more significant. Consequently, as labour markets become more integrated and ever more dependent on large and more footloose multinational enterprises, there may be a need for a "more transparent, coherent and balanced framework" at the global level to ad-

Larger financial flows have added uncertainty to the international trading system

A coherent and balanced multilateral framework could help address the employment dimension of globalization ...

Box II.2

Agriculture and the multilateral trading system

There is broad agreement that the system of protection for agriculture in advanced countries that has grown over the past 40 years has been detrimental to agricultural development in many developing countries, though it is only one of many factors that have contributed to food insecurity in some of these countries. For much of that time, the agriculture sector and international agricultural trade remained outside the normal rules and disciplines of the old multilateral trading system under the General Agreement on Tariffs and Trade (GATT). The Declaration of Punta del Este of 1986 launching the Uruguay Round of multilateral trade negotiations resulted in the 1994 Agreement Establishing the World Trade Organization;[a] the Agreement on Agriculture[a] provided for a change of course and fundamental reforms directed towards market-oriented agricultural trade and related subsidy and support programmes.

Towards this end, the Agreement on Agriculture had provided for quantifying in monetary terms all kinds of agriculture support measures—domestic, border measures and exports—and reducing such support over a period of years. After an initial agreed quantum/percentage of reduction commitments (on domestic support, border protection and export subsidies) over an initial six-year period (1995-2000), the Agreement on Agriculture envisaged a continuation of the reform process, for which negotiations were initiated in 2000. The parameters for the negotiations for continuing the process of long-term reforms as set out in article 20 of the Agreement are:

- Experience from implementing the reduction commitments (from 1995-2000);
- Effects of the reduction commitments on world trade in agricultural trade;
- Non-trade concerns, special and differentiated treatment to developing-country members, and the objective to establish a fair and market-oriented agricultural trading system, and other objectives and concerns mentioned in the preamble to the Agreement;
- What further commitments are necessary to achieve the above mentioned long-term objectives.

As a quid pro quo for the developed countries to continue their long-term reform process in agriculture, developing countries have already paid an advance price by undertaking new commitments (GATT disciplines, the agreement on Trade-related Aspects of Intellectual Property Rights,[a] the General Agreement on Trade in Services,[a] etc). The parameters and conditions for negotiations on further agriculture reforms do not call for any new market access concessions from the developing countries whether on services or on non-agricultural (industrial) goods trade.

The likely impact on food security of any multilateral agreements to further liberalize agricultural trade is uncertain in the short and medium term, given the fact that the likely upward impact on world market prices would have a negative impact on net food importers, and the fact that the small scale of agricultural production in most developing countries limits their prospects for competing in global markets. In both respects, very significant increases in aid, compensatory finance and development support will be needed to ensure that there are widespread gains.

Moreover, the reforms to the current system of protection for agriculture in the United States of America, in countries of Europe and in other developed countries are being carried out for their own benefit and in response to domestic political considerations and budgetary factors, with the aim of enhancing economic efficiency and competitiveness and generating domestic welfare gains. These can be carried out independently of what happens in the multilateral negotiations.

a   See *Legal Instruments Embodying the Results of the Uruguay Round of Multilateral Trade Negotiations*, done at Marrakesh on 15 April 1994 (GATT Secretariat publication, Sales No. GATT/1994.7).

dress the employment dimensions of globalization.[22] Whether or not that materializes, a strategy of lifting all boats (and avoiding beggar-my-neighbour responses) requires a faster pace of investment in the advanced countries, including, in particular public investment in infrastructure development and investments in low-carbon technologies consistent with commitments to mitigating the adverse impact of climate change. Moreover, a more bal-

---

22   See the discussion in International Labour Organization, 2004b.

anced pattern of domestic demand will be achieved only when rising wages (in line with productivity gains) rather than increased levels of debt provide a solid basis for expanding domestic market demand. The challenges ahead will also require economies to continuously increase their skill and knowledge base in order to successfully integrate themselves into the global production process; to ensure that the net effect of globalized production is not simply the displacement of workers; and to uphold core labour standards in order to ensure decent and productive work for all.

... along with domestic
policies designed to
stimulate investment,
job creation and
social protection

Active labour-market policies (including skill development) should be strengthened to better prepare workers for the future job market. When temporary dislocation of workers cannot be avoided, appropriate social protection measures can be introduced to provide worker security. In all cases, the benefits that global production can bring should be properly weighted against the costs, and these costs can be minimized only through active involvement of all the major actors (International Labour Organization, 2005a).

Appendix

A. External shocks and domestic adjustment decomposition methodology

The decomposition of shifts in current-account balances into different types of external shocks and domestic adjustment mechanisms is based on a methodology originating in the work of Balassa (1981) and subsequent refinements by Avila and Bacha (1987) and FitzGerald and Sarmad (1997). The analysis in chapter II follows the latter specification.

Decomposing the current account

The methodology is based on the decomposition of the current-account deficit (D) in any one year (t) between imports of goods and non-factor services (M), net payments of factor services to abroad (V), exports of goods and non-factor services (E) and unrequited transfers received from abroad (T):

$$D_t = M_t + V_t - E_t - T_t \tag{1}$$

Imports and exports are disaggregated between price indices (P_m, P_x) and volumes (J, X) at constant domestic currency prices:

$$M_t = P_{mt}.J_t \tag{2}$$

$$E_t = P_{xt}.X_t \tag{3}$$

Import volume is linked to real domestic absorption (A) - in other words, consumption (C) plus investment (I) - by a single coefficient (j):

$$J_t = j_t.A_t \tag{4}$$

$$A_t = C_t + I_t \tag{5}$$

Export volume (X) is linked to world trade volume (W) by an "overall export coefficient" (x) which, in effect, measures export penetration as the country's share of world trade:

$$X_t = x_t.W_t \tag{6}$$

Finally, factor services payments to abroad (V) are broken down into net interest payments to abroad (V_i), net investment income payments to abroad (V_d) and net workers' remittances from abroad (R). Net interest payments to abroad are defined as the product of the current dollar interest rate (r) and the debt stock (in local currency at the official exchange rate) from the previous year (F_{t-1}):

$$V_t = V_{it} + V_{dt} - R_t \tag{7}$$

$$V_{it} = r_t.F_{t-1} \tag{8}$$

It should be recalled that all the coefficients (x, j, r) are in practice derived from these equations, so that the definitional identities always sum to the observed current-account deficit (D).

Substituting (2) to (8) in (1) and dividing through by national income at current prices yields the complete decomposition formula:

$$D_t/Y_t = p_{mt}.j_t(C_t - I_t)/Z_t + r_t.F_{t-1}/Y_t + (V_{dt} - R_t)/Y_t - p_{xt}.x_t.W_t/Z_t - T_t/Y_t \tag{9}$$

where national income at current prices (Y) is equal to the product of national income at constant prices (Z_t) and the implicit gross national product (GNP) deflator (P_{yt}) and:

$$Y_t = P_{yt}.Z_t \qquad (10)$$

$$p_{mt} = P_{mt}/P_{yt} \qquad (11)$$

$$p_{xt} = P_{xt}/P_{yt} \qquad (12)$$

Finally, a base year or years (s) is chosen in order to separate out the partial derivatives (d) of the variables, which then define the following separate effects:

$$d[D_t/Y_t] =$$

$[j_s.A_s/Z_s]dp_{mt} - [x_s.W_s/Z_s]dp_{xt}$	terms-of-trade effect
$+ [F_{s-1}/Y_s]dr_t$	interest-rate shock
$- x_s.p_{xs}.d[W_t/Z_t]$	world-trade effect
$+ r_s.d[F_{t-1}/Y_t]$	debt accumulation burden
$+ d[(V_{dt} - R_t - T_t)/Y_t]$	other external variables
$+ j_s.p_{ms}.d[A_t/Z_t]$	domestic absorption
$+ [p_{ms}.A_s/Z_s]dj_t$	import replacement
$- [p_{xs}.W_s/Z_s]dx_t$	export penetration
$+ $ *interaction terms*	(13)

The first three phrases define the exogenous "external shock"; the next two are "debt accumulation burden" and "other external variables", which respond to both internal and external conditions but are taken as autonomous; and the last three, although defined as "domestic policy response" in the original version of the methodology, should, more appropriately, be termed "domestic adjustment", since the changes may be caused both by policy intervention and by private adjustment behaviour. The difference between the sum of the explicitly defined terms and the observed change in the normalized current-account deficit is defined as "interaction terms". These interaction terms are spelled out in full in the FitzGerald-Sarmad version of the methodology. The size of this "residual term" can be rather significant when shocks are large and hence a further decomposition of the residual can provide meaningful additional detail. This is not spelled out here, because it is not part of the analysis in this chapter. Those more specific results can be found in the background paper by Vos and Parra (2008).

Data and country coverage

Three main data sources were used for the application of the methodology. National accounts and world trade data were obtained from the United Nations Statistics Division database. Capital flow, debt stock, interest rate and other financial variable data were obtained from the International Monetary Fund (IMF) International Financial Statistics and the World Bank Global Development Finance databases. It is important to clarify that the estimation of the current-account balance (deficit) was based on the national accounts data. Because of statistical discrepancies, those estimates do not necessarily coincide with those reported in the IMF Balance-of-Payments Statistics.

For the sake of the comparative analysis, the periods have been harmonized, even though the timing of major shocks may differ from country to country.

Because of data limitations, not all developing countries could be covered in the analysis. The analysis in the text covers 21 countries in Latin America and the Caribbean, 12 in Asia, 26 in Africa and 12 small island developing States. The sample of countries by (sub)region is as follows:

Latin America and the Caribbean:

South America: Argentina, Bolivia, Brazil, Chile, Colombia, Ecuador, Paraguay, Peru, Uruguay and Venezuela (Bolivarian Republic of)

Central America: Costa Rica, El Salvador, Guatemala, Honduras, Mexico, Nicaragua and Panama

Caribbean: Barbados, Dominican Republic, Jamaica and Trinidad and Tobago

Asia:

East Asia: China, Malaysia, Philippines and Thailand

South Asia: Bangladesh, India, Nepal, Pakistan and Sri Lanka

Western Asia: Jordan, Syrian Arab Republic and Turkey

Africa:

Northern Africa: Morocco and Tunisia

Least developed countries in Sub-Saharan Africa: Benin, Burkina Faso, Burundi, Gambia, Lesotho, Madagascar, Malawi, Mali, Niger, Rwanda, Senegal, Sierra Leone, Sudan, Togo and Uganda

Other countries in sub-Saharan Africa: Botswana, Cameroon, Congo, Côte-d'Ivoire, Gabon, Ghana, Kenya, Nigeria and Swaziland

Small island developing states:[a]

Small island developing States that are least developed countries: Cape Verde, Maldives, Samoa and Vanuatu

Other small island developing States: Belize, Dominica, Grenada, Mauritius, Papua New Guinea, Saint Lucia, Saint Vincent and the Grenadines and Seychelles

---

a　Estimates for small island and developing States in table A.1 also include Saint Kitts and Nevis, Barbados and Trinidad and Tobago.

B. Figures

Contents

Figure A.1
Growth of GDP per capita, East Asia, 1971-2006

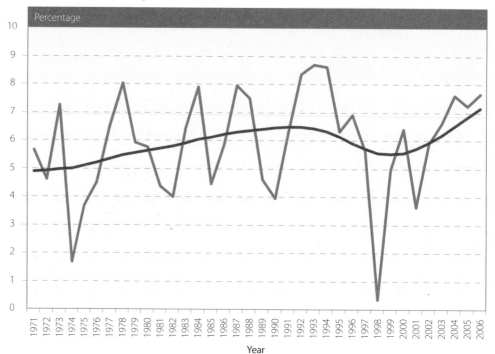

HP-filtered growth ▬▬▬
Observed growth ▬▬▬

Source: UN/DESA, based
on United Nations Statistics
Division, National Accounts
Main Aggregates database.

Note:

The red line is a smooth
trend on the rate of growth
of GDP per capita calculated
with a Hodrick-Prescott Filter
(HP). It removes short-term
fluctuations from longer-
term trends. Following the
literature, the long-term trend
in the figure was calculated
with a lag of 1 and $\mu = 100$, as
suggested for yearly data.

Figure A.2
Growth of GDP per capita, East Asia, excluding China, 1971-2006

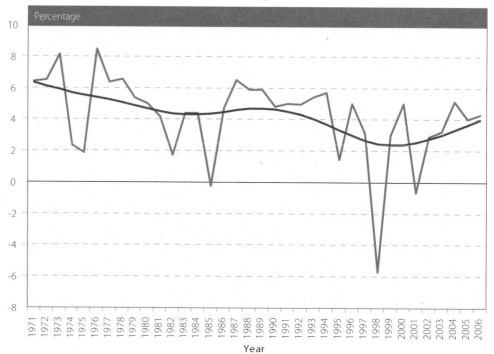

Figure A.3
Growth of GDP per capita, South Asia, 1971-2006

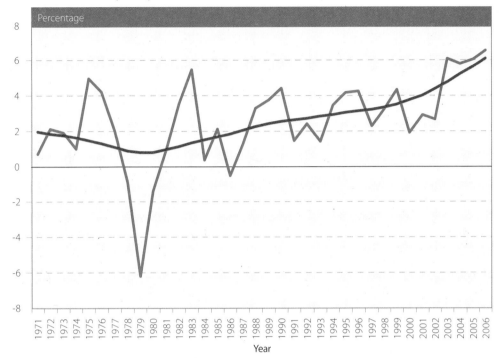

Figure A.4
Growth of GDP per capita, South Asia, excluding India, 1971-2006

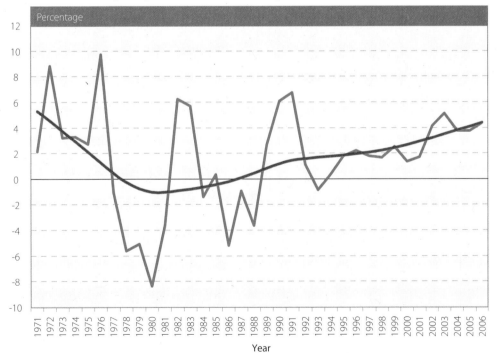

———— HP-filtered growth
———— Observed growth

Source: UN/DESA, based on United Nations Statistics Division, National Accounts Main Aggregates database.

Note:
The red line is a smooth trend on the rate of growth of GDP per capita calculated with a Hodrick-Prescott Filter (HP). It removes short-term fluctuations from longer-term trends. Following the literature, the long-term trend in the figure was calculated with a lag of 1 and μ = 100, as suggested for yearly data.

Figure A.5
Growth of GDP per capita, Western Asia, 1971-2006

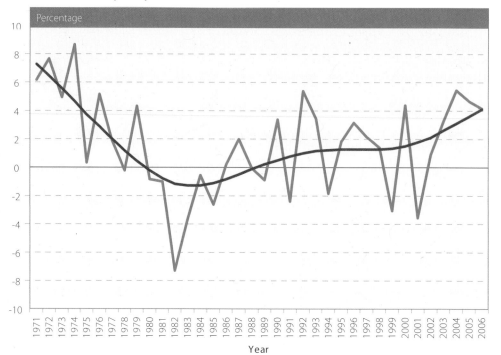

HP-filtered growth ▬▬▬
Observed growth ▬▬▬

Source: UN/DESA, based
on United Nations Statistics
Division, National Accounts
Main Aggregates database.
Note:
The red line is a smooth
trend on the rate of growth
of GDP per capita calculated
with a Hodrick-Prescott Filter
(HP). It removes short-term
fluctuations from longer-
term trends. Following the
literature, the long-term trend
in the figure was calculated
with a lag of 1 and μ = 100, as
suggested for yearly data.

Figure A.6
Growth of GDP per capita, Northern Africa, 1971-2006

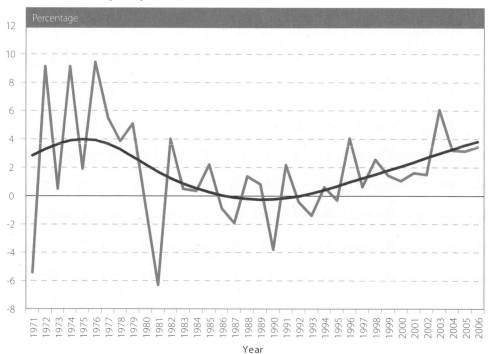

Figure A.7
Growth of GDP per capita, sub-Saharan Africa, 1971-2006

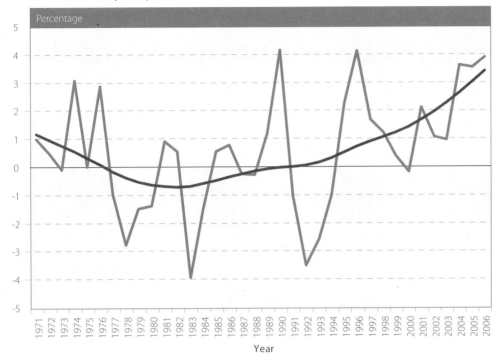

HP-filtered growth
Observed growth

Source: UN/DESA, based on United Nations Statistics Division, National Accounts Main Aggregates database.

Note:
The red line is a smooth trend on the rate of growth of GDP per capita calculated with a Hodrick-Prescott Filter (HP). It removes short-term fluctuations from longer-term trends. Following the literature, the long-term trend in the figure was calculated with a lag of 1 and $\mu = 100$, as suggested for yearly data.

Figure A.8
Growth of GDP per capita, Latin America and the Caribbean, 1971-2006

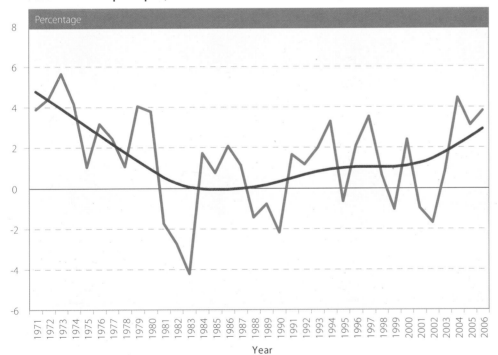

Figure A.9
Twelve-month volatility of commodity prices, December 1980-August 2008

Metals ——
Food and beverage ——
Agricultural raw ——

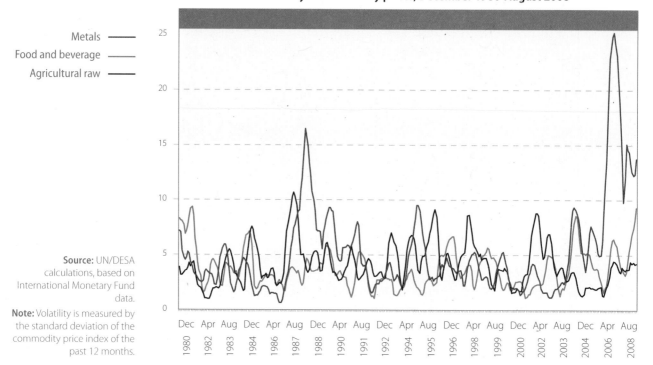

Source: UN/DESA calculations, based on International Monetary Fund data.

Note: Volatility is measured by the standard deviation of the commodity price index of the past 12 months.

Figure A.10
Net transfer of resources as percentage of GDP per capita growth, 1975-2005

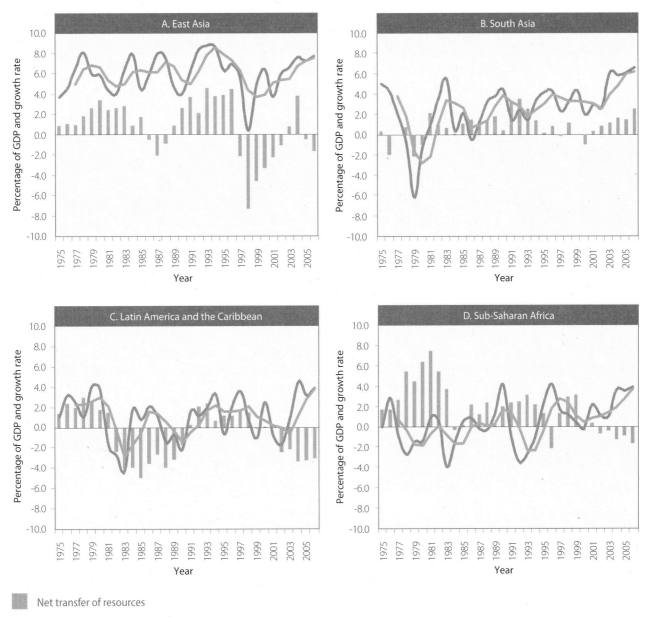

Net transfer of resources

Per capita GDP growth rate

3 period moving average (per capita GDP growth rate)

Sources: UN/DESA calculations, based on data from UN/DESA and International Monetary Fund (IMF) International Financial Statistics (IFS) online database.

C. Tables

Contents

Table A.1
Incidence of shocks per region,[a] 1980-2005

Percentage								
Type of external shock and domestic adjustment	_1986-1990_ _1980-1985_		_1991-1995_ _1986-1990_		_1996-2000_ _1991-1995_		_2001-2005_ _1996-2000_	
	Negative	_Positive_	_Negative_	_Positive_	_Negative_	_Positive_	_Negative_	_Positive_
A. Developing countries, 72 countries[b]								
Terms of trade	38	21	33	22	11	28	31	21
Interest-rate shock	3	17	0	8	3	1	0	6
World trade	14	43	10	61	0	89	4	79
Debt accumulation burden	17	4	11	1	3	0	7	0
Other external variables	31	14	31	22	18	19	26	22
Domestic spending	6	29	19	14	17	13	21	11
Trade ratios	31	43	65	13	78	11	72	10
Import ratio	33	32	57	19	51	22	38	32
Export penetration	31	33	36	28	56	18	64	14
B. Asia, 12 countries								
Terms of trade	8	25	17	17	8	17	33	17
Interest-rate shock	0	8	0	8	0	0	0	8
World trade	17	25	25	17	0	75	8	67
Debt accumulation burden	8	0	8	0	8	0	8	0
Other external variables	25	0	17	8	8	17	17	17
Domestic spending	0	25	8	8	0	33	8	25
Trade ratios	17	50	25	25	67	17	67	8
Import ratio	33	17	83	0	67	25	50	8
Export penetration	8	33	8	50	17	33	50	42
C. Latin America and the Caribbean, 19 countries								
Terms of trade	42	16	42	21	11	26	26	21
Interest-rate shock	11	42	0	11	11	0	0	5
World trade	0	63	5	68	0	100	0	100
Debt accumulation burden	21	16	32	5	5	0	16	0
Other external variables	32	16	21	47	11	32	16	32
Domestic spending	5	11	11	5	16	0	11	11
Trade ratios	53	16	84	0	100	0	68	5
Import ratio	42	11	79	11	74	11	42	21
Export penetration	26	32	21	37	58	21	58	0
D. Africa, 26 countries								
Terms of trade	50	23	46	19	15	35	35	23
Interest-rate shock	0	12	0	12	0	4	0	8
World trade	8	46	4	73	0	88	4	65
Debt accumulation burden	23	0	4	0	0	0	0	0
Other external variables	38	4	27	19	23	19	31	27
Domestic spending	4	38	19	12	8	15	19	8
Trade ratios	19	50	73	8	62	19	77	8
Import ratio	19	58	46	31	31	27	42	31
Export penetration	50	23	54	12	62	12	62	12

Table A.1 (cont'd)

Type of external shock and domestic adjustment	1986-1990 1980-1985		1991-1995 1986-1990		1996-2000 1991-1995		2001-2005 1996-2000	
	Negative	Positive	Negative	Positive	Negative	Positive	Negative	Positive
E. Small island developing States, 15 countries								
Terms of trade	33	20	13	33	7	27	27	20
Interest-rate shock	0	0	0	0	0	0	0	0
World trade	40	27	13	67	0	87	7	87
Debt accumulation burden	7	0	0	0	0	0	7	0
Other external variables	20	40	60	7	27	7	40	7
Domestic spending	13	40	40	33	47	7	47	7
Trade ratios	33	60	60	27	87	7	73	20
Import ratio	47	27	27	27	47	27	13	67
Export penetration	20	53	47	27	73	13	87	13

Source: UN/DESA calculations, based on United Nations Statistics Division, World Bank Global Development Finance and International Monetary Fund International Financial Statistics online databases.

a Number of sizeable shocks and domestic adjustment shifts per period, over total number of countries per region. Sizeable shocks are larger than 2 per cent of GNP (period average); negative shocks refer to contributions to rising current-account deficit.

b Including all countries listed in section A of the appendix.

Table A.2.
Decomposition analysis of the current account of the balance of payments, East and South Asia, Latin America and the Caribbean, Africa, Western Asia and small island developing States, 1981-2005

Percentage of GNP								
From:	*1981-1985*	*1986-1990*	*1991-1995*	*1996-2000*	*1981-1985*	*1986-1990*	*1991-1995*	*1996-2000*
To:	*1986-1990*	*1991-1995*	*1996-2000*	*2001-2005*	*1986-1990*	*1991-1995*	*1996-2000*	*2001-2005*
	A. East and South Asia[a]							
	East Asia without China				South Asia without India			
Observed deficit increase	-3.84	3.65	-9.80	-1.50	-1.51	0.52	-0.62	-1.13
External shocks	0.09	2.16	-11.16	-8.09	0.31	-0.87	-4.61	1.65
Terms-of-trade deterioration	0.67	-0.61	-1.70	2.75	0.35	0.47	-0.89	3.37
Imports price effect	-0.28	-3.60	4.91	3.12	0.38	0.13	0.58	2.29
Exports price effect	0.96	2.98	-6.61	-0.37	-0.03	0.34	-1.48	1.08
Interest-rate shock	-1.22	-0.68	-0.13	-0.83	-0.13	-0.21	-0.12	-0.31
World trade retardation	0.63	3.45	-9.33	-10.01	0.09	-1.13	-3.60	-1.40
Other external variables	1.49	-1.05	1.24	-0.06	1.83	1.34	0.68	-1.86
Debt accumulation burden	0.87	-0.68	1.29	-0.66	0.31	0.12	0.08	-0.09
Change in direct investment income	0.54	-0.44	-0.25	1.40	0.25	0.28	0.38	0.23
Change in remittances	0.11	0.05	0.23	-0.71	1.23	0.95	0.24	-1.96
Change in official transfers	-0.03	0.01	-0.03	-0.10	0.03	0.00	-0.03	-0.04
Domestic adjustment	-6.03	-0.31	2.35	6.28	-3.41	0.20	2.41	-1.16
Domestic spending	-2.43	3.34	-4.94	-3.60	-0.43	0.04	-0.03	-0.67
Consumption contraction	-1.53	-0.86	-1.30	1.05	-0.09	-0.04	0.03	-0.56
Private consumption	-0.89	-0.31	-1.11	0.53	-0.33	0.12	0.13	-0.54
Public consumption	-0.65	-0.55	-0.19	0.52	0.24	-0.15	-0.10	-0.01
Investment reduction	-0.89	4.20	-3.63	-4.64	-0.35	0.08	-0.07	-0.11
Trade ratios	-3.60	-3.65	7.28	9.87	-2.98	0.16	2.44	-0.50
Import replacement	9.55	14.76	9.51	7.57	-1.00	2.12	-0.03	0.64
Export penetration	-13.14	-18.40	-2.23	2.31	-1.99	-1.95	2.47	-1.14
Interaction effects	0.61	2.85	-2.23	0.38	-0.24	-0.16	0.90	0.24
	China				India			
Observed deficit increase	-0.34	-0.42	-1.51	-0.93	0.12	-1.00	-0.44	-0.95
External Shocks	-2.39	-0.67	0.16	5.57	0.44	-0.63	-0.63	1.56
Terms-of-trade deterioration	-4.53	-2.80	-1.16	3.14	0.01	-0.01	0.49	1.92
Imports price effect	5.47	-1.31	-0.23	-0.32	0.10	-0.37	-0.54	1.08
Exports price effect	-10.00	-1.49	-0.92	3.46	-0.10	0.35	1.04	0.84
Interest-rate shock	-0.12	-0.12	-0.18	-0.18	0.09	-0.20	-0.13	-0.01
World trade retardation	2.26	2.24	1.49	2.60	0.34	-0.42	-1.00	-0.35
Other external variables	0.71	0.84	0.90	-0.90	0.68	0.22	-1.23	-0.61
Debt accumulation burden	0.67	0.33	0.10	-0.11	0.36	0.54	-0.31	-0.09
Change in direct investment income	-0.02	0.49	0.92	-0.70	-0.01	0.28	0.09	0.00
Change in remittances	0.07	0.04	0.10	-0.03	0.33	-0.56	-1.03	-0.52
Change in official transfers	0.00	-0.01	-0.02	-0.05	0.00	-0.04	0.02	0.00
Domestic adjustment	-0.33	-0.79	-2.67	-10.00	-1.09	-0.26	1.49	-2.13
Domestic spending	-0.63	0.61	-0.67	-0.55	-0.04	-0.22	-0.17	-0.22
Consumption contraction	-0.51	-0.23	-0.98	-1.14	-0.17	-0.32	-0.26	-0.32
Private consumption	-0.34	-0.53	-0.72	-1.14	-0.27	-0.26	-0.32	-0.25
Public consumption	-0.17	0.30	-0.26	0.00	0.10	-0.06	0.06	-0.07

Table A.2 (cont'd)

From:	1981-1985	1986-1990	1991-1995	1996-2000	1981-1985	1986-1990	1991-1995	1996-2000
To:	1986-1990	1991-1995	1996-2000	2001 2005	1986-1990	1991-1995	1996-2000	2001-2005
Investment reduction	-0.12	0.84	0.30	0.59	0.13	0.09	0.09	0.10
Trade ratios	0.30	-1.40	-2.00	-9.45	-1.05	-0.03	1.66	-1.91
Import replacement	0.29	2.19	1.39	10.78	-0.24	3.37	3.56	1.26
Export penetration	0.02	-3.59	-3.39	-20.23	-0.81	-3.40	-1.90	-3.17
Interaction effects	1.66	0.20	0.10	4.41	0.09	-0.33	-0.07	0.23

B. Latin America and the Caribbean[a]

	South America				Central America without Mexico			
Observed deficit increase	-0.84	2.61	0.61	-4.83	-0.34	-2.86	-0.41	-1.93
External shocks	4.75	-1.00	-4.82	-5.31	-5.68	-5.82	-8.86	-4.54
Terms-of-trade deterioration	3.43	2.10	-0.98	-0.34	-1.14	-1.74	-1.13	1.58
Imports price effect	0.75	-0.96	-2.07	3.97	-0.70	-0.95	0.45	-0.11
Exports price effect	2.68	3.06	1.09	-4.30	-0.45	-0.79	-1.58	1.70
Interest-rate shock	1.57	-1.02	-0.15	-0.78	-1.51	0.09	0.37	-0.29
World trade retardation	-0.25	-2.08	-3.68	-4.20	-3.03	-4.18	-8.10	-5.83
Other external variables	-1.59	4.87	0.89	2.82	0.45	-3.71	-0.73	-5.03
Debt accumulation burden	-2.54	6.31	1.36	1.38	0.25	1.21	-0.58	0.18
Change in direct investment income	1.01	-1.27	-0.38	1.75	0.89	-0.20	0.50	-0.54
Change in remittances	-0.03	-0.17	-0.12	-0.30	-0.48	-4.79	-0.74	-4.66
Change in official transfers	-0.03	0.01	0.02	-0.02	-0.21	0.07	0.10	-0.01
Domestic adjustment	-2.04	4.12	5.01	-0.06	4.72	7.63	8.17	6.58
Domestic spending	-0.90	0.02	0.09	-0.24	-0.96	0.53	0.69	-0.72
Consumption contraction	-0.66	-0.03	0.06	-0.04	-0.37	-0.79	-0.47	0.23
Private consumption	-0.70	0.11	0.18	-0.06	-0.17	0.52	0.04	0.27
Public consumption	0.04	-0.14	-0.13	0.03	-0.20	-1.31	-0.51	-0.04
Investment reduction	-0.24	0.05	0.03	-0.20	-0.59	1.32	1.16	-0.95
Trade ratios	-1.13	4.10	4.93	0.18	5.68	7.10	7.48	7.30
Import replacement	-0.44	4.58	3.92	-0.35	3.92	7.94	2.96	1.82
Export penetration	-0.69	-0.48	1.00	0.53	1.76	-0.84	4.52	5.48
Interaction effects	-1.97	-5.38	-0.47	-2.28	0.17	-0.95	1.02	1.06

	Mexico				Caribbean			
Observed deficit increase	4.57	2.84	-1.90	-1.36	-3.79	-2.80	2.01	-1.82
External shocks	2.57	-5.95	-5.43	-7.77	-11.47	-11.32	-14.24	-6.67
Terms-of-trade deterioration	8.60	-2.15	0.92	-1.55	-0.83	-1.07	-2.55	-0.51
Imports price effect	4.42	-5.81	-2.00	-8.21	-6.46	-5.32	2.15	3.13
Exports price effect	4.18	3.66	2.92	6.66	5.62	4.25	-4.69	-3.64
Interest-rate shock	-2.27	-0.80	-0.34	-0.41	-1.82	-0.41	0.03	0.15
World trade retardation	-3.76	-3.00	-6.01	-5.81	-8.82	-9.83	-11.72	-6.31
Other external variables	0.62	0.30	-0.24	-1.80	3.29	-1.16	-1.93	-0.65
Debt accumulation burden	0.88	-0.80	0.44	-0.80	2.61	-0.60	-0.92	-0.02
Change in direct investment income	0.21	0.96	-0.41	-0.11	1.96	1.20	-0.01	1.22
Change in remittances	-0.47	0.12	-0.27	-0.90	-1.28	-1.85	-0.99	-1.79
Change in official transfers	0.00	0.02	0.00	0.01	0.00	0.08	-0.02	-0.05

Table A.2 (cont'd)								
From:	*1981-1985*	*1986-1990*	*1991-1995*	*1996-2000*	*1981-1985*	*1986-1990*	*1991-1995*	*1996-2000*
To:	*1986-1990*	*1991-1995*	*1996-2000*	*2001-2005*	*1986-1990*	*1991-1995*	*1996-2000*	*2001-2005*
Domestic adjustment	0.39	11.30	5.49	8.79	5.55	23.92	13.90	3.70
Domestic spending	-0.38	0.56	-0.81	0.76	-1.04	-1.10	3.02	0.82
Consumption contraction	0.03	0.13	-1.03	0.58	-1.29	-0.68	1.69	1.29
Private consumption	-0.02	0.24	-0.81	0.99	0.14	0.54	1.80	1.37
Public consumption	0.05	-0.11	-0.22	-0.42	-1.44	-1.23	-0.11	-0.08
Investment reduction	-0.41	0.43	0.23	0.18	0.26	-0.42	1.33	-0.47
Trade ratios	0.77	10.74	6.29	8.04	6.60	25.02	10.87	2.88
Import replacement	2.02	12.41	14.37	7.20	9.56	27.80	-1.54	-6.20
Export penetration	-1.25	-1.66	-8.08	0.84	-2.97	-2.78	12.42	9.08
Interaction effects	0.99	-2.82	-1.72	-0.57	-1.16	-14.24	4.29	1.79

	C. Africa excluding Nigeria[a]							
	Africa excluding Nigeria				Northern Africa			
Observed deficit increase	-3.82	-0.89	2.29	1.02	-0.44	0.15	-0.11	-0.13
External shocks	-0.38	-12.06	-10.20	-7.30	0.10	-0.14	-0.56	-0.34
Terms-of-trade deterioration	3.25	-1.03	-0.23	-0.09	0.28	0.14	0.00	-0.04
Imports price effect	3.11	0.52	-0.44	0.43	0.11	-0.05	0.02	0.12
Exports price effect	0.14	-1.55	0.21	-0.52	0.18	0.19	-0.01	-0.15
Interest-rate shock	-0.94	-1.65	-0.16	-0.58	-0.09	0.05	-0.04	-0.03
World trade retardation	-2.69	-9.38	-9.81	-6.63	-0.09	-0.33	-0.52	-0.28
Other external variables	-0.16	1.15	0.06	-0.24	0.06	-0.01	0.06	-0.12
Debt accumulation burden	0.41	0.29	-0.02	0.02	0.10	-0.03	-0.03	-0.01
Change in direct investment income	0.55	0.76	-0.18	1.42	0.02	-0.02	0.06	0.01
Change in remittances	-1.23	0.16	0.08	-1.73	-0.05	0.04	0.03	-0.12
Change in official transfers	0.11	-0.07	0.18	0.07	0.00	0.00	0.00	0.00
Domestic adjustment	-3.37	7.28	10.21	8.03	-0.57	0.29	0.30	0.33
Domestic spending	-1.54	3.08	-0.53	-0.07	-0.22	0.04	-0.08	0.01
Consumption contraction	-1.00	4.23	-0.74	-0.65	0.01	0.02	-0.07	0.01
Private consumption	-0.19	4.47	-0.45	-0.04	-0.01	0.00	-0.06	0.00
Public consumption	-0.81	-0.23	-0.28	-0.61	0.01	0.01	-0.01	0.01
Investment reduction	-0.54	-1.15	0.21	0.58	-0.22	0.03	-0.01	0.00
Trade ratios	-1.83	4.19	10.74	8.10	-0.35	0.24	0.38	0.31
Import replacement	-3.33	-5.32	4.72	5.48	-0.04	0.24	0.00	0.14
Export penetration	1.50	9.52	6.02	2.62	-0.31	0.00	0.38	0.17
Interaction effects	0.08	2.75	2.22	0.53	-0.04	0.01	0.09	0.01

	Least developed countries in sub-Saharan Africa				Remainder of countries in sub-Saharan Africa			
Observed deficit increase	-4.56	-8.01	12.87	5.68	-11.86	3.41	-1.88	-0.70
External shocks	-13.82	-40.74	-28.98	-15.36	10.99	-14.35	-16.82	-16.99
Terms-of-trade deterioration	4.77	4.20	1.68	1.66	9.37	-8.40	-2.55	-1.86
Imports price effect	4.92	8.68	0.23	2.43	8.78	-5.68	-2.13	-0.50
Exports price effect	-0.15	-4.48	1.45	-0.80	0.59	-2.72	-0.42	-1.37
Interest rate shock	-3.09	-7.05	-0.90	-1.84	-1.12	-0.68	0.19	-0.77
World trade retardation	-15.51	-37.89	-29.75	-15.17	2.74	-5.27	-14.46	-14.36

Table A.2 (cont'd)

From:	1981-1985	1986-1990	1991-1995	1996-2000	1981-1985	1986-1990	1991-1995	1996-2000
To:	1986-1990	1991-1995	1996-2000	2001-2005	1986-1990	1991-1995	1996-2000	2001-2005
Other external variables	-1.54	2.22	-0.09	-6.88	0.69	2.90	0.29	5.41
Debt accumulation burden	0.27	1.50	0.00	0.34	1.41	-0.09	-0.04	-0.23
Change in direct investment income	0.07	2.65	-0.26	3.73	2.30	0.83	-0.60	2.65
Change in remittances	-2.05	-2.00	-0.58	-11.35	-3.36	2.51	0.87	3.06
Change in official transfers	0.14	0.06	0.76	0.41	0.34	-0.35	0.06	-0.08
Domestic adjustment	9.79	16.86	33.68	27.32	-23.01	15.59	12.75	9.17
Domestic spending	4.79	4.40	-2.30	0.57	-10.85	9.19	-0.10	-0.85
Consumption contraction	2.62	10.80	-2.63	-3.74	-6.72	8.28	-0.70	0.63
Private consumption	4.04	13.15	-0.42	-2.94	-4.51	7.13	-1.51	2.52
Public consumption	-1.42	-2.35	-2.21	-0.80	-2.21	1.15	0.81	-1.89
Investment reduction	2.19	-6.40	0.36	4.30	-4.13	0.91	0.60	-1.48
Trade ratios	5.00	12.46	35.96	26.75	-12.16	6.40	12.85	10.02
Import replacement	-16.47	-26.95	18.04	21.48	0.85	1.66	3.74	3.74
Export penetration	21.47	39.41	17.91	5.29	-13.01	4.74	9.11	6.28
Interaction effects	0.99	13.67	8.25	0.59	-0.52	-0.73	1.90	1.71

D. Nigeria and Western Asia[a]

	Nigeria				Western Asia			
Observed deficit increase	-32.12	28.62	-23.16	3.46	-1.26	1.90	-0.72	-0.37
External shocks	-1.43	10.63	-22.78	-13.00	-1.09	0.51	-2.58	-7.76
Terms-of-trade deterioration	1.13	10.42	-8.44	-7.41	-0.29	2.38	2.10	-0.80
Imports price effect	7.57	-7.10	4.44	-7.01	-1.40	2.40	-0.38	-2.87
Exports price effect	-6.44	17.52	-12.88	-0.40	1.11	-0.03	2.48	2.07
Interest-rate shock	-0.48	-1.26	-0.64	0.38	-0.53	0.11	-0.23	-1.15
World trade retardation	-2.08	1.47	-13.70	-5.97	-0.28	-1.98	-4.45	-5.82
Other external variables	6.27	-1.04	-1.39	0.09	1.70	0.34	-0.18	3.34
Debt accumulation burden	4.30	-0.43	-0.74	0.61	0.57	-0.15	0.64	1.54
Change in direct investment income	2.42	0.27	0.24	0.40	0.49	0.14	-0.65	0.46
Change in remittances	-0.46	-0.86	-0.92	-0.92	0.53	0.33	-0.20	1.33
Change in official transfers	0.00	-0.01	0.03	0.00	0.11	0.01	0.02	0.01
Domestic adjustment	-28.12	21.19	-15.50	15.11	-1.65	1.55	2.46	5.18
Domestic spending	-13.52	2.16	-12.54	4.45	-0.47	-0.29	-0.80	-1.14
Consumption contraction	-11.06	2.04	-12.06	3.22	-0.45	-0.83	-0.67	-0.50
Private consumption	-4.73	5.06	-11.17	2.51	-0.36	-0.70	-0.61	-0.52
Public consumption	-6.33	-3.02	-0.89	0.71	-0.10	-0.13	-0.06	0.02
Investment reduction	-2.47	0.12	-0.48	1.23	-0.02	0.52	-0.14	-0.64
Trade ratios	-14.60	19.03	-2.95	10.66	-1.17	1.85	3.26	6.31
Import replacement	5.77	20.04	-33.46	-1.53	2.21	4.08	6.43	8.87
Export penetration	-20.37	-1.01	30.51	12.19	-3.39	-2.23	-3.17	-2.56
Interaction effects	-8.84	-2.16	16.50	1.26	-0.21	-0.50	-0.42	-1.12

Table A.2 (cont'd)								
From:	1981-1985	1986-1990	1991-1995	1996-2000	1981-1985	1986-1990	1991-1995	1996-2000
To:	1986-1990	1991-1995	1996-2000	2001-2005	1986-1990	1991-1995	1996-2000	2001-2005
	E. Small island developing States[a]							
	Least developed country small island developing States				Remainder of small island developing States			
Observed deficit increase	-4.13	1.46	-2.00	8.98	-5.78	-2.62	2.59	5.14
External shocks	5.61	-3.43	-5.96	-3.91	3.64	4.15	-20.27	-10.40
Terms-of-trade deterioration	-1.62	-2.15	-1.50	1.94	3.07	5.96	-6.60	0.95
Imports price effect	-4.00	-0.89	-2.12	0.15	3.04	-2.68	-2.39	-0.37
Exports price effect	2.38	-1.25	0.63	1.79	0.03	8.63	-4.20	1.32
Interest-rate shock	-0.92	-0.37	-0.07	0.21	-1.15	-0.88	-0.31	-0.30
World trade retardation	8.14	-0.90	-4.41	-6.07	1.72	-0.92	-13.36	-11.05
Other external variables	-2.97	3.40	3.08	3.34	-0.34	4.89	-1.13	2.58
Debt accumulation burden	-0.37	-0.07	0.04	0.35	0.36	-0.48	-0.01	0.35
Change in direct investment income	-2.73	1.36	-1.43	0.15	0.11	2.28	0.12	1.30
Change in remittances	-0.40	1.96	4.40	3.31	-1.25	2.98	-1.28	1.05
Change in official transfers	0.53	0.14	0.06	-0.48	0.44	0.10	0.05	-0.13
Domestic adjustment	-9.28	0.50	0.51	7.85	-8.50	-13.16	20.05	10.90
Domestic spending	-1.49	2.07	-1.56	3.83	-2.69	-7.84	5.37	1.88
Consumption contraction	-0.97	1.85	-0.02	1.84	-4.05	-7.08	4.68	2.85
Private consumption	-0.93	1.57	0.33	0.38	-2.55	-6.47	5.55	2.84
Public consumption	-0.04	0.27	-0.36	1.46	-1.50	-0.61	-0.87	0.00
Investment reduction	-0.51	0.23	-1.54	1.99	1.36	-0.77	0.69	-0.96
Trade ratios	-7.79	-1.57	2.07	4.02	-5.82	-5.32	14.68	9.01
Import replacement	0.19	-0.48	0.34	-2.94	7.49	6.49	0.20	-1.71
Export penetration	-7.99	-1.09	1.73	6.96	-13.30	-11.81	14.48	10.72
Interaction effects	2.51	0.99	0.37	1.70	-0.58	1.50	3.94	2.07

Source: UN/DESA calculations, based on United Nations Statistics Division, World Bank Global Development Finance and International Monetary Fund International Financial Statistics online databases.

Note: A positive sign refers to an increase in the deficit and an adverse external shock.

a Regions defined in section A of the appendix. Regional averages are weighted by GNP.

Table A.3
Technological classification of exports,[a] by regions and countries, 1980-2005

Percentage of total exports of goods							
		1980	*1985*	*1990*	*1995*	*2000*	*2005*
A. East and South Asia							
East Asia excluding China[b]							
Primary products		33	24	12	8	7	7
Resource-based manufactures	Agro-based	11	9	8	7	5	5
	Other	11	9	7	5	6	8
Low-technology manufactures	Textile, garment and footwear	14	16	19	14	12	8
	Other products	7	8	10	10	8	7
Medium-technology manufactures	Automotive	1	1	1	2	3	5
	Process	4	5	6	7	6	6
	Engineering	9	13	13	14	12	14
High-technology manufactures	Electronic and electrical	6	11	19	29	38	36
	Other	1	2	1	2	2	3
Others		3	3	2	3	1	2
China							
Primary products			60	21	10	7	4
Resource-based manufactures	Agro-based		5	5	5	4	3
	Other		11	6	6	5	5
Low-technology manufactures	Textile, garment and footwear		14	30	31	26	18
	Other products		3	11	16	16	14
Medium-technology manufactures	Automotive		0	6	1	2	2
	Process		4	5	7	6	6
	Engineering		1	10	11	12	14
High-technology manufactures	Electronic and electrical		0	4	11	20	31
	Other		2	2	2	2	3
Others			0	2	1	1	1
South Asia excluding India							
Primary products		42	35	22	12	11	14
Resource-based manufactures	Agro-based	10	5	3	3	2	5
	Other	13	5	3	1	1	6
Low-technology manufactures	Textile, garment and footwear	33	46	62	73	76	63
	Other products	1	2	3	3	3	4
Medium-technology manufactures	Automotive	0	0	0	0	0	0
	Process	1	3	4	5	5	4
	Engineering	1	2	2	2	2	2
High-technology manufactures	Electronic and electrical	0	0	0	0	0	1
	Other	0	0	1	0	0	1
Others		1	1	1	1	1	1
India							
Primary products		32	29	20	19	14	12
Resource-based manufactures	Agro-based	3	3	2	4	3	2
	Other	16	25	25	23	25	34
Low-technology manufactures	Textile, garment and footwear	29	28	32	30	29	18
	Other products	4	3	5	7	9	11

Table A.3 (cont'd)		1980	1985	1990	1995	2000	2005
Medium-technology manufactures	Automotive	3	1	2	3	2	3
	Process	3	2	4	5	6	7
	Engineering	4	4	4	3	4	6
High-technology manufactures	Electronic and electrical	1	1	2	2	2	2
	Other	2	2	3	2	3	3
Others		3	2	2	2	2	1
B. Latin America and the Caribbean							
South America							
Primary products		52	48	52	41	43	47
Resource-based manufactures	Agro-based	9	10	11	15	11	10
	Other	20	16	11	14	15	14
Low-technology manufactures	Textile, garment and footwear	5	6	6	6	5	3
	Other products	3	4	4	5	4	4
Medium-technology manufactures	Automotive	2	2	2	4	4	5
	Process	3	5	6	6	6	7
	Engineering	3	4	4	5	4	5
High-technology manufactures	Electronic and electrical	1	1	1	1	2	2
	Other	0	1	1	1	3	2
Others		1	1	1	2	3	3
Central America excluding Mexico							
Primary products			69	51	42	37	30
Resource-based manufactures	Agro-based		10	13	13	14	15
	Other		8	15	8	9	9
Low-technology manufactures	Textile, garment and footwear		4	6	13	7	14
	Other products		3	4	6	7	8
Medium-technology manufactures	Automotive		0	0	0	0	0
	Process		3	3	6	5	6
	Engineering		1	1	5	5	6
High-technology manufactures	Electronic and electrical		0	1	1	14	10
	Other		2	2	2	3	3
Others			1	3	3	1	1
Mexico							
Primary products			47	49	18	13	18
Resource-based manufactures	Agro-based		4	4	3	3	3
	Other		7	7	4	3	4
Low-technology manufactures	Textile, garment and footwear		3	2	6	7	5
	Other products		6	5	9	8	8
Medium-technology manufactures	Automotive		5	12	15	17	15
	Process		4	6	6	4	4
	Engineering		14	10	19	17	18
High-technology manufactures	Electronic and electrical		8	4	19	26	23
	Other		1	1	2	2	3
Others			0	1	1	0	1

Table A.3 (cont'd)

		1980	1985	1990	1995	2000	2005
Caribbean							
Primary products			28	22	15	22	34
Resource-based manufactures	Agro-based		9	9	10	8	5
	Other		41	47	29	49	45
Low-technology manufactures	Textile, garment and footwear		3	5	19	3	0
	Other products		5	6	4	6	3
Medium-technology manufactures	Automotive		0	0	0	0	0
	Process		5	6	8	9	10
	Engineering		2	2	8	1	1
High-technology manufactures	Electronic and electrical		5	1	2	0	0
	Other		1	1	1	1	0
Others			0	1	2	0	0
C. Africa							
Africa excluding Nigeria							
Primary products		60	55	44	43	35	31
Resource-based manufactures	Agro-based	10	9	11	13	9	11
	Other	15	12	11	12	20	25
Low-technology manufactures	Textile, garment and footwear	8	13	19	18	19	14
	Other products	1	2	2	3	2	2
Medium-technology manufactures	Automotive	0	0	1	0	1	1
	Process	4	5	7	5	3	4
	Engineering	1	2	3	3	3	6
High-technology manufactures	Electronic and electrical	0	1	2	1	2	2
	Other	1	1	0	0	0	1
Others		0	0	0	1	4	3
Northern Africa							
Primary products		47	38	27	21	20	18
Resource-based manufactures	Agro-based	6	8	9	10	7	9
	Other	17	15	14	13	11	12
Low-technology manufactures	Textile, garment and footwear	17	24	30	37	41	33
	Other products	1	1	2	3	2	4
Medium-technology manufactures	Automotive	0	1	1	1	1	1
	Process	9	9	10	8	6	5
	Engineering	1	3	4	5	7	11
High-technology manufactures	Electronic and electrical	0	1	2	2	5	5
	Other	0	0	1	0	1	1
Others		0	0	0	0	0	0
Least developed countries in sub-Saharan Africa							
Primary products		75	63	66	61	40	27
Resource-based manufactures	Agro-based	7	12	16	9	6	5
	Other	13	14	10	16	25	51
Low-technology manufactures	Textile, garment and footwear	2	3	3	4	14	4
	Other products	1	2	2	2	2	2

Table A.3 (cont'd)		1980	1985	1990	1995	2000	2005
Medium-technology manufactures	Automotive	0	0	1	1	1	1
	Process	0	1	2	3	3	3
	Engineering	1	2	1	1	1	2
High-technology manufactures	Electronic and electrical	0	0	1	0	1	0
	Other	0	1	0	0	0	1
Others		0	0	0	5	8	5
Remainder of countries in sub-Saharan Africa, excluding Nigeria							
Primary products		67	75	69	63	44	38
Resource-based manufactures	Agro-based	13	8	12	18	12	12
	Other	13	8	6	7	29	35
Low-technology manufactures	Textile, garment and footwear	1	1	2	2	2	2
	Other products	2	2	2	4	2	1
Medium-technology manufactures	Automotive	0	0	2	0	1	1
	Process	1	2	2	3	2	3
	Engineering	1	1	2	1	1	3
High-technology manufactures	Electronic and electrical	0	1	1	0	0	0
	Other	1	0	0	0	0	0
Others		0	1	0	1	6	5
D. Small island developing States							
Small island developing States							
Primary products		23	24	13	10	25	11
Resource-based manufactures	Agro-based	28	21	20	28	14	28
	Other	34	21	24	4	29	10
Low-technology manufactures	Textile, garment and footwear	7	17	25	46	25	29
	Other products	1	1	2	3	1	4
Medium-technology manufactures	Automotive	0	0	0	0	0	0
	Process	1	1	1	2	1	2
	Engineering	2	2	4	4	3	3
High-technology manufactures	Electronic and electrical	0	0	0	0	0	10
	Other	0	0	2	1	1	1
Others		4	12	9	0	1	2
Least developed country small island developing States							
Primary products		..	..	..	15	24	35
Resource-based manufactures	Agro-based	..	..	..	33	19	13
	Other	..	..	..	13	16	33
Low-technology manufactures	Textile, garment and footwear	..	..	..	23	30	4
	Other products	..	..	..	0	1	1
Medium-technology manufactures	Automotive	..	..	..	0	0	0
	Process	..	..	..	8	3	5
	Engineering	..	..	..	6	4	4
High-technology manufactures	Electronic and electrical	..	..	..	1	1	1
	Other	..	..	..	0	1	2
Others		..	..	..	0	0	2

Table A.3 (cont'd)		1980	1985	1990	1995	2000	2005
Remainder of small island developing States							
Primary products		22	24	13	10	25	9
Resource-based manufactures	Agro-based	28	21	20	28	14	29
	Other	35	21	24	3	30	8
Low-technology manufactures	Textile, garment and footwear	7	17	25	47	25	31
	Other products	1	1	2	3	1	5
Medium-technology manufactures	Automotive	0	0	0	0	0	0
	Process	1	1	1	2	1	2
	Engineering	2	2	4	4	3	2
High-technology manufactures	Electronic and electrical	0	0	0	0	0	11
	Other	0	0	2	1	1	1
Others		4	12	9	0	1	2

Source: UN/DESA calculations, based on United Nations Comtrade online database (United Nations Commodity Trade Statistics Database).

a   Classification based on Lall (2001), as detailed in *World Economic and Social Survey 2006* (United Nations, 2006), appendix to chap. III.

b   Regions are defined in section A of the appendix. Hong Kong Special Administrative Region of China, Singapore, the Republic of Korea and Indonesia are also included in this table.

Chapter III
Forces of nature? the climatic threat to economic security

Introduction

The capricious force of nature can have a devastating impact on the livelihoods of households and communities across the world. For some, particularly those living on small islands and in poor agricultural economies, such disasters often pose the single greatest threat to their security and welfare. Moreover, these are the communities most at risk with respect to the rising incidence of disasters, which are striking more than four times as frequently today as in the 1970s, and costing, on average, almost seven times as much.

Although hurricanes, tsunamis, earthquakes and floods are natural events, the disasters they trigger are not. In the case of developing countries, particularly the least developed, the adverse effects from natural hazards occur within a context of structural vulnerabilities associated with high rates of poverty, high levels of indebtedness, inadequate public infrastructure, lack of economic diversification, and the like. On some accounts, these factors make it difficult for the State in developing countries to respond effectively to the risks associated with natural hazards. Instead, much attention has been given in recent years to strategies for pooling and transferring disaster risk and smoothing household incomes through market-based financial instruments. New insurance products, and other hedging instruments, have been developed to meet some of the needs of developing regions, with strong backing from the donor community and international financial institutions.

> In developing countries, death rates from disasters are 20 times higher than in developed countries

The present chapter will examine the strengths and weaknesses of such responses. It will suggest that, though such instruments can play a role in managing disasters, it would be wrong to view them as a panacea, particularly in poorer developing countries. Indeed, as discussed in chapter II, addressing economic insecurity by extending the influence of financial markets has intrinsic flaws. What is needed instead is a more integrated approach to disaster management in the context of wider socio-economic vulnerabilities. Achieving this requires more emphasis on (ex ante) investments to better prepare for hazards and to reduce those vulnerabilities that can turn hazards into disasters, along with more effective (ex post) coping strategies.

When countries are unable to guarantee economic security through their own resources, part of the burden falls on humanitarian relief and development assistance, which, apart from ethical motivations and geopolitical considerations, can be in the donor community's self-interest if they help break the vicious circle that keeps these countries locked in a hazard-vulnerable and aid-dependent growth trap. To date, the emphasis has been on emergency relief. Making progress requires that the international community give much greater attention to large-scale investment in disaster prevention and mitigation and adopt a more consistently multilateral approach to financing such investments, including through reforms to the aid architecture.

Identifying and measuring "natural" disasters

Natural hazards are predominantly either geologic events (earthquakes, volcanoes) or hydro-meteorological ones (floods, droughts, windstorms, tsunamis) (see box III.1). Both

Box III.1

Definitions of disasters, terminology and data sources

Following the criteria of the International Strategy for Disaster Reduction (UNISDR), disasters are events where (a) at least 10 people are reported as having been killed, (b) at least 100 people are affected, (c) a state of emergency is declared or (d) a request for international assistance is made by the national Government.

The most frequently used source of disaster-related data is the Emergency Disasters Data Base (EM-DAT), provided by the Centre for Research on the Epidemiology of Disasters (CRED) at the Université Catholique de Louvain in Brussels. These data are compiled from a number of sources, including United Nations organizations, non-governmental organizations, insurance companies, research institutes and the press; nevertheless, there are large data gaps resulting from the lack of concerted efforts to systematically collect disaster-related data.

For instance, for more than 63 per cent of registered disasters, a figure is not reported for the damages caused. Hence, reported figures do not provide a comprehensive picture of the impact of disasters. Moreover, owing to different sources and methodologies for assessing damages, cost estimates must be used with caution. In particular, while reasonable estimations of direct costs are often available soon after a disaster, indirect costs tend to be more difficult to assess and are consequently often underreported.

Political interests with respect to mobilizing more foreign aid, and inadequate information systems, might also prompt overestimations of the actual costs of the damages. In general, methodologies used for assessing costs can have policy implications in terms of whether to focus on repair and rehabilitation or on preventive and reconstructive investment for development (Vos, 1999; and Vos, Velasco and de Labastida, 1999). The cost estimates referred to by the literature and quoted in this chapter refer mostly to the alleged damages relating to repair and rehabilitation.

Natural hazards are differentiated into hazards of hydro-meteorological origin, such as windstorms, wave surges, drought, floods and extreme temperatures, and those of geologic origin, such as earthquakes, volcanic eruptions and landslides. Although natural hazards also comprise wild fires, insect infestations, extreme temperatures and epidemics, these are not considered in this chapter primarily owing to the unreliability and patchiness of data.

There are in principle seven distinguishing characteristics of natural hazards, regardless of their origin, (Albala-Bertrand, 1993): (a) *magnitude*, (b) *frequency*, (c) *duration*, (d) *areal extent*, (e) *spatial dispersion pattern*, (f) *speed of onset* and (g) *regularity*. Different hazards have different implications in terms of direct damages and indirect losses.

Geologic disasters such as earthquakes are infrequent events which often cause significant damage to assets (or *stock variables*), with fewer indirect damages, particularly in economies based on agriculture, and are associated with a more rapid recovery. Poor housing structures and conditions in poor urban neighbourhoods often entail a high human cost in terms of displaced, homeless and injured populations.

Climatic disasters, such as severe windstorms, flooding and drought, occur more frequently, have a wider impact, with particularly devastating consequences for the rural economy, usually have a greater effect in terms of indirect losses (or *flow variables*), and make for a longer recovery time. Droughts are more likely to affect rain-fed agricultural economies: a severe reduction of rainfall impacting output and income can generate food insecurity and increased health risks. In a pastoral economy, stressed selling of livestock at low prices will probably increase both income and food insecurities.

Floods can be equally devastating for rural and urban economies. Loss of harvests, able-working lives, and homelessness and displacement might signify reduction of household income and loss of jobs and livelihoods. Income insecurity can be the outcome of the loss of boats by fishing communities while informal workers and day labourers may see their opportunities become reduced or vanish as commerce and transportation are disrupted.

types can have potentially devastating consequences for the communities they strike. However, hydro-meteorological events pose a greater threat of becoming large-scale (catastrophic) disasters and also account for much of the rising trend of reported disasters in recent decades (see figure III.1). The remainder of this chapter concentrates primarily on such events.

Figure III.1
Frequency of disasters, 1970-2006

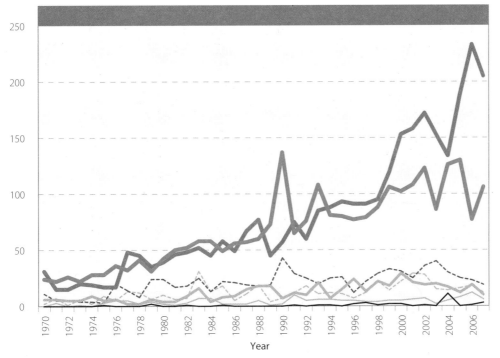

Drought
Earthquakes
Floods
Slides
Volcanoes
Waves/surge
Windstorms

Source: UN/DESA, based on data from the OFDA/CRED International Disaster Database (EM-DAT) (available at www.emdat.net), Université Catholique de Louvain, Brussels.

On average, according to official figures, 78 disasters per year had occurred during the 1970s. That figure rose to 351 per year during 2000-2006. By contrast, the average number of people killed in any single disaster has been on a long-term declining trend, leaving the total number of deaths each year from disasters fairly constant. However, the increased frequency has contributed to a large increase in the number of persons affected by disasters and in the estimated costs of damages (see figure III.2): damages have averaged $83 billion per year since 2000 compared with an average of $12 billion per year in the 1970s.[1] As disasters have become less life-threatening, they have become more threatening to the well-being of the communities that are hit.

Despite the fact that the threat from natural hazards is a shared one, the human cost measured in terms of both the number of persons affected and the losses of human lives is significantly higher in developing countries, albeit with regional variations (see tables III.1, III.2 and III.3). The large number of persons killed per event in Africa in the 1970s and 1980s was primarily due to the devastating effects of drought: in Ethiopia, more than 100,000 people perished in 1978 and at least 300,000 perished during the drought of 1983-1984.[2] In the Sudan and Mozambique, the drought of 1985 caused the

As disasters have become less life-threatening, they have become more threatening to the well-being of the communities that are hit

---

1   Figures adjusted to constant 2005 United States dollars.

2   Food relief has greatly improved over recent years, contributing significantly to the fall in the number of deaths resulting from disasters. Food insecurity, however, remains a concern in many regions.

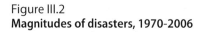

Figure III.2
Magnitudes of disasters, 1970-2006

Source: UN/DESA, based on data from the OFDA/ CRED International Disaster Database (EM-DAT) (available at www.emdat.net), Université Catholique de Louvain, Brussels.

a Millions of persons.
b Billions of constant 2005 United States dollars.

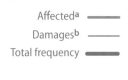

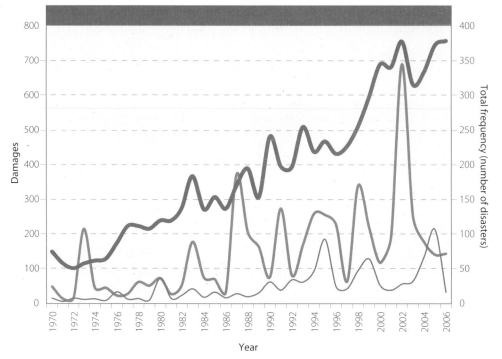

death of 150,000 people and 100,000 people, respectively. The high figure for Asia in the 1970s reflects the impact of the cyclones that hit Bangladesh in 1970, killing more than 300,000 people, and the earthquake in China, which killed more than 240,000 people in 1976. In fact, in the period 1970-2006, 95 per cent of all deaths resulting from disasters occurred in low-income and lower middle income countries, compared with just 1.5 per cent in high-income countries (see figure III.3). Controlling for population size, it appears that people in low-income countries are 20 times more likely to die from natural hazards than those in high-income countries.

Similarly, while more than 60 per cent of the total damages resulting from disasters occurred in high-income countries (see figure III.4), the estimated cost of disasters as a share of GDP was greatest in smaller economies (see table III.4). In the case

Table III.1
Average number of affected people per disaster, by country group according to level of development, 1970-2006

Thousands				
	1970-1979	*1980-1989*	*1990-1999*	*2000-2006*
High-income: non-OECD	108	126	314	68
High-income: OECD	3 994	6 628	28 117	9 276
Upper middle income	25 297	52 906	23 914	26 143
Lower middle income	55 535	291 601	1 364 179	916 552
Low-income	450 054	884 370	535 887	753 023
Unclassified	102	49	91	6

Source: UN/DESA, based on data from the OFDA/CRED International Disaster Database (EM-DAT) (available at www.emdat.net), Université Catholique de Louvain, Brussels.

Table III.2
Average number of persons killed per disaster, by region, 1970-2006

Thousands				
	1970-1979	*1980-1989*	*1990-1999*	*2000-2006*
Africa	1 344	3 008	37	28
Asia	2 098	147	352	387
Europe	67	41	15	4
Latin America and the Caribbean	728	161	144	32
Northern America	57	20	9	18
Oceania	10	6	27	2
Overall average	1 324	521	202	186

Source: UN/DESA, based on data from the OFDA/CRED International Disaster Database (EM-DAT) (available at www.emdat.net), Université Catholique de Louvain, Brussels.

Table III.3
Selected disaster statistics for various regions, 1970-2006

	Number of disasters	Killed (thousands)	Affected (millions)	Killed per 100 000	Affected per 100 000
Africa	951	702	316	78	35 168
Asia	2 984	1 561	4 888	41	127 331
Europe	844	16	31	2	4 263
Latin America and the Caribbean	1 308	244	165	44	29 790
Northern America	601	11	13	3	3 911
Oceania	380	4	15	13	44 553
Total	7 068	2 538	5 428	40	85 052

Source: UN/DESA, based on data from the OFDA/CRED International Disaster Database (EM-DAT) (available at www.emdat.net), Université Catholique de Louvain, Brussels.

of Grenada and the Cayman Islands, for example, damages amounted to several times their GDP. In contrast, Hurricane Katrina and the Kobe earthquake caused damages of less than 2 per cent of the GDP of the United States of America and Japan, respectively.[3] In fact, no upper middle income country has been ranked in the top 100 for most costly disasters relative to GDP;[4] over half of the 20 most costly disasters occurred in predominantly agrarian economies, while 4 hit least developed countries, and 3 occurred among the heavily indebted poor countries (HIPC).[5]

---

[3]   The damages caused amounted to approximately 1.3 per cent of GDP for Hurricane Katrina and 1.9 per cent of GDP for the Kobe earthquake.

[4]   Having suffered damages amounting to approximately 4.3 per cent of GDP owing to an earthquake on 23 November 1980, Italy ranked as the first high-income OECD country in one hundred twenty-eighth place.

[5]   The least developed countries were Vanuatu, Maldives and Samoa (which was ranked twice among the top 20), while the heavily indebted poor countries were Nicaragua, Tonga and Guyana.

Figure III.3
**Distribution of total deaths resulting from disasters,
by country group according to level of development, 1970-2006**

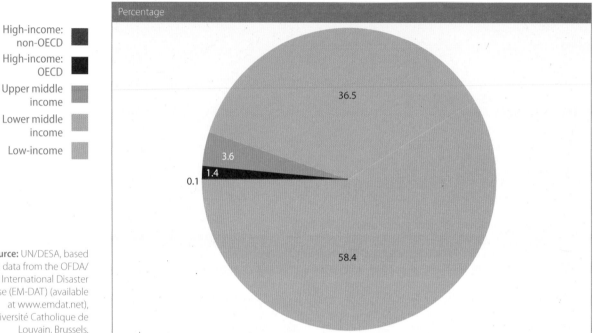

High-income:
non-OECD

High-income:
OECD

Upper middle
income

Lower middle
income

Low-income

Source: UN/DESA, based
on data from the OFDA/
CRED International Disaster
Database (EM-DAT) (available
at www.emdat.net),
Université Catholique de
Louvain, Brussels.

Figure III.4
**Distribution of damages resulting from disasters,
by country group according to level of development, 1970-2006**

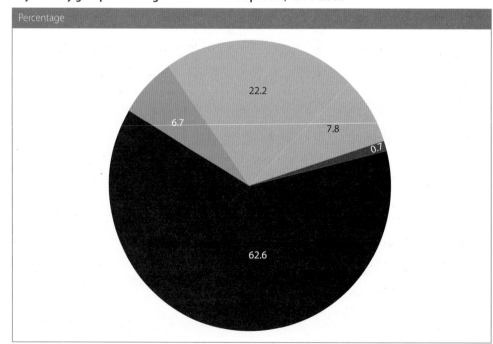

High-income:
non-OECD

High-income:
OECD

Upper middle
income

Lower middle
income

Low-income

Source: UN/DESA, based
on data from the OFDA/
CRED International Disaster
Database (EM-DAT) (available
at www.emdat.net),
Université Catholique de
Louvain, Brussels.

Table III.4
Top 20 disasters in terms of costs and fatalities (absolute and relative), 1970-2006

Country or area, year	Damage[a]	Country, year	Damage[b]	Country, year	Total deaths	Country, year	Deaths[c]
Democratic People's Republic of Korea, 1995[d]	309	United States of America, 2005[e]	158.2	Bangladesh, 1970[e]	300 317	Mozambique, 1985[g]	0.76
Cayman Islands[e]	224	Japan, 1995[f]	78.1	Ethiopia, 1985[g]	300 000	Ethiopia, 1984[g]	0.71
Grenada, 2004[e]	203	United States of America, 2004[e]	55.9	China, 1976[f]	242 000	Sudan, 1985[g]	0.64
Saint Lucia, 1980[e]	183	Italy, 1998[f]	50.4	Indonesia, 2004[e]	165 708	Peru, 1970[f]	0.51
Vanuatu, 1985[e]	146	United States of America, 1992[e]	45.0	Sudan, 1985[g]	150 000	Bangladesh, 1970[e]	0.46
Samoa, 1991[e]	139	Turkey, 1999[f]	38.1	Bangladesh, 1991[e]	138 987	Nicaragua, 1972[f]	0.42
Dominica, 1979[e]	101	United States of America, 1994[f]	37.5	Ethiopia, 1978[g]	100 000	Somalia, 1976[g]	0.42
Samoa, 1990[e]	99	Democratic People's Republic of Korea, 1994[d]	36.6	Mozambique, 1985[g]	100 000	Guatemala, 1976[f]	0.36
Nicaragua, 1972[f]	96	China, 1998[d]	36.0	Pakistan, 2005[f]	73 338	Ethiopia, 1978[g]	0.28
Dominica, 1995[e]	89	Japan, 2004[f]	27.1	Peru, 1970[f]	66 823	Honduras, 1974[e]	0.27
Antigua and Barbuda, 1995[e]	81	United States of America, 1995[e]	25.3	Iran (Islamic Republic of), 1990[f]	40 021	Honduras, 1998[e]	0.24
Honduras, 1998[e]	73	China, 1996[d]	21.6	Sri Lanka, 2004[h]	35 399	Sri Lanka, 2004[h]	0.18
Maldives, 2004[e]	62	China, 1994[g]	19.1	Venezuela (Bolivarian Republic of), 1999[d]	30 005	Venezuela (Bolivarian Republic of), 1999[d]	0.13
Saint Kitts and Nevis, 1998[e]	61	China, 2003[d]	17.1	Bangladesh, 1974[d]	28 700	Bangladesh, 1991[e]	0.13
Guyana, 2005[d]	59	Italy, 1976[f]	16.7	Iran (Islamic Republic of), 2003[f]	26 797	Honduras, 1973[j]	0.10
Democratic People's Republic of Korea, 2000[e]	57	United States of America, 2003[e]	16.0	Iran (Islamic Republic of), 1978[f]	25 045	Solomon Islands, 1975[h]	0.10
Afghanistan, 1998[f]	54	United States of America, 1999[e]	16.0	Guatemala, 1976[f]	23 000	Swaziland, 1983[g]	0.08
Honduras, 1974[e]	52	Germany, 2002[d]	15.7	Colombia, 1985[i]	21 800	Indonesia, 2004[h]	0.08
Tonga, 2001[e]	39	United States of America, 1993[d]	15.7	India, 2001[f]	20 005	Iran (Islamic Republic of), 1990[f]	0.07
Zimbabwe, 1984[g]	39	France, 1999[e]	15.6	China, 1974[f]	20 000	Nicaragua, 1998[e]	0.07

Source: UN/DESA, based on data from the OFDA/CRED International Disaster Database (EM-DAT) (available at www.emdat.net), Université Catholique de Louvain, Brussels.

a   Percentage of GDP.
b   Billions of constant 2005 United States dollars.
c   Percentage of population.
d   Floods.
e   Wind.
f   Earthquakes.
g   Droughts.
h   Waves.
i   Volcanoes.
j   Slides.

Disaster dynamics: risks, vulnerabilities and vicious circles

The development dimension

Natural hazards generally are difficult to predict and almost impossible to control. This makes them risky events, but just how risky depends, in part, on the frequency, strength and predictability of the particular hazard involved. For instance, droughts, windstorms and floods may occur relatively frequently, build over time and are relatively easy to track. In contrast, earthquakes and volcanic eruptions occur less frequently, hit instantaneously and are much more difficult to predict. However, both types are potentially catastrophic and, unlike other risks, such as illness, accidents and crime, can hit a large number of households simultaneously and cause disruptions across large swathes of economic activity. This combination of "catastrophic" and "covariant" risk is particularly difficult to assess and even more difficult to price, even in countries with sophisticated financial markets.

The threat to economic security from such events depends less, however, on the particular hazardous event itself and much more on the ability of households, communities and Governments to prepare for such events, to mitigate their impact and to deal with their aftermath. Higher levels of per capita income are strongly correlated with a lesser threat to economic security from disasters, particularly in terms of loss of life. Poorer countries and communities, by contrast, face these events with a series of economic deficits closely associated with low income per capita, including low levels of savings and other asset holdings, shortage of secure and decent employment, lack of access to credit, poor infrastructure, including schools and hospitals, etc., which limit their capacity to prepare for, respond to and recover from disasters.

The impact of hazards are exacerbated by poor response capabilities

Reduced vulnerability to natural hazards in wealthier countries also reflects changes in economic structure as those countries diversify into a wider range of productive activities, beginning with a shift away from agriculture, which is particularly vulnerable to a range of hydro-meteorological hazards. It is also a reflection of the depth and breadth of institutions. According to some assessments, this is a matter mainly of the presence of institutions of political voice, but others claim it is more one of strong property rights, lower levels of corruption and deeper financial markets.[6] No matter the precise nature of institutional strength, the general appreciation is that, with a better-functioning institutional environment, countries will be more resilient in respect of coping with disasters. Poor information, inadequate access to finance and poor social networks will affect resilience adversely, reducing the quality and effectiveness of societies' response capacities and exacerbating the impact of the hazard (United Nations Human Settlements Programme (UN-Habitat), 2007). What matters with regard to all of these factors is the State's capacity, both administrative and financial, to prepare for disasters and organize recovery.

The threat to economic security and well-being associated with natural hazards in developing countries reflects a broad range of structural vulnerabilities. These expose poorer countries and communities not just to potentially catastrophic large-scale disasters but also to frequent smaller-scale disasters which occur seasonally or annually, such as regular flooding in Bangladesh or windstorms in the Caribbean and Pacific region. In-

---

6   Amartya Sen has argued that a key factor in averting famines following a natural catastrophe is the ability of the affected population to give "voice" to its predicament and to maintain pressure on Governments to respond rapidly and effectively to social and economic distress (Sen and Drèze, 2006). Drawing on the example of India, he identified this factor with the presence of democratic government. Others, however, have argued that it may not be sufficient to avert disaster.

deed, smaller disasters often prove to be the more difficult to manage, placing a permanent constraint on resource mobilization in many developing countries and short-circuiting the possibility of their making full recoveries (Oxfam International, 2007a).

The relationship between development and vulnerability to natural hazards is not straightforward. Evidence suggests that some countries may face increased vulnerability as they move up the development ladder: the strengthening of economy-wide linkages between sectors (such as the agriculture sector and the agricultural-processing industry) that takes place at early stages of development may in fact increase susceptibility to natural hazards, as has been reported in some African countries (World Bank, 2001, chap. 9). Similarly, demographic transitions, which accompany rising income levels, can add new vulnerabilities, as can the transition from a rural to an urban economy, as land use, in both rural and urban areas, comes under increasing strains, with environmental degradation adding a further dimension to an already vulnerable and insecure situation. The livelihoods of an estimated 80 per cent of the poor in Latin America, 60 per cent in Asia and 50 per cent in Africa are dependent on low-quality land vulnerable to natural hazards (Hardoy, Mitlin and Satterthwaite, 2001).

Geographical factors add another dimension of vulnerability. Country size, location and remoteness can matter greatly, with 8 of the 10 relatively most costly disasters having been registered in small island developing States, a group of highly vulnerable but not necessarily low-income countries (Heger, Julca and Paddison, 2008). Indeed, as Rasmussen (2004, p. 7) notes, relative to land area, countries in the Eastern Caribbean Currency Union are among the most disaster-prone countries in the world (see box III.2).

The vulnerability of poorer countries to disasters is reflected in the difficulty experienced by those countries in mobilizing the resources needed to reduce their exposure to hazards, to build up their resilience and to make a rapid recovery after disasters strike. This is a development challenge which can be properly met only through large-scale investments and strategic policies that strengthen economic and social capacities at the local and national levels and that can draw on as wide a range of coping and recovery options as possible when disaster strikes.

The vulnerability of poorer countries to disasters is heightened by difficulties in mobilizing domestic resources

The impact of disasters on economic insecurity

Disasters heighten economic insecurity through three principal channels: the immediate (and more lasting) damage to the stock of productive assets (crops ready for harvest, livestock, irrigation works, plants and machinery, etc.), public infrastructure (roads, bridges, etc.), residential property and human capital (through loss of lives, injuries, interrupted schooling, etc.); the loss of income flows associated with the interruption in normal economic activity and transactions (including the displacement of populations); and the threat to growth prospects from increased economic volatility and heightened uncertainty. In fact, even the threat of disasters can impact upon economic security: for instance, rural banks may deny farmers access to financial services owing to high (perceived) disaster risk.

Capital assets, both physical and human, can be seriously damaged during a disaster, with long-term implications for employment creation and productivity performance. Damage to the capital stock varies significantly across hazards, and can be particularly severe with geologic shocks. The immediate burden is felt at the level of the household, firm and farm; however, the resulting impact as regards economic insecurity very much depends on the effectiveness of the mitigation and recovery strategies at the

Box III.2

Small isn't always beautiful:
small island developing States and the disaster threat

The unique characteristics of many small island developing States and their special challenges have been recognized in the international development agenda.

Despite their economic and social diversity, many of them still share common characteristics such as a narrow resource base, geographical remoteness and lack of competitive economic activities and economies of scale, which have partly translated into high transportation and communication costs, contributing further to their marginalization in the global economy. Owing to these structural features, the majority of small island developing States are highly vulnerable to natural hazards (Rasmussen, 2004).

On one measure, devised by the Commonwealth Secretariat and the World Bank (combining economic diversification, export dependence and the portion of the population affected by disasters), 26 of the 28 most vulnerable countries are small States (18 of them islands). In fact, damages resulting from disasters exceeding 50 per cent of GDP in individual countries are common: 12 of the 20 most costly disasters (relative to GDP) have occurred in small island developing States. While larger or more complex economies, for example, those with highly competitive industrial and service sectors, can spread the burden of adjusting to disasters over time as well as over space, the ability to "bounce back" is more limited for smaller countries. Thus, some part of the structural vulnerability of small island developing States is beyond the control of stakeholders, and cannot be easily reduced by policies or actions (Guillaumont, 2007).

The issue of climate change is particularly relevant for small island developing States. For one, the increasing incidence of disasters (from 64 during the 1970s to 166 for the seven-year period covering 2000-2006) and their intensity are set to continue. The occurrence of tropical typhoons and cyclones may increase by as much as 50–60 per cent (NASA Goddard Institute for Space Studies, 2001) and their intensity may increase by 10–20 per cent. In the short term, rising sea levels will contribute to greater storm damage. In the long term, they may lead to the submersion of large proportions of many small island developing States.

The greatest challenge of climate change, however, may lie in the implications for water supply, particularly for islands in the Pacific. Increasing storm surges, rising sea levels and global warming will significantly impact upon the availability of potable water owing to saltwater intrusion into freshwater supplies. Already less than half of the population in Kiribati has access to safe water; for the rural population in Papua New Guinea, the proportion is less than 10 per cent (Hoegh-Guldberg and others, 2000). Thus, water scarcity may make many small island developing States uninhabitable long before they are covered as a result of the rising sea level.

household, community and State levels in keeping costs to a minimum and in bringing about a rapid return to pre-disaster levels of activity.

At the macroeconomic level, disasters typically result in an immediate drop in output and employment. Increased imports of intermediate goods and raw materials are likely once the process of repair and reconstruction is under way, contributing to a worsening of the trade balance which is likely to be exaggerated by decreased exports, particularly when one or two commodities account for a large share of foreign-exchange earnings, and when the sector(s) concerned are significantly affected by the disaster. For instance, much of export production was lost as approximately 50 per cent of planted banana trees were swept away in Honduras by Hurricane Mitch in 1998; in 2004, Hurricane Ivan devastated Grenada's nutmeg crop, representing one of the economy's principle export sectors; in Sri Lanka, it was the fishing sector, one of the country's primary sources of income, that was hardest hit by the 2004 tsunami.

In the context of widespread poverty and in the absence of economic diversification, intense floods and windstorms not only destroy harvests and the livelihoods of farmers but also may severely erode the financial capacity of Governments to respond effectively. Not only will the public sector experience damage to its assets, but revenue will also be squeezed, even as that sector faces a growing expenditure bill from the damages incurred. Public reconstruction may be accelerated by borrowing abroad; but the resulting rising stock of debt may, over the longer run, adversely affect the country's credit rating and the future cost of borrowing. This, along with the increase in macroeconomic volatility, is likely to adversely affect overall investment levels at a time when resources need to be channelled towards repairing the damaged capital stock.

A number of studies have found that vulnerability to disasters, especially in terms of the proportion of the population affected, is closely associated with high volatility of income, consumption and fiscal balances, a large agricultural sector, a low investment-to-GDP ratio and an open current account.[7] Moreover, a squeeze on public finances can trigger inflationary pressures, and pose problems for the management of the public debt. Where large inflows of assistance occur in response to the disaster, these can also introduce sources of macroeconomic volatility, particularly where the flows are unpredictable (United Nations, 2005a).

In countries where existing structural vulnerabilities are significant, existing economic insecurity associated with fragile food, health and employment conditions will not only be compounded by disasters, but also slow the recovery process. Families will quickly exhaust coping mechanisms, such as savings, credits, sale of assets and migration, etc., and be forced into more risk-bearing survival strategies—for example, child labour and high-cost loans—which further perpetuate vulnerability. This will adversely impact on private investment.

While vulnerability to climatic shocks and other natural hazards suggests a poor growth environment, the available econometric evidence is inconclusive. Several studies focusing on the Caribbean region found that, although growth slows in the year of disaster, it tends to rebound in subsequent years mainly owing to post-disaster reconstruction activity which can spill over to other sectors. For instance, following a growth rate of over 7 per cent in 2003, GDP contracted by 7.4 per cent in 2004 in Grenada following Hurricane Ivan in 2004, but it subsequently expanded by 13.2 per cent in 2005 owing to reconstruction (United Nations, Economic Commission for Latin America and the Caribbean, 2007a). Thus, an overall positive, though not always significant, correlation between disasters and GDP growth may be found in this region. In contrast, other studies have reported a more strongly negative impact of disasters on *long-term* growth; no significant impact at all (Caselli and Malhotra, 2004); or an impact that in fact depends on the type of disaster.[8]

[7] See Auffret (2003) and Gassebner, Keck and Teh (2006). A high degree of openness can work through volatility of terms of trade and tends to be associated with a more specialized trade pattern, as is found in smaller economies.

[8] Differentiating more generally among disasters, climatic disasters were found to be positively associated with growth, whereas with geologic disasters, the association was negative (Toya and Skidmore, 2007). Climatic disasters might be assumed to shift relative returns in favour of human capital, which some suggest is a more important source of long-term growth, whereas the bias following geologic disasters is towards more physical capital, explaining their differing growth effects. However, Benson (1994) argues precisely the opposite, namely, that geologic disasters require larger reconstruction programmes, which may spur growth for greater periods. Arguably, neither argument offers a fully convincing analysis of accumulation dynamics where rents are the motivating force. Another problem is that such exercises often simply pick up the influence of unobserved variables unrelated to the disaster-growth nexus itself, a problem that is more likely to arise when stock and flow variables are mixed together, as is often the case.

Poverty and lack of diversification can weaken Governments' capacity to respond to disasters

A vicious circle of vulnerability and insecurity

Any pronounced and lasting impact of disasters on economic insecurity therefore appears to arise from the presence of feedback mechanisms that work to deepen structural vulnerabilities and expose populations to the threat of future disasters. This in turn heightens the risks from future shocks, with adverse consequences for investment planning and further threats to economic security. From a policy perspective, identifying such mechanisms would appear to be key to finding more effective responses to disaster planning and mitigation.

The poorest households and communities suffer the most from disasters, as they are already deprived of the basic ingredients of a more secure livelihood

Poverty is one such feedback mechanism. Rising levels of poverty have been reported after disasters and while comprehensive studies are missing, the impact can be significant. As already suggested, the poorest households and communities suffer the most from disasters, as they are already deprived of the basic ingredients of a more secure livelihood. However, the impact of disasters may push previously secure groups into the ranks of the vulnerable, if the available coping strategies collapse under large-scale or repeated shocks; according to World Bank estimates, anywhere between one fifth and two thirds of people in developing countries are vulnerable to falling into extreme poverty. Liquidating productive assets, defaulting on loans, withdrawing children from school to work on farms or tend livestock, severely reducing nutrient intake and over-exploiting natural resources, can, in these circumstances, become unavoidable but self-defeating strategies. One recent study of south India, for example, found that all segments of the population, landed and landless, upper and lower castes, were vulnerable to poverty after crop shocks (Gaiha and Imai, 2004). Moreover, disasters can compound other problems which add to the threat of heightened poverty. For example, the disaster resulting from the El Niño phenomenon in Ecuador in 1997-1998 provoked a downturn, especially in agriculture, which was further compounded by the fall of oil prices and an extremely fragile banking sector, leading to a full-blown economic crisis in 1999 (Parandekar, Vos and Winkler, 2002).

The resilience of social networks, which may be of an informal nature, can be another critical factor in dampening or perpetuating the costs of adjustment following a disaster. For instance, although the majority of flood-prone communities in the Malamulele district in South Africa share characteristics of insecure livelihoods, including food insecurity which often goes hand in hand with non-access to land, and a limited access to formal non-farm employment, the Menele community was found to have fared better than the Mavambe community because of employment opportunities linked to a rural elite with access to cropland, livestock and farm equipment (Kandelhela and May, 2006). Such networks may also involve more formal public service providers.

Lack of well-built health infrastructure and facilities such as hospitals and emergency attention centres located near vulnerable populations, as well as insufficient medical doctors, equipment and supplies, often contributes to the vulnerability of exposed populations, particularly as disasters often reduce infrastructural capacities while increasing the demand for them. In this respect, the resilience of social networks is closely linked to wider levels of inequality.

Immediately after disasters, young and older persons count among the most fatalities and injuries, with survivors dependent on family and public resources for immediate resettlement and relief

At least one study reports a strong relation between a country's level of inequality and the scale of the impact from disasters (Roberts and Parks, 2007). This can often assume a regional dimension and will likely include horizontal inequalities, such as those associated with gender and ethnic discrimination. For instance, following a disaster, pressures for women's additional work rises as the amount of unpaid work and family care likely increases, while their coping and resilience mechanisms are typically weak or further eroded by unequal public relief distribution practices (Ngo, 2001; Bunyavanich and others, 2003). Similarly, young and older persons are physiologically and socially more vulnerable to disasters, given their lower coping capacities. Immediately after disasters, young and older persons therefore count among the most fatalities and injuries, with survivors dependent on family and public resources for immediate resettlement and relief.[9]

Constraints on the supply of food could be another factor reinforcing vulnerability to the impact of natural hazards.[10] Food insecurity can be the result of geographical pressures, as is the case in small island economies, or economic pressures, linked to deforestation, overgrazing and inadequate management practices, particularly as agricultural activities crowd into increasingly fragile areas. In the immediate aftermath of a disaster, food insecurity is often significantly heightened, leading to distress sales of productive assets or the resort of using children as a source of family income so as to maintain nutritional levels. Such coping responses can reinforce poverty traps at the household level, thereby perpetuating vulnerability to future disasters. Responding to food insecurity by increasing imports of foodstuffs, however, can potentially enhance structural import dependence if it destabilizes domestic and local markets and erodes the production capacity of the local agriculture sector.[11]

While vicious circles of this kind are a persistent feature of the development landscape, there are reasons to believe that they have intensified in recent years. In particular, climate change and shifting patterns of development have contributed to a growing link between disasters and heightened economic insecurity.

Although the socio-economic impact of climate change is the subject of ongoing research, there is broad agreement that, with rising temperatures and ocean levels, longer and more severe dry periods will be experienced in some already drought-prone areas and more intense rainfall can be expected in some already flood-prone and coastal areas (United Nations Development Programme, 2007, pp. 90-107). Much of the likely cost of these changes will be borne by some of the world's poorest countries and communities. However, even the chairman of Lloyd's of London has identified climate change as its number one issue, and Europe's largest insurer, Allianz, has stated that "climate change stands to increase insured losses from extreme events in an average year by 37 per cent within just a decade while losses in a bad year could top 1 trillion" (quoted in Mills, 2007).

The increased concentration of human settlements in vulnerable urban areas has been another factor heightening the disaster-insecurity nexus. Urbanization has been growing at a tremendous pace in the developing world in recent years (United Nations Human Settlements Programme (UN-Habitat), 2007); yet it is not urbanization per se, but rather the nature of the process, that determines whether vulnerability increases or not. Particularly in developing countries, urbanization is often characterized by an increase in unstable and precarious living environments, for example, slums and shanty towns. These settlements are frequently located in high-risk areas, for example, on steep slopes which are prone to landslides, or on flood plains or in ravines, contributing to the vulnerability to hazards such as flooding and landslides. Moreover, the lack of enforcement of building regulations in the construction of such settlements exacerbates their vulnerability.

Responding to food insecurity with imports can potentially enhance structural import dependence

Climate change could increase insurance losses in a bad year to over $1 trillion

---

9   See United Nations Human Settlements Programme (UN-Habitat) (2007, p. 181).

10   More often than not, natural hazards often expose multiple vulnerabilities. In August 1999, after a major earthquake had struck the north-western part of Turkey, a survey of 230 households from the four communities worst affected revealed that the greatest immediate need for most families was shelter requirements (37 per cent), followed by food (23 per cent) and hygiene requirements (19 per cent). Ten days after the earthquake, basic environmental health needs of food, shelter and hygiene still predominated in this displaced population (Daley, Karpati and Sheik, 2001).

11   This includes vulnerability to price increases. Following an increase by 10 per cent in 2006, the food import bill of developing countries was estimated to have increased by 25 per cent in 2007 owing to higher food prices (Food and Agriculture Organization, 2006); see also box II.1.

However, as the report of UN-Habitat has made abundantly clear, this pattern of growing urban vulnerability owes a good deal to the failed development policies of the past three decades and, in particular, to those that have orchestrated a "retreat of the state". The report states (pp. 189-190):

> "Urban risk accumulation was accelerated by the debt crisis and subsequent structural adjustment programmes of the 1980s and 1990s that forced Governments throughout Latin America, Asia and Africa to slash subsidies on food, electricity and transportation and to retrench public-sector workers ... Neo-liberal policies ... have scaled down State responsibilities for risk reduction and response and place greater emphasis on the role of private citizens and companies".

One clear aspect of this shifting emphasis has been fiscal retrenchment and the accompanying decline in public investment across much of the developing world over the past two and half decades (United Nations Conference on Trade and Development, 2003, chap. IV). In some cases, this has been directly responsible for the stalled diversification of production and income sources, which remains a key component of building protection against disaster shocks. It has also led to the erosion of infrastructure for transportation, communications, energy supplies, and social services, which adds to the vulnerability of many communities. Also investments aimed at disaster preparedness and adaptation, such as in flood defences and early warning systems, have been cut back in such contexts.

Strategies to increase resilience and diminish disaster impact

Coping mechanisms include market and non-market strategies

The discussion in previous sections suggests that there is, in many developing countries, a growing threat to economic insecurity from a rising incidence of disasters. To manage these shocks, households, farms, businesses and Governments rely on both market and non-market strategies to cope with the consequences when they do hit and to aid reconstruction in their aftermath. Table III.5 illustrates observed practices on pre- and post-disaster risk financing arrangements.

Coping measures such as improved insurance and relief constitute ex post responses that leave the underlying and fundamental causes of disasters untouched. To be of lasting effect, these measures need to be part of a broader rethinking of development strategies in vulnerable countries, focused on preparedness and preventive actions. Such actions require ex ante approaches to disaster management that can more effectively reduce and mitigate the risks associated with hazard shocks, as well as strengthen resilience directed against these shocks' becoming disasters, along with a better linking from ex post coping strategies to medium-term recovery.

Disaster risk reduction

The highest priority in managing disasters must be to reduce, through increased investment in preparation and adaptation measures, the risk of natural hazards' turning into disasters

The highest priority in managing disasters must be to reduce, through increased investment in preparation and adaptation measures, the risk of natural hazards' turning into disasters. This is a multidimensional challenge. Mitigation measures comprise, inter alia, appropriate land-use planning, improved infrastructure design, and more integrated water management systems. They should also involve stronger regulation with respect to, for example, building codes. In many cases, new institutional arrangements will be needed that

Table III.5
Examples of pre- and post-disaster risk financing arrangements

	Security for loss of assets (households/businesses, non-farm)	Food security for crops/livestock loss (farms)	Security for relief and reconstruction (Governments)
Post-disaster (ex post)			
	Emergency loans; moneylenders; public assistance	Sale of productive assets, food aid	Diversions; loans from World Bank and other international financial institutions
Pre-disaster (ex ante)			
Non-market	Kinship arrangements	Voluntary mutual arrangements	International aid
Inter-temporal	Microsavings	Food storage	Catastrophe reserve funds, regional pools, contingent credit
Market-based risk transfer	Property and life insurance	Crop and livestock insurance (also index-based)	Insurance or catastrophe bonds (also index-based)

Source: Linnerooth-Bayer and Mechler (2007).

can better respond to emergencies through more effective monitoring and warning systems, and better-trained and equipped personnel. Measures will also likely involve more far-sighted environmental planning for adaptation to expected climate change.

Disaster risk planning and matching targeted expenditures constitute other critical elements of disaster mitigation. The first steps in a risk reduction plan involve identification of vulnerabilities and risks and their ranking or prioritization. Box III.3 gives two examples of community-based preparedness and risk assessment plans, the first based on activities undertaken to better withstand floods in West Bengal, India, and the second on actions taken to reduce risk of droughts in rural communities of southern Ethiopia and northern Kenya.

Unfortunately, disaster risk reduction has been a priority neither in many vulnerable countries nor among donors. Approximately only 2 per cent of disaster management funds are spent by bilateral and multilateral donors on proactive disaster risk reduction; the remaining 98 per cent are spent for relief and reconstruction (Mechler, 2005). Such skewed expenditure stands in stark contrast to potential benefits of disaster risk reduction. For instance, a retrospective analysis of 4,000 mitigation projects in the United States of America reported an average benefit-cost ratio of 1 to 4 (Multihazard Mitigation Council, 2005). Similarly, the Red River Floodway which was constructed in the 1960s in Canada from an initial cost of approximately Can$ 62.7 million is estimated to have prevented $6 billion in damages in 1997 alone. This Floodway has been used more than 20 times since construction to reduce the impact of floods and has prevented overall damages estimated at $10 billion. While it was initially built to withstand a 1-in-90-years flood, it has since been upgraded to withstand a much more severe 1-in-300-years flood (Manitoba Floodway Authority, 2006). Similarly, investments of approximately $3.15 billion on flood control in China are seen to have averted estimated losses of approximately $12 billion (Benson, 1998). According to the U.S. Geological Survey, the economic losses worldwide from disasters in the 1990s could have been reduced by

The economic losses worldwide from disasters in the 1990s could have been reduced by $280 billion through investing in disaster risk reduction

Box III.3

Community-based preparedness and risk assessment: India, Ethiopia and Kenya

The Government of West Bengal, India, together with an inter-agency group, had developed a community-based project to prepare regional communities, individually and collectively, for the next *flood* disaster which, when it did arrive, became similar to the one that had devastated the region in 2000. The project assumed that communities had to live with natural hazards, and that no external intervention should change the lifestyles of their members. Using a participatory approach, each community prepared an action plan. The plan included a community vulnerability map, which identified safe places, low-risk areas, highly vulnerable areas and the estimated number of families residing in each zone, as well as the number and location of vulnerable populations, such as the aged, the disabled, lactating mothers, pregnant women, seriously ill persons and small children. Then, the plan took note of priority elements at risk, such as life, health, property, livestock and livelihood; listed the resources at hand as well as those required to bring down the level of risk; and, last, outlined key activities that the community would carry out before, during and after a disaster.

When the next flood arrived, in 2004, the results were remarkable. Based on a comparison of damages and losses for one village from two floods, one that had occurred in 2000 and the other in 2004, the project proved to be quite effective. In 2000, the village had lost over 700 cattle, while in 2004, it lost none. In 2000, nearly 3,000 families had lost or suffered damage to other valuable assets, while in 2004, none of the families reported any such loss or damage. The village also relied primarily on food preparedness: each family had stockpiled food for from 7 to 10 days to meet its immediate needs. Furthermore, in 2004, the village experienced almost no outbreak of disease. Observing how the project benefited the community, especially the poor and most vulnerable groups, local authorities requested expansion of this project to other vulnerable areas.

Similarly, a team of researchers developed a systematic approach to classifying and ordering the sources of *drought* risk faced by pastoral populations in arid and semi-arid districts of southern Ethiopia and northern Kenya. The researchers created a robust community participatory method which was less costly and time-consuming than full surveys. The method, which was tested in the field over six months in 1998, involved 120 groups (59 groups of women and 61 groups of men). The responses identified 15 major sources of risk, ranging from availability of food and water to banditry. The most frequently mentioned problems were insecure access to food and water, livestock disease and access to health clinics. Food and water shortages were the only risks mentioned by a majority of informants, indicating that the extent of the other risks varied considerably across the region and its population, even though some (for instance, malaria and conflict) were certainly severe in many places.

Source: United Nations, International Strategy for Disaster Reduction, and World Bank (2007).

$280 billion through investing some $40 billion in disaster risk reduction (International Federation of Red Cross and Red Crescent Societies (IFRC, 2001), a figure below the annual average flow of aid in that decade.

Low expenditure on disaster risk reduction programmes may be a consequence of the difficulty of assessing the costs and benefits of disaster risk reduction. It is also, however, a consequence of short-sighted policy design, as well as lack of political will. The floods in Tabasco (Mexico), for example, which left 1 million people homeless could have been avoided if planned investments in a modern flood-control infrastructure and other preventive measures and programmes had been undertaken. Policymakers and the international community may be unwilling to spend large sums on disaster risk reduction when faced with limited budgetary resources and when unable to show immediate returns. This is also made apparent by the insufficient levels of private investment in disaster risk reduction. For instance, despite extensive public awareness campaigns, studies show that only about 10 per cent of earthquake- and flood-prone households have adopted loss-reduction measures in the United States (Kunreuther, 2006). Public awareness campaigns and more effective training of emergency personnel will be required to address this gap.

Linking relief to development

An effective approach to reducing vulnerability may be to link medium-term development strategies to relief activities, as relief measures alone may save lives but not necessarily livelihoods. For many developing countries, diversification of production and livelihoods is a key component of such an approach.

Relief must be linked to development strategies

As discussed earlier, many vulnerable countries tend to be highly dependent on a limited number of export commodities. Such dependence amplifies their vulnerability to natural hazards. It is therefore important that reconstruction efforts promote alternative, sustainable livelihood opportunities for those affected. From an individual farmer's point of view, alternatives to monocultures are not always feasible owing, for example, to lack of access to credit which limits a farmer's ability to plant multiple crops or the availability of complementary inputs. Consequently, a combination of public investment and cheap credit is often critical to shifting towards a more diversified pattern of development.

Repairing and reconstructing basic infrastructure are important steps in moving from relief to medium-term recovery, but must be carried out in such a way as to prevent further vulnerabilities from emerging. Following the prompt provision of water and sanitation in the Indonesian communities affected by the 2004 tsunami, some communities, for instance, still did not have electricity after two years of resettlement. Similarly, while by 2006, Sri Lanka had rebuilt over 60,000 houses, much of the housing stock as well as infrastructure such as hospitals, schools and bridges had not yet been repaired (Birkmann, 2007). In the haste to build new infrastructure, well-intentioned mitigation programmes can overwhelm communities' capacities rather than leverage them, overlooking local and regional conditions for dealing with natural hazards. For instance, approaches to disaster risk reduction which are focused on, for example, investment in dams and large infrastructure without adjustment to local geographical conditions have been harmful in Bangladesh: the "cordon approach", where flood plains are cordoned off from the neighbouring river channels through construction of solid embankments, has in fact resulted in less area for the monsoon river-water to spread over as more cordons are built. Consequently, flood levels in these areas have risen (Islam, 2001).

Adequate infrastructural investment, institutional capacity and access to finance are often missing in vulnerable countries and populations. In addition, the absence of adequate transportation networks to provide access to vulnerable populations in case of earthquakes, and the need for availability of sensitive weather communications systems for early warning in case of hurricanes and tsunamis, highlight the variety of challenges that must be tailored to local conditions (see box III.4).

Because disasters may increase food insecurity, preventive measures designed to deal with food vulnerability are crucial in pre-disaster preparedness and recovery activities. These should include mapping by early warning systems of food-insecure households, classified by degree of malnutrition and deficiencies in food consumption, and medium-term policies such as cash transfers and issuance of food stamps, as well as active support to small- and medium-scale crop agriculture, for example, subsidies to agricultural inputs. Prolonged reliance on the distribution of food aid after the disaster may have adverse effects on local farmers, thereby deepening poverty and increasing economic insecurity.

Preventive measures designed to deal with food vulnerability are crucial in pre-disaster preparedness and recovery activities

Urban populations settled on hill slopes and terrains are vulnerable to heavy rains and floods, as are those living in fragile housing and under crowded conditions. Dealing with chronic housing crises and insufficient regulations are therefore essential to

Fragile housing conditions amplify vulnerabilities

Box III.4

Technology and early warning systems

On 26 December 2004, a massive tsunami in the Indian Ocean claimed about 220,000 lives, injured over 500,000, left 3 million-5 million homeless and cost billions of dollars in damage. The scale of the tragedy could have been substantively reduced if there had been proper early warning systems.

Technical innovations arising from better understanding of the physical causes of disasters, improved forecasting and prediction, and better monitoring and modelling of hazard-related factors represent key elements for mitigating the adverse effects of natural hazards. Technology should therefore be used appropriately to provide effective early warning systems designed to reduce vulnerabilities and enhance adaptive capacity to natural hazards.

Translating available technologies and knowledge into useful tools presents many challenges for developing countries. Technological, financial and institutional factors mainly determine the level of adaptability and responsiveness. For example, it is possible to forecast flash floods as they develop by weather radar. Such radar technology is, however, often absent in African, Asian and Caribbean developing countries where flash floods are more likely to occur.

To reduce some of these shortcomings, several global organizations are assisting developing countries in building up effective early forecasting systems. For example, the collaborative efforts of the World Meteorological Organization (WMO) and the National Meteorological and Hydrological Services (NMHS) are playing a critical role in the reduction of death from disasters in some countries. Similarly, the Food and Agriculture Organization of the United Nations (FAO) Global Information and Early Warning System on Food and Agriculture (GIEWS) and the Food Insecurity and Vulnerability Information and Mapping System (FIVIMS), both related to floods and droughts, are providing useful information for risk reduction plans for developing countries. Broadly, international financial support, knowledge-sharing, capacity-building, training, research and development to address gaps and shortcomings of developing countries can provide guidance for effective early warning systems in these countries. Along these lines and following the devastating floods in South Asia in 2004, an Emergency Flood Damage Rehabilitation Project (EFDRP) with international support has been set up at a cost of $180 million to improve the technological aspects and effectiveness of early warning systems in the region (United Nations, International Strategy for Disaster Reduction, 2006).

Low-cost technologies can make a difference in the functioning of early warning systems in developing countries. For instance, in the Dominican Republic, warnings are issued on national radio and TV. Relevant maps are delivered to municipal civil defence officials and cellphones and local sirens are utilized to warn the population. The early warning system in Cuba has also proved its effectiveness by reducing dramatically the number of human losses (International Federation of Red Cross and Red Crescent Societies (IFRC), 2006): for instance, four persons had been killed when Hurricane Charley hit the island in 2004, while no one perished when Hurricane Ivan struck one month later. Hurricane Charley had killed 10 persons in Florida, while Ivan killed 52 persons in the United States, 39 in Grenada and 15 in Jamaica.

Similarly, use of low-cost technology has contributed to a significant reduction of cyclone-related deaths in Bangladesh: although 10,000 persons perished during Cyclone Sidr in November 2007, this figure is significantly lower than the 139,000 deaths caused by a similar cyclone in 1991.

There is, however, ample room for improvement. More lives could have been saved in Bangladesh if existing and widely used low-cost technologies had been integrated into the national early warning system. Along the same lines, despite a weather forecast system, heavy rains triggered devastating landslides on the mountainous border between the Dominican Republic and Haiti in May 2004, leaving hundreds of people dead and thousands homeless.

International collaboration and investment on early warning systems have increased. The meteorological institute of Cuba shares information with the United States National Hurricane Center (NHC) and produces regional models to forecast storms and other natural hazards. The institute issues regular scientific-based meteorological information and early warning news on the evolution of a natural hazard and risk. During a hurricane season, the media, local civil protection committees, and regional coordinators are mobilized to disseminate storm updates and related information

Box III.4 (cont'd)

to high-risk areas. Public transportation, designated shelters and civil society groups comprising, for example, women, small businesses and doctors are brought together to persuade vulnerable people to relocate and to facilitate relocation, while providing essentials such as food, water and blankets. At the local levels, disaster coordinators are equipped with low-cost technologies to maintain successful coordination of efforts extending from the national to the local level. In this regard, Zambia has an extensive system set up for early risk-mapping of natural hazards. It prepares vulnerability assessment in advance and is mobilizing resources at a wider level as international aid agencies have also become part of the early warning system.

pre-disaster preparedness, as unsafe buildings and lack of enforcement of building codes amplify vulnerabilities (United Nations, International Strategy for Disaster Reduction, and International Recovery Platform, 2007). For instance, the fact that building codes established in the 1980s had required buildings to have steel frames meant that buildings constructed more recently were less affected by the 1995 Kobe earthquake than older buildings. The lesson was learned: since then, older constructions have also been required to comply with the new codes in preparation for future earthquakes (Kawamura, 1995).

There is also a role for legislation and planning in terms of direct risk reduction measures of a non-structural nature. These should encompass risk evaluation programmes, provision of information to people on measures to reduce risk (for example, relevant information on disaster risk and means of protection for people residing in high-risk areas), resettlement plans, establishment of early warning systems, and the inclusion of disaster risk reduction subjects and training programmes in schools and within communities. A recent survey (United Nations, International Strategy for Disaster Reduction, 2006) indicates that effective early warning systems must be people-centred and must comprise four elements: (a) knowledge of the risks faced, (b) a technical capacity, monitoring and warning service, (c) dissemination of meaningful warnings to those at risk and (d) public awareness and preparedness to act. For example, the early warning system in Cuba proved its effectiveness by reducing dramatically the number of human losses relative to those of its neighbours.

Standard use of environmental impact assessments as part of public investment and development programmes would greatly improve the effectiveness of actions directed towards disaster mitigation. For example, the Government of Viet Nam with the support of the International Federation of Red Cross and Red Crescent Societies invested in a "mangrove project" by planting and protecting 12,000 hectares of mangroves along almost 200 kilometres of coastline. While the planting and protection cost about $1.1 million, the project helped to reduce the cost of dyke maintenance by $7.3 million per year, and to improve the resilience with respect to further hazards of 7,750 families through their selling of crabs, shrimps and mollusks (United Nations Environment Programme, 2007). Thus, naturally occurring mitigation measures involving, for example, mangroves, seagrass beds and reeds play an important role in reducing the adverse impact of natural hazards.

Pooling risk

To some degree, disaster insurance schemes can be effective coping mechanisms. Though such insurance will not reduce the direct impact of disasters, it can provide indemnification against damages incurred, enabling those covered to replace lost and repair damaged assets. As such, it can smooth consumption, reduce economic insecurity and prevent the establishment of an unstable post-disaster investment climate.

As noted earlier, the combination of catastrophic and covariant risks associated with many natural hazards makes their pooling and transfer, through market-based financial instruments, administratively difficult or prohibitively expensive. Even so, the extent to which households, enterprises and States choose to manage disaster risk through insurance varies significantly, even among developed countries.

Typically, insuring public assets against disasters is quite different from insuring against damages incurred by households or firms, as Governments are believed to be able to socialize risk through levying taxes. Although insurance of public assets is not widespread and is actually illegal in some developed countries, it can be an attractive option in small, low-income or highly exposed countries where fiscal capacity is weak, and publicly owned assets account for a large share of the capital stock, or where infrastructure risks are highly correlated (Linnerooth-Bayer and Mechler, 2007). While sovereign insurance instruments such as catastrophe bonds are becoming more widely used (see box III.5), the global market is relatively small, with total coverage having reached $5 billion in 2003 (Guy Carpenter, 2006).

The availability of disaster insurance to households and firms varies greatly across hazard type: it is most common in the case of storm risk, where it is often bundled with home or business property insurance, but is much rarer in the case of earthquake risk and is virtually non-existent for other types of natural hazards. Moreover, although it is more widespread than insurance of public assets, its uptake on a global level has been rather low: only approximately 1 per cent of damages are covered this way in low-income countries, and even in high-income countries, coverage is less than one third.[12] While insufficiently developed financial markets and lack of appropriate regulatory frameworks have contributed to low insurance penetration in developing countries, households and businesses are often unable to afford commercial insurance, even if it is available, or may not consider disaster insurance a priority, or may simply not trust providers (Linnerooth-Bayer and Mechler, 2007; Syroka, 2007). Consequently, even in high-income countries, households and businesses must often rely extensively on public assistance to recover from the impact of disasters.[13]

Responding to the unwillingness of private insurers to fully underwrite these risks, several countries legislated State involvement in the insurance industry, which has often taken the form of public-private national insurance systems, with the State acting

The combination of catastrophic and covariant risks associated with many natural hazards makes market-based financial instruments, administratively difficult or prohibitively expensive

Insufficiently developed financial markets and lack of appropriate regulatory frameworks have contributed to low insurance penetration in developing countries

[12] In fact, insurance penetration varies greatly across regions: the average catastrophe insurance premium per person in Africa and Asia amounts to less than US$ 5, approximately 1 per cent of the corresponding amount in the United States, parts of Europe and Australia. Moreover, there is virtually no coverage at all in a number of countries in Africa compared with a per capita premium in South Africa of $160 (Munich Re, 2005; Swiss Re, 2007).

[13] Significant covariant risk implies that large reserves are required to avoid the threat of insolvency, which can threaten even well-capitalized and diversified insurance companies in developed-market economies, as has recently been the case following hurricane damage in the south-eastern United States. There is, for instance, evidence that insurance companies are not renewing insurance contracts in northern States in the United States owing to the effects of the 2005 hurricane season, although these States were not affected. Likewise, reinsurance premiums increased in Caribbean islands following the impact of Hurricane Andrew in Florida in 1992, although these islands had not suffered extensive damage. In response to perceived greater threats, some insurers in States of the United States have introduced percentage deductibles in lieu of dollar deductibles to limit exposure to catastrophic losses from natural disasters and mandatory deductibles for natural hazards in certain areas.

Box III.5

Pooling risks in different contexts: examples of innovative public and private insurance: Mexico and Malawi

In 2006, the Government of Mexico insured its catastrophe reserve fund, FONDEN (Fondo Nacional de Desastres Naturales), against major earthquakes with a mix of reinsurance and a catastrophe bond. The contract is linked to a parametric trigger in terms of magnitude and depth of seismicity for the three-year period 2007-2009 and aims at protecting three regions in Mexico considered to be at highest risk. It pays an interest spread of 230 basis points above the London Interbank Offered Rate (LIBOR) if an insurance claim is not triggered by an earthquake in one of the specified zones with specified magnitude and depth and if an official declaration of a disaster is made by a federal agency.

The Government of Mexico financed the transaction out of its own means, though it did receive technical assistance from the World Bank and the Inter-American Development Bank. Costs for the catastrophe bond transaction, however, were about 2 per cent of cover, approximately twice those usually associated with traditional reinsurance (Lane, 2004). Reduction of costs by substituting outside consultancy firms with internal expertise in estimating risks appears to be a feasible course of action in the future. In Turkey (another earthquake-prone country), for example, universities are developing their capacity to carry out sophisticated catastrophe modelling as a basis for risk assessments.

The potential market for catastrophe bonds is large, as the lack of risk correlation between catastrophe bonds and financial markets makes these instruments particularly interesting for investors. However, as with other hazard-indexed instruments, the major disadvantage is basis risk, which is the lack of correlation of the trigger with the loss incurred. Moreover, there is no guarantee that post-disaster bond payments will reach those most in need.

While the catastrophe insurance in Mexico is publicly financed, a private sector approach has been taken in Malawi, which is one of the more drought-prone countries in the Southern African region. In 2004-2005, the country experienced a devastating drought, throwing 40 per cent of the smallholder population into a dependence on food aid. In fact, although 20 per cent of the country's area is covered by water (Lake Malawi), food insecurity is chronic, particularly as most farmers have small holdings, ranging from 0.5 to 3 hectares.

Loan recovery rates ranged from 50-70 per cent that year; one bank, two micro-finance institutions and a Government- and donor-led agricultural lending programme stopped operating owing to drought-related defaults. In 2005, the Insurance Association of Malawi agreed to offer an index-based weather insurance policy, linked with credit supply, to small-scale farmers. One of the groups interested in testing this approach was the National Smallholder Farmers' Association of Malawi. Groundnut was chosen for the pilot, as the crop is relatively drought-sensitive and as farmers have been reluctant to invest in adopting new varieties because of the high costs of seed.

In accordance with the policy, the farmer enters into a loan agreement with a higher interest rate that includes the weather insurance premium, which the bank pays to the insurer, the Insurance Association of Malawi. The insurance payments are index-based, depending on precipitation measured at one of three weather stations within the region of the pilot programme.

Depending on location, premiums amounted to 6-10 per cent of the insured cost-of-seed values, an amount easily repayable from the increased productivity of the seeds (estimated at about 500 per cent). In the event of a severe drought, the borrower pays a fraction of the loan and the rest is paid by the insurer directly to the bank. The fact that the farmer is less likely to default has a stabilizing effect on the bank's portfolio and risk profile. Without this assurance, banks rarely loan to high-risk, low-income farmers. The advantage for the farmers is that they obtain needed credit to invest in the seeds and other inputs necessary for higher-yield crops.

A survey of 168 farmers participating in the 2005-2006 pilot programme provides reason for both optimism and caution in respect of this scenario. Although the sample was not fully representative (owing to exclusion of defaulting participants), the responses were indicative of farmers' perceptions about the weather insurance scheme. The results showed that, although almost all participating farmers had reported that they would join the scheme if offered the opportunity again, only 55 per cent of respondents reported having understood the scheme before joining it. In addition, over one quarter of respondents did not consider the rainfall measurements from the local stations to be trustworthy.

Source: Linnerooth-Bayer and Mechler (2007).

as the provider of last resort, as in Japan's earthquake programme and national flood insurance in the United States.[14] In many low-income countries, microfinance institutions are taking a more prominent role in providing disaster insurance programmes, often with donor encouragement and support.

Although other types of micro-insurance do exist (see chap. V), the primary focus of microfinance institutions dealing with natural hazards has been on agriculture and crop insurance designed to respond to the threat of food insecurity and the inability to cope with the consequences of destroyed crops, reduced yields and decimated livestock herds. This is particularly relevant when the livelihoods of large proportions of the population are based on subsistence farming and nomadic herding activities.

Global insurance of
agriculture is small
and skewed

There has, in fact, been a long and well-documented experience with crop insurance products in general. However, the global market remains relatively small, with the total global insurance premiums of agricultural insurance programmes having amounted to approximately $8 billion in 2006, a mere 0.5 per cent of total value added in agriculture. Moreover, crop insurance is highly skewed, with the North American market accounting for over two thirds of that total (see table III.6).[15] The African continent, excluding South Africa, accounts approximately for less than 1 per cent of total premium payments, despite the fact that it accounts for approximately 13 per cent of global agricultural GDP.

The traditional crop insurance products are *named peril* and *multiple peril* insurance: the former covers particular hazards and in the case of hail, for example, has been available in North America and Europe for over 100 years. The latter establishes an insured yield as a percentage of the historical average yield and, in the event of disaster, pays an indemnity proportional to the difference between the two.[16] However, the high information content and high administering and running costs associated with these schemes have contributed to the large subsidies provided in many developed economies.[17] To avoid expensive verification of claims at the individual-farm level, several countries are piloting *index-based* or parametric schemes where payouts are contingent on an easily verifiable, objective physical trigger which is usually related to weather, such as rainfall measured at a regional weather station (see box III.5).[18]

The current structure of index-based insurance schemes, and their essentially pilot status, raises questions, however, as to their resilience with respect to large-scale

---

14   Japan's earthquake programme, for instance, is backed by Government reinsurance and taxpayers. Similarly, the Government of the United States serves as the primary insurer in the United States National Flood Insurance Program (NFIP). In France, catastrophe insurance is offered as part of an all-hazards policy bundled with property insurance.

15   Table III.6 lists the 10 largest programmes in the world by agricultural premium for risk that is transferred to the international reinsurance market. It does not take Government-retained risk into account.

16   Such schemes are the basis for most federal crop insurance programmes in the United States, and most Provinces of Canada, and also exist, for instance, in Italy, Spain, Portugal, Austria, Brazil and Japan.

17   To reduce the cost to farmers of purchasing such insurance, significant subsidies exist. For instance, the United States Federal Government subsidizes approximately 70 per cent of the total cost of the federal crop insurance programmes, costing taxpayers $3 billion per year.

18   Other indices, however, are equally possible. In Mongolia, livelihoods of nearly half the population depend on livestock farming. This has given rise to an index-based livestock insurance scheme where the trigger is based on the overall mortality rate of adult animals in a given county, which has enabled herders to protect themselves against livelihood losses from extreme weather conditions, such as a harsh winter (*dzud*) (Mahul and Skees, 2007).

Table III.6
Estimated agricultural insurance premium payments, top 10 countries

	Estimated insurance premiums	
Country	Millions of United States dollars	Percentage of global total
United States of America	4 600	57.5
Canada	900	11.3
Spain	550	8.9
Italy	350	4.4
France	300	3.8
Germany	200	2.5
South Africa	100	1.3
Australia/New Zealand	100	1.3
China	80	1
Republic of Korea	60	0.8
Total	7 240	90.5[a]

Source: Carpenter (2006).

a   Discrepancy due to rounding.

impacts in the face of major catastrophic events, as well as the extent to which they can be relied upon to reduce farmers' insecurity.[19]

The benefits of providing access to insurance against the threat of disasters are clear: indemnification against damages encourages investment, contributes to income growth and reduces income insecurity. However, high costs limit the reach of insurance, particularly in the case of poorer countries and communities. Also, serious questions have been raised regarding the likelihood of keeping disaster insurance schemes solvent, given the catastrophic and covariant nature of the risks involved (see note 13 above). Consequently, the role of the insurance types discussed may be more relevant to smaller-scale disasters. Moreover, competent regulatory bodies are needed to monitor conditions for both insurers and clients and ensure that the market provides sustainable insurance contracts. In this respect, it is worth remembering that deeper financial markets are as much a consequence as a cause of sustained economic development. Therefore, pooling risks against disaster through financial markets cannot be the only pillar of an effective coping mechanism.

> Serious questions have been raised regarding the likelihood of keeping disaster insurance schemes solvent, given the catastrophic and covariant nature of the risks involved

Multilateral initiatives for disaster relief and prevention

The international community has intensified its efforts towards reducing the adverse effects of natural hazards and man-made disasters. Building on the 1994 Yokohama Strategy for

> Focus is moving from relief and emergency action to increasing resilience

---

19   As triggers are essentially one-dimensional, for example, based only upon rainfall, insured crops must be highly correlated with the object underlying the index. Otherwise, the lack of correlation of the trigger with the loss incurred (*basis risk*) is high. Some crops may therefore need a more broad-based index. Moreover, constructing a weather index requires consistent historical records of daily weather data, ideally covering at least 25-30 years, as well as historical production and yield data. Data in few countries are likely to meet these requirements. Finally, coverage of many piloted index-based schemes reduces the financial impact of hazards only by paying off insured farmers' loan obligations, rather than by paying direct indemnification to farmers. They therefore do not provide greater income security per se or address the plight of the agriculture sector when crops are wiped out.

a Safer World: Guidelines for Natural Disaster Prevention, Preparedness and Mitigation and its Plan of Action[20] and as a follow-up to the International Decade for Natural Disaster Reduction, the International Strategy for Disaster Reduction has promoted public awareness and commitment, expanded networks and partnerships, and improved knowledge of causes of disaster and options for risk reduction. The international community has thus been moving away from a relief and emergency action approach towards a broader strategy for increasing resilience of vulnerable populations and countries which includes prevention and preparedness as well as a focus on medium-term recovery and mitigation mechanisms.[21] The key objectives of the United Nations Millennium Declaration of 8 September 2000[22] form an important pillar of strengthening resilience with respect to hazards by reducing vulnerability on a general level.

However, there is still a long way to go. Indeed, as noted earlier, only a tiny fraction of international funding is directed towards strengthening resilience against hazards through investments in disaster resilience and adaptation, and in planning. Moreover, the large proportions of funding mobilized in response to disasters that are directed towards providing basic essentials such as food and health highlight the reactive nature of these responses.[23]

Climate change is sharpening socio-economic vulnerabilities of already fragile populations and countries such as those in sub-Saharan Africa and small island developing States, while testing the coping mechanisms of other previously less vulnerable groups (United Nations Development Programme, 2007; Intergovernmental Panel on Climate Change (IPCC), 2007). For example, increased adverse effects of droughts and floods threaten to be long-lasting and adversely affect biodiversity and human settlements. Multilateral programmes have been created to support these countries. For instance, the United Nations Convention to Combat Desertification in Those Countries Experiencing Serious Drought and/or Desertification, Particularly in Africa,[24] adopted in 1994, and the Programme of Action for the Least Developed Countries for the Decade 2001-2010,[25] adopted in 2001 by the Third United Nations Conference on the Least Developed Countries, call for greater priority to be given to substantive programmes and related institutional arrangements. Similarly, in 2005, the International Meeting to Review the Implementation of the Programme of Action for the Sustainable Development of Small Island Developing States called for increased commitments to reduce the vulnerability of small island developing States due to their limited capacity to respond to and recover from disasters.

Further international cooperation for sharing information, raising awareness and building capacities, however, is still needed. In particular, as suggested by the Plan of Implementation of the World Summit on Sustainable Development ("Johannesburg Plan of Implementation"),[26] actions for an integrated approach to address vulnerability, disaster risk management and mitigation as "an essential element of a safer world in the

Climate change is sharpening vulnerabilities of fragile populations

---

20   A/CONF. 172/9, chap. I, resolution 1, annex I.

21   The Agenda for Humanitarian Action adopted by the International Conference of the Red Cross and Red Crescent in December 2003 includes, for instance, goals and actions aimed at reducing the risk and impact of disasters and improving preparedness and response mechanisms.

22   See General Assembly resolution 55/2.

23   In 2006, for instance, more than 55 per cent of funding of appeals was directed to food (United Nations, Office for the Coordination of Humanitarian Affairs, 2008).

24   United Nations, Treaty Series, vol. 1954, No. 33480.

25   A/CONF. 191/13, chap. II.

26   *Report of the World Summit on Sustainable Development, Johannesburg, South Africa, 26 August-4 September 2002* (United Nations Publications, Sales No. E.03.II.A.1 and corrigendum), chap. I, resolution 2, annex.

twenty-first century" (para. 37) are needed. The General Assembly has echoed this call and encouraged the Intergovernmental Panel on Climate Change to continue to assess the adverse effects of climate change on the socio-economic and disaster reduction systems of developing countries.

These above-mentioned initiatives provide necessary, albeit essentially normative frameworks at the broader institutional level. However, they need to be translated into specific actions at national and regional levels to reduce the vulnerability to disasters and yield tangible outcomes.

In this respect, greater attention is being placed by donors and national Governments on specific programmes to reduce income insecurity. Cash transfer programmes have formed an important component of these efforts: they have, for instance, been introduced in several developing countries to reduce poverty among older persons and the poor (United Nations, 2007a). These developments are also affecting the international community's response to disasters.

Greater attention is being placed by donors and national Governments on specific programmes to reduce income insecurity

Cash transfers

The principal response to dealing with the impact of disasters has in general focused on the provision of goods and services, particularly in developing economies. This has included supply of food, subsidized loans, work-for-cash and work-for-food programmes and other cash-similar tools such as vouchers, direct food and housing support.[27] Providing support by granting direct cash handouts has traditionally been shunned, however, by international donors and national politicians.

Nevertheless, there is growing evidence that, in the medium term, cash transfers to affected households may be preferable to in-kind support, and interest is growing in this respect among international development agencies, bilateral donors, non-governmental organizations and national Governments. Commodity-based aid is likely to remain the primary response in dealing with the immediate aftermath of a disaster so as to ensure that basic commodities are available. However, cash-based transfers constitute a viable alternative to in-kind aid once the local capacity for providing basic goods and services has been restored: as households are more likely to know their most urgent needs, providing a cash transfer enables them to purchase the goods and services most needed. This contributes to greater aid effectiveness. In addition, evidence suggests that cash transfers can be less expensive to administer than in-kind handouts (such as food aid) (Barrett, Holden and Clay, 2001), and thus increase the efficiency of aid. They also offer a faster and more transparent mode of delivering support (Standing, 2007) and are better able to sustain recovery, since there is one portion that is invested rather than consumed and because more is spent on goods and services produced locally (Department for International Development, 2005).

Cash transfers may be preferable to in-kind support

Recent examples of the use of large cash transfer schemes to respond to the aftermath of disasters have been provided by Maldives and Sri Lanka (in response to the 2004 tsunami), by Pakistan (in response to the 2005 earthquake in Pakistan-administered Kashmir) and by Turkey (in response to the 1999 Izmit earthquake). In each case, payment was conditional on the impact of the disaster, involving determining whether, for example, household members were injured or killed in Pakistan or whether houses were damaged or destroyed in Maldives, and so on. Transfers per individual were equivalent to

---

27   For instance, officially designating an event a disaster has significant implications in the United States, as a wide range of the above-mentioned forms of assistance are then made available to the affected area. Up to $25,000 in federal assistance can be provided to individuals and households (Federal Emergency Management Agency (FEMA), 2007, p. 44).

approximately 2.9 per cent of annual GDP per capita in Sri Lanka, and ranged between 1.5 and 4.5 per cent of annual GDP per capita in Maldives, and between 3.4 and 8.6 per cent of annual GDP per capita in Turkey. Owing mainly to generous compensation for deaths and injury, payments were considerably more generous in Pakistan, reaching up to 48.3 per cent of annual GDP per capita (Heltberg, 2007). Other successful schemes have been employed in response to drought in Ethiopia and floods in Mozambique (see chap. V).

International pooling initiatives

Individual countries
have difficulty managing
disaster risk with their
own resources

The ability of a single country to manage disaster risk is often limited by serious resource constraints. Accordingly, international institutions, including at the regional level, have an important role to play, as they are often better able to employ pooling strategies, realize synergies and hence cope with covariant risk.

Seeking formal mechanisms for transferring risks is one option for donors and international organizations. Incurring an annual payment to address financial risk rather than responding to irregular and unpredictably large requests for post-disaster aid can enable donors to leverage their commitments. The Turkish Catastrophe Insurance Pool, launched in 2000, represented the first such pool of its kind to tackle the problem of insurance affordability in a middle-income developing country. Within the Turkish Catastrophe Insurance Pool, earthquake insurance is obligatory for all property owners in Istanbul and other urban centres at high seismic risk (poorer property owners in rural areas are therefore excluded). While premiums are based upon risk, they are made more affordable owing to a contingent loan facility with favourable conditions provided by the World Bank.

In a similar vein, several members of the Caribbean Community (CARICOM) established in 2007 the Caribbean Catastrophe Risk Insurance Facility (CCRIF) under the auspices of the World Bank. This is in fact the first multi-country catastrophe insurance pool and is intended as a pilot for other regions. The objective of the facility is to pool risks relating to natural hazards and hence provide a mechanism through which to assist affected members in absorbing the adverse impact of disasters. To do so, the programme provides budgetary support by bearing up to 20 per cent of estimated government losses resulting from earthquakes and hurricanes.[28] The need for such a mechanism is particularly acute for Caribbean countries, as they are prone to various types of natural hazards (see box III.2) and as the impact of those hazards often exceeds an individual country's ability to deal with them exclusively thorough its own means. In its first year, the Facility was able to secure $110 million of total coverage. While the Facility itself retains responsibility for the first layer of claims (approximately $10 million), the remaining $100 million are transferred to international markets through reinsurance as well as a catastrophe swap provided by the World Bank.

Transferring the responsibility for estimating losses to the Caribbean Catastrophe Risk Insurance Facility eliminates the risk of losses' being overstated so as to obtain higher payouts. However, as estimates of losses are based upon a hazard index and on predetermined models of damages that vary with wind speed, basis risk remains a major concern of the Facility.

---

28   These include damages to government buildings and infrastructure, estimated losses in tax revenue and government relief expenditures. Claims are contingent on a trigger depending on an index for hurricanes (wind speed) and earthquakes (ground shaking) and payments are provided immediately in the event of a disaster. Annual contributions to the facility range between $200,000 and $4 million, depending on the size of the country. Payouts are available up to a predetermined limit: Jamaica has the highest premium ($4 million) and the highest coverage ($95 million), of which $50 million relates to hurricanes. To jump-start the reserve fund, the Governments of Bermuda, Canada, France and the United Kingdom of Great Britain and Northern Ireland, as well as the Caribbean Development Bank and the World Bank, have pledged a total of US$ 47 million.

An action that could be quickly implemented by the international community to assist countries affected by disasters would be to introduce a simple mechanism for extending a moratorium on debt servicing. Debt relief has occasionally been offered to countries affected by disasters: for instance, the Paris Club offered debt relief to a number of countries affected by the 2004 Indian Ocean tsunami; the deferred payments were to be repaid over five years, with a one-year grace period.

A moratorium on debt servicing could assist countries affected by disasters

Such a simple mechanism must be one that is not dependent upon an International Monetary Fund (IMF) programme to avoid new conditionality. Rather, a meeting of all creditors should be coordinated to carry out the process in a single operation rather than through bilateral agreements with all Paris Club and non-Paris Club creditors (Schneider, 2008). Moreover, the mechanism would need to waive interest payments for the period of emergency in order to prevent both a bunching of repayments and future rescheduling and borrowing in order to meet repayment obligations. In doing so, such a mechanism would enable affected countries to address their domestic needs related to reconstruction and rehabilitation in a timelier manner. Through the easing of the revenue constraint, the need to divert previously earmarked budgets to accomplish these tasks decreases. This would also enable the Government to protect spending, for example, on education, health and water and sanitation, that benefits the poor in particular. Moreover, introducing such a procedure would remove the political considerations that arise in the process of disbursing funds and reduce the time lags in obtaining these funds, as well as eliminate the negative signals that acceptance of ad hoc offers could send to markets.[29] This mechanism might indeed benefit heavily indebted poor countries with significant debt servicing; on the other hand, countries with lower debt-servicing commitments would be less affected.

A global disaster mechanism

The international community, through both public and private organizations, is often quick to respond to emergency calls following large-scale disasters. However, there has been a persistent tendency for pledges to fall short of delivery, while funds requested by the United Nations for disasters have consistently failed to reach the desired level: for instance, in 2007 only 72 per cent of requested funds through consolidated and flash appeals materialized, leaving a shortfall of $1.4 billion (United Nations, Office for the Coordination of Humanitarian Affairs, 2008). In addition, the fact that funds for such appeals frequently come from existing budgets results only in a reallocation of existing resources. This financial uncertainty hampers disaster relief planning. Moreover, the scale and direction of international disaster relief aid appear to be heavily influenced by economic and geopolitical interests, including colonial ties and geographical proximity, and by biases in news coverage. The consequences are significant. According to one estimate, such biases may have reduced the flow of funds to disasters in Asia by over one third, to disasters in Africa by over one fifth and to disasters in South America by more than one sixth (Strömberg 2007, p. 220). Moreover, the tied nature of such aid and the conditionalities attached to it remain a significant obstacle to its effectiveness.

Pledges of funds often fall short of delivery

Financing a more integrated approach to disaster management is likely to be best undertaken through a *global disaster mechanism*. This could begin with a move to consolidate the current existing approaches to financing disaster emergencies. A proposal for a $4 billion-$5 billion fund was put forth in 2006 by the then Chancellor of the

A global disaster mechanism is needed

---

29   In fact, Thailand did not sign up for the moratorium offered by the Paris Club: the potential spillover effect on the country's credit ratings may have been an underlying reason.

Exchequer of the United Kingdom, Gordon Brown, as part of a wider plan to "make poverty history" (Brown, 2006). However, until very recently, this plan had not moved beyond the conception stage.

Several compensatory financing facilities were proposed in the recent past. Most were too small, however, to be really effective. For instance, an ACP-EU Natural Disaster Facility has been created to strengthen disaster risk reduction and management as well as improve disaster preparedness, mitigation and post-disaster rehabilitation in African, Caribbean and Pacific (ACP) States. The 12 million euros of seed capital provided by the European Development Fund falls short, however, of the funding called for, amounting to at least 250 million euros, to assist ACP States (ACP-EU Joint Parliamentary Assembly, 2007). Similarly, the Inter-American Development Bank has an Emergency Reconstruction Facility which can provide loans of up to $30 million to assist members affected by disasters. It also has a Disaster Prevention Fund which provides grants for disaster risk management activities; the maximum grant for individual projects is limited, however, to US$ 1 million.

A Global Facility for Disaster Reduction and Recovery has been set up under the International Strategy for Disaster Reduction to develop and implement the Hyogo Framework for Action 2005-2015: Building the Resilience of Nations and Communities to Disasters[30] through coordinated programmes designed to reverse the trend in disaster losses by 2015. As reducing vulnerability is its core objective, the Global Facility seeks to provide technical and financial resources for disaster risk research with an annual budget of $5 million. It also aims at incorporating disaster risks into development strategies through, for example, risk management, research and establishing recovery financing mechanisms with an estimated $350 million for a 10-year period. It further aims to provide fast and reliable financing for recovery, primarily to low-income high-risk countries through a Standby Recovery Financing Facility.

The World Bank has most recently introduced a Catastrophe Risk Deferred Drawdown Option (CAT DDO) facility (World Bank, 2008a). Targeted at low-income countries affected by disasters, this facility provides rapid access to funds. Disbursements, however, take the form of loans and although they can reach up to $500 million, they are limited to a maximum of 0.25 per cent of the country's GDP.

Financing must be quick and automatic

These examples of multilateral facilities serve to highlight the importance that vulnerability to disasters is beginning to receive. However, considering the magnitude of the damages that disasters can cause, measured either in nominal terms or in relation to GDP (as outlined above), it is clear that any multilateral facility must be well funded so as to provide *sufficient* financing *quickly* and *automatically*. Existing facilities fail to pass this acid test. Creating a *global disaster mechanism,* possibly under the auspices of the United Nations, could bring together and scale up in a more holistic manner the existing fragmented resources available for large-scale disaster relief. While the details would need to be worked out, the proposed global disaster mechanism could be set up under the following guiding principles.

Access to the global disaster mechanism would be linked to predetermined triggers so as to remove the distortions associated with the current practices of disbursing relief. More specifically, as the aim of the facility would be to provide financing for countries significantly affected by disasters, the following three proxy variables are proposed to measure the impact of the disaster and identify disasters that would qualify for access to the facility:

---

30   A/CONF. 206/6 and Corr. 1, chap. I, resolution 2.

(a)   The total population affected as a percentage of the country's total population, to capture the scope of the disaster;

(b)   The resulting damages expressed as a percentage of the country's total public revenue, to highlight the potential strain on public resources;

(c)   The resulting damages as a percentage of the country's total GDP, to highlight the economic scale of the impact.

To assist in reconstruction and recovery, the mechanism should disburse to affected countries an amount equivalent to 25 per cent of damages caused. Any disaster meeting one of the following conditions would trigger eligibility with respect to the mechanism:

(a)   It has affected 5 per cent or more of a country's population;

(b)   It has caused damages equal to 5 per cent or more of GDP;

(c)   It has caused damages that exceed 10 per cent of government revenue.

Using the global experience of disasters since the turn of the millennium, approximately one third of countries experiencing a disaster during the period 2000-2006 would have been eligible if the mechanism had been in place. Moreover, the selected thresholds would have implied average financing requirements for that period of $2.5 billion per annum.

Funding for the global disaster mechanism should be based on assessed contributions with more developed countries contributing relatively more than less developed ones. This would spread the cost of the facility more equitably. Hence, while high-income non-OECD countries would pay a proportion of their GDP equal to 80 per cent of that paid by high-income OECD countries, upper middle income countries would pay a proportion of GDP equal to 75 per cent, and lower middle income countries would pay a proportion of a GDP equal to 50 per cent, of that of high-income OECD countries. Low-income countries would be exempted from contributing. Under such a financing scheme, high-income countries would have contributed less than 0.007 per cent of their GDP annual over the period 2000-2006. For the United States, this would have translated into an annual contribution equal to approximately $800 million ($2.7 per person), less than 3 per cent of its total official development assistance (ODA) provided in 2005. In contrast, a lower middle income country such as Guyana, which is also classified as a heavily indebted poor country, would have contributed on average $27,000 per year to the facility ($0.04 per person), yet would have been a net recipient of $158 million over the total period 2000-2006 (net payments to such a proposed facility for low-income and lower middle income countries are given in table III.7).

Given what has been said about the links between relief, recovery and development in countries prone to disasters, this mechanism should, however, ultimately aim to assume a much larger role in financing ex ante investments in disaster planning and preparedness, including a range of services to assist in disaster recovery. Such services could include disseminating best practises and related capacity-building and monitoring environmental protection and regulatory standards to the extent that they related to the threat of disasters.

The global disaster mechanism should therefore eventually coordinate the delivery of funds, and could act as an umbrella mechanism for unifying existing mechanisms and responsibilities, such as those outlined above, with their respective institutions. In any case, the importance of such a mechanism would be to automatically provide predictable funds needed for reconstruction, risk mitigation and recovery from shocks.

This mechanism must ultimately aim at disaster planning and preparedness

Table III.7

Hypothetical net payments[a] of selected low-income and lower middle income countries and areas to the proposed global disaster mechanism for the period 2000-2006

Millions of United States dollars			
Country or area	Net payments	Country or area	Net payments
Low-income			
Afghanistan	0.00	Viet Nam	-78.60
Lao People's Democratic Republic	-0.30	Mozambique	-119.50
Mongolia	-30.00	Myanmar	-130.00
Cambodia	-47.10	India	-284.70
Tajikistan	-50.50	Bangladesh	-666.70
Sudan	-60.90	Pakistan	-1 300.00
Madagascar	-69.10	Democratic People's Republic of Korea	-1 609.40
Lower middle income			
Indonesia	61.10	Lesotho	0.30
Colombia	27.00	Suriname	0.30
Egypt	22.10	Cape Verde	0.20
Ukraine	17.00	Bhutan	0.20
Peru	16.90	Djibouti	0.20
Morocco	11.60	Samoa	0.10
Iraq	7.80	Vanuatu	0.10
Ecuador	7.40	Micronesia, Federated States of	0.10
Dominican Republic	6.40	Marshall Islands	0.00
Tunisia	6.30	Kiribati	0.00
Belarus	6.10	Moldova	-12.20
Syrian Arab Republic	6.00	Tonga	-19.10
Angola	5.50	Azerbaijan	-30.00
Cameroon	3.70	Armenia	-35.00
Jordan	2.70	Thailand	-36.80
Bolivia	2.20	Maldives	-120.20
Bosnia and Herzegovina	2.10	Guyana	-158.30
Honduras	1.80	Georgia	-202.50
Albania	1.80	Guatemala	-239.80
Paraguay	1.50	Philippines	-243.80
Turkmenistan	1.40	Jamaica	-251.00
Namibia	1.30	Sri Lanka	-359.60
The former Yugoslav Republic of Macedonia	1.30	Cuba	-543.10
Congo	1.20	El Salvador	-617.80
Nicaragua	1.10	Iran (Islamic Republic of)	-1 073.40
West Bank and Gaza	0.80	Algeria	-1 674.00
Fiji	0.70	China	-5 590.40
Swaziland	0.60		

Source: UN/DESA, based on data from the OFDA/CRED International Disaster Database (EM-DAT) (available at www.emdat.net), Université Catholique de Louvain, Brussels.

a   Insurance premium minus indemnization.

Any proper design of a global disaster mechanism would need to deal with several critical issues. For one, independent assessments of damages would be important to prevent overinflation of figures.[31] In this regard, and notwithstanding the availability of various methodologies for assessing damages, valuing damaged assets at replacement cost, including the cost of disaster mitigation and prevention to reduce vulnerability to future similar events, might be preferable (United Nations, Economic Commission for Latin America and the Caribbean, 2003), as it would automatically introduce an important disaster risk reduction component to the facility. This component could be strengthened by explicitly making the facility responsible for investment in disaster planning and mitigation (through, for example, earmarking a certain percentage of disbursements for mitigation). Moreover, through consolidation of existing resources, such as those listed above, and involvement of the insurance industry and international organizations, available funds could be greatly enhanced. Combining these financing responsibilities with various technical assistance and capacity-building responsibilities, as well as information gathering and monitoring, would enable countries to reduce their vulnerabilities to natural hazards and would reinforce the public-good dimension of the global disaster fund. Sufficiently well funded, such a facility could also go a long way towards increasing the likelihood of sustained recovery from large-scale events. However, to eliminate problems of adverse selection, participation of countries would have to be as wide as possible. Pooling risks across *all* countries would contribute to increased financial sustainability of the facility as well as highlight the collective challenge associated with climatic shocks.

Dealing with disasters

Natural hazards are not preventable, and the risks surrounding them are intrinsically difficult to manage. However, this cannot be said of the damage and insecurity that they can cause. Rather, the threat to economic insecurity from disasters is the result of compounded socio-economic vulnerabilities which expose particular communities and countries to this danger.

High priority must be given to disaster risk reduction in the design and implementation of national development strategies. One of the principal components of disaster risk reduction must be increased investment in hazard-mitigation measures. Moreover, vulnerability assessments will play an important role in identifying risks and those groups that are the most vulnerable in order that concrete policies may be designed.

The development dimension of disasters underlines the need, however, for a more integrated approach which combines development and risk management. Countries that are vulnerable to disasters must therefore not only be given sufficient policy space within which to design the appropriate integrated development strategies but also have access to adequate funding. For many countries, a fundamental challenge remains, namely, how to mobilize funds and resources for ex ante disaster mitigation in an environment where financial resources are already scarce. Regional and international cooperation will likely be critical in providing such resources. Cooperation ahead of time is also needed for designing policies and procedures for information exchange, strengthening linkages

[31] The United Nations has undertaken numerous independent disaster assessments, involving national and international experts, since the early 1970s, mainly in the Latin American and Caribbean region but, more recently, also on a more global basis (see United Nations, Economic Commission for Latin America and the Caribbean, 2007b, and United Nations Development Programme, 2007).

between scientific and technical institutions, and building mutual understanding among national disaster agencies.

There are a number of strategies available to households, communities and Governments for dealing with the threat that disasters pose to economic insecurity. These strategies will differ, however, according to development level and can comprise market- as well as non-market-based approaches. For instance, non-market strategies designed to strengthen coping capacities of households and communities ex ante may involve voluntary mutual arrangements. In more developed economies, relevant market-based arrangements are likely to involve property and life insurance, while in developing economies, crop and livestock insurance may be more relevant. In developed economies, at the national level, taxation may be the implicit form of insurance, while for less developed countries, formal insurance through, for example, catastrophe bonds, or in fact reliance on aid, may be the only feasible alternative.

In this regard, there is a role for pooling individual, or national risk through financial markets. Its potential, however, should not be overstated. For one, risk transfer in the form of public and/or private insurance through market-based strategies is often a real option only at higher levels of development. While high- and middle-income countries have more degrees of freedom for including insurance programmes as part of a set of mitigation tools for disaster risk reduction, insurance is less relevant to countries with underdeveloped financial sectors and in contexts of widespread income insecurity. Moreover, while non-market community-based strategies can quickly be exhausted even by small-scale localized disasters, the covariant nature of larger-scale disasters and the resulting impact can threaten even well-capitalized insurance markets. More formal mechanisms of pooling risks through (financial) markets are therefore unable to address the risks posed by large-scale catastrophic disasters.

Transferring the responsibility for sufficient protection against disasters to individuals by merely ensuring that risk transfer and risk pooling, such as insurance, are *available* can therefore not be the primary pillar for addressing the insecurity challenge. Rather, the main responsibility for strengthening economic security must lie with *Governments* and must focus on decreasing vulnerability by reducing economic and social risk to hazards ex ante.

This chapter has therefore proposed the creation of a global disaster mechanism as key to a more integrated approach to disaster management. The mechanism might begin by providing disaster relief but should quickly gear up to assume a wider set of responsibilities linked to disaster mitigation. Moreover, particularly in the light of climate change, the function of this facility should be perceived as encompassing more than a response to challenges in poorer countries. Recent experiences stand as a reminder that the threat to economic security from disasters is not one faced exclusively by the poorest countries. Indeed, more than one half of the world's population is now highly exposed to at least one natural hazard yearly and the impact of Hurricane Katrina in the United States in 2005 highlights not only the vulnerability of communities even in the richest parts of the world, but also the enormity of the challenge of repairing the damage to the social and economic fabric that such events can inflict. Indeed, to the extent that, as the Intergovernmental Panel on Climate Change has already suggested, the increased incidence of disasters is linked to man-made climate changes, finding more effective ways of managing climatic shocks, at both the national and international levels, would appear to be essential for ensuring a more secure future for everyone.

Chapter IV
Things fall apart: the vicious circle of economic insecurity and civil conflict

Introduction

The previous chapters have argued that preventing economic shocks and natural disasters from becoming endemic sources of insecurity requires an integrated policy approach. This will include a more prominent role for public goods and stronger regulations in creating and preserving more secure spaces where individuals, communities and countries can pursue their activities with a reasonable degree of predictability and stability, and with due regard for the aims and interests of others.

For some countries, however, where increased economic insecurity has been woven into a pattern of deep social cleavage and political instability, such spaces have essentially disappeared. Under these circumstances, the State runs the danger of losing its ability not only to deliver basic services, but also, often, to maintain its traditional monopoly over the forces of law and order. The result is that the "normal" channels through which negotiation and compromise are effected have given way to shocking, even genocidal levels of violence. Oftentimes, the international community is pulled into these conflicts through both military involvement and emergency relief, with the United Nations increasingly on the front line; during the 1990s, it carried out four times as many peacekeeping missions as in its previous 40 years.

For countries in conflict, renewing the policy dialogue must essentially wait for the fighting to stop. However, even when this has happened, post-conflict countries will remain particularly fragile societies, where deep social and economic vulnerabilities come with the added threat of a return to full-scale civil war. This possibility adds a distinct dimension to the policy challenge in such countries.

The present chapter examines some of the links among economic insecurity, political collapse and post-conflict recovery. The first section sketches the changing trends in conflict over the past 40 years and examines some of the economic threats and vulnerabilities associated with civil wars. This is followed by discussions of the costs of such conflict at the household level and the ways in which those costs can heighten existing vulnerabilities, potentially trapping countries in a state of prolonged conflict. A good deal of the recent analysis of civil conflict has speculated on whether greed or grievance has been the underlying force behind such conflict traps. The third section adopts a different focus by examining how threats to the social contract can give rise to prolonged conflicts. With this in mind, the next section examines the institutional support and policy space needed to accelerate post-conflict recovery. It suggests that a more strategic and integrated developmental approach to repairing the social contract depends on re-establishing an effective State which can move from aid dependence to mobilizing domestic resources in a manner that does not reignite previous tensions. In many post-conflict situations, the international community will have, for reasons given later in the present chapter, to play a key role. To date, the debate has been about how long that role might last. The final section suggests that, while time is certainly of the essence, the real task is making economic security as much of a strategic priority as military security. It suggests that, in this regard, the international community can still learn much from the principles that made the Marshall Plan a successful post-conflict recovery programme after the Second World War.

Armed conflict since the Second World War

Until the mid-1970s, most of the casualties of war had been soldiers fighting in inter-State wars. Since then, the vast majority of conflicts have been civil wars, in which the fighting has been much more irregular and most of the victims have been non-combatants (figure IV.1). Fearon and Laitin (2003) estimate that, since 1945, civil wars have resulted in three times as many deaths as wars between States. The number of these conflicts peaked in the early 1990s, but continued to be high for the remainder of the decade (two or three times the number recorded in the early 1970s), before dropping off at the start of the millennium. An estimated 5.5 million people were killed in 35 civil wars during the 1990s, making it the deadliest decade since the 1940s.[1]

The main factor behind the steady rise in civil conflict since the early 1970s has been the persistence of existing conflicts, rather than any substantial increase in the number of new wars (figure IV.2). In the early 1970s, civil conflicts had lasted on average for just two and a half years, by the mid-1980s the duration had lengthened to four years and by the early 1990s it had more than doubled to a peak of over nine years; by the start of the millennium, conflicts were lasting on average about seven years.

Protracted conflicts have been most common in Asia and have involved full-scale civil conflicts as well as secessionist struggles confined to geographical subregions. Africa has also been a region of protracted conflicts, more so since the early 1980s, when long-standing struggles going back in some cases to the post-independence period (the number of conflicts peaked in the late 1960s) were compounded by "ethnic" conflicts (figure IV.3). Over two thirds of countries in sub-Saharan Africa have experienced a civil war episode during the past 25 years. Elsewhere, conflicts that might have been expected to diminish with the end of the cold war have persisted and even intensified, most notably in the Middle East. The experience of civil war had returned also to Europe in the late 1980s, in the aftermath of the break-up of the former Yugoslavia and the dissolution of the Soviet Union, but this phenomenon proved short-lived. Latin American conflicts peaked in the late 1980s, with a heavy concentration in Central America, but have been on a steadily declining trend ever since.

The declining incidence of inter-State wars has coincided with a declining trend in the annual average number of battle-related deaths. As can be seen from figure IV.4, that decline has been associated with four (progressively less intense) peaks at the end of the 1940s, the 1960s, the 1970s and the 1990s, respectively.[2]

The number of deaths on the battlefield has been on a declining trend, but the impact of civil conflicts measured in terms of transnational refugees (including asylum-

---

1   Collier and others (2003) suggest that the decline from the peak of the early 1990s reflects the surge of peace settlements associated with the end of the cold war, possibly owing to a drying up of finance and greater scope for peacekeeping missions; but they also worry that this may have been a one-off drop.

2   The first two peaks were generated by the revolution in China and the Korean War and, later, by the conflicts in South-East Asia, the third peak was generated by rising tensions in the Middle East, and the final peak by an intensification of conflicts in Africa.

Figure IV.1
The trend in armed conflicts since 1945

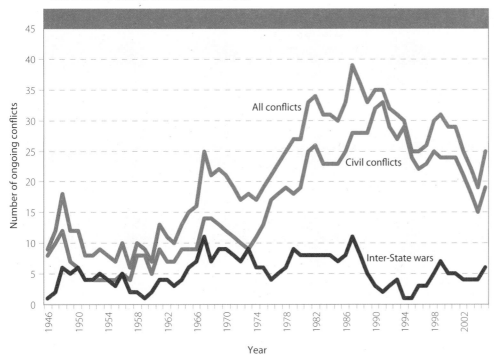

Source: UCDP/PRIO Armed Conflict Dataset (2007). Abbreviations: UCDP, Uppsala Conflict Data Programme at the Department of Peace and Conflict Research, Uppsala University, Uppsala, Sweden; PRIO, International Peace Research Institute, Oslo (Centre for the Study of Civil War).

Figure IV.2
Onsets of armed conflicts versus long-lasting crises, annual numbers, since 1945

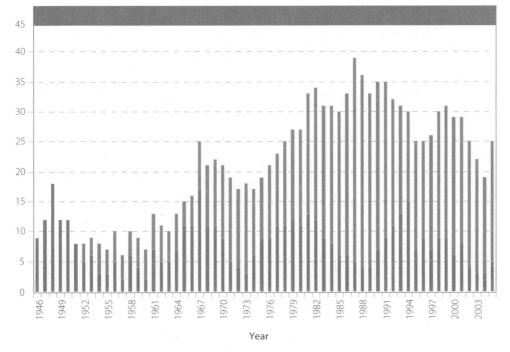

Conflict types:

▨▨▨ Ongoing conflicts having lasted more than five years

▬ Ongoing conflicts having lasted from one to five years

▨▨▨ Onsets

Source: UCDP/PRIO Armed Conflict Dataset (2007). Abbreviations: UCDP, Uppsala Conflict Data Programme at the Department of Peace and Conflict Research, Uppsala University, Uppsala, Sweden; PRIO, International Peace Research Institute, Oslo (Centre for the Study of Civil War).

Figure IV.3
Regional trends in armed conflicts in the post-Second World War period

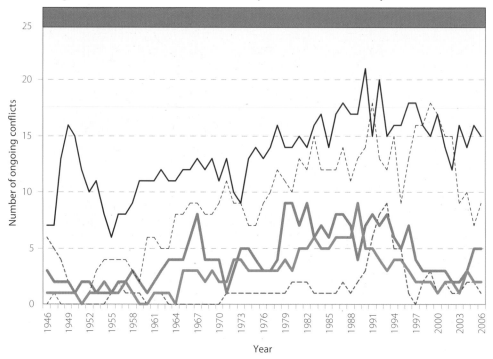

Source: Robert H. Bates and others, "Political Instability Task Force report: phase IV findings (McLean, Virginia, Science Applications International Cooperation, 2003).

Figure IV.4
Battle-related deaths in civil conflicts in the post-Second World War period

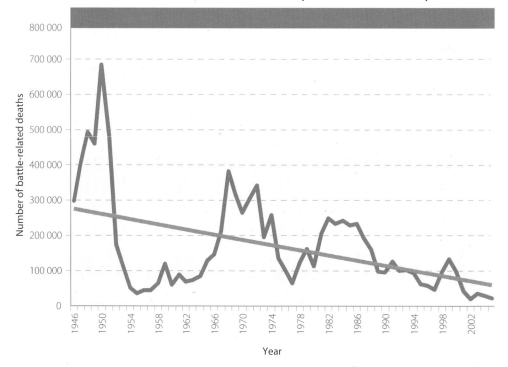

Source: UCDP/PRIO Armed Conflict Dataset (2007).

Abbreviations: UCDP, Uppsala Conflict Data Programme at the Department of Peace and Conflict Research, Uppsala University, Uppsala, Sweden; PRIO, International Peace Research Institute, Oslo (Centre for the Study of Civil War).

seekers) and internally displaced civilians has increased sharply since the early 1980s (see figures IV.5 and IV.6). No less than 24.5 million people were displaced in 2006, half of them in Africa (United Nations High Commissioner for Refugees, 2007).

Figure IV.5
Transnational refugees and internally displaced civilians, 1965-2000

Source: U.S. Committee for Refugees and Immigrants, 2007).

Figure IV.6
Transnational refugees and internally displaced civilians, by region, 1965-2000

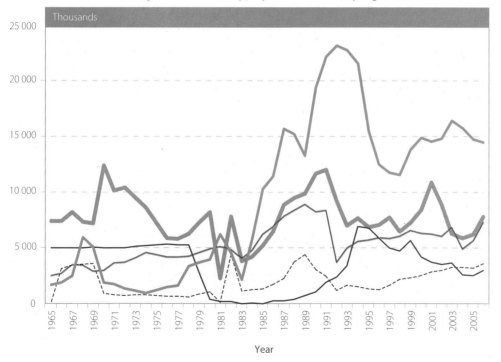

Source: U.S. Committee for Refugees and Immigrants, 2007).

Civil wars undermine social
cohesion, threaten the
norms and institutions
of the State, and create a
sense of fear and distrust
among its citizens

The picture that emerges from a consideration of these broad trends is one of increasingly *protracted* and disruptive civil conflicts, fought principally inside national borders.[3] As a consequence, civil wars are much more likely to generate deep and cumulative divisions that undermine social cohesion, threaten the norms and institutions of the State, and create a sense of fear and distrust among its citizens. These developments, in turn, further exacerbate internal tensions and violence, making such conflicts strongly path-dependent. In fact, a good deal of cross-country evidence indicates that countries that have endured a period of conflict in the past are more likely to experience repeated conflict in the future. According to World Bank estimates, a country with a record of conflict is 2 to 4 times more likely to experience a subsequent war than one without, and the risk may be 10 times for a country that has just ended a war (see Collier and others, 2003).

All civil conflicts are, of course, shaped by local conditions and particular histories (Ballentine and Sherman, 2003). There appears, however, to be a number of broad characteristics, in addition to a prior history of conflict, that make countries more vulnerable to civil wars. On the economic side, these include a low level of income, a slow pace of economic growth and a weakly diversified economic structure. There is also some evidence to suggest that highly unequal societies are more prone to lasting civil conflicts (United Nations, 2005b; Collier, 2007a). The risk of conflict also appears to be lower both in well-established democracies and in autocracies, perhaps because of the presence of greater State capacity. Conversely, that risk is at its highest during transitions to and from democracy, when State capacity is weak, and also in fledgling and imperfect democracies.

For an idea of some of the vulnerabilities noted directly above, it is worthwhile examining a few of the stylized facts regarding conflict across developing countries. Table IV.1 presents 17 countries with very high conflict incidence since 1960,[4] with their average annual long-term growth rates of per capita income, the typology of their economies (according to their resource endowments and principal exports) and their most frequently occurring political regime types.

Manufacturing exporters
are least likely to
experience outright
civil war

The conflicts were predominantly separatist struggles or were, at least, geographically confined. Generally speaking, these conflicts occurred in poor countries with an annual per capita income (in 2000) below $3,000, with poor growth performers experiencing more conflict years. Only five of the countries in table IV.1 had a per capita income growth rate of more than 2 per cent per annum: Colombia, India, Indonesia, Sri Lanka and Uganda. Only four economies (India, Mozambique, the Philippines and Sri Lanka) were not point-sourced (that is to say, economies whose production relies on an intensive exploitation of a few key resources, such as oil or diamonds, located in specific geographical areas) or coffee/cocoa-based economies. This lends some support to the arguments regarding conflict and its association with natural resources across countries. Murshed (2007) points out that only four point-sourced and three coffee/cocoa-based economies have had per capita income growth rates of more than 2 per cent per annum. Botswana and Indonesia are the best-performing point-sourced economies. Furthermore, only three point-sourced countries and four coffee/cocoa-based economies have not de-

---

3   The threat of regional contagion is also present, particularly in cases where borders have been drawn by colonialist expediency, although the spillover effect is not always direct (see Murdoch and Sandler, 2004).

4   We have excluded Israel with 49 years of conflict, as it is a rich country when one excludes the occupied Palestinian territory, as well as Cambodia (36 years) and Yemen (23 years) because of the paucity of economic data. Note also that countries can have more than one year of civil war in any given calendar year if there are several conflicts taking place within the nation simultaneously (as has been the case for Angola, Ethiopia, India, Iraq, Myanmar and the Philippines).

Table IV.1
Growth, polity and economic typology during the years of conflict for selected countries, 1965-2000

Country	Conflict incidence in years	Regime type most frequent	Average annual per capita income growth rate (1965-1999) (percentage)	Economic typology
Myanmar[a]	177	1	1.5	Diffuse, point-sourced
India	104	3	2.4	Manufacturing
Ethiopia	81	1	-0.3	Coffee/cocoa
Philippines	59	1, 2, 3	0.9	Diffuse, manufacturing
Iraq	57	1	-3.5	Point-sourced
Angola	43	1	-2.1	Point-sourced
Iran (Islamic Republic of)	41	1, 2	-1.0	Point-sourced
Algeria	37	1, 2	1.0	Point-sourced
Chad	36	1	-0.6	Point-sourced
Colombia	35	3	2.1	Coffee/cocoa
Indonesia	32	1	4.8	Point-sourced, manufacturing
Guatemala	31	1, 2	0.7	Coffee/cocoa
Sudan	31	1, 2, 3	0.5	Diffuse, point-sourced
South Africa	31	2	0	Point-sourced
Mozambique	27	1	1.3	Diffuse
Uganda	23	1, 2	2.5	Coffee/cocoa
Sri Lanka	22	3	3.0	Diffuse, manufacturing

Source: Murshed and Tadjoeddin (2008).

Note: The code for entries under the heading "Regime type most frequent" is as follows: 1 for autocracies (those countries with an autocracy score below -4); 3 for democracies (those with a democracy score above 4); and 2 for "autocracies", which have both autocratic and democratic characteristics (those with a score between -4 and 4).

a Formerly Burma.

scended into some form of civil war. Diffuse economies (where natural resources tend to be spread across the national economy) have also experienced conflict, including Myanmar and the Philippines in Asia and Mozambique and Zimbabwe in Africa. Eight out of 30 diffuse economies have avoided civil war, which represents a better record than that for point-sourced and coffee/cocoa-based economies. India notwithstanding, manufacturing exporters are least likely to experience outright civil war, perhaps because they tend to generate stronger economic growth and to develop better institutions (Gelb, 1988, Auty, 1990; Gylfason, 2001). Those economies also tend to be more diversified and hence more capable of withstanding commodity price and other external shocks.

According to one recent econometric analysis of 38 conflicts in sub-Saharan Africa between 1981 and 1999, declines in both lagged and current growth as well as an increase in economic shocks were all significant determinants of civil war in that region, albeit with varying degrees of intensity (Miguel, Satyanath and Sergenti, 2004). More recent empirical evidence from Brueckner and Ciccone (2008) also suggests that downturns in the price of international commodities were partly responsible for the high level of societal strife in sub-Saharan Africa between 1980 and 2003, increasing the likelihood of both the incidence and onset of civil wars.

In many of these cases, economic shocks became caught up in a perverse and vicious circle of falling State revenue, declining political authority, expanding illegal and informal activity and further declines in revenue, "a pattern of incentives that could only increase violence" (Putzel, 2004, p. 8). This pattern has been traced by Mkandawire (2002, p. 192) to poorly designed adjustment programmes which exerted enormous pressure on "the African body politic" and in some cases caused an "unraveling of the social pacts" that had provided a degree of national cohesion in the post-colonial era.[5] They have frequently led to increased income inequality, often quite sharp, and a worsening of the level of human development, producing a growing sense of alienation in many sections of the population, and spawning a degree of resentment unseen before, in many cases, in the period following the gaining of their political independence (Keen, 2005).

Food riots and other violent demonstrations against adjustment measures have been extensively recorded (Jeong, 1996), along with episodes of heightened religious and racial tensions (Paris, 2004, p. 167).[6] However, cases of outright collapse into civil war remain relatively small in number. That threat appears greater when the adjustments also serve to hollow out the middle-income sectors (students, professors, civil servants, etc.) which usually form the backbone of a strong social contract. Woodward (1995), for example, has argued that the erosion of economic security among the Yugoslav middle class, in the wake of adjustment programmes during the 1980s, was an important catalyst of subsequent conflict in the Balkan region. This has also been seen as one important aspect of the Rwandan conflict in the early 1990s (Andersen, 2000).

Prominent outliers such as Colombia and India notwithstanding, most conflict-prone countries are neither stable democracies nor autocracies, which lends support to the findings of Hegre and others (2001) that conflict risk is greatest when the political regime is in transition from, say, autocracy to democracy. As illustrated in figure IV.7, those countries characterized by weaker civic societies along the transition tend to give rise to Governments that are incapable of effectively enforcing the law or of creating an environment where parties can negotiate and avoid destructive confrontations.[7] Countries

5 Despite the failure of adjustment programmes in the majority of Latin American countries, a failure analogous to the failure of such programmes in sub-Saharan Africa, these countries have proved to be more resilient with respect to civil strife, although there was a spike in the late 1980s. This might reflect a higher level of ethnic homogeneity, and somewhat more diversified economic structures than in sub-Saharan Africa, as well as a deeper pool of social capital which had been built up over the previous three or four decades (Astorga, Berges and Fitzgerald, 2005) and in some respects allowed social indicators to continue to improve even as the economic downturn began to bite after the debt crisis of the early 1980s (Hirschman, 1995). Moreover, in Latin America, many of the reforms included in the structural adjustment programmes were owned and supported by the economic and political elites. In sub-Saharan Africa, in contrast, the structural adjustment programmes-sponsored economic reforms were generally perceived to have been externally designed and imposed.

6 For a scholarly assessment of these packages, see Easterly (2005). It is worth noting that most of the countries listed in table IV.1 have struggled to establish a strong link between economic growth and human development. Using health and education indicators as a measure of the latter, Ranis and Stewart (2007) classified 69 countries within four performance categories of virtuous, vicious and two categories of lop-sidedness, depending on the balance between growth and human development. They tracked that performance on a decade-by-decade basis for the period from 1960 to 2000. Most of the countries in table IV.1 for which Ranis and Stewart also provided data shifted between vicious and lopsided development patterns for most of that period, though some had seen a deterioration from more virtuous to lopsided performances in the 1980s and 1990s.

7 Quality of governance is measured by the point estimate of the fifth cluster of the World Bank measure (see Kaufman, Kraay and Mastruzzi (2004)), where higher values correspond to better outcomes. The countries in the sample are classified within one of two groups, the "good governance" group and the "bad governance" group, depending on whether they have performed better or worse than the average. This is intended as an indicative exercise rather than an exhaustive one, which would have required a much more nuanced discussion of the governance concept than that based on utilization of these measures.

in this transition also appear likely to experience increased levels of corruption (Rock, 2007). The environment in such countries is particularly vulnerable as regards the capacity of normal conflicts associated with the development process to generate abnormal levels of social discontent which in turn threaten a vicious cycle of rising economic insecurity and political violence.

Figure IV.7
Third-wave Democracies: relationship between the kind of transition to democracy and the quality of economic governance

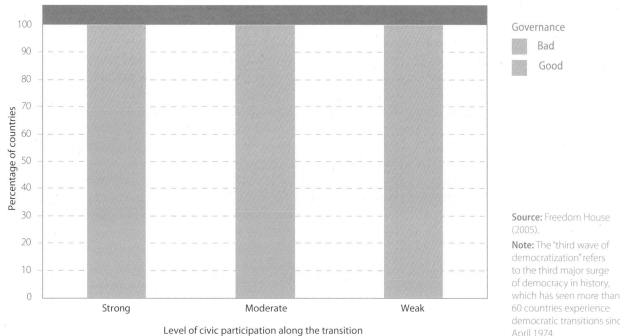

Governance

Bad

Good

Source: Freedom House (2005).

Note: The "third wave of democratization" refers to the third major surge of democracy in history, which has seen more than 60 countries experience democratic transitions since April 1974.

The devastating impact of civil strife on economic security

Direct impact of armed conflict on household welfare

Civil wars are deeply disruptive of economic life. They endanger personal security and civil liberties, seriously damage the environment and create health crises and famines. The World Bank has appropriately described them as exemplifying "development in reverse" (Collier and others, 2003, p. 32). The recent empirical literature has begun to document in more detail the economic costs to the countries involved. Comparatively less attention has been devoted, however, to estimating the effects of violent conflicts on household welfare, owing, to a large extent, to a paucity of useful, reliable data which would enable researchers to explore the relationship between armed conflict and household welfare in a rigorous fashion.[8]

Civil wars are deeply disruptive of economic life

---

8   Significant, albeit infrequent, evidence-based studies have slowly started to surface (see, for instance, recent research programmes at the Households in Conflict Network (HiCN) (www.hicn. org), A Micro Level Analysis of Violent Conflict (MICROCON) (www.microconflict.eu) and the Centre for Research on Inequality, Human Security and Ethnicity (CRISE) (http://www.crise.ox.ac.uk)).

Violent conflicts kill and injure civilians and combatants alike and cause severe psychological damage to those involved in fighting, to those living in war-torn communities and to displaced populations.[9] Armed civil conflicts are also highly correlated with increases in infant and maternal mortality rates, a higher proportion of untreated illnesses, reductions in nutritional levels and so forth, even when such impacts are not directly caused by the initial conflict (World Health Organization, 2002; Stewart, 2004). These effects are often aggravated by a variety of factors, even after the end of the conflict, including the breakdown of health and social services (which increases the risk of transmission of diseases such as HIV/AIDS, particularly in refugee camps), decreased food security (possibly resulting in famines), increased insecurity in living conditions and the loss of social capital and political trust (Grein and others, 2003).

The most visible direct impact of armed civil conflict on household welfare is the destruction of human capital, including the lives of young men in prime working age, though a large number of conflicts have been accompanied by violence against civilians, often children, women and the elderly (see, for example, Dewhirst, 1998; Woodward, 1995). Indeed, some studies suggest that the long-run impact on mortality levels is as great or even greater for these vulnerable groups (Li and Yang, 2005).[10] The death of household members of working age means that the household will be left with severely depleted earning capacity. Often, this is enough to push already vulnerable households (particularly households with widows, orphans and disabled individuals) into extreme forms of poverty, which may well become persistent if the household is unable to replace the lost labour (see Justino and Verwimp, 2006; and Binzel and Brück, 2006).

Injuries, the spread of infectious disease and increases in permanent disabilities caused by violence and conflict may also result in large decreases in household welfare. The fact that households may have to draw on existing savings to pay for medical expenses will impose severe financial burdens on already vulnerable households (Oxfam International, 2007b). Consequences in terms of household labour decisions can also be dramatic and long-lived. In many circumstances, the household may have little choice but to replace dead or injured males with children. Children are then removed from school, which may in turn deplete the household stock of human capital, reducing future earnings (for evidence, see Ghobarah, Huth and Russett, 2003; Alderman, Hoddinott and Kinsey, 2004; de Walque, 2006). This situation is made worse when the health status of children is also badly impaired by the conflict.

Food insecurity is a serious problem in conflict situations

Anti-personnel mines may raise the threat of food insecurity by making much of agricultural land unusable. For this reason, as much as 39 per cent of the land in Cambodia, for instance, could not be used after the conflict there. Similar problems have been experienced by Angola, Mozambique and other African States regarded generally as being "among the most landmined countries in the world" (Date-Bah, 2001, p. 36). Roads, bridges, railways and ports would face similar hazards, making the distribution of agricultural and other goods and services, as well as exports, both difficult and risky.

During violent conflicts, productive assets are stolen, damaged or destroyed through heavy fighting and looting. In Rwanda, during the 1994 genocide the cattle stock decreased by 50 per cent on average (Verpoorten, 2003). In Tajikistan, the homes and live-

---

9   An extensive literature on the psychological aspects of conflict has documented some of these individual responses to conflict-related trauma which include changes in political action and beliefs (see Tedeschi and Calhoun, 1996; Powell and others, 2003).

10   There are also lasting consequences from heightened sexual violence which often accompanies conflicts.

lihoods of about 7 per cent of households were damaged during the civil war which lasted from 1992 to 1998 (Shemyakina, 2006). The Burundi conflict in the 1990s was associated with severe asset depletion (Bundervoet and Verwimp, 2005).

The destruction of assets by armed conflict will also impact significantly on the ability of affected households to recover their economic and social position in post-conflict settings. On the other hand, armed civil conflicts take place because there is something worth fighting for, implying that some groups and individuals will benefit from violence through looting, redistribution of assets during conflict and (for those who "win" the conflict or support winning groups during the conflict) privileged access to market and political institutions. These effects are as important in understanding processes of armed conflict as the more negative ones from fighting, as both types of effects will have a significant bearing on the sustainability of peace during the post-conflict period.

Armed conflicts are typically accompanied by large population movements. Civilian populations are often targets for both armies and rebel groups that are trying to expand their territorial control, weaken population support for opponent groups, increase their own support base and/or add to their resources through looting and appropriation of valuable assets and sites (Kalyvas, 2004). This will lead to flights of populations from areas of more intense fighting or from areas where the outbreak of violence is expected.

The impact on the household is made worse by the accompanying destruction of social networks and the consequent depletion of important elements of the social, economic and political capital of the poor. Refugees from conflict areas and displaced populations are found among those living under the most difficult forms of socio-economic exclusion and deprivation (Chronic Poverty Research Centre, 2005). The literature has distinguished between different types of displaced persons, including those forced to migrate, asylum-seekers and refugees. Asylum-seekers and forced migrants are, to a large extent, young, economically active household members. Traditionally, these have always been the members of society most likely to migrate. In conflict settings, this effect is compounded by the fact they are also the most probable targets for violence and forced recruitment into armies or rebel groups (see Czaika and Kis-Katos, 2007). Other displaced groups such as the elderly, women and children are overrepresented among refugees from conflict areas.

Yet, little is known about the effects of violent conflict as regards the experience of displaced households and individuals, the breakdown of societies and the destruction of social networks. Ibáñez and Moya (2006) have found that forced displacement led to significant asset losses among Colombian households. This limited their ability to generate new sources of income and disrupted risk-sharing mechanisms among affected communities. The displaced Colombian households had to rely on costly strategies in order to maintain minimum consumption levels. Displacement may also affect employment conditions, impeding the recovery of households from welfare losses during the conflict. In the context of the displacement of Bosnians during the 1992-1995 war, Kondylis (2007) has shown that displaced populations were less likely to work in the post-conflict period: during that time, displaced men and women were less likely to be engaged in work by 7 and 5 percentage points, respectively, in relation to the remaining population.

These factors can have important long-term impacts. Displaced populations (as well as demobilized combatants) experiencing social exclusion may provide the basis for opposition to political factions that continue to resort to violence or for criminalization (Van Hear, 2003; Steele, 2007). The demobilization of troops and returned refugees and displaced populations may also create competition for available scarce resources (such as jobs, land, assets, and available services like health care), which may, in turn, create new forms

Armed conflicts are typically accompanied by large population movements

The establishment of sustainable patterns of peace depends largely on the successful integration of displaced populations into society

of exclusion and become sources of renewed instability. Evidence also exists suggesting that productivity levels of returnees tend to be lower than the productivity levels of those who stayed. This may cause difficulties in terms of reintegration of returnees into their original communities (Kondylis, 2005). In contrast, in the context of the situation of young Congolese men in Ugandan refugee camps, Clark (2006; 2007) has shown that conflict may offer the opportunity of access to new forms livelihood strategies, as these young people were no longer bound by pre-conflict traditions. In a pioneering study using a unique data set, Deininger, Ibáñez and Querubin (2004) analysed return patterns of displaced populations during the Colombian conflict. Their results show that the desire to return is very much influenced by particular characteristics of the household and the displacement process. In general, agricultural employers, in the origin and reception sites, families with access to land and households with a dense social network in the origin will be more willing to return to their village. On the other hand, vulnerable families, such as those in households with one parent, with female heads or with large dependency ratios (often found overrepresented among the chronically poor), show a strong preference for settling in the reception site. Households tend to be less willing to return to their place of origin when displacement was caused by distressing events or if security-related fears are still present.

Indirect impact of armed civil conflicts on household welfare

In addition to the direct impacts on household welfare, armed conflicts have substantial effects on the wider economic and political environment in which firms, farms and households operate, including on such intangible factors as trust, tolerance, solidarity, loyalty, etc., all of which are necessary in order for a market economy to flourish. In this respect, civil conflicts can shape the institutional framework well beyond the end of the military operations. There will also be an immediate impact on the welfare and well-being of households via the effects of conflicts on economic performances at the country level, including macroeconomic and growth conditions, as well as the distribution of income and wealth.

Conflict will generally lead to an informalization of economic activity, as well as to the rise of criminal activities, including smuggling

Conflict will generally lead to an informalization of economic activity, as well as to the rise of criminal activities, including smuggling. At the same time, people and assets will look for safer locations, given the threat of theft and the mounting level of economic uncertainty that accompanies the interruption of normal economic activity and transactions. In many cases this will trigger capital flight, both financial and human, on a large scale. The fact that both informalization and capital flight are particularly difficult to measure, even in relatively tranquil times, certainly adds to the difficulty of auditing with any great precision the wider economic impact of conflict. Still, a number of observers have attributed the rise in capital flight from Africa over the past three decades, either directly or indirectly, to prolonged conflict across the region; according to Boyce and Ndikumana (2001), for example, capital flight from 25 African countries between 1970 and 1996 was estimated to have been $193 billion.[11]

Civil conflicts lead to a sharp drop in income and a large increase in absolute poverty

Civil conflict is likely to lead to a drop—possibly a sharp one—in income. On one estimate, the typical conflict of seven years duration reduces incomes by 15 per cent, implying an increase of approximately 30 per cent in the incidence of absolute poverty (Collier, 1999). Ten years after the genocide, it was estimated that the Rwandan gross

---

11   Analogously, Fielding (2003) estimates that the fraction of Israeli capital wealth held outside the country is highly correlated with the intensity of the Palestinian-Israeli conflict. According to the author, this correlation is a consequence of a causal link that runs in both directions: more violence leads to more capital flight, but more capital flight is also a predictor of higher future levels of violence.

domestic product (GDP) was 30 points lower than it would have been if the genocide had not occurred. The level of poverty was well above what it would have been without the conflict: 60 per cent instead of 42-47 per cent for the population as a whole and 42 per cent instead of 26-28 per cent for those living in extreme poverty are struggling to satisfy their basic needs (Panić, 2008). On another recent estimate (Oxfam International, 2007b), Africa lost $18 billion per year between 1990 and 2005 owing to conflict (about 4 per cent of average yearly GDP).

Consumption levels are likely to follow declining incomes, although, in some cases, these can by maintained by running down savings or relying on overseas income sources such as remittances, or aid flows. A stronger and more pronounced trend is a drop in investment, both private and public. This will occur because of the heightened uncertainty and volatility brought on by war, by the likely rise in prices and interest rates, by a drying up in foreign investment, and by the decline and shifting composition of government expenditure. The likely magnitude will depend on the scale and duration of the conflict; however, on one estimate, civil war will cut investment by as much as 0.4 per cent of GDP annually, with private investment most adversely effected (Imai and Weinstein, 2000).

The tradable goods sector is also likely to contract, with exports dropping more quickly than imports, particularly where production is diverted towards domestic markets. However, as regards disruption, this sector will be particularly sensitive to the nature of the conflict and the structure of the economy, as well as the existence of access to foreign credit. Key commodities may even see a boost in production where Governments, in an effort to generate foreign exchange, provide additional protection to the sector. In some circumstances, the regulation of trade may also be altered by the monopolization of distribution channels by different warring factions, with an uncertain impact on output (Humphreys, 2003).

Declining trade volumes will also have a direct bearing on the fiscal position of the State in many countries experiencing conflict, given the reliance of poorer countries on tariff revenues. That position will almost certainly deteriorate with the onset of conflict. Government revenue as a proportion of GDP tends to fall sharply in countries in conflict, though this is not inevitably the case; according to Stewart (2004), for example, revenue in Mozambique rose during its conflicts. However, in almost all cases, revenue will lag expenditure, leading to a widening of budget deficits, increased indebtedness and inflationary pressures. Conflict also produces a general shift in the composition of government spending, as military expenditure is maintained or increases alongside falls in other discretionary expenditures, particularly for social services, but also for public infrastructure.

The longer civil war continues, the more damaging are the economic and social consequences. However, the impact on long-run growth prospects is less clear-cut. Indeed, to the extent that the main impact of war is the destruction of existing physical capital and temporary reduction of human capital accumulation, conventional models predict a rapid burst of post-war growth as the economy returns to its steady-state path. In fact, to the extent that post-war investments consist of more recent and better-quality capital, economic performance could eventually exceed that of the pre-war economy and thus regions that had suffered more from the war might eventually overtake regions that suffered less.[12]

In the absence of clear-cut theoretical predictions, the analysis of the net impact of civil conflicts on economic growth becomes mainly empirical in nature. The recent

Conflict usually leads to falling expenditures on social services

---

[12]   See Gilchrist and Williams (2004), who discuss the cases of Japan and Germany after the Second World War.

literature tends to agree on the overall growth-reducing impact of civil wars. Knight, Loayza and Villanueva (1996), for example, have estimated that civil wars lead, on average, to a permanent income loss of about 2 per cent of GDP. In addition, Collier (1999) has calculated, using cross-sectional evidence for 92 countries between 1960 and 1989, that one year of conflict reduces a country's growth rate by 2.2 per cent (see, also, Hoeffler and Reynal-Querol, 2003). On most assessments, the longer-term growth impact will depend on the structure of the economy—with some sectors (agriculture) being not only more vulnerable to conflict than others (construction, finance, manufacturing) but also less quick to recover—and on the geographical scope of the conflict. Estimates are of course made difficult by not knowing what would have happened in the absence of conflict, given that the onset of conflict often occurs in the context of some degree of economic turmoil.

The persistence of civil conflicts

The conflict trap

The previous sections have suggested that the presence of certain general social, political and economic vulnerabilities make some countries more susceptible to armed civil conflict. Moreover, once the conflict begins, the short- and long-term depletion of social, physical and human capital is bound to intensify existing vulnerabilities and create forms of destitution from which households will find it difficult to recover. This may in turn impact upon the household's activity choices and lead to an increased preference for low-risk, low-return activities, limiting the household's capacity to accumulate assets.

Countries vulnerable to conflict can become trapped in a vicious circle

This suggests that countries vulnerable to conflict can become trapped in the kind of vicious circle familiar from the development literature, whereby interdependent and cumulative processes work to reinforce existing vulnerabilities. In most conflict situations, the likelihood is that such traps will have multiple dimensions. Capital flight, both human and financial, and the shortening of investment horizons in the face of uncertainty, are likely to deepen those traps in countries experiencing conflict. The negative impact of conflict on health, nutritional levels and education, particularly during childhood, can further erode human capital and readily reinforce the structural vulnerabilities behind conflict, as can the rising incidence of hunger and falling nutritional levels which tends to be a marked feature of conflict environments.

Traps can also emerge in factor markets. The return to subsistence agriculture which is fostered by civil strife (Teodosijević, 2003) diminishes the capacity of households to accumulate profits and therefore hinders the release of household labour to off-farm employment. In Latin America, violence has significantly affected the efficiency of farm holdings owing to the disruption of rural labour markets and the limits imposed on the operation of bigger farms.[13] These effects may be further amplified by the displacement of households and the death and injury of household members, which will limit the labour-market participation of vulnerable households (Verwimp, 2005). Ibáñez and Moya (2006) report that, in the case of conflict, it is not necessarily low skill levels that limit labour-market participation, but rather the impossibility of using skills owing to the destruction of social networks and the difficulty of integrating into new environments. Although some of these households could in principle accumulate assets and avoid poverty, they are un-

---

13   See González and Lopez (2007) on Colombia.

able to do so when they become trapped below the minimum asset threshold needed to achieve a viable accumulation strategy (see Barrett and Carter, 2006). In particular, the conflict dynamics that turn different groups against each other often result in changes in and/or the breakdown of social relations and social cohesion and the loss of risk-sharing arrangements. The impact of this on household welfare can be dramatic, as households will no longer be able to rely on community relations in times of difficulty, will not be able to access particular employment or credit arrangements based on informal ties, and may even be excluded from operating under new norms and in new institutional processes.

The capture, abuse and erosion of social capital may help feed conflict. Pinchotti and Verwimp (2007) illustrate this clearly in the case of Rwanda. Armed civil conflict also crucially alters the structure of political institutions, both local and national, as well as their ability to provide public goods and guarantee the establishment of property rights, the rule of law and security. Violent conflicts frequently result from and/or lead to forms of State and governance failure (see, for example, Zartman, 1995; King and Zheng, 2001); but they also offer important opportunities for new classes of local and regional leaders to challenge political powers (see, for example, Reno, 2002). In most conflicts, a number of actors (leaders and members of militias, political elites, businessmen, and petty traders, and also households and various other groups) have tried to improve their position and to exploit the opportunities offered. Changes may arise through the emergence of "ethnic entrepreneurs" who exploit inter-communal distrust as a means of building and consolidating political support (Paris, 2004, pp. 161-162) or through the emergence of local "governance" structures in places where "government" is absent. In such circumstances, there exists what the available literature usually refers to as State "collapse" (Zartman, 1995).

> Civil conflict weakens the authority of the State and its ability to provide public goods and guarantee the establishment of property rights, the rule of law and security

Reappraising the "greed hypothesis"

One explanation for why these traps have tightened in recent years focuses on the choices made by calculating rebel leaders regarding whether to maximize their profits through normal lines of production or through the violent appropriation of existing assets. According to this view, the combination of economic failure and the presence of valuable natural resource rents provide a fertile environment for conflict as well as the financial means by which rebel organizations can maintain their activities.

The greed hypothesis has an intuitive appeal and has been extremely influential in donor policy circles: Civil wars occur in poverty-stricken, failed States that are characterized by venal, corrupt and inept regimes, which underinvest in social protection and the rule of law, and are sustained by a kind of behaviour akin to banditry. This suggests how a conflict trap can persist and also provides an agenda for breaking the circle once the fighting ends, namely, through direct intervention so as to prevent failing States from completely collapsing, combined with measures to strengthen property rights, root out past corrupt practices and bring price incentives back to normal (Collier and others, 2003).

However, the evidence mustered in support of this approach has cast serious doubts on its value for policymakers (box IV.1). Moreover, rational choice theories of conflict rest on dubious assumptions and (an) abstraction from history (Cramer, 2002). As Mkandawire (2002) points out, the desire reflected in such an approach to impose a one-dimensional and static analysis on what is an inherently complex and dynamic problem reveals it to be particularly insensitive to the origins of most rebel movements in Africa; in addition, such an approach provides few clues as to why the structural vulnerabilities

Box IV.1

Greed is not enough

Cross-country regression studies have suggested that dependence on primary commodity exports is highly correlated with the risk of civil war. This has been used to argue that natural resources constitute the "booty" of those propelled by a rational but essentially criminal motivation for civil war (Collier and Hoeffler, 2002; 2004). How empirically valid is the simple version of the greed hypothesis?

The World Bank's own assessment of this work criticized "its lack of an appropriate conceptual and empirical framework … and poor execution" (Banarjee and others, 2006, p. 64). The cross-country studies have been extensively criticized for a lack of robustness in the econometric specification. This includes sample bias weighted towards African countries with particularly unreliable or missing data having a potentially distortionary effect on quantitative analysis (Lemke, 2003). Others have pointed to the lack of consistency in the use of proxy variables (Cramer, 2002), as well as to the narrow meaning assigned to these proxies; according to Nathan (2005), variables that can reflect either greed or grievance dynamics are casually attributed to one or the other. There are also problems with the definition of the key variables. Primary commodities include both agricultural commodities and minerals/fuels, but crucially exclude illegal substances (cocaine and heroin) as well as illegal alluvial diamonds. As illicit gemstones and drugs are arguably more crucial to financing rogue conflict entrepreneurs in a greed-based conflict, their omission is a serious flaw (Lujala, Gleditsch and Gilmore, 2005). In the same vein, Humphreys (2005) argues that, in some instances, it is better to utilize data on oil deposits, rather than oil exports, to study the resource-civil war nexus.

Another set of methodological concerns about the greed research are linked to endogeneity and causality problems. Correlation is not causation, and in any complex system, two-way causality is endemic and correlation might be due to a third variable. These possibilities appear to have been insufficiently investigated. Thus, civil wars might "cause" resource dependence by, for example, undermining investment in the manufacturing sector. There may also be mechanisms that exist between natural resource endowments and the risk of civil war, and that help explain why an abundance of certain types of resources actually lead to war. Two promising explanations among a plethora proposed by Humphreys (2005) include an undiversified economy and weak State capacity. Snyder and Bhavnani (2005) argue that the causal mechanism operating between conflict and lootable resources entails, broadly speaking, a government revenue effect. This requires examining how the State obtains its revenues and determining, for example, whether or not taxing the mineral sector (which may or may not be lootable) is important to the State. Even if a lootable sector exists, it may not be important for State revenues if other revenue sources exist side by side with it. The mode of extraction—whether artisanal or industrial—also matters, since only artisanal techniques render resources lootable.

Finally, of most importance is how Governments spend their revenue: If the State allocates its revenues to social welfare, military expenditure and growth enhancing investment, conflict is less likely than if it appropriates revenues for factional and kleptocratic purposes, as has been the case for Sierra Leone, for example. Prior to 1985, its alluvial diamonds had been extracted in an industrial fashion, rather than by artisans, making them non-lootable; it did not descend into civil war until after that. Dunning (2005) compares Zaire (now the Democratic Republic of the Congo) under Mobutu (1965-1997) to Indonesia under Suharto (1965-1998). In both Indonesia and Zaire, resource flows were volatile. However, Suharto chose diversification and high growth rendering policies, as well as policies aimed at equalization and poverty reduction so as to contain political opposition; Mobutu, on the other hand, did not because he felt that diversification and investment in infrastructure would loosen his grip on power and strengthen political opposition to him based on ethnicity.

around which conflict builds up have deepened in recent years, and depends instead on such deus ex machina-type influences as leadership quality, propaganda and the irrational behaviour of combatants to explain why conflict persists.

Since conflicts typically do involve a large cost in terms of lost and wasted resources, the opposing parties, if operating rationally, should in principle be able to reach an agreement that satisfies all sides. The inability to reach such an agreement is therefore an essential ingredient in explaining the emergence of armed conflicts. Modern States have typically established a collection of rules and institutions for conflict management and dispute resolution, including constitutions, courts and arbitration bodies, as well as fostered a set of values such as compromise and trust to keep the costs of conflict management within bounds. Such institutions channel contests for power through economic competition and political bargaining instead of through armed and disruptive conflicts, give legitimacy to the distribution of the rewards, and generally provide people with the assurance that problems will be resolved without recourse to violence. In most stable societies, these institutions have evolved in response to an array of pressures and tensions, including many that are generated by market forces. As Albert Hirschman (1994) has observed, conflict can be either a "glue" or a "solvent", depending on whether or not society learns to manage it.

Even if large resource rents do constitute a sizeable prize, violent conflict is unlikely to take hold as long as the country has a framework of viable rules, both formal and informal, that govern the allocation of resources and the peaceful settlement of any kind of potential grievances. In the end, the absence of such rules cannot be explained in terms of economic motive or opportunity alone, inasmuch as it involves the complex interplay of political, social and cultural factors.

Violent conflict is unlikely where the country has a framework of viable rules that govern the allocation of resources and the peaceful settlement of grievances

The breakdown of the social contract

A society with a balanced distribution of social and economic resources is generally better able to manage tensions with less risk of resorting to violence and conflict than a society characterized by poverty and sharp socio-economic divisions. In this regard, at least three key demands—legitimacy, order and fairness—must be satisfied if a social system is to endure. *Legitimacy* encompasses the basic justification of a Government's authority over its citizens (or of an international or supranational body over its members), the procedures by which that authority is created and exercised, and, more generally, the manner in which political, social and economic institutions are rooted in and reflect the values and traditions (or, in the words of Adam Smith, the "moral sentiments") of the population or community concerned. The means by which the justification of authority is achieved has obviously changed over time and still varies among communities. The dominant principle governing modern politics is that legitimate authority is based in some way or another on discussion with and approval by those over whom that authority is exercised. Although this democratic principle is core, there is still plenty of scope for variation in the ways in which it is put into practice and, indeed, for disagreement as to how far it should go in emphasizing the concepts of individual liberty and free choice and that of equality.

Order encompasses the agreed laws, rules, social norms and informal conventions that govern the relations among the various members of a society, or the international relations of independent States whether within or outside formal institutions. The structure of incentives embedded in these laws, norms and standards defines the acceptable forms of behaviour throughout the system and provides for sanctions against those that are unacceptable. Clearly, for laws to be observed and for citizens to be able to pursue their legitimate aims, appropriate and effective institutions of enforcement must be in place. Well-ordered and effectual legislative and judicial systems are crucial for meeting this requirement of stability; but, more fundamentally, laws and rules will stand only when a majority of those subject to them agree to observe them voluntarily because it is in their interest to do so, and not because of the threat of being caught breaking them or of being sanctioned for doing so.

Finally, *fairness* encompasses the capacity of the system to meet the needs of all its members, and the recognition that popular support for institutions and the system as a whole will not be sustained if economic performance fails to generate an adequate standard of living, or falls persistently below expectations, or if too many citizens are left behind in poverty or regard the distribution of the benefits and costs of economic change as unjust.

Competitive markets do not spontaneously guarantee the legitimacy, order and fairness they need to function effectively. Moreover, they are sources of social disruption and tend to be caught up in processes of cumulative change which can lead to rising incomes for some but which can just as easily relegate others to low levels of security and well-being. Consequently, their stability depends on an effective social contract and a set of related institutions that help build trust and tolerance, manage conflicts and extend participation in the decision-making process. When such institutions do exist and function well, the legitimacy, order and fairness of social outcomes will be guaranteed. However, problems will arise if social contestation becomes so intense that it cannot be managed by the existing institutions.

A good deal of attention has been given to how collective violent action arises from issues of ethnic identity, whether based on race, language, religion, tribal affiliation or regional differences, and how significant differences among ethnic groups in their access to economic and political resources may mark the beginning of a process that can ultimately lead to the breakdown of the social contract and the explosion of an open conflict. More generally, Stewart (2002) defines differences in groups' access to economic, social and political resources as "horizontal inequalities", in contrast with the traditional "vertical inequality" which ranks individuals in terms of different income classes. Horizontal inequalities are multidimensional. The economic dimension involves more than just income differences and also includes access to employment and to a variety of assets (land, finance); the social dimension encompasses access to services (for example, health care and water) and to social protection (including personal safety); and the political dimension includes access to power at the top (presidency, cabinet) and at lower levels (parliamentary assemblies, local governments) as well as at the levels of bureaucracy, the army and the police. These inequalities are likely to be more dangerous where they are compounded across all three dimensions simultaneously.

Available empirical evidence confirms that horizontal inequalities, in contrast with purely vertical inequalities, can give rise to political mobilization and to levels of dissatisfaction that turn more quickly to violence.[14] The proportion of conflicts attributable to ethnic violence has been steadily increasing in the post-Second World War period (figure IV.8).[15]

14   See for example Mancini (2005) on Indonesia and Murshed and Gates (2005) on Nepal.

15   The Center for Systemic Peace (Severn, Maryland) divides armed conflicts into three categories: Civil intra-State conflicts involving rival political groups; ethnic intra-State conflict involving the State agent and a distinct ethnic group; and international inter-State conflict (usually between two or more States or a distinct polity resisting foreign domination, that is to say, colonialism). The "proportion of incidence" indicates the number of conflicts classified as ethnic divided by the total number of conflicts year by year. The Center for Systemic Peace also proposes an indicator of the destructive impact of each conflict on a scale of 1 (smallest) to 10 (greatest). This indicator, known as "magnitude", reflects multiple factors including State capabilities, area and scope of death and destruction, population displacement, and episode duration. The "proportion of total magnitude" indicates, accordingly, the proportion of the total magnitude (that is to say, the sum of magnitude scores across all the active conflicts) attributable to ethnic conflicts year by year.

Figure IV.8
Incidence and magnitude of ethnic conflicts since 1945

Source: Stewart and Brown (2008).

Violence is likely to intensify when competition and conflict reinforce deep and cumulative social cleavages of an exclusionary kind, and individuals and households are compelled by social pressure or threats to give up normal multiple identities and "take sides". In this regard, researchers have suggested that conflict is often driven by *polarization* rather than by inequality per se. Income polarization, for example, is higher when the gap between rich and poor is greater (resulting in greater alienation between the two) and when within-group inequality is low, resulting in greater identification with others in the same income group (Esteban and Ray, 1999, p. 401). Furthermore, when economic polarization aligns with social polarization, the potential for violent conflict may be multiplied. Duclos, Esteban and Ray (2004) speculate that a "hybrid" measure of polarization, one that combines social and economic considerations, may be a better predictor of social conflict than "pure income" or "pure social" measures confined to distribution measured on a single attribute; and Montalvo and Reynal-Querol (2005) offer empirical support for the proposition that what they term "ethnic polarization"—which attains a maximum when the population is divided into two ethno-linguistic groups of equal size—is a statistically significant predictor of the likelihood of civil war.

When economic polarization aligns with social polarization, the potential for violent conflict may be multiplied

Post-conflict recovery and economic priorities

Post-conflict countries constitute a diverse group. However, a good deal of the policy challenge in all cases centres on three goals: security, reconciliation and development.[16] At first blush, the challenge seems to be one of short-term expediency versus long-term goals. Yet, it goes much deeper.

The most immediate demands once the fighting stops centre on providing essential humanitarian and emergency relief along with measures to rebuild and maintain basic levels of order and physical security

The most immediate demands once the fighting stops centre on providing essential humanitarian and emergency relief to the war-ravaged society along with the creation of an effective and professional military and/or police presence to rebuild and maintain basic levels of order and physical security. According to a paper issued by the Government of the United Kingdom of Great Britain and Northern Ireland, the poor in post-conflict States regard the absence of internal security to be as major a threat to their existence as "hunger, unemployment and lack of drinking water" (quoted in McDonald, 2005, p. 29). However, that threat can be eliminated only with the creation of an impartial, well-trained judiciary and police force that enjoy the trust and respect of the whole community as well as mechanisms for civilian control and oversight of those forces. This will encompass an ongoing process of rebuilding domestic civil authority, and one that, from a fairly early date, will also include an agenda for returning to a more normal pattern of economic activity.

It has often been suggested that the process of post-war reconstruction has to start with reconciliation at the socio-political level (Sardesai and Wam, 2002; McKechnie, 2003). However, it would be a mistake to be too rigid or dogmatic about a correct ordering of the "key priorities"—"social policies first, followed by sectoral policies and macro policies last" (Collier, 2002). Social policies and institutional reforms *are* essential in post-conflict countries. However, they will achieve little in the way of reconstruction, even less in the way of development and, certainly, no lasting peace, without social reconciliation (Panić, 2005). Equally important, there will be little social reconciliation and no sustainable development if inappropriate macroeconomic policies increase economic insecurity and socio-economic inequalities. Given that the cleavages created by economic inequalities will often take much longer to overcome than some of the legal and social barriers to expanded opportunity, lasting economic security will depend on establishing and sustaining a long-run development path which can generate fast and more inclusive growth. This will require the State to establish the rules that allow markets to function by reducing transaction costs, arbitrating commercial disputes, regulating non-competitive practices and market failures and, more generally, managing economic rents.

At the end of civil war, confidence in government is likely to be low and any recovery agenda must be designed with this legitimacy deficit in mind

The public domain is not, of course, synonymous with State activities. Still, many of the most important changes that the post-conflict State needs to achieve entail the provision of public goods. No major economic reconstruction and development effort is possible without the strengthening of State institutions; and without reconstruction and

16   The relation between these has attracted a good deal of attention in the wake of the 2001 terrorist attacks on New York and Washington, D.C., but the issue has had a much longer history. In his criticism of the Treaty of Versailles (1919), Keynes (1919, p. 134) rebuked its authors for not understanding that "the most serious of the problems which claimed their attention was not political or territorial, but financial and economic, and that the perils of the future lay not in frontiers and in sovereignties but in food and coal and transport". President Roosevelt made the connection between economic well-being, internal stability and international peace in his State of the Union Message of 6 January 1941 naming the four freedoms (from fear and want, and of worship and speech). A quarter of a century later, Robert McNamara (1968, p. 149) argued that "(I)n a modernizing society security means development" and that "(w)ithout internal development of at least a minimal degree, order and stability are impossible".

development, future conflicts are unavoidable. However, at the end of civil war, confidence in government is likely to be low and any recovery agenda must be designed with this legitimacy deficit in mind. How that is done will depend not only on the manner of the Government's accession to power, its constitutional accountability, and its willingness and ability to carry out the required institutional changes for the benefit of the whole community, but also on the priorities it sets for itself and its citizens and whether or not these are fulfilled within a reasonable time frame.

State-building and economic reconstruction: policies and priorities

A distinction needs to be made at the outset between the ultimate goals and matters of principle (where generalizations are possible) and the programmes and policies necessary to achieve or implement them (where, invariably, country-specific solutions are required). As no two countries are identical, even when they pursue the same ends the means to achieve these ends will differ, often significantly. Moreover, no matter how successful institutions and policies are in one period of a country's history, they cannot, under dynamic economic and social conditions, be expected to remain so indefinitely. New problems and priorities will require changes in the existing institutions and policies. The "permanence" of permanent peace will be determined in the end by the timing of these changes and their sensitivity to the needs and aspirations of the whole population, not just those of a privileged minority.

The process of economic recovery begins with efforts to consolidate the gains achieved in the early phase of transition from war to peace and progresses through the gradual rehabilitation and reconstruction of the economy and supporting institutions. It continues until the country establishes a development path determined largely by its own priorities and resources. Specific actions to this end will vary from country to country depending on the country's needs, priorities and available resources. However, five basic objectives of economic policy were agreed in the 1940s and enshrined, to a significant extent, in the Charter of the United Nations (Panić, 2005). Countries were urged: to strive to achieve high levels of employment and job security; to maintain adequate levels of growth to sustain the employment levels achieved; to maintain macroeconomic stability through reasonably stable prices and low inflation; to achieve a fair distribution of the gains from economic progress and maintenance of a minimum level of standard of living that would be socially acceptable for everyone in the society; and, finally, to maintain sustainable external balances primarily to preserve the country's economic sovereignty and to support the other goals.

It was the inclusion of these economic goals as a formal part of the post-conflict security agenda that distinguished the period after 1945 from that after 1918 and the speed with which they were achieved was one of its great triumphs. In light of the features discussed earlier, it is likely that today's post-conflict States will take much longer to attain satisfactory levels of economic security.

Markets cannot be expected to attain this situation by themselves. Indeed, the absence of the requisite framework of incentives, rules and regulations needed for markets to work effectively and to make their operation compatible with social stability and cohesion means that they will likely play a subordinate role in the initial recovery period. After a lifetime of studying the experience of countries at different stages of development, Charles Kindleberger (1996, p. 220) concluded that when economies are "moving

The process of economic recovery begins with efforts to consolidate the gains achieved in the early phase of transition from war to peace and progresses through the gradual rehabilitation and reconstruction of the economy and supporting institutions

on trend", a decentralized form of economic organization is likely to be more effective, but in times of crises, when fundamental changes are required, it is centralization and coordination of economic activity that are essential (see, also, Panić 2003, part II).

The enormity of the security challenge facing many post-conflict societies stems from the fact that moving back to trend occurs simultaneously with efforts to repair trust in public institutions and authority, and to re-establish a wider institutional framework of customs and laws not just to enforce contracts and protect private property, but to fashion a view of national interest that is broader and longer-term than that held by those with privileges and positions rooted in the past. Doing so will require an integrated recovery strategy, including an explicit role for distributive policies. Failure to address the grievances that remain in the society after the fighting ends may quickly lead to renewed social and political unrest and a reversion to conflict. This has been the experience of many countries that remain trapped in vicious cycles of conflict, deprivation, despair and persistent insecurity.

Filling the institutional gaps in post-conflict economies will require sufficient time and (policy) space for undertaking appropriate reforms and adjustments in the light of specific circumstances. In this respect, insistence on a correct "sequencing" of reforms runs the risk of substituting political choices shaped by local values and conditions for general technocratic solutions.[17] Rather, what is needed is a period of "democratic gradualism" during which a mixture of political and economic mechanisms can be developed to forge a broad national agenda, to handle a wide variety of adjustment costs that accompany reforms and policy choices in pursuit of economic recovery, and to establish a tradition of conflict management and peaceful dispute resolution [18] The results may not be economically or socially optimal according to some preconceived criteria of efficiency and there is always the danger of capture by specific interests; but these problems can be dealt with, in part, through the accompanying evolution of transparency in the policymaking process, the setting of credible adjustment targets and the design of effective sanctions if those targets are not met.

Creating a national identity that encompasses the community as a whole, and not just a particular social group, private interests, or a particular locality or region, is the responsibility of the central Government. It is also the responsibility of the Government to ensure the character and goals of the State and to make sure that everyone is working towards achieving the same widely desired aims. This is particularly important in fragile States where a lack of social responsibility, and corruption and negligence, tend to be common and therefore not confined to just the organs of the central Government. Even when this is not the case, there is a danger that a highly decentralized effort towards post-war reconstruction and development will concentrate on local issues, ignoring wider problems which affect the country as a whole.

As resources are scarce and unequally distributed between regions and localities, some of these regions and localities will make much greater and faster progress in the reconstruction than others. In the absence of an effective central authority to manage interregional transfer of resources, the disparities could do more than just make it virtually impossible to create a feeling of national unity and purpose, with everyone making a contribution towards achieving the same goals: Horizontal inequalities would sooner or later trigger renewed conflicts, especially if the regions differ significantly in their ethnic,

17   This, of course, holds true for countries that are implementing large-scale reforms even if they have not experienced a prior period of civil conflict (see Rodrik (2004)).

18   On the idea of "democratic gradualism", see Kozul-Wright and Rayment (1997).

racial or religious composition. It would not take long in this case for the disparities to be regarded as the result of a deliberate act carried out by the State, designed to favour interests of certain groups at the expense of others. Delegating a major responsibility for the reconstruction and development to non-governmental and civil society organizations may also hinder the re-establishment of central authority. By their very raison d'être, most of these organizations concentrate on specific issues that promote interests of particular groups only. In other words, they tend to lack the impartiality as well as the resources that are essential to achieving a permanent solution to the problems common to post-conflict countries.[19] For similar reasons, it is impossible to solve one of the most serious problems in all fragile and post-conflict States—that of lawlessness and lack of personal safety—by delegating the task of achieving internal order to private organizations. The reason for such a delegation of responsibility is usually either widespread lack of confidence in the police or the inadequacy of the Government's financial resources for training and running an effective, impartial police force. Such a course of action is unlikely, however, to achieve a satisfactory, lasting solution to the problem of personal security. Inasmuch as it excludes those who cannot afford to pay for private protection, and who in fact constitute the vast majority of people in these countries, private provision of "security" is completely incompatible with one of the most important characteristics of the maintenance of internal order as a public good.

Perhaps the key idea to be kept in mind when thinking about the links between State-building and economic recovery in post-conflict situations is that of "adaptive efficiency", the capacity to develop institutions that provide a stable framework for economic activity but at the same time are flexible enough to provide maximum leeway for policy choices at any given time and in any given situation in response to specific challenges. The emphasis on flexibility and the need to experiment reflects the realities of operating in a fragile and uncertain context typical of post-conflict situations, which certainly rules out the privileging of a set of predetermined policy instruments (be they rapid trade liberalization and privatization, on the one hand, or high tariff protection and nationalization, on the other) to be employed in post-conflict situations regardless of actual circumstances.

This has an important bearing on the choice of economic policies designed to start and sustain the recovery process. Attempts to build a durable peace often require policies, including macroeconomic measures, that fly in the face of conventional wisdom. For example, the International Monetary Fund (IMF), in its pursuit of the objective of macroeconomic stabilization, often requires the borrower Government to cut its budget deficit to target levels before successive instalments of an IMF loan can be disbursed. Whatever the wisdom of these deficit-reduction targets—itself often a matter of debate—in regions emerging from civil war, their feasibility and desirability must be viewed through the distinctive lens of the requirements of establishing a viable peace. To the extent that the usual macroeconomic prescriptions of IMF clash with the aim of building peace, there is a compelling case for rethinking those prescriptions.

The need to rethink conventional wisdom emerged quite clearly in the early years of Cambodia's reconstruction efforts. Instead of cutting public employment, the coalition Government expanded it by about 15 per cent so as to accommodate job seekers who had belonged to the former opposition. In an effort to appease the donors, the Government trimmed the budget deficit by cutting non-salary expenditures. "The outcome was '*remarkable progress*' on the macroeconomic balances", the World Bank (1998a) observed in a subsequent evalua-

---

19   This can be part of a more general problem with non-governmental organizations (see Mkandawire (2007)).

tion, "combined with continued erosion of non-maintained infrastructure and of health, education and other services" (italics in original).

Similar tensions between fiscal austerity and reconstruction efforts arose in post-war Mozambique. Asserting that macroeconomic stabilization was an "absolute prerequisite", IMF pressed in 1995 for spending cuts and a rollback in a scheduled increase in the minimum wage. Fearing that these moves would jeopardize the long-term goals of economic recovery and political stabilization, the ambassadors of the United States of America, the Netherlands and Canada, and the resident representatives of the European Union (EU), the United Nations Development Programme (UNDP), Finland and Switzerland, took the unusual step of writing a joint letter to the Fund to voice their concerns (Hanlon, 1996; Ball and Barnes, 2000).[20] In the end, a compromise was hammered out: the spending cutbacks were slowed and the minimum wage increase remained in place.

Proponents of macroeconomic discipline argue that inflation can undermine political stability as well as economic recovery, and that inflation often hits the real income of the poor especially hard. These are good reasons to control inflation by means of fiscal and monetary discipline. However, policymakers do not face an all-or-nothing choice between hyperinflation and draconian austerity: fiscal and monetary stringency is invariably a matter of degree. It is true that beyond a certain point, profligate spending and soaring deficits could trigger rapid inflation and spark economic distress and political unrest. However, most studies find a fairly high threshold level of inflation, falling anywhere between 20 and 40 per cent depending on regional differences, below which there is little evidence of a negative impact on growth performance (United Nations, forthcoming). In the range between moderate deficits and none at all, however, a trade-off often exists between the size of the deficit on the one hand and the social tensions generated by inadequate public expenditure on the other. Within this intermediate zone, higher government budget deficits can *reduce* social tensions by financing peace-related expenditures (Pastor and Boyce, 2000).

Building fiscal capacity

The speed and sustainability of recovery of the post-conflict economy will depend critically on the availability of resources needed to fund recovery and rehabilitation activities. The size of government revenue relative to gross domestic product (GDP) in war-torn societies typically is far below the average for other countries with similar per capita income.[21] A crucial issue during post-war transitions must therefore be the building of State capacities to raise revenue to provide sustainable funding for new democratic institutions and for expenditures to improve human well-being, strengthen public security, and ease social tensions. Filling the gap will come, in part, through external support, and depending on the overall cost of the conflict, reconstruction and the early stages of economic development will be a responsibility shared between the receiving country and its donors. Ultimate success or failure will be determined, therefore, by how each side discharges its part of that shared responsibility.

Sidebar: Policymakers do not face an all-or-nothing choice between hyperinflation and draconian austerity

Sidebar: A crucial issue during post-war transitions must be the building of State capacities to mobilize domestic revenue to fund new democratic institutions, improve well-being, strengthen security, and ease social tensions

20   Donor statement dated 6 October 1995, cited by Christian Michelsen Institute, *Evaluation of Norwegian Assistance to Peace, Reconciliation and Rehabilitation in Mozambique* (Oslo, Ministry of Foreign Affairs, 1997), p. 49.

21   Gupta and others (2004) find a negative relationship between government revenue and conflict in a sample of low- and middle-income countries. Addison, Chowdhury and Murshed (2004) report that the intensity of conflict, as well as its presence, negatively affects the tax/GDP ratio.

Given that international aid is likely to account for between one third and half of GDP, and in some cases even more, managing it will be among the first economic policy issues for many post-conflict States. Such flows pose a range of technical and institutional challenges for policymakers from developing countries, regardless of whether or not they are in a post-conflict recovery; these concern, inter alia, the divergence between commitments and disbursements, the volatility of aid flows, the costs of tied aid, the lack of donor coordination, etc. (United Nations, 2005a; United Nations Conference on Trade and Development, 2006). Traditionally, donors have preferred to finance specific projects linked to the provision of various public goods. In this respect, routing the major portion of external assistance outside the government gives rise to a "dual public sector": an internal public sector that is funded and managed by the government, and an external public sector that is funded and managed by the donors. In sheer monetary terms, the latter frequently dwarfs the former. This has several adverse consequences. Most evident is the opportunity cost of failing to tap these resources for the purpose of building State capacities to allocate and manage public expenditure. Less obvious, but no less serious, is the "crowding out" effect as professionals are recruited into the external public sector, often at salaries that the government cannot match.[22] Ironically, aid donors then point to lack of capable government personnel as a rationale for continuing to bypass the State.

The fact that the "external" public sector is managed by numerous agencies, each with its own priorities, also poses enormous coordination problems. This leads to the waste of scarce administrative resources, as government ministries cope with the different reporting systems of multiple funding sources. There are no institutional mechanisms, however, that can make donor agencies accountable to the local citizenry.[23]

The problem of the dual public sector would be reduced, however, if donors were to channel a greater share of their resources through the State's budget allocation process instead of bypassing it. Key stumbling blocks to doing so are the problems of combating corruption and need to ensure fiduciary responsibility. Dual-signature systems designed to approve all spending decisions (one from the Government side and the other from an external monitoring agency) have been found to be effective in addressing both the corruption and the accountability concerns. Dual-signature systems have been implemented in the Governance and Economic Management Assistance Programme (GEMAP) in post-conflict Liberia (Dwan and Bailey, 2006) and the Afghanistan Reconstruction Trust Fund, a World Bank-administered account through which donors help to fund the Government's recurrent budget (Scanteam, 2005).

> The problem of the dual public sector would be reduced if donors were to channel a greater share of their resources through the State's budget allocation process

---

22 In the case of Rwanda, for example, Obidegwu (2003, p. 20) observes: "With the flood of international NGOs, relief and development agencies into Rwanda after the genocide, the government service could not compete for the few qualified people available." In the case of Afghanistan, Ghani and others (2007, p. 10), in contrasting the salaries of $1,000 per month paid by donor agencies with the $50 per month paid by the Government, remark: "Unsurprisingly, there has been a brain drain from the managerial tier of the government to menial positions in the aid system. The people might have judged it to be fair had the disparity in wages resulted from a competitive market; however, the problem is that both bureaucracies are funded from the resources of the aid system and the rules for remuneration are arrived at by bureaucratic fiat rather than by open processes of competition."

23 Voicing the last two of these concerns in an analysis of aid to Mozambique, Arndt, Jones and Tarp (2006, p. 1) conclude: "(T)he proliferation of donors and aid-supported interventions has burdened local administration and there is a distinct need to develop government accountability to its own citizens rather than donor agencies."

Experience has shown that aid can "crowd out" domestic revenue mobilization, reducing the incentive for the government to tax its own populace.[24] If, instead, aid is to "crowd in" domestic revenue, conscious efforts need to be made to this end. The international community can support government efforts to mobilize domestic resources in several ways: by linking some of its aid to progress in domestic revenue performance, by helping to curb extra-legal revenue exactions and by providing technical assistance.

On the expenditure side of fiscal policy, it is not unusual for donors to require "counterpart funding" by the Government as a condition for the disbursement of aid to specific projects, a strategy intended to ensure domestic "buy-in" and to counteract fungibility (whereby aid merely frees government money for other uses). On the revenue side, however, conditionality of this type has been rare. It would be a straightforward matter to link certain types of aid—notably budget support—to progress in meeting domestic revenue targets. Such a policy is akin to the provision of "matching grants" by private foundations. In both cases, the aim is to strengthen incentives for aid recipients to seek further resources.[25] The EU conditioned its budget support to the Government of Mozambique in 2002 on increases in domestic revenue. One of the benchmarks in the Afghanistan Compact signed in London in early 2006, which sets out the framework for international assistance to that country over the period 2007-2011, was to increase the revenue/GDP ratio from 4.5per cent in 2004/05 to 8 per cent in 2010/11.[26] Nevertheless, conditionality with respect to revenue mobilization remains the exception, not the rule (for a discussion, see Carnahan, 2007).

Curbing extra-legal revenue exactions is a task located on the cusp between public finance and security. When profits from the exploitation of nominally public resources flow into private pockets, this not only deprives the State of revenues but also often finances quasi-autonomous armed groups that threaten the peace (Le Billon, 2000 and 2008). When local warlords levy "taxes"' on trade, sometimes including trade in narcotics, as in Afghanistan, they undermine the State's monopoly not only on revenue collection but also on the legitimate exercise of force. Curtailing such activities may require substantial international assistance, but it will also often require a much more careful assessment of the links between strategic military objectives and long-term development goals (for further discussion, see Sedra and Middlebrook, 2005; Ahmad, 2006; House of Commons, International Development Committee, 2008).

Fiscal policymaking in post-war settings requires careful attention to questions of priorities, especially when targeting expenditures. In the face of many pressing needs—for spending in areas such as public safety, the demobilization and reintegration

24   Examining evidence from a large sample of developing countries, Gupta and others (2003) found that grant aid, in particular, tends to lower revenue efforts: in countries with high levels of corruption, "the decline in revenues completely offsets the increase in grants". A recent IMF study (Heller, 2005, pp. 4 and 21) cites disincentives to mobilize domestic resources as a "moral hazard" of external aid flows, observing that "some African countries with among the highest ratios of aid to GDP are also those that have stubbornly low tax ratios".

25   Visiting Guatemala in May 1997, a few months after the signing of that country's peace accords, the Managing Director of IMF, Michel Camdessus, took a broad step in this direction when he stated that the Fund's only condition for a standby agreement would be that the Government comply with its peace-accord commitments, including a 50 per cent increase in the revenue-to-GDP ratio. Camdessus warned that without a significant increase in the tax effort, Guatemala could not expect to receive substantial international aid, and noted that IMF would have preferred an even more ambitious revenue target (see Boyce (2002, pp. 41-42) and Jonas (2000, pp. 185-186)).

26   See The Afghanistan Compact, London Conference on Afghanistan, 31 January–1 February 2006, p. 12. Available at http://www.unama-afg.org/news/_londonConf/_docs/06jan30-Afghanistan Compact-Final.pdf. See also document S/2006/90, annex.

of ex-combatants, health, education, and the rehabilitation of economic infrastructure—trade-offs will be unavoidable. The aim must be to maximize returns defined in terms of conventional development indicators and to pursue post-conflict objectives in building a durable peace.

When viewed through a conflict lens, public expenditure cannot be divorced from the issue of grievances rooted in distributional inequalities which are often important drivers of conflict, and which also often worsen during conflict. Two sets of distributional issues are particularly relevant to post-conflict public expenditure decisions. The first is how to incorporate vertical and horizontal equity concerns into spending decisions. The second is how to allocate expenditures across the political landscape so as to bolster incentives for the implementation of accords and the consolidation of peace (box IV.2). Conflict impact assessments could be one means to address both sets of issues. These are analogous to environmental impact assessments, first introduced in the 1970s, with the difference that here the concern is the social and political environment rather than the natural environment. Just as environmental impact assessment aims to incorporate "negative externalities" of pollution and natural resource depletion into expenditure policies, so conflict impact assessment aims to incorporate the "negative externalities" of social tensions and violent conflict. Yet efforts to incorporate distributional considerations into expenditure decisions in post-conflict countries are still at a very early stage of development.[27] Information on vertical inequality—the distribution of benefits across the poor-to-rich spectrum—is sometimes collected and sometimes used as an input into policymaking. In many cases, however, even such basic data are not available. In the case of horizontal equity—distribution across regions and groups defined on the basis of race, ethnicity, language or religion—the paucity of information is even more severe. At best, conflict impact assessment today stands roughly where environmental impact assessment stood three decades ago—its importance is accepted in principle, but it has a long way to go in terms of developing the tools and capacities for implementation in practice.

The phenomena of between-group alienation and within-group identification also have implications for the role of "social capital" in the dynamics of conflict and peace-building. Social capital—trust, norms and networks that facilitate coordination and cooperation—is often regarded as an entirely wholesome and beneficial entity; but it can also have a "dark side", insofar as it enables some groups to cooperate more effectively to the detriment of others. During war-to-peace transitions, therefore, an important aim of public expenditure, and of public policies more generally, is not simply to build generic social capital but rather to build specifically those types of social capital that reduce inter-group alienation. In some cases, trade unions can serve as important arenas for cooperation across ethnic and religious cleavages (Kanbur, 2007); hence, reducing the power of trade unions to advance efficiency gains, itself a doubtful proposition, could have particularly damaging longer-term consequences in terms of rising insecurity and group tensions. Other mechanisms, such as cooperatives and marketing boards, can play a similar role in rural economies.

Distributional impacts also need to be considered on the revenue side of fiscal policy in post-conflict countries. The primary revenue goal of post-war government authorities, and of the international agencies that seek to assist them, has been to increase the volume of collections; the secondary goal has been to do so as "efficiently" as possible. Neglect of the distributional impacts of taxation, however, can subvert both of these goals.

The starting point for any effort to address this lacuna must be careful documentation of the distributional incidence of revenue instruments both vertically and

Distributional issues are particularly relevant to post-conflict public expenditure decisions

---

27   For an assessment, see Goodhand (2006).

Box IV.2

Peace conditionality

A key issue in mobilizing external support revolves around the question of the conditionalities attached to aid, understood broadly as "the means by which one offers support and attempts to influence the policies of another in order to secure compliance with a programme of measures" (Buira, 2003, p. 3). Aid pledged to post-conflict countries will be conditional from its inception, in the sense that maintaining peace is necessary for unlocking the pledges. Subsequent aid disbursements are inherently conditional, too, insofar as resumption of violence would trigger suspension of aid, and failure to make progress towards building peace would jeopardize future aid commitments; but in addition, a good deal of aid is still conditional in the sense that it is extended with the explicit aim of shifting policymaking in recipient countries towards more market-friendly development strategies. The record in terms of both implementation and achievements has been a poor one, and crafting lending along such lines is particularly inappropriate for post-conflict countries.

There is a growing consensus that conditionality must not go beyond factors directly affecting the objectives of the programme being financed and that countries must have at their disposal a range of policy options for carrying out reforms and adjustment. This is particularly germane to post-conflict countries where good policies and State capacities to implement them tend to be in short supply. On some assessments, conditionalities might still be used to reduce social tensions, induce conflict resolution and encourage the implementation of peace accords. In practice, however, reorienting lending practices towards these ends has been the exception rather than the rule.

Peace conditionality essentially seeks to calibrate the flow of support for the peace process by tying specific aid agreements to specific steps towards building peace. The term was coined in a study that suggested that in post-conflict settings, following a negotiated peace accord, donors can and should tie reconstruction and development aid to the concrete steps to be taken to implement the accord and consolidate the peace (Boyce, 2005). In the case of El Salvador, the Government's failure to implement key aspects of the 1992 peace accord—including the provision of adequate funds for high-priority peace programmes, such as the land transfer programme for ex-combatants and the creation of a national civilian police force—jeopardized the peace process. Hence, the study recommended that the international financial institutions should apply peace conditionality to encourage the Government to mobilize domestic resources to fulfil its commitments.

Peace conditionality can be applied to reconstruction and development aid, but most observers agree that, for both ethical and practical reasons, it should not be applied to humanitarian assistance. Ethically, it would be untenable to punish vulnerable people for the sins of their leaders; and practically, the leaders may not be terribly sensitive to humanitarian needs. Since conditionality usually involves specific aid agreements rather than across-the-board cut-offs, there is room for flexibility in deciding which types of aid will carry which conditions. A starting point for the application of conditionality would be those types of aid that are most valued by political leaders and are least crucial for the survival of at-risk populations.

The application of peace conditionality to fiscal policy does not require a great stretch for institutions like IMF and the World Bank, which have a long history of applying conditionality to macroeconomic stabilization and economic reform programmes. In the fiscal arena, peace conditionality simply involves a reorientation of objectives towards the goal of building peace. In some cases, this may mean relaxing budget deficit targets so as to permit Governments to finance high-priority peace programmes. In other cases, it means paying more attention to the composition of public expenditures, the level of tax revenues, and the distributional impacts of expenditure and taxation.

Peace conditionality can be applied at the local level, too. In its "Open Cities" programme in Bosnia and Herzegovina, for example, the Office of the United Nations High Commissioner for Refugees allocated reconstruction aid to municipalities that demonstrated a commitment to the right of refugees and internally displaced persons to return to their homes. The aim had been to use aid to reward local authorities who sought to implement the General Framework Agreement for Peace in Bosnia and Herzegovina, and the annexes thereto, initialled at Dayton, Ohio, on 21 November 1995 (Dayton accord),[a] to penalize those who obstructed implementation, and to encourage vacillators to get off the fence.

a See document A/50/790-S/1995/999. See *Official Records of the Security Council, Fiftieth Year, Supplement for October, November and December 1995*, document S/1995/999.

horizontally. Collecting the necessary data will be a non-trivial task, for today there is a paucity of such information even in "normal" developing countries, let alone in war-torn societies.[28] Technical assistance from the international community could play a valuable role in filling this information gap. Documentation is only the first step. The second is to incorporate this information into policymaking. In choosing the mix of revenue instruments—the balance among tariffs, value-added taxes and income taxes, for example—their distributional incidence must be considered alongside their revenue potential, administrative feasibility, and efficiency effects. One option that would be likely to receive much more attention, once revenue is seen through the distributional lens, is luxury taxation. Taxes on items such as private automobiles and private aircraft can combine the attractions of ease of administration, distributional progressivity, and substantial revenue. Remarkably, these rarely feature in discussions of revenue policies.

Information on the distributional impacts of revenue instruments, and on the ways that government policies are taking these into account, should be disseminated widely to the public, so as to guard against misperceptions and facilitate compliance by legitimizing the policies. The importance of this was demonstrated vividly in Guatemala, where the peace accords set explicit targets for increasing Government revenue and social expenditure. To this end, the first post-conflict Government attempted to increase the tax on large property owners. This effort was scuttled, however, in the face of protests not only from estate owners but also from small-scale indigenous farmers who thought that the tax would burden them (Rodas-Martini, 2007, p. 90; Jonas, 2000, pp. 171-172). The lesson is clear: successful revenue policymaking cannot be a purely technocratic preserve but must be part and parcel of the process of learning how to handle conflicting interests and trade-offs.

How external resources are spent today often has implications for how domestic resources must be spent tomorrow. This is true both for recurrent expenditures, including salaries, and for capital expenditures that will require spending for operation and maintenance in future years. Hence, there is an evident need to think about the long-term fiscal implications of current decisions. In the aftermath of war, attention to pressing short-term needs is perfectly natural, and perfectly valid; but this does not imply that the future consequences of today's decisions can or should be shunted aside for others to handle later. Although much can be done to enhance domestic revenue capacities, prudence demands recognition that budget constraints will always be a fact of life. In the building of new government institutions and infrastructure, this reality must be borne in mind. It would be a mistake to rely on a transitory flush of external funds to create structures that are not fiscally sustainable. Past experience suggests that this is often ignored in post-conflict reconstruction activities, particularly with respect to total security expenditures which often far exceed forecast domestic revenue (World Bank, 2005a, p. 47). Capital investments with high operation and maintenance costs can also generate fiscal burdens down the road. "Donor-driven investments in public hospitals are sometimes referred to as 'Trojan horses'", notes a recent World Bank report (2005b, p. 52), "because of their large operating costs which crowd resources out of priority areas such as the basic package of health services".

Closely related to this problem is the bias of many aid-funded projects in favour of excessive reliance on imports. In deciding on the extent to which the goods and services purchased for relief, recovery and reconstruction should be imported, rather than procured locally, donors face another tension-laden choice between short-run expediency and

28 For a review of the rather sparse literature on the distributional impacts of taxation in developing countries, see Gemmell and Morrissey (2005).

long-run capacity-building—the capacity in this case being in the private sector. Again, there are undoubtedly cases where the former trumps the latter: those, for example, where local sourcing would require large investments with long gestation periods; but there are also cases where local procurement could do more to stimulate economic recovery, and perhaps enable money to be saved in the process. [29]

Household-level reconstruction policies

From an early stage, policies aimed at promoting sustainable peace structures must address seriously the breakdown of households and communities caused by armed conflicts. In particular, displaced populations and demobilized soldiers left without outside social and economic options are likely to turn into a group of people with little to gain from a return to peace. Unless their conditions are improved noticeably, this can well undermine attempts for sustainable conflict resolution (Sandler and Enders, 2004).

> Cash payments can act as an "inducement" to lay down weapons and as an interim measure to ease the return to the civilian community and reduce the likelihood of rearming

One issue of particular importance in this respect is the reintegration of young people who oftentimes form the backbone of fighting units. Although wide attention has been given to the thorny issue of child soldiers, less attention has been paid to the role of young people as political actors in the post-conflict period (Clark, 2007). Various programmes have been designed to facilitate the disarmament of these ex-combatants, the demobilization of their former fighting units and their reintegration into the social, economic and political life of civilian communities (DDR). While mainly in-kind assistance has been adopted in the past, in the last decade the use of cash transfers has become increasingly widespread (Isima, 2004). Despite the controversies that surround the ethical case to be made for cash and, indeed, any form of assistance aimed exclusively at ex-combatants (Archibald and Richards, 2002), cash payments have been regarded by practitioners and students as potentially more reliable both as an "inducement" to lay down weapons and as an interim measure to ease the return to the civilian community and reduce the likelihood of rearming (Tanner, 1996; Berdal, 1996; Keener and others, 1993). The potential benefits of using cash in disarmament, demobilization and reintegration are much the same as those that obtain in the context of natural disasters, as discussed in chapter III, and perhaps those benefits may even be greater, given the poor infrastructure and institutional capacity in post-conflict environments. Lastly, cash payments are seen as boosting local institutional capacity-building, for example, by encouraging local banks to manage large amounts of money (Knight, 2001). The specific design of disarmament, demobilization and reintegration programmes is critical, however, in determining whether or not cash payments will speed up and reinforce the ongoing peacebuilding process, rather than trigger community resentment, corruption or cross-border arms movements (Willibald, 2006).

> Post-conflict policies must create mechanisms to support those that suffered the greatest welfare losses

Post-conflict policies must also create mechanisms to support those that suffered the greatest welfare losses, revive sustainable income-generation processes, strengthen property rights and regulate (and, in many circumstances, rebuild) credit and insurance markets. Well-defined property rights influence significantly the potential for economic growth in any given country through investment incentives (resulting from larger certainty of future returns to capital and labour), increased credit market access and in-

---

29   The supposed efficiency advantages of foreign sourcing can be illusory. In respect of Afghanistan, for example, where United States Agency for International Development funds for rebuilding schools and health clinics were routed through a New Jersey-based private contractor, press reports revealed inordinate delays and shoddy construction, and, in the words of one Agency official, "extraordinary costs" (Stephens and Ottaway, 2005; see, also, Rohde and Gall, 2005).

creased land productivity (see Deininger, 2003). However, the role of property rights in both the onset of armed conflict and in the post-conflict period is less well understood. Strengthening property rights is not likely to be a linear process which results inevitably in lower levels of conflict (Velásquez, 2007). In a recent study, Butler and Gates (2007) show that simply increasing property rights without addressing equity issues can in fact increase the level of conflict in society, since it may add to existing grievances. Successful efforts to strengthen property rights in post-conflict settings must comply with issues of fairness and equity in order to address biases that either exist or may arise through the granting of property titles (for instance, through granting land titles to small farmers who work the land but do not hold formal titles). This finding has significant implications for international organizations and peace treaties that encourage State governments to focus on strengthening property rights institutions without addressing central issues of equity, fairness and social justice (ibid.).

In addition to the issue of property rights, recovery programmes must also address the challenge of rebuilding credit and other financial markets, as one possible means of lifting households affected by armed conflict out of potential poverty traps and of averting further marginalization of excluded groups. Microfinance services, including savings, credit and insurance facilities, have been used in specific circumstances to address the issue of the economic security of households in the post-conflict period, support the return to farming of rural populations that may not have access to the formal financial sector (which may itself have been destroyed by the conflict) and aid the reconstruction of key financial institutions and capital and insurance markets at the community level. Venkatachalam (2006) offers evidence for the success of these policies in the period after the civil war in Tajikistan. Yet, while household-level post-conflict policies must carefully consider the role that this and other financial instruments can play in reconstructing livelihoods and spurring economic activity, these instruments should not be seen as a substitute for the larger set of elements needed to make up a coherent development strategy in insecure and fragile economies (see chap. V).

A related mechanism which might also be employed in some countries is that involving remittances. Remittances can play a crucial role in rebuilding credit and other financial markets. The international community has paid enormous attention to limiting international income transfers in order to limit the funding of armed groups or terrorist groups by diasporas (see Lindley, 2007, on Somalia). However, income or in-kind transfers from migrant, refugee or asylum-seeking populations may play a significant role in helping populations in post-conflict settings to rebuild their livelihoods and recover their pre-war consumption levels, as well as move out of poverty traps (see chap. V).

Aid effectiveness in post-conflict countries: lessons from the Marshall Plan

Civil wars do more than inflict heavy human and material costs. They also diminish the capacity of a country to deal effectively with their underlying causes, thereby increasing the risk of future, even more costly and debilitating, conflicts. What is more, the longer they persist the greater the danger that they will destabilize, and even spill over into, other States, making whole regions vulnerable in the process to inter-communal divisions, violence and wars. This makes the objectives of foreign aid and the conditions under which it is provided and implemented in post-conflict countries of critical importance because of their effect on the distribution of gains from any improvements in economic performance that external assistance makes possible. Indeed, as was made clear in the previous section, particularly in the initial stages of recovery, managing external assistance is difficult to distinguish from implementing the normal domestic policy agenda.

Still, such foreign aid will do little to confront the underlying causes of conflict without the presence of an institutional framework with the responsibility and capacity to reduce inequalities to the levels that are generally regarded as legitimate and fair. Attempts to transplant that framework from one environment to another are unlikely to be successful if they ignore local conditions and strangle the process of trial and error that is the hallmark of successful recovery episodes. As sustainable, permanent peace is the most important goal that foreign aid can help post-conflict countries achieve, the effectiveness of all forms of external assistance has to be judged by how far they contribute towards achieving that overriding objective.

It is particularly important that donors listen to the needs of local representatives and their ideas about what can be done to address them

It is particularly important that, instead of imposing their own institutional models and policy preferences on the receiving countries, the donors help them utilize "local knowledge and perceptions and listen to the needs that are articulated by conflict-affected countries and their ideas abut what can be done to address them" (United Nations, 2004). They should also assist the countries in "building on the capacities that exist" rather than try to duplicate "or displace locally developed initiatives" (ibid.). To ensure that all these conditions are met, it is essential that progress on each be monitored carefully and fully discussed among the various stakeholders, including those from the private sector (box IV.3). Given the past record in this area, the responsibility for monitoring could be assigned to independent assessors working for or on behalf of international organizations not directly involved in providing external assistance to the country concerned (United Nations Conference on Trade and Development, 2006).

The Marshall Plan is a model that can still be employed by the international community

Recognizing the need for a framework of organizing principles intended to ensure that aid is used more effectively and to encourage policymakers to forge a new kind of social contract in post-conflict economies, many observers continue to see the Marshall Plan as a model that can still be employed by the international community.[30] When United States Secretary of State George Marshall made his famous speech at Harvard on 5 June 1947, the economic and political outlook for Europe was far from encouraging. The post-war recovery in output appeared to have stalled and there were fears of rising social unrest and of communist parties' winning elections in several countries. Marshall stated explicitly that, uppermost in his mind, was the economic dimension of security: "Our policy is directed against hunger, poverty, desperation and chaos … so as to permit the emergence of political and social conditions in which free institutions can exist." Marshall clearly viewed insecurity as a possible incubator of conflict and considered that free institutions would emerge from "economic health", not the other way round. When critics object to proposals for "new" Marshall Plans for certain countries on the grounds that they are not democracies or do not possess market economies, they forget that the Marshall Aid was not so demanding: Italy and West Germany adopted democratic institutions only in 1948 and 1949, respectively, and in Italy, many of their provisions were ignored as part of the strategy to keep the communists out of power. Although most of the institutions of a market economy did not have to be built from scratch, the various European economies were highly regulated and subject to direct controls for the best part of a decade; and with large sections of the population still suffering considerable privation, quick fixes and shock therapy for a return to "normal" market conditions were considered neither economically feasible nor politically acceptable.

---

30   See also Panić (1992); Kozul-Wright and Rayment (2007, chap. 7).

Box IV.3

Monitoring aid effectiveness

The need for careful monitoring of aid and of the way that it is organized will depend also on who is providing it and how. An important problem with bilateral assistance, for example, concerns the fact that it may be used in support of special interests in either receiving or donor countries. If that is the case, those providing the aid are likely to give control over its implementation to individuals and groups who support their aims. Bilateral aid needs, therefore, to be monitored carefully by independent assessors.

The advantage of multilateral aid, apart from avoiding multiplication of effort and the waste that it causes, is that it is better positioned to induce collective action among donors. Nevertheless, with many donors and the risk of major differences in their motives for providing assistance, multilateral aid may also require a more careful monitoring than bilateral aid and an independent assessment of its effectiveness. Special monitoring arrangements and close cooperation among the receiving country, donor Governments and international aid agencies will also be needed in those economic and social activities in which transnational corporations or non-governmental organizations play an important role, especially if significant exploitation of natural resources is involved.

The so-called natural resource curse and Dutch disease have received considerable attention, often for the wrong reasons. Generally, misunderstandings of the experience of a few countries have led some analysts to a conclusion that seems to imply that the worst fate that can befall a country is to be rich in natural resources. If this were the case, Scandinavian countries, Canada and the United States of America, to give a few examples, would still be poor, conflict-ridden States instead of members of that exclusive club comprising countries with the most advanced economies in the world. The "curse" and the "disease" refer, in fact, to something quite different: the result of institutional failures, wrong policies, corrupt Governments and/or the inability of small or poor countries to defend their interests against powerful, predatory foreign corporations and their Governments. It would not take long for a more equitable sharing of the revenues between the two sides to dispel the curse. However, this would require something that has proved far from easy to achieve, namely, an agreement between Governments of post-conflict countries and foreign corporations to avoid the short-term approach to the exploitation of natural resources which ignores long-term development of the countries concerned and the consequences of its failure. An effective agreement of this kind is possible only if private corporations, their Governments and Governments of post-conflict countries regard peace as a global public good in which all of them have an important stake.

The basis for full cooperation between Governments of the corporations' countries of origin and Governments of developing countries already exists in international agreements and national laws. Cooperation is therefore possible provided, of course, that the Governments observe and enforce those instruments. The Antiterrorism, Crime and Security Act of 2001, for example, gives courts of the United Kingdom of Great Britain and Northern Ireland the power to prosecute "UK-registered companies and UK nationals … in the UK for any act of bribery or corruption committed overseas" (McDonald, 2005, p. 15). In 1999, members of the Organization for Economic Cooperation and Development had agreed that "they would all legislate to make bribery of a public official in a foreign country an offence" (Collier, 2007b, p. 137). As a number of well-publicized cases show (ibid., chap. 9), adverse publicity is another powerful weapon in making transnational corporations and banks act in such a way as to promote peace rather than cause conflicts. To be effective, however, the publicity must also include mention of the suppliers of these corporations; otherwise, there is nothing to prevent transnationals from outsourcing, as many of them do, the worst aspects of irresponsible, exploitative behaviour to small firms in post-conflict countries and disclaiming any responsibility for, or even knowledge of, the actions of those firms.

With this background in mind, there are at least seven major virtues of the Marshall Plan which provide useful lessons for rebalancing the policy environment facing countries that are emerging from conflict today. First, it set a time frame for the post-war adjustment process that was more realistic than that envisaged by the United States Treasury or by an IMF programme. Instead of thinking in terms of 18 months, the timescale was changed to from 4 to 5 years.[31] Second, Marshall made it clear that there was to be an end to piecemeal assistance which had suffered from a lack of coordination and had less impact than expected in stimulating economic recovery. A key requirement, therefore, was that each State recipient of aid had to produce a four-year outline plan for recovery, setting out targets for the main economic variables and providing an account of how the Government intended to achieve its objectives. Third, Marshall insisted that these plans, together with estimates of the need for assistance, had to be drawn up by the Western Europeans themselves: "It would be neither fitting nor efficacious for (the United States) to undertake to draw up unilaterally a program designed to place Europe on its feet economically. This is the business of Europeans ... The role of this country should consist of friendly aid in the drafting of a European program and of later support of such a program..." Marshall thus acknowledged the existence of national sensibilities, admitted that the recipient countries were better informed about the facts of their situation than outsiders, and generally showed a deference towards European traditions and preferences that has subsequently been conspicuously absent from the attitudes of the rich countries and international institutions towards the rest of the world.

A fourth feature of the Marshall Plan was the release of aid in tranches that depended on the countries' intermediate targets' being met. The removal of the recovery programme from the Bretton Woods framework did not therefore imply an escape from conditionality, but only that the Marshall Plan conditions were different and more flexible and were to be met over a longer period than that allowed by IMF rules.[32] Fifth, the Marshall Plan acknowledged that the damage to European productive capacities and the great disparity in economic strength between the United States and Europe meant that rapid liberalization of trade and payments would quickly lead to European payments-related crises. It was accepted that Europe would gradually dismantle a wide range of direct and indirect controls on its trade between 1950 and 1958 according to an agreed timetable within the framework of the European Payments Union. This gradual liberalization of trade provided European producers with protection against competition from the United States and gave them time for, and encouragement in, the reconstruction of enterprises capable of producing competitive substitutes for dollar imports. At the same time, the United States agreed to a more rapid improvement in access to its own market for European exports, a policy of asymmetric liberalization which stands in marked contrast to the present approach of EU and the United States which insists on a rapid opening of developing countries' markets and on restricting the range of policy options available for their development.[33]

Sixth, effective leadership requires generosity. Marshall Aid consisted largely of grants and the small proportion of loans contained a large element of grant: they were usually offered for 35 years at 2.5 per cent interest with repayments starting in 1953. It is worth emphasizing this structuring of financial help at a time when the terms "aid" and "assistance" are used loosely to cover everything from gifts to loans at market (or above-market)

31   For a discussion of the consequences of the premature withdrawal of aid in contemporary post-conflict situations, see World Bank (2008).

32   Conditionality was important not simply to ensure that the aid was being used effectively but also to gain, and sustain, the support of the United States taxpayer.

33   Another, largely forgotten aspect of American restraint towards the relative economic weakness of Europe in 1947 was a moratorium on foreign investment in Germany until monetary equilibrium had been more or less achieved (Kindleberger, 1996). The prospect of United States investors' buying up Mercedes, Siemens and other major companies at derisory prices did not appear to the State Department as a useful contribution to winning the "hearts and minds" of a defeated population and a future ally.

rates of interest. The wisdom of adding to the debts of already heavily indebted economies is highly questionable—all the more so when they are grappling with economic restructuring and institution-building, which is typically the case for countries trying to accelerate their development or to recover from the chaos that normally follows the end of violent conflict. A generous supply of grants, monitored within and conditional on a coherent economic programme along the lines of the Marshall Plan, can be more effective than loans in lifting countries out of a "stagnation trap" where heavy debt-servicing obligations hold back the domestic and foreign investment that could improve the longer-run performance of the economy, including its capacity to service debt. Another advantage of grants is that they are not usually subject to the long and complex negotiations, legal and financial, associated with the provision of loans. This is important inasmuch as one of the lessons of the Marshall Plan is that prompt assistance at the start of a promised programme can help to sustain positive expectations, which most likely will have been raised by politicians, and generate a momentum for change that will stand a chance of becoming self-reinforcing.

Lastly, yet another virtue of the Marshall Plan that is still relevant to attempts to tackle current problems is its insistence that there should be a degree of united and cooperative effort among the Europeans themselves, and that the plans of the 16 recipient countries and the allocation of aid should be coordinated within a regional body. This requirement partly reflected United States foreign-policy objectives with regard to a more integrated Europe, and also provided a structure for cooperation in areas where there are significant externalities, economies of scale and other transboundary issues. The peer review of national programmes provided national policymakers with a regional perspective on their own policies and encouraged a culture of regular contact and cooperation among national bureaucracies which is today taken for granted in Europe.

Focusing on these *principles* of the Marshall Plan can help to provide a coherent framework for coordinating economic recovery and development plans with international assistance. Without the provision of an articulate account of a Government's macroeconomic objectives and their relation to detailed programmes for infrastructure investment, education, health, housing, etc., it is difficult to see how limited supplies of foreign assistance, financial and technical, could be really effective. Official assistance is essentially a form of intervention designed to ease shortages, bottlenecks and other constraints on growth and structural change, but it is difficult to target aid towards the areas where it will be most effective without some idea of priorities and the potential marginal effect of, say, removing one bottleneck before another. Such programmes would also make it easier to provide general, non-project assistance to government budgets or the balance of payments, as was done for a number of European countries under Marshall Aid. Development (even more than reconstruction) programmes essentially deal with deep-rooted structural problems and both fiscal and current-account deficits are usually unavoidable if constructive long-run adjustment is to be achieved.

The provision of financial assistance to deal with long-term imbalances is usually seen by the international financial institutions as offering evidence of a weak commitment to reform and as encouraging a slackening of discipline by postponing necessary adjustment. This was not the view of the Marshall Planners, who regarded such assistance as an investment in social cohesion and structural change and as providing Governments with the breathing space required to bring difficult and often painful policies to success. When such policies threatened to cause social upheaval on a scale that might upset the adjustment process, as was the case in post-war Italy at one point, Marshall Aid was available to cushion the social costs through support to the Government budget.

The wisdom of adding to the debts of already heavily indebted economies is highly questionable

Another major attraction of a Marshall Plan framework is that it can serve an important political function. A multi-year programme of economic and social objectives, presenting their interrelationships and the means to achieve them and demonstrating that they are contingent on outside assistance, effectively sets out the Government's vision of the structure of the society at which it is aiming. That is highly political, and so the proposed programme provides a basis for the democratic discussion and the negotiation between competing views that should take place. This will not always result in what the international financial institutions regard as the "best" policies, but the advantage of democratic processes, as was suggested earlier, is that they generate pressures necessary to correct mistakes: they may achieve the "best" policy more slowly than if they had been driven by autocratic outsiders, but, politically speaking, the slow route may be superior. The creation of a "new Marshall Plan" could thus provide a concrete operational basis for such concepts as "ownership" and "partnership", which otherwise risk degenerating into empty slogans. Moreover, the existence of a coherent national programme with popular support, indicating where outside assistance could be most effective, ipso facto constitutes a powerful and persuasive argument to potential donors for responding to national priorities rather than following their own preferences.

Conclusion

Under stable political and social conditions, the rising threat of economic insecurity can be met through the established channels of political representation, negotiation and bargaining. Where those are weak or absent, the danger exists that insecurity will turn to violence and possibly to civil conflict. The threat arises of a vicious circle of economic insecurity, social cleavage and political collapse, which appears to be more likely in countries that are undergoing economic and political transitions and where tensions and grievances among groups are compounded along multiple lines of exclusion.

Such violence is likely to remain a presence in post-conflict societies as policymakers seek to address security, reconciliation and development challenges. Indeed, once the conflict has ended, the absence of social consensus means that these challenges must be addressed simultaneously and under the threat of a return to violence. This makes the task of the State in post-conflict societies a particularly onerous one, the more so as it seeks to repair its own legitimacy and struggles to mobilize domestic resources to meet the demands that are placed on it.

A crucial issue during post-war transitions will be the building of State capacities to mobilize domestic revenue to provide sustainable funding for new democratic institutions and for expenditures to improve human well-being, strengthen public security, and ease social tensions. Depending on the overall cost of the conflict, reconstruction and the early stages of economic development will be heavily dependent on external resources. Ultimate success or failure will be determined, therefore, by how each side discharges its part of the shared responsibility for recovery. From the recipient side, innovative policy responses to fiscal management will be required. The donors must resist imposing their own institutional and policy preferences on the receiving country. The Marshall Plan remains a relevant set of principles in this regard, and one that helped restore economic security in war-torn European countries. These principles retain their relevance today, even though the security, reconciliation and development challenges are a good deal more demanding than those facing war-torn Europe after 1945.

Chapter V
Poverty, insecurity and development risks

Introduction

Previous chapters have pointed to the growing threat in recent decades of serious downside economic risks facing individuals, communities and countries. Heightened exposure has been associated with financial shocks, natural disasters and social conflicts. Yet the deepening sense of insecurity has had just as much to do with the lack of effective policy responses. The *Survey* associates this failure, in part, with a policy bias built around the misguided idea of a self-regulating market economy. There is a clear and urgent need for a new balance between the market and the public interest along with a more integrated social and economic policy framework which can provide and preserve a secure and stable economic future.

It is also clear from the earlier discussions that exposure to downside risks has not been distributed evenly both across and within countries. The poorest households and communities are particularly vulnerable and all too often their only available response is through short-term coping and survival strategies which tend to increase their exposure to future risks. In many cases, poverty turns what should have been transient shocks or disturbances into chronic insecurity.

The present chapter looks at some of the policy challenges centered around the poverty-insecurity trap in developing countries. The first section examines the institutional conditions that help embed markets in a stable, secure and more inclusive process of development. The gap left when these institutions are weak or missing is a major source of exposure to downside risks. The following section examines the role of the developmental State in filling that gap, which has traditionally been associated with measures to socialize the risks faced by an emerging class of domestic investors in return for their channelling resources towards the industrial sector, as a means of expanding formal employment opportunities and reducing poverty. These measures remain the basic ingredients for alleviating poverty in most developing countries. However, they may not always address the vulnerabilities facing poor households and communities. Accordingly, the next sections will look selectively at some of the mitigation, adaptation, and coping measures that might help achieve a more secure and inclusive growth path. The final section considers whether measures to break the poverty trap in developing countries are best applied universally or when targeted at those most vulnerable.

Poverty often turns transient shocks into chronic levels of insecurity

Markets and social cohesion

In the years following the Second World War, the major achievement of the Western democracies was to avert a resurgence of the waste, despair and violence that had scarred the interwar landscape by promoting economic growth, driven mainly by market forces, combined with full and stable employment and steadily rising wages. Governments set out to improve the efficiency of the market system by correcting failures of markets, especially non-competitive markets, and to accelerate growth by promoting collaboration among enterprises, representatives of organized labour and public agencies in the areas of long-term investment, research and development, education and training, and so on. This approach involved utilization of a new set of policy instruments, which ranged from indicative planning and income policies at one extreme to trade liberalization and tax breaks at the other. Such policies, in combination with Keynesian demand management, laid the basis for what was known at the time as the mixed economy and created what is now, in retrospect, often perceived as a golden age. At the same time, the welfare State consolidated advances in social policy made over the previous half-century. In doing so, it replaced fragmented systems of social protection (which had collapsed in the face of the economic shocks of the 1920s and 1930s) with a more reliable and cohesive system of public services and social insurance built around the idea of universal citizenship. The Universal Declaration of Human Rights[1] set the benchmark by proclaiming:

> Everyone has the right to a standard of living adequate for the health and well-being of himself and of his family, including food, clothing, housing and medical care and necessary social services, and the right to security in the event of unemployment, sickness, disability, widowhood, old age or other lack of livelihood in circumstances beyond his control.[2]

Yet none of the above should be taken to imply that the golden age was free from shocks and stresses, which was clearly not the case, or that there were no State failures.[3] Indeed, mounting fiscal pressures on the welfare State were already apparent in many countries in the 1970s, even as they faced new demands for extended coverage. What is being suggested, however, is that modern capitalist economies are most productive when embedded in a political and social system where the more destructive characteristics of the market are subject to effective constraints.

Markets need to be embedded in appropriate socio-political institutions

Markets, as Adam Smith recognized long ago, are above all social constructs, which need to incorporate various shared norms, habits and values (extending beyond those of self-interest, competition and risk-taking) if they are to be part of an effective economy and stable polity. As suggested in chapter IV, these include legitimacy, order and fairness, which cannot be provided by the market itself. This entails far more than simply claiming that markets are invariably imperfect, whether because of overpowerful economic actors, asymmetric information, externalities and so on. Rather what is implied is that markets are always in some sense managed, most fundamentally by the values and social constraints of the society in which they operate. The "varieties of capitalism" (Hall and Soskice, 2001), both in their evolution over time and at any given period of time, are intertwined with the variegated institutional expression of such different values and constraints.

Markets need to be "governed" and "civilized"

The institutions that must be in place if markets are to emerge and function in an orderly manner include those responsible for granting and protecting property rights and reducing transaction costs. They also include regulatory bodies established to monitor and correct abuses of market power as well as effective coordination mechanisms to stabilize markets, particularly by averting short-run macroeconomic imbalances. At the same time, various institutions are needed to provide support and incentives for long-term growth and innovation in cases where market failures are rife. Together, these institutions constitute the means to "govern markets" in such a way as to foster their creative role and support risk-taking (Wade, 1990).

---

1   General Assembly resolution 217 A (III).

2   Ibid., article 25, para.1.

3   In a recent assessment, Reich (2007) has referred to the "not quite golden age".

However, unleashing the creative potential of markets must be matched by efforts to temper their more destructive impulses which can threaten political stability and social cohesion. The institutions that aim at "civilizing markets", that is to say, at making their operation compatible with social cohesion and political stability, include, first of all, those responsible for guaranteeing such provision of goods and services to all the members of a society as the society considers adequate and, particularly, those institutions that improve social welfare. Redistributive institutions, which aim at modifying the structure of wealth ownership and income so as to raise distribution to levels considered desirable or at least tolerable by society, and bargaining institutions, which aim at reducing the conflicts generated by the normal functioning of markets, provide an additional source of social cohesion. Finally, institutions of voice are needed to strengthen participation in decision-making processes, relating not only to distributive outcomes but also to the functioning and scope of the markets themselves.

Within this wider context of unleashing, governing and civilizing markets, public policies are best understood as stimulating collective action in pursuit of a common interest, rather than as being linked exclusively to the actions of the State. Although the responsibility for leadership often falls on the State, the institutions that may be developed to carry out the public functions outlined above include non-State actors and must take into account not only market failures but also government failures (and those of other forms of collective action). Recognizing these complexities of governance underscores the importance of creating a strong institutional framework—a high institutional density—with active participation of multiple social actors and with adequate accountability. In its absence, the spaces that communities and countries rely on for providing security and stability are likely to be fragile or absent.

The erosion of such spaces appears to have accompanied the deregulation of market forces and the rolling back of the State, whether in developed, developing or transition economies. That process has advanced at differing rates in different countries, although the pace and depth have often been greatest in developing and transition economies (Glyn, 2006; Mkandawire, 2004). Underlying this shift was the belief, infused with considerable optimism, that by getting price incentives right, income gaps (within and across countries) would close and any future adjustments would be smaller and easier to manage. Moreover, the institutional vacuum left by the withdrawal of State welfare guarantees would quickly be filled through an influx of more informed individuals, benefiting from stronger property rights and improved access to market services.

In fact, the record in terms of closing income gaps has, as discussed in previous *World Economic and Social Surveys*, been uneven, and has taken place against the backdrop of a generally slowing global economy (figure V.1). Moreover, the expectation that these forces would generate more stable outcomes has not been supported by the recent record of boom-bust cycles, gyrating asset, currency and commodity prices, and ever larger economic shocks, as discussed in chapter II. Indeed, the process of deregulating markets has brought forth new distortions and biases which are creating new sources of insecurity.

Deregulation of markets and rolling back of the State have aggravated insecurity

The developmental State and social policy

The mixed economy model which had emerged after the Second World War acquired distinct characteristics in developing countries. These were often linked to a politically charged development agenda adopted by newly independent countries under pressure to close the economic and social gaps distinguishing them from those higher up on the de-

Figure V.1
Global per capita growth, 1961-2006

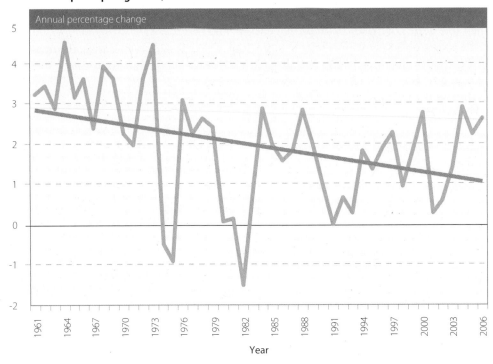

Annual percentage change

Year

Source: World Bank, World Development Indicators.

velopment ladder; but they also tended to be associated with the forging of a very different kind of social contract than had previously existed—one in which a much more prominent place was given to managing industrial development and achieving fast-paced capital formation so as to meet those goals. The historical record suggested that social policy could play a prominent role not only in recasting notions of solidarity and citizenship but also, if properly designed, in catching up with those higher up on the economic ladder.

The experience with finding the right balance of social and economic policies in developing countries for promoting a more inclusive and secure growth path has been mixed. In many cases, the resources needed to extend social protection have lagged too far behind policy pronouncements and intentions, leaving large gaps in quality and coverage. Oftentimes, limited State resources have been captured by special interests with little interest in using social policy as an effective tool for enhancing economic development, let alone for addressing the vulnerabilities of wider constituencies. More recently, a narrow conception of what constitutes good development policy has closed down the search for a more integrated economic and social policy agenda.

In any economy where the market plays a prominent role in managing resources, a large share of income accrues to a small minority of owners of productive assets. The size of that share can and does vary significantly and there is a good deal of ongoing debate about the exact links between inequality and economic growth. However, there is no reason to doubt that the spending behaviour of this minority is a major determinant of growth performance and social stability,[4] inasmuch as it is to the owners of these productive assets that the choice falls of how to spend the profits they generate, that is, how to distribute them among personal consumption, purchasing financial assets abroad or

---

4   See Keynes (1919) for a description of how this fitted into the pre-1914 European social contract.

reinvesting them in existing lines of economic activity, and expanding into new areas of wealth creation.

In this context, investment can provide an important social as well as an economic justification for the concentration of income in the hands of a minority, acting as a kind of social tax on profits that restricts their use for personal consumption. However, the ideal level of investment does not reveal itself automatically. Indeed, the connection between profits and investment can be a particularly difficult one to establish in poorer countries where the investing class is often relatively small and the investment climate particularly risky. Experience has shown that building a strong nexus between profits and investment is one of the hardest challenges facing policymakers in developing countries (United Nations Conference on Trade and Development, 1997). The discussion in chapter II has suggested that the challenge has, if anything, become even harder in recent years.

Success stories have been closely associated with the East Asian experience, where developmental States adopted a series of measures to socialize investment risk and to raise profits above those generated by competitive market forces. The long-term success of these countries rested on the State's forging a social contract in which the nascent entrepreneurial class accepted, in return for State support, some degree of direction with respect to its investment decisions. This was both to ensure expansion of jobs in labour-intensive manufacturing as a means of absorbing unskilled labour (including from the rural sectors) and reducing poverty, and to effect a shift to more technologically demanding activities which were more likely to guarantee rising living standards in the future.

Given the generally more capital-intensive nature of late industrialization, such an approach often required a heavy export bias in policy support (along with managed entry of competitors, both domestic and foreign, into key growth sectors) which allowed employment expansion beyond the limits set by the domestic market (United Nations Conference on Trade and Development, 2003). Similar measures were taken after 1945 in other successful catch-up economies, notably Japan, as well as some of the smaller economies on the European periphery such as Finland, Ireland and Portugal (Vartiainen, 1995; Reinert, 2007).

These successful late industrializing economies all have mixed economic policies featuring various social measures, including the universal provisioning of social services, designed to manage the strains and stresses associated with rapid growth and structural change. Many European countries, for example, introduced flat-rate pensions at a comparatively early stage of their development in response to various political tensions, at a time when those countries had a per capita income and economic structure similar to those of many middle-income developing countries today.[5]

There is no doubt that specific social, political and economic factors play an important role in shaping policy options in the development process. However, developing governmental capacity and institutions for promoting welfare, and the adoption of universal policies for the general level of welfare carry broader relevance. And, it is precisely in contrasting different models of the developmental State that it is possible to see how different social and economic arrangements can lead to similar outcomes (box V.1).

> Profits need to be invested in expanding domestic productive capacity

> East Asian countries succeeded through socializing investment risk

> Late industrializing countries, both in Asia and in Europe, mixed targeted economic policies with social measures

---

5   Many late industrializing European States were ahead of the early starters in terms of social policy, with a clear sequence running from workplace insurance through health and maternity insurance to old age and disability provision and, finally, unemployment insurance and family allowances. For a brief history, see Pierson (2003); for relevant discussions, see also Vartiainen (1995).

Box V.1

Social policies in late industrializing economies

The early roots of Scandinavian social policy, which included establishing and developing social security, health and educational systems, was fostered by a strong and independent farmers movement, and the consequent establishment of peasant political parties during the first two decades of the twentieth century. Compulsory schooling had been introduced as early as 1814 in Denmark and in the 1840s in Sweden and Norway, well before industrialization took off. However, this progress in education proved instrumental in the achievement of rapid industrialization and subsequent economic upgrading, and also provided a strong political base for universal social protection (Hort and Kuhnle, 2000, p. 4).

Still, during the interwar years, Scandinavian countries were still highly rural economies characterized by high levels of inequality, where agriculture accounted for between one third and one half of the active labour force (Vartiainen, 1995, p. 158). In Norway, for example, as late as the 1930s, the richest city was 60 times wealthier than the poorest rural municipality and 10 times wealthier than the poorest city; and there was a 15-fold gap between the richest and poorest rural municipality (Falch and Tovmo, 2003). Scandinavia also had some of the highest levels of industrial conflict in Europe and high levels of unemployment and underemployment, particularly in the rural areas. The task of alleviating poverty, easing social tensions, reducing unemployment and raising growth fell to newly elected social democratic Governments in the 1930s and was achieved through a combination of universal social policies, active labour-market policies and collective wage bargaining at the industry level in cooperation with Government and employer organizations (Moene and Wallerstein, 2006, p.149). A centralized wage bargaining system essentially limited profits in declining low-productivity sectors (by setting a relatively high wage) while expanding profits in high-productivity sectors (by setting a relatively low wage). This contributed both to a more egalitarian income structure and to a fast pace of growth thanks to the reallocation of labour and capital to high-productivity sectors. Increasing productivity and wages, in turn, provided the fiscal base for an expanding social sector that ensured that those facing adjustment would receive appropriate protection and support, which was extended on a universal basis to create a more encompassing notion of solidarity and citizenship (Moene and Wallerstein, 2006, p. 155; Chang and Kozul-Wright, 1994, pp. 866 and 874).

Social policy was institutionalized in the Republic of Korea and Taiwan Province of China at lower levels of socio-economic development than had been the case in the European countries (Hort and Kuhnle, 2000, p. 167) and was used principally to promote selective social investments by the developmental State in support of a fast pace of overall growth and political objectives set within a largely authoritarian political structure. This produced a more targeted approach than the welfare developmentalism of Scandinavia. The role for general social protection of the vulnerable was initially left to families so as to avoid welfare programmes. For instance, social insurance programmes such as occupational welfare programmes and vocational training were initially limited to industrial workers (Yi and Lee, 2003) and were introduced mainly to ensure that workers remained loyal to their firms and the labour force remained well trained. This, in turn, explains the introduction of compulsory education at an early stage of industrialization in the Republic of Korea and the large investments in secondary education, tertiary education and research and development (Lall, 1991). Such social measures essentially emphasized job capability rather than job security, and social development was subordinated to the overall economic development strategy in the Republic of Korea and Taiwan Province of China.

However, the emphasis of that strategy on strong employment growth in the manufacturing sector along with improvement of the economy's skills base did imply an expansion of social protection. The concept of universality, on the other hand, emerged amid more recent developments in the Republic of Korea and Taiwan Province of China and must be understood in terms of both the process of greater political democratization and, in the former case, as a response to the economic crisis at the end of the 1990s, as the latter highlighted the inadequacy of existing social protection mechanisms which were based on strict means tests and did not help the poor. Universal coverage of national health insurance was thus introduced in Taiwan Province of China in 1995. It was extended to the whole population of the Republic of Korea as late as 2000 (Kwon, 2005, p. 9). Nevertheless, while social inclusion is now given greater emphasis in these two countries, social policy is still primarily subordinate to economic development.

Poverty and vulnerability to downside risks

A basic lesson to be drawn from successful development experiences is that sustained poverty reduction depends on a fast pace of growth. However, the connection between growth and poverty is not a direct one. Some fast-growing economies have failed to tackle poverty, while some slower-growing economies have had a more successful record in this area (figure V.2). Two crucial mediating variables which determine the nature of the growth-poverty nexus are the distribution of income and the employment content of growth.

Fast aggregate growth is a necessary but not a sufficient condition for poverty reduction

Figure V.2
Growth and poverty reduction, 1981-2004[a]

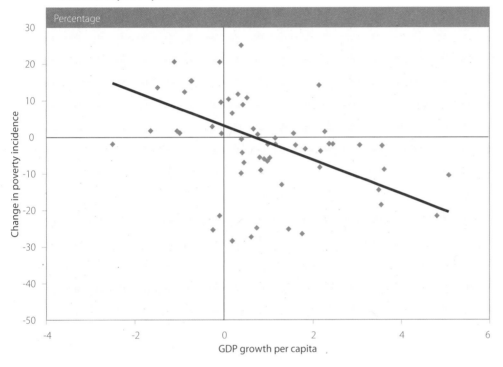

Sources: UN/DESA, based on United Nations Statistics Division, National Accounts Main Aggregates database; and World Bank, PovcalNet.
Note: The measurement of poverty corresponds to the poverty line of $1 a day (PPP).
a Developing countries with available data.

The East Asian experience confirms that countries with a more equal distribution of assets (particularly land) and income can grow faster than countries with a higher degree of inequality. Various growth enhancing channels arising from redistribution, including higher productivity among smallholders, human capital investments, scale economies linked to larger domestic markets and political stability, have been identified. On this basis, Dagderiven, van der Hoeven and Weeks (2001) found, for a group of 50 developing countries, that in a large number of mainly middle-income developing and transition countries, redistribution had been more effective than growth in eliminating poverty; that in others, a mixture of redistribution and growth was most effective; and that in yet other, mainly very poor countries, fast growth alone was the most effective mechanism.

The other link between growth and poverty is employment intensity of growth. In a recent study of 13 developing countries, Khan (2007) found that the East Asian experience, characterized by a rapid expansion in the industrial workforce and a drop in agricultural employment as growth accelerated, had not been replicated to the same extent in some of the more recent fast-growing Asian economies (China, Viet Nam, India and

Cambodia) either because inequality worsened and/or the employment intensity of growth was weak. The declines in poverty were, as a consequence, lower than might have been expected given their headline growth figure, and in one case, Cambodia, poverty actually increased. In the case of China, after 1995, the rate of poverty reduction decelerated as growth became more urban centred and inequality increased. In other cases (Bangladesh and Uganda), a more moderate growth performance was compensated by unorthodox sources of employment creation in the rural economy with some (albeit tenuous) positive impact on poverty alleviation.

These links among growth, distribution and employment can be obscured if there is an undue focus in the policy discussion on levels of abject poverty. In this respect, the dollar-a-day benchmark may not provide the best guide to policymakers for addressing the structural vulnerabilities that determine whether or not growth translates into poverty reduction.[6] In recent years, there has been a shift from a *physiological* model of deprivation, focused on the non-fulfilment of basic material or biological needs, to a *social* model of deprivation, focused on such elements as lack of autonomy, powerlessness, lack of self-respect and dignity, human rights, etc.[7] The latter links poverty alleviation much more strongly to a larger development agenda; however, it should avoid confusing poverty with insecurity.

Poverty and insecurity are interrelated

Insecurity is associated with being vulnerable to falling into poverty or falling into greater poverty. This "downside risk" is a combined function of the *exposure* and *response* to adverse pressures, which include idiosyncratic events such as illness, and workplace accidents and crime, as well as covariant events such as climatic shocks, harvest failure and economic downturns. Exposure to these downward threats varies with the size, frequency, timing and bunching of the particular shocks in question, as well as the spatial proximity to them (and the threat of contagion), but is also linked to the systemic or more cumulative stresses determined by the pattern of relations among growth, distribution and employment.

These systemic stresses were exposed by the Asian financial crisis, in countries that had fared quite well in reducing long-term chronic poverty (United Nations, 2005b). More recently still, Perry and others (2006), reviving the language of Gunnar Myrdal, have suggested that the Latin American region is caught in a vicious circle of persistent poverty, insecurity and unstable growth, which has been perpetuated by a persistent and widespread tendency to underinvest in productive assets and social capital.[8] This conclusion has been confirmed for other developing regions by a growing body of research (Jomo and Baudot, 2006).

Breaking the poverty-insecurity trap requires going beyond aggregate growth promotion

It follows that efforts to break the poverty-insecurity trap will require a policy framework that not only generates higher growth but also examines how investment strategies adopted by both the public and private sectors address the underlying vulnerabilities which expose households and communities to larger downside risks. The main operational objective is to devise long-term poverty reduction strategies for addressing these "root" causes of chronic poverty through a mixture of measures that not only target the vulnerabilities leading to economic security but also allow for better management of the risk through mitigation and coping measures (table V.1).

---

6   A recent study by Pritchett (2005) has concluded that effective poverty reduction strategies require a large enough poverty target to address systemic challenges. He suggests that a global poverty agenda should establish an upper global poverty level of about $10 a day. The number may or may not be appropriate; the underlying rationale, however, is clearly important for policy evaluation purposes.

7   On some assessments, this has entailed picking up the basic needs agenda which had dominated poverty discussions for a short period of time in the 1970s but was dropped after the debt crisis of the early 1980s.

8   See, also, Lopez and Perry (2008).

Table V.1
Managing risks and vulnerabilities

Macropolicies	*Social security and social protection programmes*
Mitigation	**Mitigation**
Macroeconomic policies (growth-oriented, counter-cyclical and pro-poor)	Social security and pension mechanisms
Agricultural development policies Infrastructure investment	Structural cash transfer programmes Targeted price subsidies
Financial regulation and supervision	
Adaptation	**Adaptation**
Asset transfers (land, credits)	Public health and education
Development of savings mechanisms for the poor and vulnerable	Access to microfinance schemes
	Minimum wage and labour-market policies
Coping	**Coping**
Migration and remittances (policies)	Workfare programmes (which are triggered when unemployment rises)
Credits, debt restructuring, debt relief	Disaster relief
	Food subsidies
	Cash transfers

Risk reduction measures are taken in advance of an emerging shock or stress and aim to reduce the likelihood that the shock or stress will occur. The central aim (for the problem at hand) is to make societies and people more resilient towards shocks and insecurity by giving them the assets and means to better manage risks. Examples include macroeconomic policy measures to reduce the risk of financial crises, as well as labour-market policies that improve employment standards. Mitigation measures are taken in anticipation of a shock with a view to minimizing its deleterious consequences. At the individual or community level, there are many informal mechanisms of risk mitigation including diversification of sources of income, producing large families for farm labour or for income-generation, adopting contractual arrangements, such as sharecropping, which trade off profits for insurance. Examples from a public policy perspective include extension of microfinance and provision of social insurance.

Coping measures are those that take effect only after a shock occurs. Such measures can include informal mechanisms for coping with risk such as selling assets, drawing on savings or stocks of grain, obtaining help through remittances from family members abroad, accessing credit from informal moneylenders and so on, along with more formal responses, whether through the market, (for example, various insurance mechanisms) or in terms of public policy (through transfers under, for example, social assistance schemes and price subsidies). Many of these schemes are identical to those aimed at the chronic dependent poor.

Non-catastrophic events can be frequent but with non-severe effects (transitory illness, temporary unemployment) and households can cope with those mostly from their savings, loans, family transfers or private insurance. For very poor households, however, such events may still be devastating and require a "welfare"-type response to prevent them

Measures are needed for reducing downside risk and coping with the consequences

from turning into personal and community disasters. Still, given resource constraints and depending on the nature of risks and exposures, a balance may have to be sought between policies that reduce or mitigate risks, and make households more resilient towards shocks and capable of better managing risks, for example, through strengthening their assets (adaptation), and those that provide support in alleviating the immediate distress caused by shocks (coping).[9]

Some of the strengths and limitations of coping instruments have been examined in the context of specific challenges discussed in previous chapters. This chapter will focus on a selection of reduction (pro-poor macroeconomic), adaptation (microfinance) and coping (transfers) measures.

Risk mitigation

Risk reduction measures lower the probability and severity of negative income shocks

Risk reduction (or mitigation) measures aim to lower the probability and severity of negative income shocks. Though there is much that can be done in this regard at the individual and community levels, a prominent role still belongs to the government, which can use various macroeconomic and other policies to reduce negative income shocks.

Macroeconomic policies

Macroeconomic policies that can be used by Governments for risk reduction have been discussed in more detail in chapter II. Generally, these policies need to be counter-cyclical, pro-investment and aimed at greater social cohesion through strong job creation. They should benefit the poorest communities in developing countries which are particularly vulnerable to downside risk associated with economic shocks and growth stagnation; they can also acquire a stronger pro-poor dimension if tailored to local conditions and the constraints on growth.

Rapid growth of labour-intensive industries is the key

In this respect, policies should direct resources to sectors that employ and provide livelihoods for the poor. Rapid employment growth in labour-intensive sectors is key. In most developing countries, the majority of the poor are employed in agriculture and small enterprises, which will be a strong focus of pro-poor policies, as discussed in the next section. Macroeconomic policy must avoid an anti-rural bias and stimulate activity in labour-intensive agriculture. Many traditional adjustment programmes have failed in this regard. Still, with rapidly expanding urban populations across the developing world, labour-intensive manufacturing (and related services) will be key to addressing poverty challenges over the longer term.

The experience of the 1990s has shown that strong growth will not materialize if macroeconomic policies do not target a competitive and stable real exchange rate and low-to-moderate real interest rates which encourage investment in labour-intensive tradable sectors (see chap. II; and Cornia, 2007). Strong institutions for the regulation of the financial and banking sector are also required, with financial policies integrated with more traditional industrial policy measures so as to ensure that the growth process is driven by sectors with a labour-intensive bias. This also allows capital accumulation to be funded through the mobilization of domestic resources and encourages stronger local financial intermediaries, thereby avoiding some of the dangers of pro-cyclical capital inflows.

---

9   For an earlier discussion about links between poverty and insecurity, see World Bank (2001).

In many cases, a pro-poor policy position will require a much stronger focus on public investment, including infrastructure and human capital, given its strong propensity to crowd in private investment at lower levels of development. However, more than anything, developing countries need the requisite space within which to combine macroeconomic, trade and industrial policies into a consistent strategy.

A pro-poor policy position will require a much stronger focus on public investment

Agricultural development policies

Of the developing world's 5.5 billion people, about 3 billion live in rural areas with half in smallholder (agricultural) households. The food crisis that has emerged in 2008 demonstrates yet again the vulnerability of this population to adverse long-term trends and unexpected shocks. Historically, most successful cases of industrialization began with progress in agriculture. In more recent years, the experiences of China, India and Viet Nam also show how agricultural growth can lay the basis for subsequent growth of industry and the rest of the economy. Cross-country analyses further show that growth originating in the agricultural sector is oftentimes much more effective in reducing poverty and insecurity than growth originating in non-agricultural sectors. In the case of China, for example, it has been found that growth originating in agriculture was 3.5 times more successful in reducing poverty than growth in non-agricultural sectors; and the figure has been found to be even higher for South Asia (United Nations, Economic and Social Commission for Asia and the Pacific, 2008, p. 127). In Latin America, this ratio was found to be 2.7.[10] In fact, reduction of rural poverty from 37 to 29 per cent between 1993 and 2002 (while the rate of urban poverty remained constant at 13 per cent) has been the main factor behind the recent decline in overall poverty from 28 to 22 per cent over the same period. It is also important to note that about 80 per cent of the reduction in rural poverty was due to improvement in rural areas themselves rather than to outmigration.[11] It is unfortunate, therefore, that many developing countries have neglected the agricultural sector in recent years. The adoption of adjustment programmes imposed on many countries, particularly in sub-Saharan Africa, after the debt crisis of the early 1980s has not corrected this bias, and in many cases may have actually made it even worse (United Nations Conference on Trade and Development, 1998).

There are no quick policy fixes, but an effective set of incentives must be in place to provide farmers with a predictable financial surplus and encourage them to invest some of it so as to raise productivity and diversify output. Extension services need to focus on specific supply-side problems, improving the technical knowledge of farmers, and making it easier to obtain inputs as well as credit. Such specific measures to strengthen productivity and extend markets can be greatly enhanced by infrastructure investment and greater research and development. A shift in the ratio of public spending to gross domestic product (GDP) in the agriculture sector is an urgent priority in many developing countries. This ratio currently stands at just 4 per cent for "agriculture-based" economies (those with 30 per cent or more of their GDP originating from agriculture) compared with 12 per cent for more "urbanized" economies (which derive less than 10 per cent of their GDP from agriculture).

Agricultural growth requires incentives, extension services, and investment in infrastructure and human capital

The Economic and Social Commission for Asia and the Pacific (United Nations, Economic and Social Commission for Asia and the Pacific, 2008) has recently estimated that raising the average agricultural productivity of the Asia-Pacific region to that

---

10   See World Bank (2007, p. 6) for further details.

11   Ibid., p. 3, for the statistics presented here.

of Thailand could take 218 million people out of poverty and would reduce inequality, as measured by the Gini coefficient, by 6 per cent. Agricultural research and development, education of the rural population and rural infrastructure, particularly electricity and roads, are the key determinants of labour productivity; and investment in these areas would have a major impact on poverty reduction.

In addition to these general policies, different forms of agricultural production may require specific support measures. For example, in countries where agriculture comprises mainly smallholders, improving their productivity is an important task. Accomplishment of this task may in turn require improvement of their access to such resources as land, water, education and health. Promotion of producer associations may also be important in such settings for achieving more efficient farming operation and for uncovering marketing opportunities and actually making use of them. On the other hand, in agriculture characterized by massive un- and underemployment, expansion of non-farm employment and facilitation of rural-urban migration may assume priority. Finally, in urbanized countries, more importance may need to be attached to switching to product items that are higher in the value chain, utilization of the increasing switch to supermarkets as the main outlet for agro-produce, reduction of the rural-urban income gap, and preservation of the environment and ecology. Developed countries also need to consider reducing subsidies offered to their farmers so as to improve access to their markets by agricultural producers of developing countries, as well as reducing the wasteful use of their own agro-ecological resources.

Risk adaptation

Despite efforts at the national, regional, community and individual levels to reduce risks, it is difficult to expect that they can be completely eliminated. It is therefore important to take measures that can help people live with risks. These measures are classifiable into two types: ex-ante or *risk adaptation* measures; and ex-post or *risk coping* measures, that is, measures that one can take when negative income shocks have already occurred. The distinction between these two types is somewhat problematic, because what one can do ex post often depends on what one has done ex ante. Thus, some of the measures described as risk coping could also be described as risk-adaptive, and vice versa.

Asset distribution

An egalitarian land
distribution has beneficial
effects on economic
security

An unequal distribution of productive assets is one of the root causes of poverty and insecurity. Improving land distribution can therefore be an important policy instrument for reduction of economic insecurity. As research has shown that small farmers can often be more productive than large farmers (Ray, 1998; United Nations, Economic and Social Commission for Asia and the Pacific, 2008), a more equal land distribution would therefore allow a higher volume of total output. It would also allow the poor to have better access to education, health and other social services, thereby helping them to build up human capital. A more healthy and educated labour force in turn helps to raise agricultural productivity by facilitating introduction of new technology and crops. Finally, a more equal distribution of assets also allows the poor to participate more meaningfully in the country's political process, which in turn helps to increase their share of the country's budgetary resources.

International experience bears out the proposition regarding a positive link between egalitarian distribution of land and a better growth outcome. Most of the reduction in rural poverty has been the result of progress made in East Asia and the Pacific, where the number of rural poor declined from 1,036 million in 1993 to 883 million in 2003. By contrast, the number of the rural poor actually increased in both sub-Saharan Africa and South Asia over this period. Observers generally agree that the land reforms carried out in East Asian economies in the 1940s and 1950s had created a more egalitarian land ownership pattern that allowed a wider participation and sharing in the growth process, and that similar success has been registered with subsequent land reforms in the region (United Nations, 2006, chap.V). In the latter reforms, however, the transfer of property rights was more limited than in the earlier ones, and reforms were tailored to prevailing socio-economic conditions, producing a variety of experiences.

Land redistribution is often difficult to achieve politically and can usually be undertaken only under extraordinary circumstances, for example, following a revolution or war. However, there are land reform models which are politically more feasible, such as South Africa's Settlement and Land Acquisition Grant (SLAG), set up to enable rural households to purchase arable land (see box V.2).

Box V.2

Land redistribution in South Africa

Various measures have been taken by the Government of South Africa aimed at providing the disadvantaged and the poor with land for residential and productive purposes. In particular, a single, yet flexible, grant mechanism providing up to a maximum of 16,000 rand (R) (equivalent to approximately US$ 2,000) per household was established to enable beneficiaries to purchase land from willing sellers. Land redistribution has taken several forms (for example, group settlement with some production; group production; commonage schemes; on-farm settlement of farm workers; and farm worker equity). A range of additional financial resources, such as the planning grant and facilitation and dispute resolution services, supported the basic grant.

This approach has not involved prior acquisition of land by the State. Limits were set with regard to both the amount of grant that a particular household could obtain and the household income, so as to ensure that the programme benefited many and reached low-income households.[a] The sellers in the market could be large landowners themselves or property developers who would take land from landowners, divide it up into parcels of suitable size and sell to potential beneficiaries. The buyers, in their turn, often grouped together in order to obtain the grant, design projects, and acquire land collectively. The Communal Property Associations Act enacted in 1996 encouraged such group formation. However, the paternalistic implementation of such collective acquisitions by the Department of Land Affairs (DLA) led to centralization, bureaucratization and long delays, thus interfering with the spirit and goals of the programme. As a result, between 1995 and 2000, only 0.6 per cent of the country's commercial farmland had willingly been sold under the programme, and the number of beneficiaries remained limited to 60,000. This achievement compared poorly with the original target of transferring almost 30 million hectares (about 30 per cent of the country's arable land) under the programme. Apart from the paternalistic and bureaucratic modus operandi, there were other objective obstacles, such as (a) non-coverage of upfront costs by the grants, (b) lack of human capital on the part of beneficiaries needed to practise modern farming, (c) inertia acting against geographical mobility and (d) inadequate rural and extension services.

To accelerate the land transfer process, in 2001 the Government launched a revised programme, entitled "Land Reform for Agricultural Development", which decentralized implementation and thus helped to speed up the process. In addition, all beneficiaries were now required to make a contribution (in cash, in labour or in kind), the purpose of which was to strengthen their commitment to the project.[b] However, the introduction of the contribution requirement also meant that the

a Originally, under the Settlement and Land Acquisition Grant (SLAG), the monthly income of potential beneficiary households was supposed not to exceed R1,500. For further details, see *World Economic and Social Survey 2003* (United Nations, 2003), chap. VII.

b The minimum personal contribution required for the minimum grant was set at R5,000 (about US$ 650 in 2003).

Box V.2 (cont'd)

c The *2003 Survey* (p. 215) concludes: "What is required is the political will to give greater priority to redistributive land reform within broader rural development strategies and to invest in the infrastructure and services required to support the activities of land redistribution beneficiaries, with the aim of turning many rural people into landowners."

revised programme would be targeted more towards expansion of small and medium-sized commercial farms than towards poor peasants without any land or assets.

These factors notwithstanding, the South African market-based land reform programme provides significant evidence that the obstacles to land reforms may not be as politically insurmountable as they are often perceived to be. The experience of South Africa also demonstrates that market-based land reform need not be fiscally onerous. Data show that the annual capital expenditure on the original South African land redistribution programme in the peak fiscal year (1998/99) was equivalent to only 0.2 per cent of the total annual Government budget. However, success of land reform requires complementary efforts towards providing better infrastructure, input delivery and extension services. The experience of South Africa indicates that costs for providing such complementary services remained less than 1 per cent of the general Government expenditure in 2001. Thus, given the political will, market-based land reforms are financially feasible and can play an important role in enhancing economic security of the poor.c

Minimum wage policies

The working poor are also very insecure

Even with successful land reform, the majority of the poor rely on wage labour as their only means of generating income. Over 50 per cent of the labour force in developing countries is engaged in work in agriculture, much of which is very poorly paid and insecure. Improving employment conditions for these workers would have a large and direct impact on improving household security.[12] In general, the political representation of these workers is very poor and the likelihood of effective formal legislation is limited. Expanding non-farm rural employment does appear to have offered the opportunity for improving conditions in Asia and Latin America, though less so in Africa (Demeke, Guta and Ferede, 2003; Gordon and Craig, 2001). However, as mentioned above, over the longer term, promotion of labour-intensive industrialization is key to poverty reduction in generally labour-surplus economies.

Productivity growth is not translating into wage growth

Mere expansion of employment, however, may not be enough to achieve poverty alleviation and insecurity reduction even in this sector (International Labour Organization, 2005b, p. v). In a world dominated by the working poor, a key concern is whether rising productivity levels translate into rising wages. This is not necessarily the case. An example is provided by India, where, between 1980 and 1999, per capita GDP in purchasing power parity (PPP) terms increased from about $750 to about $2,500, while the real manufacturing wage index declined from about 140 to 70 (ibid., p. 53, table 4). In Mexico, while the North American Free Trade Agreement (NAFTA) has led to an expansion of employment in maquiladoras from 446,436 to 1.3 million persons between 1990 and 2000, there has been virtually no growth in wages (ibid., p. 89).

Low or declining wages can provide a temporary growth boost, particularly as linked to expanding export sectors. However, sustained economic growth depends on productivity improvements and a growing domestic market. In this respect, to the extent that minimum wage legislation encourages wage growth, it has been seen as a possible way to help achieve alleviation of poverty and reduction of economic insecurity, which in turn can have a positive knock-on impact on productivity growth. Empirical evidence on these connections is scarce. A positive impact on wages in large enterprises in the formal sector due to minimum wage legislation is reported in most studies. Some have also reported a similar impact on wages in smaller enterprises, including in the rural sector, with an accompanying positive effect on poverty reduction (Lustig and McLeod, 1997; Gindling and

---

12   See Mugrai and Ravallion (2005).

Terrell, 2005), although others find this to be conditional on a strong growth performance (Morley, 1992). However, even when legislation is present, there remain serious enforcement problems in many developing countries and many see it as, by itself, a particularly blunt instrument for providing more secure livelihoods (United Nations, 2007b).

Microfinance

One of the ways in which the poor and vulnerable can adapt to risk and insecurity is through improved access to financial markets. The poor have historically been excluded from the world of formal credit and other financial services and relegated to that of usurious moneylenders. This often results, for the poor, in a condition of perpetual indebtedness and ultimately the loss of whatever collateral was offered to obtain a loan. Attempts to provide modern credit services to the poor have generally foundered in the face of high transaction costs and their lack of any assets that could be offered as collateral.

> The poor are often excluded from formal financial services

Microcredit represents an attempt to solve these twin problems through the innovative use of group lending, whereby peer pressure serves as a substitute for collateral and group responsibility serves to minimize transaction costs. Microcredit financing had begun on an experimental basis in Bangladesh in the late 1970s; in 2006, there were more than 7,000 microcredit institutions in operation, serving about 500 million people in more than 50 countries, including some developed countries. These aim for a more virtuous cycle, whereby a rise in income enables a household to take some risks, which in turn allows it to raise its income still further.[13]

Though microcredit programmes are not insurance programmes per se, they can play such a role through income and consumption smoothing.[14] Of course, such a diversion can upset investment planning and the danger exists that, through financial, social, and psychological penalties imposed on loan default, microcredit could even increase the vulnerability of the poor. In view of these limitations, according to some scholars, straightforward insurance programmes can be more effective in helping the poor to deal with insecurity.[15]

Attempts at providing insurance services to the poor have generally foundered in the face of difficulties related to administration, high transaction costs, and the familiar problems of adverse selection and moral hazard. Still a "repressed demand" for such services has been documented (Mosley, 2007).[16] It is therefore not surprising that the

> Micro-insurance programmes are spreading

---

13   Evidence for the effectiveness of such programmes in achieving sustained poverty reduction is mixed; for a review, see Morduch (1994, 1995, 1999b).

14   There was, in fact, a formal insurance element in some microcredit programmes designed to ensure the recovery of the loan in case of death or incapacitating injury suffered by the borrower. This covered risks of the lender and not those of the borrower. The fact that microcredit is used for consumption smoothing purposes is also well recognized. Referring to Pitt and Khandker (1998), Morduch (1999b, p. 1605), for example, indicates that "(M)icrofinance borrowing is shown to improve the ability to smooth consumption across seasons, and *entry into the programmes is partly driven by insurance concerns*" (emphasis added). Further, he reports that his own investigation confirmed the consumption smoothing effect of microcredit programmes and concludes (p. 1606) that "(S)ubstantively, the results suggest that benefits from *risk reduction may be as important as (or more important than) direct impacts on average levels of consumption*" (emphasis added).

15   See Clarke and Dercon (2008) for further details.

16   By "repressed demand", Mosley means unmet insurance demand in general, but does not dwell on the issue of the prices at which demand and supply are evaluated. In this regard, Mosley speaks of "substantial thwarted demand for insurance services". He also expresses the view that whatever insurance services were offered were meant for or targeted at the male population only, indicating a gender aspect to the repressed demand.

organizational innovation that allowed credit to reach the poor has proved attractive as a delivery mechanism for insurance services, too. Churchill (2006), for example, provides a large compendium of micro-insurance programmes which lists as many as 74 programmes from across the world. So far, the majority of micro-insurance programmes have focused on life and health risks, although more recent programmes have expanded into areas such as crop insurance (see chap. III for an assessment). Mosley (2007) offers an examination of a selection of programmes and reports having found a positive impact, including to those who were not direct buyers.[17]

Many micro-insurance programmes arose as a side activity of microfinance institutions otherwise focused on microcredit. However, with time, "standalone" micro-insurance organizations have also emerged. Institutions offering micro-insurance may be classified also on the basis of their motivation and, from this viewpoint, may be categorized as either "for profit" or "non-profit". For-profit institutions are similar to commercial companies; non-profit institutions, however, may operate either as companies or as non-governmental, social or cooperative organizations.

Micro-insurance
programmes face
difficulties in initial take-up
and other hurdles

Despite the spread of micro-insurance programmes, as described above, overall the insurance needs of the poor still remain, for various reasons, largely unmet (see Clarke and Dercon, 2008; Mosley, 2007). First of all, insurance is a more complicated product than credit; hence the take-up is slow and low.[18] This causes a problem of financial viability: low take-up increases the cost of insurance, keeps the insured risk pools smaller, and makes reinsurance costlier, which in turn reduces take-up.[19] In fact, there seems to be an inverse relationship between the break-even premium and the portfolio size. The trade-off suggests that there are basically two means of overcoming the problems faced by micro-insurance programmes: one is to raise premiums, which is self-defeating; the other is to subsidize such programmes until the self-sustaining level of uptake is reached (see box V.3).[20]

In face of the hurdles noted above, micro-insurance programmes in different parts of the world are experimenting with different options. It may be too early to derive definitive lessons from these experiments. However, in general, they point to the necessity of focusing on single risks, piggybacking on existing microfinance operations, and so on. In view of the positive externalities of micro-insurance programmes and of their initial survivability problem, the use of subsidies to such programmes would seem justifiable.

There needs to be a shift
in focus towards micro-
savings programmes

Building up savings can be an effective way of adapting to risks. Many researchers have shown that even the poor want to and can save, and that appropriate mechanisms can help realize this potential. In fact, Hulme, Moore and Barrientos (2007) are

---

17   Mosley (2007) tabulates findings from case studies of the following five programmes: (a) Foundation for International Community Assistance (FINCA), Uganda, (b) Bangladesh Rural Advancement Committee (BRAC), (c) Grameen Kalyan (Grameen welfare organization), (d) Society for Social Services (SSS), Bangladesh and (e) Bhartiya Samruddhi Investments and Consulting Services (BASICS), Ltd, India. The first four are health schemes, while the fifth is a weather scheme. He suggests the following channels through which positive externalities may be generated: (a) knowledge achieved by experimentation; (b) "bonding social capital" benefits achieved through lower individual and group vulnerability; (c) "linking social capital" benefits achieved through an improvement in clients' awareness of service quality; and (d) "beneficial contagion" effects.

18   The general problems with insurance, as alluded to above, are: (a) information asymmetry, (b) transaction costs, (c) enforcement constraints and (d) ambiguity aversion. Even microfinance institutions find it hard to overcome these hurdles.

19   See Clarke and Dercon (2008, p. 10).

20   Such a trade-off between scale and unit cost does apply to other microfinance services, and, in fact, for most business propositions. However, the trade-off may be particularly stark for the business of micro-insurance.

Box V.3

Subsidizing microfinance programmes

Even though microfinance programmes are formally private sector operations, they often require explicit or implicit State subsidies. The issue of subsidies has provoked various responses. First, many microfinance institutions claim that they break even financially and even produce some surplus. In fact, according to *The MicroBanking Bulletin* of July 2003, 66 out of 124 (about 50 per cent) micro-lenders surveyed were financially sustainable. Second, other microfinance institutions claim that even though they are not yet financially solvent, they are steadily progressing to that stage, and soon will be fully financially independent. The argument for providing a temporary subsidy to microfinance institutions until they can reach the scale and efficiency necessary for them to break even financially is essentially an "infant industry" protection argument.

However, a third response takes the view that it is unreasonable to demand that microfinance institutions break even financially. According to this view, the utility and usefulness of microfinance programmes should not be judged by narrow financial yardsticks. Instead, a broader view is required in order to evaluate the multidimensional role that microfinance programmes play in the life of the poor. Furthermore, proponents of this view contend that the emphasis on financial viability will force microfinance institutions to move away from the poor and focus attention on the non-poor or the not-so-poor, thus thwarting the initial mission of microfinance institutions. They therefore perceive an inconsistency between the criticism that microfinance institutions are not reaching the extreme poor and the criticism that those institutions are not demonstrating financial viability. In fact, it is microfinance institutions that serve poorer categories of households that are generally more subsidy-dependent. According to the survey mentioned above, the financial viability rate among microlenders focusing on the low end was 37 per cent (18 out of 49).

To argue for subsidies for microfinance, Morduch (2006), for example, has coined the expression "smart subsidies", while recognizing that the term may appear to be a "contradiction in terms". He explains that "smart subsidies maximize social benefits while minimizing distortions and misplaced targeting" (p. 11) and presents the following four lessons:

(a)   Subsidized credit does not equal "cheap credit";
(b)   Profitability does not equal efficiency;
(c)   Profitability does not equal sustainability;
(d)   Profitability does not guarantee access to commercial finance.

Morduch (2006) suggests that these lessons show that if appropriately designed, subsidies can preserve the free market efficiency outcomes, such as hard budget constraint, a clear bottom line, and competitive pressure, and yet help increase the scale of microfinance outreach, access to commercial finance, and depth of outreach to the poor (pp. 10-11).[a]

Morduch (2006) does not want to limit microfinance subsidy to the start-up phase only, believing as he does that if subsidies are reasonable for the start-up phase, then they are also reasonable when microfinance institutions try to expand to "wholly new areas". He therefore argues against the five-year limitation on subsidies suggested by the Consultative Group to Assist the Poor (CGAP) donor guidelines. He also demonstrates that subsidies are needed to allow borrowers to graduate from very small loans (which lenders cannot make without subsidies) to loans of larger amounts, when break-even becomes possible. He further notes that subsidies are also needed to arrange for a multidimensional assistance package, including food aid and social services, which is necessary to ensure that the microcredit programme achieves effectiveness and success with the extremely poor.

Despite his arguments for microfinance subsidies, and his contention that smart subsidies can help "achieve social objectives that are not readily achievable when working through strictly for-profit institutions", Morduch still believes that, in general, subsidies should be "time-limited" and "rule-bound", and that depending on subsidies is not a viable long-run option. Accordingly, he also seems to advocate subsidy to only "a subset of institutions", referring most likely to microfinance institutions that are more poor-focused and/or operate under relatively more difficult conditions (in, for example, remote or sparsely populated areas).

a   See also Morduch (1999a, b) and Armendariz de Aghion and Morduch (2005).

Box V.3 (cont'd)

In contrast with Morduch, Clarke and Dercon (2008) seem to offer more unconditional support to subsidies for microfinance programmes. They maintain that, given existing technologies and transaction costs, microfinance programmes will never be commercially viable, and hence need to be viewed partly as commercial programmes and partly as welfare programmes, and as thereby requiring subsidies in the long run. In other words, in their view, providing subsidies to microfinance institutions may be a cost-effective means of reaching the poor and improving their lives. Pointing to the paucity of data showing financial viability of microfinance programmes in general, Clarke and Dercon express the opinion that, given the current cost of technology and expertise, microfinance for the very poorest will never be profitable.[b] The authors believe that the pioneers of microcredit, such as Grameen, have developed loan contracts that do not "distort incentives or decisions but still manage to serve the poor". Furthermore, citing Karlan and Zinman (2007a and b), Clarke and Dercon suggest that it remains difficult for microfinance programmes to become profitable by raising prices of their product and thus take the view that subsidies may be necessary on a long-term basis.

Clarke and Dercon (2008) further note that subsidized insurance can potentially avoid the problems arising from weak safety nets, since, if such insurance is properly designed, anyone can acquire a policy and be covered themselves against the serious risks that he or she faces. Hence, subsidies should be given to encourage uptake and inclusion. They recommend that subsidies be targeted towards trialling and evaluating innovative micro-insurance programmes rather than provided directly to existing micro-insurance products.

Mosley (2007) also argues strongly for subsidies for micro-insurance programmes, particularly in view of their positive externalities and the problems of survival that they face initially.

b Clarke and Dercon (2008) note that "The costs are just too high", and suggest that "subsidizing microcredit may be a cost-efficient way of improving the lives of the poor" (p. 17).

somewhat rueful about the redirection of attention from savings to (micro) credit in recent years, for they perceive this as representing a historic shift in emphasis from thrift as the foundation of finance for the poor in the early twentieth century to a reliance on credit and debt as a way out of poverty in the early twenty-first. Along these lines, despite the fact that community-based savings groups and other informal savings systems had had a long history, microcredit organizations and institutions were for a long time barred from accepting savings from their clients.

The poor are often prevented from securing access to formal savings programmes through a mixture of unfamiliarity, distance, costs, and the indivisibility of available saving instruments in the formal banking sector. Alternative savings institutions/programmes that are more suited to the needs and capabilities of poor households can remove such barriers and allow those households to save and to use their own savings as a means of coping with risks.

Savings are often a better form of self-insurance

Savings as (self) insurance has many features that are superior to those of insurance. For example, while insurance can generally be used to cope with only certain pre-specified types of risks, savings can be used to deal with any type of risk, as long as the damages involved do not exceed the amounts of savings. Second, whereas insurance helps only ex post, savings can be used to undertake both ex ante and ex post measures to deal with risks. Thus, savings as an insurance mechanism is much more flexible. Third, use of savings does not require prior approval. Hence, savings ensure independence in respect of deciding how to deal with risks. All these advantages are in addition to the fact that savings can, while insurance programmes usually cannot, generate an "income effect". Noting the insurance role of microcredit and microsavings programmes, many have characterized these as *quasi-insurance* programmes.[21]

21   Mosley (2007) offers the following four examples of quasi-insurances: (a) risk-minimizing credits for the ultrapoor, (b) Emergency loans from "village banks", (c) Microsavings schemes and (d) Loan savings linkages.

To the extent that microcredit programmes have proved relatively more successful in reaching the poor, they are now being expanded to include delivery of savings services to the poor. The process has led to the emergence of two types of microsavings institutions. The first type comprises of those that engage in both microcredit and microsavings, producing a joint product. An early leader in this regard was Bank Rakayat Indonesia, which by 1996 was offering saving services to over 16 million households. Deposits have been small, with average balances in 1996 of $184, suggesting that the average depositor was less well off than the average borrower (with an average loan balance of over $1,000). However, this represented over $3 billion in savings and gave Bank Rakayat Indonesia a cheap source of funds for re-lending, while providing households with the means to build up assets and better smooth consumption. The second type comprises those institutions for which engagement in microsavings constitutes the sole activity. An example of the latter type is the SafeSave programme of Bangladesh. Under SafeSave, staff solicits savings from members on a daily basis, thus helping households "convert their ability to save in regular but small amounts into a useful lump of money" (Morduch 1999b, p. 1607).

Evidence gathered by Hulme, Moore and Barrientos (2007, p. 8) suggests that there are tens if not hundreds of millions of savings accounts in various classes of financial institutions that are generally aimed at markets below the level of commercial banks, and that a substantial fraction of these institutions' clients are probably poor or near poor. The market for microsavings services is therefore large. According to the microfinance virtual library, it should be possible to raise $2 billion from borrowers' savings alone. The Country-Level Savings Assessment data gathered by the Consultative Group to Assist the Poor (CGAP) show that a high proportion of both rural and urban households currently have no bank accounts, indicating a huge unrealized demand for deposit services among poor clients, many of whom report keeping savings in cash or in other informal and semi-formal institutions. Microfinance institutions therefore have a huge demand to fulfil through improved savings products. On some assessments, policymakers who are looking to strengthen their microfinance programmes would be better served by giving greater attention to microsavings schemes, making these affordable, widely available and less costly. Savings also need to be more remunerative, earning real positive interest rates (Hulme, Moore and Barrientos, 2007).

The average size of all microfinance programmes—credit, savings and insurance—are becoming larger over time thanks to several factors. First of all, these programmes generally follow the principle of graduation, so that, taking microcredit as the example, upon successful repayment of the previous loan, borrowers become eligible for a higher loan amount in the next round. Second, as microfinance institutions mature and become more secure, they introduce new loan programmes of larger size. For example, Grameen Bank Bangladesh now provides loans of large sizes which are enabling borrowers to construct or undertake capital improvement of their existing houses. Grameen is also introducing loans for small businesses. However, this larger size may strengthen the criticism that microfinance does not reach the extremely poor. At the same time, these programmes are still too small to generate an investment surge that can push an economy towards growth take-off. It remains to be seen what sort of evolution microfinance undergoes in the coming years.

There is a vast demand for savings services among the poor

Microfinance needs to aim at larger size and more investment-oriented goals

Risk coping

Risk coping, as mentioned above, refers to ex post measures that can be taken by the Government, communities and households to enable people to live through negative shocks when these have already occurred.

Workfare/employment programmes

One of the oldest measures for providing relief to people facing income insecurity entails the offer of employment through various types of workfare programmes. Though originally these programmes had mainly been undertaken as ex post emergency measures for coping with crisis situations, with time they were also being used as ex ante arrangements for helping the vulnerable to adapt to risk and even for reducing risk for them. Thus, many developing countries are expanding their workfare programmes and utilizing them as an alternative means of providing social insurance. For example, India has recently adopted a programme that guarantees 100 days of work to all who need it in rural areas.

Workfare programmes can create valuable assets for the wider community

As the experience of workfare programmes has been widely studied, an understanding of their merits and demerits is quite well established.[22] In rural areas, such works, by guaranteeing some income continuity in the face of adverse economic shocks, can spare farmers from having to run down productive stocks and can even encourage them to undertake riskier, and more productive, investments. Moreover, work done under workfare programmes, if properly planned and executed, can create valuable assets such as roads, irrigation canals, dykes, schoolhouses and storage facilities, although, in practice, the programmes are not uniform or always satisfactory in terms of their quality and productivity.[23] Further, their use in response to shocks and disasters allows the poor not only to save, but to save more productively. Empirical studies offer considerable evidence of the insurance impact of workfare programmes. For example, Cain and Lieberman (1983) find that the volume of land sales is highly correlated with floods and droughts in villages without workfare programmes, whereas no such correlation exists in villages having such programmes. Similarly, Ravallion (1991) finds that access to relief work (including the Employment Guarantee Scheme) appears to have allowed many of the poor in the villages of India to avoid sale of land as a form of adjustment. He believes that the presence of the Food-for-Work Programme helped Bangladesh prevent deaths during the 1988 floods, while the absence of such programmes was one reason why more people had died in the aftermath of the 1974 floods.

However, there has been persistent criticism regarding the high administrative costs of such schemes, their poor record in terms of providing jobs for people from the poorest and least secure households, the crowding out of comparable work from the

---

[22] See, for example, Bandyopadhyay (1988), Basu (1981), Besley (1995), Besley and Coate (1992), Narayana, Parikh, and Srinivasan (1988), Ravallion (1991, 2003).

[23] It may be noted that, in certain contexts, public workfare programmes have greater potential to create productive assets than would be possible in the private sector. For example, workfare programmes undertaken by public authorities could adopt schemes to build irrigation canals with greater ease than the private sector with its problems of coordination and cooperation and of restrictions arising from the existence of private property rights. China's success in building rural infrastructure by mobilizing surplus labour during the Maoist period and in developing Township and Village Enterprises during the post-1978 reform period points to this comparative advantage, so to speak, of public workfare programmes. However, realization of the full productive and insurance potentiality of workfare programmes depends to a great extent on the governance capability of a country, at both the central and the local level.

private sector, and their capture by powerful politicians. Another controversial issue concerns the wage paid on such schemes. Setting the wage at or even below local subsistence levels, for example, is hardly likely to address the vulnerabilities associated with poverty. Moreover, if this is intended to induce self-targeting, the result may be self-defeating, as only those with some other income source could afford to take such work. Paying such low wages could also lower the average wage in surrounding jobs.

Despite such criticism, the experience and impact assessments suggest that workfare programmes hold considerable potential for providing a form of economic security to poor families who have able-bodied members willing to work in exchange for benefits. Concerns about crowding out are probably exaggerated and can, in any case, be addressed by appropriately timing the programmes, adroitly designing them in terms of wage (benefit) level and amount of work required, ensuring that work under them proves to be productive and creates valuable assets, and ensuring that they are complementary to rather than in conflict with pre-existing benign security arrangements.

The concerns about coverage are probably more relevant, however. Workfare programmes cannot benefit households that do not have members able to undertake the work required by the programmes. For those households, other types of programmes are necessary. Moreover, countries where wages are bolstered by some regulatory device, such as a minimum wage, are probably not suited to the establishment of large-scale public works schemes intended to be a form of social protection.

Workfare programmes can be an effective tool in dealing with the economic insecurity of people left out of formal employment

Not all needy families benefit from workfare programmes

Welfare and cash transfer programmes

As noted above, workfare programmes, despite their merits, are not suitable for providing social protection to all who are in distress. Families that do not have members willing and able to undertake the work required by these programmes cannot benefit from them. Welfare programmes that do not have work requirements can fill some of these gaps. In addition, welfare programmes may focus on certain specific goals other than just current income-generation, which is generally the focus of workfare programmes. In particular, welfare programmes designed to help the poor build human capital and thus break the intergenerational cycle of poverty have become quite popular in recent years. It may be noted that even work-promotion programmes need not always take the form of public workfare and, instead, may entail subsidies that are provided for private employment and given to either workers or employers.

Welfare programmes can help to meet the general need for income as well as to achieve specific developments goals

There are a wide variety of welfare programmes. For example, in the survey by Coady, Grosh and Hoddinott (2004) of 122 programmes covering 48 countries, as many as 79 were classified as "transfer" programmes and another 23 were categorized as "subsidies".[24] Of those belonging to the transfer category, 49 took the form of "cash" transfers, 18 were "near cash" and the remaining 12 comprised in-kind "food transfers". Along the same lines, 18 of the subsidy programmes reduced the cost of food, whereas 5 entailed "non-food" subsidies. Although the programmes surveyed by these authors represent neither a census nor a random sample, they point to a wide prevalence of welfare programmes in different parts of the world.[25]

---

[24] The remaining 20 belonged to the "public works" category (of which 12 were in the "job creation" subcategory and 8 in the "programme output/social product" subcategory).

[25] The authors themselves acknowledged that "(W)hile our efforts to construct a database of targeted interventions were exhaustive (or at least exhausting), there are good reasons to believe that the database is neither a random sample nor a census of all targeted programmes and their impacts" (Coady, Grosh and Hoddinott, 2004, p. 83).

A set of challenges centre around the level and structure of benefits and the related issues concerning financing and budgeting of the programmes. Setting the benefit level low may help to increase the coverage, reduce incentives for people to enrol unduly and keep the budget manageable. However, low benefit levels may also make the programme ineffective and reduce the chances for participants to graduate. On the other hand, setting the benefit level high may lead to undue enrolment, restrict the coverage, create resentment among those left out of the programme, generate disincentives for enrollees to graduate and create undue budgetary pressure. There is also the possibility of differentiating the benefit level in accordance with household characteristics. Such differentiation, while of help in raising the effectiveness of the programmes, increases the demands placed on administration and management of the programmes. Benefit levels in welfare programmes that are currently under operation are generally thought to be on the lower rather than on the higher side.

There are a variety of options available in the design of the delivery mechanism, including cash, checks, vouchers, in-kind benefits and so on. As regards the method of transfer, in the case of cash, a service window or an ATM machine could be used. An important aspect of delivery concerns whether the recipient will have to travel to receive the benefits or whether the benefits will be delivered to his or her residence. The former arrangement has the advantage of reducing the administrative costs of the programme but it may be more discriminatory.

Affordability of welfare programmes is a hotly debated issue. This was discussed in *World Economic and Social Survey 2007* (United Nations, 2007a) in the context of pensions. The debate is rooted partly in differences of perception of the social necessity and role of these programmes. Benefits provided under welfare schemes can take both cash and in-kind forms. For a long time, however, there was opposition to cash transfers as a means of combating poverty and insecurity and even of dealing with emergency. It was argued that cash transfers would promote idleness and dependency and prove costly.[26] However, there is now a growing movement in favour of them. This switch has strong advocates among non-governmental organizations, though development agencies, both multilateral and bilateral, also seem to be catching up.

Cash transfer programmes are growing in popularity

Cash transfer programmes can be classified as either conditional or unconditional. Conditional cash transfer programmes require recipients to fulfil certain conditions such as sending children to school, attending training programmes, visiting health centres, and so on. Unconditional cash transfers do not impose any such condition on the recipients. From another point of view, cash transfer programmes may be classified into lump-sum transfer programmes and periodic transfer programmes. Most cash transfer programmes are of the "periodic" type; an example of a lump-sum cash transfer is that given for construction of houses or other such capital projects. Cash transfer programmes may also be classified from the viewpoint of the particular purpose they are to serve or the particular category of people to which they are targeted. From this viewpoint, cash transfer programmes may be grouped according to the following purposes: (a) general poverty/insecurity alleviation, (b) education promotion, (c) old age support, (d) health promotion and disability (in particular AIDS) support and (e) other.

Cash transfer programmes are easy to administer but they raise incentive issues

In general, advocates of cash transfer programmes point to their ease of disbursement, low administrative costs and ability to reach the poor directly and boost their

26   "The fear of giving money is almost pathological among aid agencies, even though, or maybe because, it would be simpler and cheaper to give cash than any other form of help" (Sesman, 2004).

self-esteem and productive capacity.[27] These are all advantages that become more apparent in the context of rising insecurity following a large-scale shock or economic downturn. However, researchers have noted some potential demerits of cash transfer programmes, too, among which are promotion of idleness and dependency, and potentially distortionary and discriminatory effects, as well as their proneness to corruption. Despite these possible drawbacks, programmes of cash transfer are spreading, albeit with some regional variations (see box V.4).

Box V.4

Cash transfer programmes

Cash transfer programmes in Latin America

Cash transfer programmes in Latin America are mainly focused on the young and aim in particular, at helping children of poor families become educated and thus break the intergenerational poverty cycle. The downside is that such programmes may appear to discriminate against families that do not have young children. *Oportunidades* is an important example of a cash transfer programme implemented in Mexico. According to Standing (2007, p. 17), the Mexican cash transfer programme is a "central part of the country's social protection system" and has evolved into "a complex mechanism of social engineering" reaching about 3 million households at any one time.

Bolsa Família, which is the flagship of Brazil's cash transfer schemes, had, by 2006, reached over 11 million households living below the official poverty line, or over 44 million people. The scheme represents the consolidation of a number of income transfer schemes, and the payment is conditional on several human development objectives and is nominally means-tested. Other cash transfer schemes of Latin America include SISBÉN *(Sistema de Identificación de Potenciales Beneficiarios de Programas Sociales)* and *Familias en Acción* (Colombia); *Programa de Asignación Familiar* (Honduras); Programme of Advancement through Health and Education (Jamaica); and *Red de Protección Social* (Nicaragua), which pre-dated the Brazilian model, having become operational in 2000.

Cash transfer programmes in Africa

In contrast with those in Latin America, cash transfer programmes in Africa have often been used as part of disaster relief and have focused on the old and sick. In view of the AIDS epidemic, it is not unexpected that support for the sick, particularly AIDS victims, has emerged as an important part of cash transfer programmes in Africa. Ethiopia's Cash for Relief (CfR), funded by the United States Agency for International Development, is an important example. Another is Ethiopia's Meket Livelihood Development Pilot Project. Evaluation shows that money received under these programmes was spent not only on consumption, but also on paying off debts, acquisition of livestock, undertaking investment to improve land productivity, etc. The cash transfer programmes implemented in Ethiopia by the United Kingdom of Great Britain and Northern Ireland-based non-governmental organization Save the Children have also been found to be cost-effective and non-inflationary.

Somalia's Emergency Cash Relief Programme has been implemented in the drought-affected and politically contested north-eastern part of the country. Some 13,380 socially vulnerable households had been each given a one-time grant of $50 under this scheme. Observers report that even this small cash grant helped people reduce their debts, purchase food and water, and invest themselves with some sense of "empowerment". It has been claimed that the cash support helped the community to survive. Other programmes of cash transfer in Africa include Zambia's Kalomo Social Cash Transfer Scheme, funded by the Deutsche Gesellschaft für Technische Zusammenarbeit (GTZ) (Eschborn, Germany) programme; and programmes especially directed towards people infected with AIDS in Namibia and South Africa.

---

27   For further details, see, for example, Standing (2007).

Box V.4 (cont'd)

Cash transfer programmes in Asia

Cash transfer programmes are becoming popular in Asia, too. Attention has been drawn to the success of the Bangladesh Food for Education programme in promoting female education. With the passage of time, food is being replaced by cash in this programme. Other cash transfer programmes in Bangladesh include Assistance for the Old and Assistance for Widows. In Mongolia, the Cash for Herders programme is claimed to have led to investments that regenerated herders' livelihoods.

Remittance policies

Remittances are a growing and relatively stable source of income

Labour migration, particularly on a significant scale, is usually a sign that the exporting economy is not generating a sufficient number of decent jobs for an expanding workforce. On the other hand, it does open the possibility for new sources of development finance (Ratha, 2007). In fact, remittances seem to have become the most important source of external finance for many developing countries, and can also improve the terms of access to international financial markets.[28] For some countries, remittances account for one third or more of gross national income (GNI) and in many cases, the figure hovers around 20 per cent (see Ratha and others, 2007). It is no wonder, then, that remittances have become an important factor in risk coping and mitigation, at both macro- and micro levels.

Remittances, at least to date, appear to be more stable than private capital flows and less subject to boom-bust cycles and can provide a counter-cyclical stimulus (Kapur, 2004). For example, Ecuador's remittance earnings increased from $643 million to $1.4 billion between 1997 and 2001, a period during which the country experienced social upheaval and political chaos (ibid.). Mexico and Argentina had a similar experience during their financial crises of 1995 and 2001, respectively. Similarly, remittances steadily increased in East Asian countries during the financial crisis of 1998-2001 (Sharma, 2008). Remittances have therefore emerged as a kind of self-insurance mechanism for developing countries in the face not only of economic downturns, but also of political crisis (as was the case for Lebanon during its civil war and Haiti) and natural disasters (as was the case for countries of Central America in the aftermath of Hurricane Mitch).

Low-income families generally benefit from remittances

Though countries differ in this regard depending on the dominant type of migrant labour, remittances generally reach low-income families, thus benefiting precisely those who are generally more insecure. This is particularly true for countries whose emigrants are primarily low- or unskilled workers. For example, evidence shows that 60 per cent of Mexican and 40 per cent of Paraguayan remittance-receiving households fall in the lowest quintile of the income distribution (Acosta, Fajnzylber and Lopez, 2007).[29] Similarly, inasmuch as most emigrants from South Asian countries are low- or unskilled labourers working in oil-rich Middle Eastern countries, their remittance money also primarily reaches low-income families. Remittances therefore generally produce a more egalitarian distribution, whereas aid-related processes (through misappropriation, etc.) often exacerbate inequality. In a sense, remittances serve as a welfare programme financed and

[28] For example, in 2001, Banco do Brasil issued US$ 300 million in bonds using the future yen remittances from Japan, and similar bonds have been used by financial institutions of Mexico, El Salvador, Panama and Turkey to raise cheaper and longer-term financing from international capital markets (Johnson and Sedaca, 2004; Sharma, 2008).

[29] However, there are countries where remittance income distribution is biased towards the rich. Examples of such countries in Latin America include Peru and Nicaragua (Acosta, Fajnzylber and Lopez, 2007).

implemented by a country's nationals working abroad. As a result of the above, it is not surprising that remittances generally have a greater impact on poverty alleviation than many other sources of national income. According to Ratha (2007), remittances have helped reduce the poverty rate by 11, 6, and 5 percentage points in Uganda, Bangladesh and Ghana, respectively.

A large part of remittances is spent directly on consumption. Surveys in several Latin American countries show that about 84 per cent of the remittance money in El Salvador and 46 per cent in Mexico is spent on household (consumption) expenses (López-Córdova and Olmedo, 2006). A significant part is spent on health and education, helping households to retain and build up human capital and thus to improve their long-term economic position.

Some researchers have suggested that the propensity to save out of remitted incomes is higher than it is for regular income (Orozco, 2003); remittances then become a source of investment financing. For example, the surveys mentioned above also show that about 10 per cent of remittances in Brazil and Guatemala were spent on business investment. Investments out of remittance money are generally small-scale, labour-intensive and geared towards the production of locally demanded goods and services. A remittance-fuelled growth is therefore likely to be more pro-poor.

Measures to strengthen remittance flows can therefore make not only a direct contribution to household security but also an indirect one by strengthening long-term growth prospects. For example, Governments might make sending remittance money easier and less costly, so that a greater proportion of earnings abroad could be sent back home as remittances. They might also adopt policies to ensure that remittances are sent through official channels, instead of through underground or illegal ones, so that it would become easier for the formal financial system to benefit from remittances. They could also take measures to leverage remittances and channel them for public purposes. For instance, in the last decade, Hispanic immigrants across the United States have organized themselves into hometown associations that finance public works projects and small businesses in the towns from which they have migrated. The Government of Mexico has taken the initiative of leveraging the remittances of hometown associations by creating a "three-for-one programme" whereby all hometown association remittances used to improve infrastructure or establish businesses are matched dollar for dollar by the Mexican Federal, State and local authorities (Kapur, 2004).

While emphasizing the beneficial effects of remittances, it should not be forgotten that growth in developing countries can suffer as a consequence of lack of human capital. The best strategy would therefore be to encourage migration by unskilled labour while creating conditions attractive enough to keep skilled and educated labour back home. However, developing-country Governments by themselves may have little control over the first component of this strategy. Moreover, remittances may also negatively affect labour participation, intensity of job search, and risk-taking at home. Research has produced mixed findings on this issue. Funkhouser (1992), based on evidence from Nicaragua, has reported a decrease in labour participation but an increase in self-employment. Yang (2005), on the other hand, has reported a positive effect of remittances on labour participation, particularly by adults. To the extent that part of it may be due to increased enrolment in schools, decrease in (child) labour participation stemming from the flow of remittances should not be treated negatively, as noted by Chami, Fullenkamp and Jahjah (2003). In general, since the income level of remittance-receiving households is still generally low, the labour-disincentive effects of remittances may not be that pronounced.

Remittances boost consumption and promote health and education

Government policies can enhance the positive effect of remittances

More important, probably, is the effect of remittances on government policy formulation. On the negative side, the availability of remittances may increase complacency and reduce the pressure on Governments to carry out reforms designed to improve efficiency and domestic resource mobilization. On the positive side, remittances may help countries reduce their dependence on aid and loans and thus free them from various conditionalities associated with aid. In Bangladesh, for example, between 1990 and 2006, while remittances as a proportion of GDP increased from 2.4 to 9.8 per cent, the corresponding ratio for official development assistance (ODA) decreased from 8 to 2 per cent (Sharma, 2008). This reduced dependence on ODA can help developing countries have more policy space, which they can use to implement pro-poor growth policies, as described above, and thus make significant strides in overcoming economic insecurity.

Towards an integrated approach to dealing with poverty and economic insecurity

Integration of arrangements across formal and informal sectors

Informal employment in developing countries is a challenge for those devising social policies

Fast growth, expansion of formal employment, with decent wages and benefits, public systems of education and health care, and so on, provide the basic foundation for a strong social safety network with broad-based coverage for the whole population. However, to the extent that the coverage of formal employment remains limited, as is particularly the case in developing countries, so that many of the poor and vulnerable are either self-employed or under- or unemployed, or to the extent that, as was the case in some East Asian countries during the financial crisis of the late 1990s, the formal economy has retreated quite sharply, it will be necessary in many poor countries to adopt various direct intervention programmes to provide income and security. Discussion in the previous sections has pointed to many such programmes and most countries will, in practice, combine several such programmes to reduce levels of insecurity. The particular combination of public and private, both formal and informal, arrangements needed to create the right social protection network will vary from country to country.

Still, in all cases, in the search for the right mixtures, there will be a need to concentrate on maximizing complementarities across the available programmes. First, there may be complementariness *across groups*. Thus, different groups of insecure people at the same time and at the same location may require different types of programmes depending on their specific characteristics and needs. For example, while in a village in times of distress, families with able-bodied working-age members may need *workfare* programmes, families without such members may need *welfare* programmes. Second, the complementariness may run *across time*. Thus, while in the immediate aftermath of a flood and the associated crop loss, a village may benefit from *food aid*, after some time (when the challenge of immediate survival has been dealt with and normal work has picked up), a programme of *cash transfer* may be more helpful. Third, the complementariness may run *across space*. Thus, villagers in a location with highly erratic rainfall may benefit more from a rainfall insurance programme, whereas residents in a locality with stable irrigation facilities may not need such a programme. Fourth, there may be complementariness between *public* and *private* sector initiatives. For example, various microfinance programmes, which are by and large private sector initiatives, may complement various workfare and welfare programmes, which are usually public sector operations. As mentioned earlier, unlike most other direct intervention programmes, microfinance originated as, and has remained, a predominantly private sector operation. So far as budget affordability is concerned, microfinance programmes can therefore provide an alternative or be a useful complement to the public sector-funded programmes. Fifth, there may be complementariness *across programme attributes*. For example, micro-insurance programmes can make microcredit programmes more beneficial. Similarly, microsavings programmes can facilitate functioning of micro-insurance programmes (box V.5).[30]

Complementariness among various microfinance programmes

Box V.5

Microfinance now encompasses programmes of microcredit, microsavings and micro-insurance. Each of these programmes has its unique niche, though a closer analysis shows that they may be complementary to each other in many ways. One dimension of this complementariness is of an *organizational nature*. For example, it was found to be expedient in many cases to have the same organization offer various microfinance services as joint products. Such an organizational set-up may be beneficial in several respects. First of all, it may reduce cost, and thus ensure the initial survivability of new programmes by letting them piggyback on already operational programmes. Second, besides permitting them to economize on overhead and transaction costs, such a set-up may help new programmes in deeper ways, for example, by allowing micro-insurance programmes to avoid problems of adverse selection and other information and enforcement problems.

A second type of complementarity arises out of the *specific roles* that different microfinance programmes can play. Even though microcredit, microsavings, and micro-insurance can all play an insurance role, the specific ways in which they play this role are different in each case. Various microfinance programmes can therefore complement each other and their functions can be combined so as to meet the specific needs of a household or community.

It has been noted that while insurance programmes are risk-specific, savings can serve as a more general-purpose insurance. Clarke and Dercon (2008, p. 11) expand the idea further by classifying risks into "small" and "large/catastrophic", suggesting that while "quasi-insurance" programmes, such as microsavings, may be effective in dealing with the former category of risk, specific micro-insurance programmes can be more effective in dealing with the latter. The actual practice indeed seems to support the notion of such a specialization. A large number of micro-insurance programmes indeed focus on risk to life.

Clarke and Dercon (2008) further note that the above-mentioned complementarities may be used to redesign the "credit life insurance" component of conventional microcredit programmes so that it becomes beneficial both to the lender and to the borrower. Such a redesigned credit life insurance can counteract the increased vulnerability that microcredit may otherwise create for certain borrowers in certain situations. More concretely, Dercon suggests that in some situations signing up for micro-insurance might be made mandatory for microcredit clients. This is basically a proposal for organizational integration using complementarity of an organizational nature as mentioned above.

However, it should be noted that there are also downsides to organizational integration of various microfinance programmes. First, people who are not interested in micro-insurance may now feel discouraged from accessing microcredit. Thus, the proposed compulsory bundling may restrict expansion of microcredit. Second, allowing such bundling may also lead to collusion among microfinance service providers and give rise to market power. Hence, caution is necessary with regard to implementing proposals for organizational/programme integration.

---

30   The BRAC Income Generation for Vulnerable Group Development (IGVGD) programme (Bangladesh) is often cited as an example of successful utilization of complementarities among various direct intervention programmes. Under the programme, extremely poor people, who are left out of conventional microcredit programmes, are provided with food aid and microsavings services, which enable them to make a "low-risk transition" from the relatively non-risky environment of the subsistence economy to the risky environment of the cash economy. In general, concrete analyses of concrete situations are indispensable for determining the right type of direct poverty and insecurity alleviation programmes necessary. In fact, such analyses may lead to new, innovative efforts or a new configuration of previously known efforts. There is therefore no substitute for concrete analysis of concrete situations utilizing the most detailed information that can possibly be gathered.

"Benign" and "pernicious"
types of traditional security
arrangements exist

One particular issue that requires closer examination is the role that pre-existing, traditional, and informal security mechanisms can play in delivering social protection. The question that is of particular interest is whether these are undermined and displaced by new, modern, and formal security arrangements or whether there can be some complementarity between these two types of security arrangements for the poor. In considering this question, it should be noted that pre-existing, traditional security arrangements can be either "benign" or "pernicious". Borrowing from friends, relatives or fellow villagers on the basis of altruism or reciprocity may be an example of the benign type of traditional security arrangement. Traditional "funeral societies", prevalent in many countries of Africa, in which members contribute on a regular basis so as to be able to obtain a lump-sum amount when death strikes, may offer another example of a traditional benign security arrangement. Similarly, Rotating Savings and Credit Associations (ROSCAs), popular in many countries, where members make regular payments in order to be able to receive a lump-sum amount in turn, may represent another such example. On the other hand, usurious borrowing from local moneylenders (in exchange for collaterals) is an example of the pernicious type of traditional security arrangement.[31]

Modern poverty alleviation programmes may complement and build on traditional "benign" security arrangements

According to some scholars, traditional security arrangements of the benign type are few and far between. They point to the very prevalence of traditional security arrangements of the pernicious type as a proof of the inadequacy of the benign type. From this viewpoint, there is not much reason to worry about the "crowding out" effect of new programmes (Morduch, 1999b; Ravallion, 1991).

By contrast, Clarke and Dercon (2008) urge caution against undermining or supplanting pre-existing security arrangements.[32] They note that traditional security arrangements are fragile and depend crucially on proper alignment of the interests of all participating members. Anything that undoes this alignment is likely to disrupt such arrangements. Clarke and Dercon therefore recommend that, in designing new programmes, effort should be made to make use of the pre-existing arrangements and to build upon them. In particular, they note that relying on groups, instead of individuals, in designing the modern interventions can be more helpful as regards preserving and making use of the pre-existing, traditional security arrangements. Certainly, in those countries that still have large rural populations, growth strategies will likely have an agrarian bias and the State sector may need to channel scarce resources towards infrastructure development. Consequently, in these situations, it is likely that support measures will need to be tailored to a more prominent role for community- and family-based support measures.

Universality versus targeting

Donors have generally promoted targeting in social policy

A good deal of controversy surrounding social policy centres on whether efforts at alleviation of poverty and increasing security should follow the principle of "universalism" or

---

31   It should be noted that the distinction between traditional and modern arrangements or between formal and informal ones is relative. For example, it is moot whether Rotating Savings and Credit Associations ought to be called traditional, since these emerged in the nineteenth century and in that sense they belong to the "modern" era. However, to the extent that these may already exist when new interventions are being considered, they may be deemed traditional. Similarly, it is not clear whether usurious borrowing from traditional moneylenders should be called informal, because generally such borrowing entailed *impersonal* contracts with clearly stipulated conditions which were often accompanied by some kind of written instrument (the signature or thumbprint of the borrower). Similarly, it is not clear whether some microfinance programmes should be characterized as formal or informal.

32   See also Dercon (2001, 2002).

that of "targeting". Since the 1980s, donor agencies have generally advocated targeting usually on both efficiency grounds and as a response to binding resource constraints. In many cases, this was a deliberate attempt to limit the role of the State, on the assumption that one can alleviate poverty with less resources (Besley and Kanbur, 1990).

However, the experience with targeting has revealed several shortcomings including high administrative and transaction costs, perverse incentives and financial non-sustainability in the face of weak political support (Mkandawire, 2007). According to a study by the Asian Development Bank Institute which examined six Asian countries: "With relatively high levels of leakage the expectation is that in practice most targeting measures are high-cost means of transferring benefits to the poor" (Weiss, 2004). Self-targeting schemes appear to be the "cheapest" but this comes at the cost of under-coverage (Mkandawire, 2007, pp. 319-320). Of particular concern is the way in which targeting, almost by definition, leads to segmentation and differentiation. In service provision, targeting can lead to a dual structure—one part created for the poor and funded by the State, the other created for the rich and supported by the private sector. Geographical targeting often leads to horizontal inequality so that the poor in one area benefits more than the poor in another, non-targeted area. As discussed in chapter IV, this combination of polarization and spatial inequality can be explosive politically and is often the basis of ethnic conflicts.

Some observers have also raised questions regarding conditionality linked to targeting, pointing to the perverse outcomes that conditionalities often generate (Standing, 2007). A tragic example is provided by programmes in Namibia and South Africa where the means-tested disability grant to AIDS victims (which reaches 20 per cent of the total affected population) is withdrawn if the patient's condition improves and his or her capacity to work increases. As a result, many AIDS patients stop taking the medication after experiencing some improvement and let their condition worsen so as to continue to receive the assistance. The expression "sickness-poverty trap" has been coined to refer to this kind of situation. According to Standing, the experience of Namibia and South Africa contrasts with that of Zimbabwe where in similar programmes, formal conditionalities are largely ignored, thereby yielding better results.

Targeting and conditionality can generate poverty traps and other perverse effects

In general, the experience points to the fact that targeting leads to reduced budgets devoted to poverty and welfare, so that "the more for the poor means less for the poor" (Gelbach and Pritchett, 1995), suggesting that the optimal policy for the poorest and most vulnerable is not necessarily the one that targets benefits as narrowly and efficiently as possible (Sen, 1995).

Targeting leads to reduced spending on poverty and welfare

In fact, most Governments tend to have a mixture of both universal and targeted social policies. In the more successful countries, however, the overall social policy has been universalistic and targeting has been used simply as one instrument for making universalism more effective (Skocpol, 1991). The particular combination appears to be linked to how the developmental State manages developments in the labour market, beginning from modest, often means-tested, programmes for limited groups of the population. However, early institutional solutions may have an effect on the later expansion and development of social programmes; for example, those first introduced based on the principle of economic means-testing may be more likely to develop into universal programmes than those established for clearly defined groups of the economically active population. In contrast, a focus on general education has proved to be of great importance for successful subsequent economic development and national wealth.

Targeting should serve universalism

Scandinavia and East Asia offer examples of different means of expanding social protection in support of development

Development strategies can never simply mirror successful experiences from the past. However, both the more "inclusive welfare developmentalism" strategy pursued in Scandinavia, and the more selective strategy used, for example, in Taiwan Province of China and the Republic of Korea, can offer useful lessons for today's middle-income countries searching for a more effective balance of social and economic policies (see box V.6).[33]

Box V.6

Some possible lessons to be derived from the Scandinavian welfare experience

Specific historical social and economic factors in Scandinavia may have been conducive to the development of a participatory political culture, consensus-building, a strong role of local and central government, and the overall support for the principle of universalism. However, developing governmental capacity and institutions for promoting welfare and the adoption of universal policies for the general level of welfare, carry broader relevance.

The scope of social planning—including establishing and developing social security, health and educational systems during the first half of the twentieth century—was clearly a result of democratic political processes aimed at balancing demands for and goals of economic growth and social justice.

A focus on general education and universal health services may prove to be of great importance for subsequent successful economic development and national wealth. State and public responsibility for a healthy population should be insisted on from the start in the context of creating national wealth and strength. The early stress on universal, compulsory education is not necessarily motivated by the urge for economic development. However, it can be instrumental for rapid industrialization, modernization of the economy and economic upgrading.

Social security and welfare State arrangements embody political and social preferences, formed by culture, traditions, economic and technological developments, social structure and social relations. There is no objectively "correct" path for governmental social policies. Values and preferences concern, among other things, perceptions about fairness, social justice, social cohesion, stability and equalization of life chances. One core challenge in respect of any social security system is how to organize it in such a way as to ensure that it provides incentives to work, which seems to be an important goal of most Governments. One possible effect of an unemployment insurance system would be its facilitation of the process of restructuring in industry and business. Economic security may reduce workers' and employees' resistance to change. Obligatory government schemes, which cover employees and workers independently of specific employment conditions or specific characteristics of firms or employers operating at a given place and time, may be advantageous with respect to labour mobility, structural economic change and economic growth. National schemes for unemployment insurance are basically work-friendly.

There is no simple link between the scope of the welfare state and taxation levels, nor between its scope and long-term economic performance (growth, employment rates, labour productivity or adjustment to economic shocks). However, a well-developed welfare State, with sophisticated social security arrangements, may get through a crisis more easily—or at least at a more moderate social cost (in terms of poverty and inequality).

In a more globalized world, we may expect more rapid changes in labour markets, greater mobility, more flexible work, and more career shifts during the period of labour-market participation. These new patterns may induce changes in pension systems designed to make them more transparent and less dependent upon the "best years" and "last years" of earnings, and thus fairer, in the sense that the pension would reflect contributions during all working years. Another lesson for other countries may be that in the era of globalization (that is, greater economic integration in the world), the need for a consolidated, national social security system is objectively greater than before.

Source: Kuhnle and Hort (2004).

---

[33] Several of today's middle-income economies have income levels and economic structures similar to those of Scandinavian economies of the 1930s.

Box V.7

Into the wild: the case for a basic minimum income

The International Labour Organization (2004a) has raised the question whether a basic minimum income—essentially a regular and unconditional cash grant from the State—could become an unconditional right for all citizens. The core objective of a universal basic income would be to protect populations against the downside risks from either idiosyncratic or covariant shocks of a non-catastrophic nature. Such ex ante schemes are generally seen to be more effective than ex post schemes in providing a minimum level of economic security, and cash transfers have generally proved to be the most rapid means of helping people in times of crisis. Given the various negative incentive problems associated with means-tested and targeted benefits, there appear to be strong grounds for a universal approach to income security. Any discussion of such a proposal immediately raises two fundamental questions: Is it politically feasible? Is it affordable?

Notions of fairness are culturally prescribed, and an unconditional grant would be unacceptable in many countries. Taking the United Kingdom of Great Britain and Northern Ireland as a case study, Atkinson (1996) proposed a "participation income" paid to all those aged 18 or over, which would reduce (so the study argues) the number of people dependent on means-tested benefits, while over 50 per cent of families would be better off, women in particular. The related idea of a "negative income tax", first suggested by Friedman (1962), has been explored at the Federal and State levels in the United States of America as an option for means-tested benefits. These explorations eventually gave rise to the so-called Earned Income Credit introduced in 1975 but, generally, it was found to be difficult to devise a scheme that would match the cash and in-kind benefits already available without undermining the incentive to work (Allen, 2002). In Belgium and the Netherlands, a minimum income guarantee is granted to people who are out of a job and do not have or have lost other entitlements, such as family allowances or pensions. The amount of income granted often varies in relation to age, family and employment situations of the beneficiaries. Ongoing discussions in these countries on the transformation of income-security programmes into unconditional minimum income schemes are of particular interest in respect of a potential universal basic income. Related schemes are already in place in some developing countries that have the full or partial aspects of a minimum basic income. These schemes are often differentiated by the scope of coverage and the specific entitlements that populations can be granted, for example, minimum income guarantee (India), food for work (Afghanistan) and Bolsa Familia for the poorest (Brazil).

The costing of such schemes also raises questions. Some of these have been dealt with in the discussion in the 2007 *World Economic and Social Survey* (United Nations, 2007a), on universal pension schemes. These schemes are often funded through general tax revenues. The *Survey* estimated that a universal pension system keeping older persons out of extreme poverty—by setting benefits at $1 per day for everyone aged 60 years or over—would cost 1 per cent of gross domestic product (GDP) or less for about two thirds of developing countries (ibid.). In other words, this would seem to be an affordable option, even for many of the poorest countries. Blackburn (2007) has taken this argument a step further and proposed a global pension fund to administer a universal pension scheme financed by a modest tax on global financial transactions and corporate wealth.

Perhaps the best known example of an operational basic income scheme is the Alaska Permanent Fund Dividend, which, since 1982, has paid an annual grant to every Alaskan, including children, who was a resident during the previous year and indicated the intention to remain. The Alaska Permanent Fund Dividend is funded from the State's oil revenues, which accounts for over 40 per cent of its value added (Goldsmith, 2001). The payment has averaged US$ 1,000 per person and in 2007 a family of four received close to $6,000. Spending has been on consumer durables as well as on savings for children and college funds.

This scheme, which on average absorbs 2.2 per cent of Alaska's GDP, provides a benchmark for replicating the basic income idea elsewhere. Few countries can count on windfall natural resource rents like Alaska. Hence, funding may have to be provided from general tax revenues or from a contributory scheme. The nature and coverage of fiscal systems vary significantly on a country-by-country basis. In principle, given that the aim would be to bolster economic security rather than redistribute incomes, the feasibility of a basic income scheme would depend on the breadth of the fiscal base.

Box V.7 (cont'd)

To obtain an idea of the affordability of a basic income scheme, one could use the taxable income of the highest quintile of the population as the financing constraint. Based on a sample of 85 countries and using the example of Alaska by setting 2.2 per cent of GDP as the constraint, the global budget for a universal basic income for 85 countries would amount to $1.1 trillion in 2007. Given that the total net income of the top quintile for the sample of countries is about $11.6 trillion, on average the tax would amount to under 10 per cent of this segment's income. That figure leans heavily, however, on the income of the rich in developed countries and in a few Latin American countries with relatively high income inequality. The tax burden on the rich in the poorest countries would likely become unrealistically high. Further estimations for 159 countries reveal that in 129 developing countries the annual payout or basic income per individual would be less than $360 (or less than $1 dollar a day). An additional $1.3 trillion would be needed to cover the shortfall and ensure that all would at least receive a basic income of one dollar per day. The rich in developing countries would probably not be able to make the larger contribution to cover this additional cost. Hence, a certain amount of resources would have to be transferred from rich to poor countries in order to make such a global basic income scheme viable. A multilateral transfer mechanism could be devised to facilitate this.

Some observers however note that the dominant welfare model is too heavily based on the twentieth century industrial wage-labour paradigm. Standing (2007) refers to this as the "old-dualistic model" and argues that in the current era of post-industrial society and globalization, the paradigm may have become less valid. According to this argument, the shift in paradigm calls for a fundamental change in the approach towards welfare. Standing (p. 22) thinks that a universal social pension is a feasible first step in the direction of establishing the universal right to income security, and thereby promoting sustainable livelihoods and personal development. He expresses the optimistic view that "sooner or later universal basic income security will emerge as the sensible and equitable objective from the experience with targeted, conditional cash transfers" (p. 27).

According to this assessment, a universal, regular and unconditional cash grant could replace the provision of means-testing which entails significant administrative, incentive and coverage problems (see box V.7 above). There are already examples of such universalistic schemes though their wider political acceptability and financial feasibility are open to question.

Bibliography

Acosta, Pablo, Pablo Fajnzylber and Humberto Lopez (2007). The impact of remittances on poverty and human capital: evidence from Latin American household surveys. World Bank Policy Research Working Paper, No. 4247. Washington, D.C.: World Bank. June 2007.

ACP-EU Joint Parliamentary Assembly (2007). Resolution on natural disasters in ACP States: EU funding for preparedness (EDF funds) and relief (ECHO funds). Available from http://www.acp-eu.gov.rw/index.php?iro=news&obj=49&details=235. November.

Addison, T., A.R. Chowdhury and S.M. Murshed (2004). The fiscal dimensions of conflict and reconstruction. In *Fiscal Policy for Development: Poverty, Reconstruction and Growth*, Tony Addison and Alan Roe, eds. Basingstoke, United Kingdom: Palgrave Macmillan, pp. 260-273.

Ahmad, S. (2006). Poverty, drugs and corruption "fueling Afghan insurgency". *Agence France-Presse*, 12 February.

Akyüz, Yilmaz (2008). Financial instability and countercyclical policy. Background paper prepared for *World Economic and Social Survey 2008*.

Albala-Bertrand, J.M. (1993). *The Political Economy of Large Natural Disasters*. Oxford, United Kingdom: Clarendon Press.

Alderman, H., J. Hoddinott and B. Kinsey (2004). Long-term consequences of early childhood malnutrition. HiCN Working Paper, No. 09. Brighton, United Kingdom: Households in Conflict Network (HiCN), University of Sussex. July.

Allen, Jodie (2002). Negative income tax. *The Concise Encyclopedia of Economics, 2002,* David R. Henderson, ed. Indianapolis, Indiana: Liberty Fund.

Andersen, R. (2000). How multilateral development assistance triggered the conflict in Rwanda. *Third World Quarterly,* vol. 21, No. 3, pp. 441-456.

Archibald, S., and P. Richards (2002). Converts to human rights? popular debate about war and justice in rural central Sierra Leone. *Africa*, vol. 72, No. 3.

Armendariz de Aghion, Beatriz, and Jonathan Morduch (2005). *The Economics of Microfinance.* Cambridge, Massachusetts: The MIT Press.

Arndt, C., S. Jones and F. Tarp (2006). Aid and development: the Mozambican case. Discussion Paper, No. 06-13. Copenhagen: University of Copenhagen, Department of Economics.

Astorga, P., P. Berges and V. Fitzgerald (2005). The standard of living in Latin America during the twentieth century. *Economic History Review*, vol. 68, No. 4, pp. 765-796.

Atkinson, A. B. (1996). The case for a participation income. *The Political Quarterly*, vol. 67, No. 1 (January), pp. 67-70.

Auffret, Philippe (2003). High consumption volatility: the impact of natural disasters. *World Bank Policy Research Working Paper,* No. 2962. Washington, D.C.: World Bank. January.

Auty, R.M. (1990). *Resource Based Industrialization: Sowing the Oil in Eight Developing Countries*. New York: Oxford University Press.

Avila, L., and E. Bacha (1987). Methodological note. In *International Monetary and Financial Issues for Developing Countries*. Geneva: United Nations Conference on Trade and Development, pp. 177-204.

Balassa, Bella (1981). The newly-industrializing developing countries after the oil crisis, *Weltwirtschaftliches Archiv*, vol. 117, No. 1 (March), pp: 142-194.

Ball, N., and S. Barnes (2000). Mozambique. In *Good Intentions: Pledges of Aid for Post-Conflict Recovery*, Shepard Forman and Stewart Patrick, eds. Boulder, Colorado: Lynne Rienner.

Ballentine, K., and J. Sherman (2003). *The Political Economy of Armed Conflict Beyond Greed and Grievance*. Boulder, Colorado: Lynne Rienner.

Banarjee, Ahbhijit, and others (2006). An evaluation of World Bank research, 1998–2005. Washington, D.C.: World Bank. Mimeo. September.

Bandyopadhyay, D. (1988). Direct intervention programmes for poverty alleviation: an appraisal. *Economic and Political Weekly*, vol. 23, No. 26 (June), pp. A77-A88.

Bank for International Settlements (BIS) (2001). *71st Annual Report: 1 April 2000 - 31 March 2001*. Basel: BIS.

Barrett, C., S. Holden and D. Clay (2001). Can food-for-work programmes reduce vulnerability? Discussion Paper, No. D-07/2004. Aas, Norway: Agricultural University of Norway. Also available in *Insurance Against Poverty*, Stefan Dercon, ed. (Oxford, United Kingdom, Oxford University Press, 2004). Additional information available from http://papers.ssrn.com/so13/papers.cfm?abstract_id=329660.

Barrett, C.B., and M.R. Carter (2006). Poverty traps and productive social safety nets: policy implications for conflict recovery. Paper prepared for the Conference on Poverty Reduction in Conflict and Fragile States: Perspectives from the Household Level, Washington, D.C., 8 and 9 November 2006, organized by the United States Agency for International Development, the Households in Conflict Network (HiCN) and the German Institute for Economic Research (DIW, Berlin).

Basu, Kaushik (1981). Food for work programmes: beyond roads that get washed away. *Economic and Political Weekly*, vol. 16, Nos.1-2, pp. 37-40.

Benson, Charlotte (1994). Book review: *The Political Economy of Large Natural Disasters with Special Reference to Developing Countries*, by J.M. Albala-Bertrand. *Disasters*, vol. 18, No. 4, pp. 383-386.

_____ (1998). The cost of disasters. In *Development at risk? natural disasters and the third world*, John Twigg, ed. Oxford, United Kingdom: Oxford Centre for Disaster Studies, pp. 8-13.

Berdal, M. (1996). *Disarmament and Demobilisation after Civil Wars*. Adelphi Paper, No. 303. Oxford, United Kingdom: Oxford University Press.

Besley, Timothy (1995). Nonmarket institutions for credit and risk sharing in low-income countries. *Journal of Economic Perspectives*, vol. 9, No. 3 (summer), pp. 115-127.

_____, and Ravi Kanbur (1990). The principles of targeting. World Bank Policy Research Working Paper, No. 385. Washington, D.C.: World Bank.

_____, and Stephen Coate (1992). Workfare versus welfare: incentive arguments for work requirements in poverty-alleviation programs. *American Economic Review*, vol. 82, No. 1 (March), pp. 249-261.

Binzel, C., and T. Brück (2006). Conflict and fragility: findings from the literature and a framework for analysis at the micro level. Paper prepared for the Second Annual HiCN Workshop: The Unit of Analysis and the Micro-Level Dynamics of Violent Conflict, Antwerp, Belgium 2006.

Birkmann, Joern (2007). Tsunami: socio-economic insecurities, direct and indirect impacts and the post-tsunami process: special focus on Indonesia and Sri Lanka. Background paper for *World Economic and Social Survey 2008*.

Blackburn, Robin (2007). A global pension plan. *New Left Review*, No. 47 (September/ October).

Borio, C., C. Furfine and P. Lowe (2001). Procyclicality of financial system and financial stability: issues and policy options. BIS Paper, No. 1. Basel: BIS.

Boyce, J.K. (2002). *Investing in Peace: Aid and Conditionality after Civil Wars*. Oxford, United Kingdom: Oxford University Press.

_____ (2005). Development assistance, conditionality, and war economies. In *Profiting from Peace: Managing the Resource Dimensions of Civil War*, Karen Ballentine and Heiko Nitzsche, eds. Boulder, Colorado: Lynne Rienner, pp. 287-314.

_____ (2008). Post-conflict recovery: resource mobilization and reconstruction. Background paper prepared for *World Economic and Social Survey 2008*.

_____, and L. Ndikumana (2001). Is Africa a net creditor? new estimates of capital flight from severely indebted sub-Saharan African countries, 1970-1996. *Journal of Development Studies*, vol. 38, No. 2, pp. 27-56.

Brown, Gordon (2006). Comment: Our final goal must be to offer a global new deal. *The Guardian,* Wednesday, 11 January 2006, p. 26. Available from http://www. guardian.co.uk/politics/2006/jan/11/debtrelief.internationalaidand development.

Brueckner, T., and A. Ciccone (2007). Growth democracy and civil war. Barcelona, Spain: Universitat Pompeu Fabra. Mimeo.

_____ (2008). Rain and the democratic window of opportunity. Barcelona, Spain: Universitat Pompeu Fabra. Mimeo.

Budnevich, Carlos (2008). Stabilization funds to mitigate economic vulnerability. Background paper for *World Economic and Social Survey 2008*.

Buira, A. (2003). The governance of the IMF in a global economy. In *Challenges to the World and IMF: Developing Country Perspectives*, A. Buira, ed. London: Anthem Press.

Bundervoet, T., and P. Verwimp (2005). Civil war and economic sanctions: an analysis of anthropometric outcomes in Burundi. HiCN Working Paper, No. 11. Brighton, United Kingdom: Households in Conflict Network (HiCN), University of Sussex. Available from www.hicn.org.

Bunyavanich, S., and others (2003). The impact of climate change on child health. *Ambulatory Pediatrics*, vol. 3, No. 1 (January-February), pp. 44-52.

Butler, K., and S. Gates (2007). Communal violence and property rights. Paper presented at the Jan Timbergen European Peace Science Conference, Amsterdam, 25-27 June 2007.

Cain, Mead, and Samuel S. Lieberman (1983). Development policy and the prospects for fertility decline in Bangladesh. *Bangladesh Development Studies*, vol. 11, No. 3, pp. 1-38.

Carnahan, M. (2007). Options for revenue generation in post-conflict environments. Public Finance in Post-Conflict Environments Policy Paper, No. 1. New York: Center on International Cooperation; and Amherst, Massachusetts: Political Economy Research Institute.

Caselli, F., and P. Malhotra (2004). Natural disasters and growth: from thought experiment to natural experiment. International Monetary Fund. Unpublished draft.

Chami, Ralph, Connel Fullenkamp and Samir Jahjah (2003). Are immigrant remittances a source of capital for development? IMF Working Paper, No. 03/189. Washington, D.C.: International Monetary Fund. September.

Chang, Ha-Joon, and Richard Kozul-Wright (1994). Organising development: comparing the national systems of entrepreneurship in Sweden and South Korea. *Journal of Developmental Studies*, vol. 30, No. 4.

Chen, Shaohua, and Martin Ravallion (2007). Absolute poverty measures for the developing world, 1981-2004. World Bank Policy Research Working Paper, No. 4211. Washington, D.C.: World Bank.

Chronic Poverty Research Centre (2005). Chronic poverty report 2004-05. Manchester, United Kingdom: Chronic Poverty Research Centre, School of Environment and Development, University of Manchester.

Churchill, Craig, ed. (2006). *Protecting the Poor: A Microinsurance Compendium*. Geneva: International Labour Office.

Clark, C. (2006). Livelihood networks and decision-making among Congolese young people in formal and informal refugee contexts in Uganda. HiCN Working Paper, No. 13. Brighton, United Kingdom: Households in Conflict Network (HiCN), University of Sussex.

_____ (2007). Understanding vulnerability: from categories to experiences of Congolese young people in Uganda. *Children and Society*, vol. 21, No. 4, pp. 284-296.

Clarke, Daniel, and Stefan Dercon (2008). Insurance, credit, and safety nets for the poor in a world of risk. Background paper prepared for *World Economic and Social Survey 2008*.

Coady, David, Margaret Grosh and John Hoddinott (2004). *Targeting of Transfers in Developing Countries: Review of Lessons and Experiences*. World Bank Regional and Sectoral Studies. Washington, D.C.: World Bank and International Food Policy Research Institute.

Collier, P. (1999). On the economic consequences of civil war. *Oxford Economic Papers*, vol. 50, No. 4, pp. 168-183.

_____ (2002). Aid, policy and growth in post-conflict countries. World Bank dissemination note, No. 2. Washington, D.C.: World Bank, Conflict Prevention and Reconstruction Unit.

_____ (2007a). Economic causes of civil conflict and their implications for policy. In *Leashing the Dogs of War*, Chester A. Crocker, Fen Osler Hampson and Pamela Aall, eds. Washington, D.C.: United States Institute of Peace Press.

_____ (2007b). *The Bottom Billion*. Oxford, United Kingdom: Oxford University Press.

_____, and others (2003). *Breaking the Conflict Trap: Civil War and Development Policy*. World Bank Policy Research Report, No. 26121. Washington, D.C.: World Bank; and New York, New York: Oxford University Press.

_____, and Anke Hoeffler (2002). On the incidence of civil war in Africa. *Journal of Conflict Resolution*, vol. 46, No. 1, pp. 13-28.

_____ (2004). Greed and grievance in civil wars. *Oxford Economic Papers*, vol. 56, No. 4, pp. 563-595.

Cornia, Giovanni Andrea (2007). Potential and limitations of pro-poor macroeconomics: An Overview. In *Pro-Poor Macroeconomics: Potential and Limitations,* Giovanni Andrea Cornia, ed. New York, New York: Palgrave Macmillan.

Cramer, Christopher (2002). *Homo economicus* goes to war: methodological individualism, rational choice and political economy of war. *World Development*, vol. 30, No. 11, pp. 1845-1864.

Cumming, Christine (2006). Review of recent trends and issues in financial sector globalisation. In *Financial Globalization. BIS Papers*, No. 32. Basel: Bank for International Settlements. December.

Czaika, M., and K. Kis-Katos (2007). Civil conflict and displacement: village-level determinants of forced migration in Aceh. HiCN Working Paper, No. 32. Brighton, United Kingdom: Households in conflict Network (HiCN), University of Sussex.

Dagderiven Hulya, Rolph van der Hoeven and John Weeks (2001). Redistribution Matters: Growth for Poverty Reduction. Employment Paper, No. 2001/10. Geneva: International Labour Office.

Daley, Randolph W., Adam Karpati and Mani Sheik (2001). Needs assessment of the displaced population following the August earthquake in Turkey. *Disasters*, vol. 25, No. 1, pp. 67-75.

Date-Bah, E. (2001). *Crisis and Decent Work: A Collection of Essays*. Geneva: International Labour Organization, In Focus Programme on Crisis Response and Reconstruction.

Davis, J., and others (2001). Stabilization and Savings Funds for Nonrenewable Resources: Experience and Fiscal Policy Implications. *IMF Occasional Paper, No. 205.* Washington, D.C.*:* International Monetary Fund.

De Ferranti, David, and others (2000). *Securing Our Future in a Global Economy.* World Bank Latin American and Caribbean Studies: Viewpoints. Washington, D.C.: World Bank. June.

de Walque, Damien (2006). The long-term legacy of the Khmer Rouge period in Cambodia. Paper presented at the First Annual Workshop, Households in Conflict Network, Berlin, 15 and 16 January 2006. Available from www.hicn.org.

Deininger, K. (2003). Causes and consequences of civil strife: micro-level evidence from Uganda. *Oxford Economic Papers,* vol. 55, No. 4, pp. 579-606.

_____, A.M. Ibáñez and P. Querubin (2004). Towards sustainable return policies for the displaced population: why are some displaced households more willing to return than others? HiCN Working Paper, No. 07. Brighton, United Kingdom: Households in Conflict Network (HiCN), University of Sussex.

Demeke, Mulat, Fantu Guta and Tadele Ferede (2003). Growth, employment, poverty and policies in Ethiopia: an empirical investigation. Issues in Employment and Poverty Discussion Paper No. 12. Geneva: Employment Strategy Department, International Labour Office. August.

Department for International Development (2005). Natural disaster and disaster risk reduction measures: a desk review of costs and benefits. Draft final report. London: DFID. 8 December.

Dercon, Stefan (2001). Conclusion. In *Insurance Against Poverty*. UNU-WIDER Studics in Economic Development. Oxford, United Kingdom: Oxford University Press.

_____ (2002). Income Risk, Coping Strategies, and Safety Nets. WIDER Discussion Paper, No. 2002/22. Helsinki: United Nations University World Institute for Development Economics Research.

_____ (2004). *Insurance Against Poverty*. Oxford, United Kingdom: Oxford University Press.

Devlin, J., and S. Titman (2004). Managing oil price risk in developing countries. *The World Bank Research Observer*, vol. 19, No. 1, pp. 119-139.

Dewhirst, P. (1998). Frozen emotions: women's experience of violence and trauma in El Salvador, Kenya, and Rwanda. *Development Update,* vol. 2, No. 2.

Dowrick, S., and J. Golley (2004). Trade openness and growth: who benefits? O*xford Review of Economic Policy*, vol. 20, No. 1 (spring), pp. 38-56.

Duclos, Jean-Yves, Joan Esteban and Debraj Ray (2004). Polarization: concepts, measurement, estimation. *Econometrica*, vol. 72, No. 6 (November), pp. 1737-1772.

Dunning, Thad (2005). Resource dependence, economic performance, and political stability. *Journal of Conflict Resolution*, vol. 49, No. 4, pp. 457-482.

Dwan, R., and L. Bailey (2006). Liberia's governance and economic management assistance programme (GEMAP). New York: Department of Peacekeeping Operations of the United Nations Secretariat; and Washington, D.C.: World Bank, Fragile States Group. Available from http://www.gemapliberia.org/files/WB_Joint_review_of_GEMAP.pdf.

Easterly, William (2005). What did structural adjustment adjust? The association of policies and growth with repeated IMF and World Bank adjustment loans. *Journal of Development Economics*, vol. 76, No. 1 (February), pp. 1-22.

_____, Roumeen Islam and Joseph E. Stiglitz (2001). Shaken and stirred: volatility and macroeconomic paradigms for rich and poor countries. In *Annual World Bank Conference on Development Economics 2000*, Boris Pleskovic and Nicholas Stern, eds. Washington, D.C.: World Bank, pp. 191-212.

Epstein, Gerald, ed. (2005). *Financialization and the World Economy*. Cheltenham, United Kingdom: Edward Elgar, chap. 3.

_____, Ilene Grabel and K.S. Jomo (forthcoming). Capital management techniques in developing countries: managing capital flows. In *IPD Capital Markets Liberalization Companion Volume,* José Antonio Ocampo, Shari Spiegel and Joseph Stiglitz, eds. Oxford, United Kingdom: Oxford University Press.

Esteban, J.M., and D. Ray (1999). Conflict and distribution. *Journal of Economic Theory*, vol. 87, No. 2, pp. 379-415.

Falch, Torben, and Per Tovmo (2003). Norwegian local public finance in the 1930s and beyond. *European Review of Economic History, vol.* 7, No. 1, pp. 127-154.

Fearon, James D. (2004). Why do some civil wars last so much longer than others? *Journal of Peace Research*, vol. 41, No. 3, pp. 379-414.

_____, and David D. Laitin (2003). Ethnicity, insurgency, and civil war. *American Political Science Review*, vol. 97, No. 1, pp. 75-90.

Federal Emergency Management Agency (FEMA) (2007). Robert T. Stafford Disaster Relief and Emergency Assistance Act, as amended, and Related Authorities. *FEMA 592*. Available from http://www.fema.gov/pdf/about/stafford_act.pdf. U.S. Department of Homeland Security. June.

Ffrench-Davis, Ricardo (2006). *Reforming Latin America's Economies: After Market Fundamentalism*. Basingstoke, United Kingdom: Palgrave Macmillan.

Fielding, D. (2003). How does civil war affect the magnitude of capital flight? evidence from Israel during the intifada. Discussion Paper in Economics, No. 03/10. Leicester, United Kingdom: Department of Economics, University of Leicester.

Fiess, Norbert (2002). Chile's new fiscal rule. Washington, D.C.: World Bank. Mimeo. May.

FitzGerald, Edward, and K. Sarmad (1997). External shocks and domestic adjustment in the 1970s and 1980s. In *External Finance and Adjustment: Failure and Success in the Developing World*, Karel Jansen and Rob Vos, eds. London and New York: Macmillan and St. Martin's Press, pp. 63-89.

Food and Agriculture Organization of the United Nations (1999). Investment in agriculture for food security: situation and resource requirements to reach the World Food Summit objectives. Rome: FAO. May.

_____ (2006a). *The State of Food and Agriculture in Asia and the Pacific, 2006*. Bangkok: FAO Regional Office for Asia and the Pacific.

_____ (2006b). *The State of Food Insecurity in the World 2006: Eradicating World Hunger—Taking Stock Ten Years After the World Food Summit*. Rome: FAO.

_____ (2008). Crop Prospects and Food Situation, No. 2 (April). Rome: FAO.

Freedom House (2005). *How Freedom is Won: From Civic Resistance to Durable Democracy*. New York, New York: Freedom House.

Friedman, Milton (1962). *Capitalism and Freedom*. Chicago, Illinois: University of Chicago Press.

Funkhouser, Edward (1992). Migration from Nicaragua: some recent evidence. *World Development*, vol. 20, No. 3, pp. 1209-1218.

Gaiha, R., and K. Imai (2004). Vulnerability, shocks and persistence of poverty: estimates for semi-arid rural South India. *Oxford Development Studies*, vol. 32, No. 2 (June), pp. 261-281.

Gassebner, Martin, Alexander Keck and Robert Teh (2006). The impact of disasters on international trade. Staff Working Paper, No. ERSD-2006-04. Geneva: World Trade Organization, Economic Research and Statistics Division. March.

Gelb, A.H. (1988). *Windfall Gains: Blessing or curse?* New York, New York: Oxford University Press.

Gelbach, Jonah B., and Lant H. Pritchett (1995). Does more for the poor mean less for the poor?: the politics of tagging. World Bank Policy Research Working Paper, No. 1523. Washington, D.C.: World Bank.

Gemmell, N., and O. Morrissey (2005). Distribution and poverty impacts of tax structure reform in developing countries: how little we know. *Development Policy Review*, vol. 23, No. 2, pp. 131-144.

Ghani, A., and others (2007). The budget as the lynchpin of the State: lessons from Afghanistan. In *Peace and the Public Purse: Economic Policies for Postwar Statebuilding*, James K. Boyce and Madalene O'Donnell, eds. Boulder, Colorado: Lynne Rienner.

Ghobarah, H.A., P. Huth and B. Russett (2003). Civil wars kill and maim people—long after the shooting stops. *American Political Science Review*, vol. 97, No. 2, pp. 189-202.

Gilchrist, S., and J.C. Williams (2004). Transition dynamics in vintage capital models: explaining the postwar catch-up of Germany and Japan. NBER Working Papers, No. 10732. Cambridge, Massachusetts: National Bureau of Economic Research.

Gindling, T.H., and Katerine Terrell (2005). The effect of minimum wages on actual wages in formal and informal sectors in Costa Rica. *World Development*, vol. 33, No. 11, pp. 1905-1921.

Glyn, Andrew (2006). *Capitalism Unleashed: Finance, Globalization and Welfare*. Oxford, United Kingdom: Oxford University Press.

Goldsmith, Scott (2001). The Alaska Permanent fund Dividen Program. Paper presented at the conference on Alberta: Government Policies in a Surplus Economy, 7 September.

González, M., and R. Lopez (2007). Political violence and farm household efficiency in Colombia. Storrs, Connecticut: University of Connecticut. Mimeo.

Goodhand, J. (2006). Conditioning peace? the scope and limitations of peace conditionalities in Afghanistan and Sri Lanka. The Hague: Netherlands Institute of International Relations ("Clingendael").

Gordon, A., and C. Craig (2001). *Rural Non-Farm Activities and Poverty Alleviation in Sub-Saharan Africa*. NRI Policy Series, No. 14. Chatham, United Kingdom: Natural Resources Institute.

Grein, T., and others (2003). Mortality among displaced former UNITA members and their families in Angola: a retrospective cluster survey. *British Medical Journal*, vol. 327, No. 7416, p. 650.

Griffith-Jones, Stephany, and José Antonio Ocampo (2008). Compensatory financing for shocks: what changes are needed? Background paper prepared for the Committee for Development Policy, New York: United Nations.

Guillaumont, Patrick (2007). Assessing the Economic Vulnerability of Small Island Developing States and the Least Developed Countries. *UNU-WIDER Research Paper*, No. 2007/40. Helsinki: United Nations University-World Institute for Development Economics Research. June.

Gupta, S., and others (2003). Foreign aid and revenue response: does the composition of aid matter? IMF Working Paper, No. 03/176. Washington, D.C.: International Monetary Fund. September.

_____ (2004). Fiscal consequences of armed conflict and terrorism in low- and middle-income countries. *European Journal of Political Economy*, vol. 20, No. 2, pp. 403-421.

_____ (2005). Rebuilding Fiscal Institutions in Post-conflict Countries. Occasional Paper, No. 247. Washington, D.C.: IMF. December.

Guy Carpenter (2006). Global agriculture insurance and reinsurance market overview. July. Available from http://www.agroinsurance.com/en/pratice/?pid=453 (accessed September 2007).

Gylfason, T. (2001). Natural resources, education, and economic development. *European Economic Review*, vol. 45, No. 4 (May), pp. 847-859.

Hall, Peter, and David Soskice, eds. (2001). *Varieties of Capitalism*. Oxford, United Kingdom: Oxford University Press.

Hanlon, J. (1996). *Peace Without Profit*. Oxford, United Kingdom: James Currey.

Hanson, G., and others (2002). Expansion strategies of US multinational firms. In *Brookings Trade Forum 2001*, S.M. Collins and D. Rodrik, eds. Washington, D.C.: Brookings Institution Press, pp. 245-282.

Hardoy, Jorge E., Diana Mitlin and David Satterthwaite (2001). *Environmental Problems in Cities of Africa, Asia and Latin America*. London: Earthscan.

Heger, M., A. Julca and O. Paddison (2008). Analysing the Impact of Natural Disasters in Small Economies: The Caribbean Case. *UNU-WIDER Research Paper*, No. 2008/25. Helsinki: United Nations University-World Institute for Development Economics Research.

Hegre, H., and others (2001). Toward a democratic civil peace? democracy political change and civil wars 1816-1992. *American Political Science Review*, vol. 95, No. 1, pp. 16-33.

Heller, P.S. (2005). Pity the finance minister: issues in managing a substantial scaling up of aid flows. IMF Working Paper, No. 05/180. Washington, D.C.: International Monetary Fund. September.

Heltberg, R. (2007). Helping South Asia cope better with natural disasters: the role of social protection. *Development Policy Review*, vol. 25, No. 6, pp. 681-698.

Hirschman, Albert (1994). Social conflicts as pillars of democratic market society. *Political Theory*, vol. 22, No. 2, p. 203.

_____ (1995). On the political economy of Latin American development. In *A Propensity to Self-Subversion*. Cambridge, Massachusetts: Harvard University Press.

Hoeffler, A., and M. Reynal-Querol (2003). Measuring the costs of conflict. Oxford, United Kingdom: Centre for the Study of African Economies, University of Oxford.

Hoegh-Guldberg, O., and others (2000). *Pacific in Peril: Biological, Economic and Social Impacts of Climate Change on Pacific Coral Reefs*. Sydney, Australia: Greenpeace, p. 36.

Hort, Sven E.O., and Stein Kuhnle (2000). The coming of East and South-East Asian welfare states. *Journal of European Social Policy*, vol. 10, No. 2, pp. 162-184.

House of Commons, International Development Committee (2008). Reconstructing Afghanistan: fourth report of session 2007-08, vol. I, Report, together with formal minutes. London: The Stationery Office Limited. Published on 14 February 2008 by authority of the House of Commons.

Hulme, David, Karen Moore and Armando Barrientos (2007). Assessing the insurance role of micro savings. Background paper prepared for *World Economic and Social Survey 2008*.

Humphreys, Macartan (2003). Economics and violent conflict. Working paper. Cambridge, Massachusetts: Harvard University.

_____ (2005). Natural resources, conflict, and conflict resolution: uncovering the mechanisms. *Journal of Conflict Resolution*, vol. 49, No. 4, pp. 508-537.

_____, and J. Weinstein (2004). What the fighters say: a survey of ex-combatants in Sierra Leone. CGSD Working Paper, No. 20. New York, New York: Center on Globalization and Sustainable Development, The Earth Institute at Columbia University.

Ibáñez, A.M., and A. Moya (2006). The impact of intra-State conflict on economic welfare and consumption smoothing: empirical evidence for the displaced population in Colombia. HiCN Working Paper, No. 23. Brighton, United Kingdom: Households in Conflict Network (HiCN), University of Sussex.

Imai, K., and J. Weinstein (2000). Measuring the economic impact of civil war. Palo Alto, California: Stanford University. Mimeo.

Imbs, Jean, and Romain Wacziarg (2003). Stages of diversification. *American Economic Review,* vol. 93, No. 1 (March), pp. 63-86.

Institute for International Economics (IIE) (2006). *China: The Balance Sheet—What the World Needs to Know Now about the Emerging Superpower.* Washington, D.C. IIE.

Intergovernmental Panel on Climate Change (IPCC) (2007). Climate change 2007: impacts, adaptation and vulnerability. Contribution of Working Group II to the Fourth Assessment Report of the Intergovernmental Panel on Climate Change.

International Federation of Red Cross and Red Crescent Societies (IFRC) (2001). *World Disasters Report 2001: Focus on Recovery.* Geneva.

_____ (2006). *World Disasters Report 2006: Focus on Neglected Crises.* Geneva.

International Labour Organization (2005a). Global employment trends brief. February. Geneva: International Labour Office.

_____ (2005b), *World Employment Report 2004-05: Employment, Productivity and Poverty Reduction.* Geneva: International Labour Office.

_____, Programme on Socio-economic Security (2004a). *Economic Security for a Better World.* Geneva: International Labour Office.

International Labour Organization, World Commission on the Social Dimension of Globalization (2004b). *A Fair Globalization: Creating Opportunities for All.* Geneva: International Labour Office.

International Labour Organization and World Trade Organization (2007). *Trade and Employment: Challenges for Policy Research.* Joint study of the International Labour Office and the Secretariat of the World Trade Organization. Geneva: ILO.

International Monetary Fund (2008). *Global Financial Stability Report: Containing Systemic Risks and Restoring Financial Soundness. April 2008.* Washington, D.C.: IMF.

Irwin, Scott H., Philip Garcia and Darrel L. Good (2007). The performance of Chicago Board of Trade corn, soybean, and wheat futures contracts after recent changes in speculative limits. May. Available from http://www.farmdoc.uinc.edu/irwin/research/CBOTFuturesPerformance.pdf.

Isima, J. (2004). Cash payments in disarmament, demobilisation and reintegration programmes in Africa. *Journal of Security Sector Management,* vol. 2, No. 3, pp. 1–10.

Islam, S. Nazrul (2001). The open approach to flood control: the way to the future in Bangladesh. *Futures,* vol. 33, Nos. 8-9 (October), pp. 783-802.

Jacobs, Elisabeth (2007). The politics of economic insecurity. Issues in Governance Studies, No. 10, Washington D.C.: The Brookings Institution. September.

Jeong, H.W. (1996). Managing structural adjustment. *SAIS Review,* vol. 16, No. 2, p. 275.

Johnson, Brett, and Santiago Sedaca (2004). Diasporas, émigrés and development: economic linkages and programmatic responses. A special study of the United States Agency for International Development (USAID). Trade Enhancement for the Services Sector (RESS) Project. Carana Corporation, Washington, D.C.: March.

Jomo K.S., and Jacques Baudot, eds. (2006). *Flat World, Big Gaps: Economic Liberalization, Globalization and Inequality.* New Delhi: Orient Longman.

Jonas, S. (2000). *Of Centaurs and Doves: Guatemala's Peace Process.* Boulder, Colorado: Westview.

Justino, P. (2008). Household-level impact of armed civil conflicts and policy responses. Background paper for *World Economic and Social Survey 2008.*

_____, and P. Verwimp (2006). Poverty dynamics, conflict and convergence in Rwanda. HiCN Working Paper, No. 16. Brighton, United Kingdom: Households in Conflict Network (HiCN), University of Sussex.

Kalyvas, S. (2004). The urban bias in research on civil wars. *Security Studies,* vol. 13, No. 3, pp. 1-31.

Kaminsky, Graciela, Carmen M. Reinhart and Carlos A. Végh (2004). When it rains, it pours: procyclical capital flows and macroeconomic policies. NBER Working Paper, No. 10780. Cambridge, Massachusetts: National Bureau of Economic Research. September.

Kanbur, R. (2007). What's social policy got to do with economic growth? *Indian Journal of Human Development* (New Delhi), vol. 1, No. 1.

Kandelhela, Masingita, and Julian May (2006). Poverty, vulnerability and the impact of flooding in the Limpopo Province, South Africa. *Natural Disasters*, vol. 39, No. 2 (October), pp. 275-287.

Kapur, Devesh (2004). Remittances: the new development mantra? G24 Discussion Paper Series, No. 29. Geneva: United Nations.

Karlan, Dean S., and Jonathan Zinman (2007a). Credit elasticities in less-developed economies: implications for micro-finance. *CEPR Discussion Paper*, No. 6071. London: Centre for Economic Policy Research.

_____ (2007b). Expanding credit access: using randomized supply decisions to estimate the impacts. *CEPR Discussion Paper*, No. 6007. London: Centre for Economic Policy Research.

Kauffmann, D., A. Kraay and M. Mastruzzi (2004). Governance matters III: governance indicators for 1996-2002. Washington, D.C.: World Bank. 5 April.

Kawamura, Hiroshi (1995). The Kobe earthquake: evaluation of economic impacts and crisis management. Department for Economic and Social Information and Policy Analysis of the United Nations Secretariat. June.

Keen, David (2005). Liberalization and conflict. *International Political Science Review*, vol. 26, No. 1, pp. 73-89.

Keener, S., and others (1993). Demobilization and reintegration of military personnel in Africa: the evidence from seven country case studies. World Bank Internal Discussion Paper, No. IDP-130. Washington, D.C.: World Bank.

Keynes, John Maynard (1919). *The Economic Consequences of the Peace.* London: Macmillan.

Khan, Azizur (2007). Growth, employment and poverty: an analysis of the vital nexus based on some recent UNDP and ILO/SIDA studies. DESA Working Paper, No. 49. New York: ST/ESA/2007/DWP/49. United Nations. July.

Khandker, Shahidur (1998). *Fighting Poverty with Microcredit: Experience in Bangladesh.* New York, New York: Oxford University Press, for the World Bank.

Kindleberger, Charles (1995). Asset inflation and monetary policy, *Banca Nazionale del Lavoro Quarterly Review*, No. 192 (March), pp. 17-37.

_____ (1996). *World Economic Primacy: 1500–1990.* Oxford, United Kingdom: Oxford University Press.

King, G., and L. Zheng (2001). Improving forecasts of State failure. *World Politics*, vol. 53, No. 4 (July), pp. 623-658.

Kletzer, Lori G. (2001). *Job Loss from Imports: Measuring the Loss.* Washington, D.C.: Institute for International Economics.

Knight, M. (2001). A one way street: defining a new approach to the disarmament, demobilisation and reinsertion of ex-combatants during the war-to peace transition. Master of Arts dissertation. York, United Kingdom: University of York. Mimeo.

_____, N. Loayza and D. Villanueva (1996). The peace dividend: military spending cuts and economic growth. *IMF Staff Papers,* vol. 43, No. 1, pp. 1-37. Washington, D.C.: International Monetary Fund.

Kondylis, F. (2005). Agricultural production and conflict refugee status: quasi-experimental evidence from a policy intervention programme in Rwanda. London: Economics Department, University of London. 8 April. Mimeo.

_____ (2007). Conflict-induced Displacement and Labour Market Outcomes: Evidence from Post-war Bosnia and Herzegovina. CEP Discussion Paper, No. 777. London: Centre for Economic Performance, London School of Economics and Political Science.

Kozul-Wright, R., and P. Rayment (1997). The institutional hiatus in economies in transition and its policy consequences. *Cambridge Journal of Economics*, vol. 21, No. 5, pp. 641-661.

_____ (2007). *The Resistible Rise of Market Fundamentalism: Rethinking Development in an Unbalanced World.* London: Zed Books.

Kuhnle, Stein, and Sven E.O. Hort (2004). The developmental welfare State in Scandinavia: lessons for the developing world. *Social Policy and Development Programme Paper,* No. 17. Geneva: United Nations Research Institute for Social Development. September.

Kunreuther, H. (2006). Disaster mitigation and insurance: learning from Katrina. *The Annals of the American Academy of Political and Social Science*, vol. 604, No. 1, pp. 208-227.

Kwon, Huck-ju (2005). Transforming the developmental welfare State in East Asia. *Social Policy and Development Programme Paper,* No. 22. Geneva: United Nations Research Institute for Social Development.

Lall, Sanjaya (1991). Explaining industrial success in the industrial world. In *Issues in Development Economics*, V. N. Balasubramanyam and S. Lall, eds. London: Macmillan.

_____ (2001). *Competitiveness, Technology and Skills.* Cheltenham, United Kingdom: Edward Elgar.

Lane, M. (2004). The viability and likely pricing of "cat bonds" for developing countries. In *Catastrophe Risk and Reinsurance: A Country Risk Management Perspective*, E. Gurenko, ed. London: Risk Books, pp. 239-268.

Le Billon, Philippe (2000). The dynamics of resource wars. In *Angola's War Economy: the Role of Oil and Diamonds*, Jackie Cilliers and Chris Dietrich, eds. Pretoria: Institute for Security Studies, pp. 21-42.

_____ (2008). Resources for peace? managing revenues from extractive industries in post-conflict environments. Public Finance in Post-Conflict Environments Policy Paper No. 4. New York: Center on International Cooperation; and Amherst, Massachusetts, Political Economy Research Institute.

Lemke, Douglas (2003). African lessons for international relations research. *World Politics*, vol. 56, No.1, pp. 120-124.

Li, W., and D. Yang (2005). The great leap forward: anatomy of a central planning disaster. *Journal of Political Economy*, vol. 113, No. 4, pp. 840-77.

Lindley, A. (2007). Protracted displacement and remittances: the view from Eastleigh, Nairobi. *New Issues in Refugee Research*. Research Paper, No. 143. Geneva: Office of the United Nations High Commissioner for Refugees.

Linnerooth-Bayer, J., and R. Mechler (2007). Insurance against losses from natural disasters in developing countries. Background paper prepared for *World Economic and Social Survey 2008*.

Lopez, J., and Guillermo Perry (2008). Inequality in Latin America: determinants and consequences. World Bank Policy Research Working Paper, No. 4504. Washington, D.C.: World Bank, Latin America and Caribbean Region. February.

López-Córdova, Ernesto, and Alexandra Olmedo (2006). International Remittances and Development: Existing Evidence, Policies and Recommendations. Occasional Paper, No. 41. Washington, D.C. and Buenos Aires: Integration and Regional Programs Department, Inter-American Development Bank. August.

Lujala, Päivi, Nils Petter Gleditsch and Elizabeth Gilmore (2005). A diamond curse? civil war and a lootable resource. *Journal of Conflict Resolution*, vol. 49, No. 4, pp. 538-562.

Lustig, Nora, and Darryl McLeod (1997). Minimum wages and poverty in developing countries: some empirical evidence. In *Labour Markets in Latin America*, S. Edwards and N. Lustig, eds. Washington, D.C.: Brookings Institution Press.

Mahul, O., and J.R. Skees (2007). Managing agricultural risk at the country level: the case of index-based livestock insurance in Mongolia. World Bank Policy Research Working Paper, No. 4325. Washington, D.C.: World Bank.

Mancini, L. (2005). Horizontal inequality and communal violence: evidence from Indonesian districts. CRISE Working Paper, No. 22. Oxford, United Kingdom: Centre for Research on Inequality, Human Security and Ethnicity, University of Oxford.

Manitoba Floodway Authority (2006). The Red River Floodway Expansion Project community newsletter, fifth edition. Winnipeg, Manitoba, Canada. December. Available from http://www.floodwayauthority.mb.ca/pdf/newsletter_winter_0607_en.pdf.

McDonald, M. (2005). Provision of infrastructures in post-conflict situations. DFID Working Paper, No. 6484. London: Department for International Development. June.

McKechnie, A. (2003). Building capacity in post-conflict countries. World Bank Social Development Notes: Conflict Prevention and Reconstruction, No. 14 (December), pp. 1-4. Washington, D.C.: World Bank.

McNamara, R. (1968). *The Essence of Security*. New York, New York: Harper and Row.

Mechler, R. (2005). Cost-benefit analysis of natural disaster risk management in developing countries. Working paper. Deutsche Gesellschaft für Technische Zusammenarbeit (GTZ), Eschborn, Germany.

Miguel, E., S. Satyanath and E. Sergenti (2004). Economic shocks and civil conflict. *Journal of Political Economy*, vol. 112, No. 4, pp. 725-753.

Milberg, William, and Deborah Scholler (2008). Globalization, offshoring and economic insecurity in industrialized countries. Background paper for *World Economic and Social Survey 2008*.

Mills, Evan (2007). Responding to climate change: the insurance industry perspective. Lawrence Berkeley National Laboratory, U.S. Department of Energy, University of California, Berkeley, California. 26 November. Available from http://www.climateactionprogramme.org/features/article/responding_to_climate_change_the_insurance_industry_perspective/.

Mishkin, F. (2006). *The Next Great Globalization: How Disadvantaged Nations Can Harness Their Financial Systems to Get Rich*. Princeton, New Jersey: Princeton University Press.

Mkandawire, Thandika. (2002). The terrible toll of post-colonial "rebel movements" in Africa: towards an explanation of the violence against the peasantry. *Journal of Modern African Studies,* vol. 40, No. 2, pp. 181–215.

_____, ed. (2004). *Social Policy in a Development Context.* Basingstoke, United Kingdom: Palgrave MacMillan.

_____ (2007). Targeting and universalism in poverty reduction. In *Policy Matters: Economic and Social Policies to Sustain Equitable Development*, J. A. Ocampo, K. S. Jomo and Sarbuland Khan, eds. London: Zed Books.

Moene, Karl Ove, and Michael Wallerstein (2006). Social democracy as a development strategy. In *Globalization and Egalitarian Redistribution*, P. Bardhan, S. Bowles and M. Wallerstein, eds. Princeton, New Jersey: Princeton University Press.

Montalvo, G., and M. Reynal-Querol (2005). Ethnic polarization, potential conflict and civil wars. *American Economic Review*, vol. 95, No. 3 (June), pp. 796-816.

Morduch, Jonathan (1994). Poverty and Vulnerability. *American Economic Review*, vol. 84, No. 2 (May), pp. 221-225.

_____ (1995). Income smoothing and consumption smoothing. *Journal of Economic Perspectives*, vol. 9, No. 3 (summer), pp. 103-114.

_____ (1999a). Between the State and the market: can informal insurance patch the safety net? *World Bank Research Observer*, vol. 14, No. 2 (August), pp. 187-207.

_____ (1999b). The Microfinance Promise. *Journal of Economic Literature*, vol. 37, No. 4 (December), pp. 1569-1614.

_____ (2006). Smart subsidies. *ESR Review*, vol. 8, No. 1 (summer), pp. 10-16.

Morley, Samuel (1992). Structural adjustment and the determinants of poverty in Latin America. Paper prepared for the Conference on Confronting the Challenge of

Poverty and Inequality in Latin America, Brookings Institution, Washington, D.C., 16 and 17 July 1992. Revised version appeared in Nora C. Lustig, ed., *Coping With Austerity: Poverty and Inequality in Latin America* (Washington, D.C., Brookings Institution Press, 1995).

_____, and Rob Vos (2006). External shocks, domestic adjustment and the growth slowdown. In *Who Gains from Free Trade? Export-led Growth, Inequality and Poverty in Latin America*, Rob Vos and others, eds. London: Routledge.

Mosley, Paul (2007). Assessing the success of micro insurance programs in Meeting the Insurance Needs of the Poor, Background paper prepared for *World Economic and Social Survey 2008*.

Mugrai, Rinku, and Martin Ravallion (2005). Is a guaranteed living wage a good anti-poverty policy? World Bank Policy Research Working Paper, No. 3640. Washington, D.C.: World Bank.

Multihazard Mitigation Council (MMC) (2005). Natural hazard mitigation saves: an independent study to assess the future savings from mitigation activities, vol. 2, Study Documentation. Washington, D.C.: Multihazard Mitigation Council.

Munich Re (2005). NatCatSERVICE, Natural disasters according to country income groups, 1980-2004. Munich, Germany: Munich Re Group.

Murdoch, J., and T. Sandler (2004). Civil wars and economic growth: spatial dispersion in Africa and worldwide. *American Journal of Political Science,* vol. 48, No. 1, pp. 138-151.

Murshed, S.M. (2006). Turning swords into ploughshares and little acorns to tall trees: the conflict growth nexus and the poverty of nations. Background paper for *World Economic and Social Survey 2006*.

_____, and M.Z. Tadjoeddin (2007). Reappraising the Greed and Grievance Explanations for Violent Internal Conflict. MICROCON *Research Working Paper No. 2*. Brighton, United Kingdom: A Micro Level Analysis of Violent Conflict, Institute of Development Studies at the University of Sussex.

_____, and Scott Gates (2005). Spatial-horizontal inequality and the Maoist conflict.

Narayana, N.S.S., Kirit S. Parikh and T. N. Srinivasan (1988). Rural works program in India: costs and benefits. *Journal of Development Economics*, vol. 29, No. 2 (September), pp. 131-156.

NASA Goddard Institute for Space Studies (2001). How will the frequency of hurricanes be affected by climate change? New York, New York. April. Available from http://www.giss.nasa.gov/research/briefs/druyan_02/.

Nathan, Laurie (2005). The frightful inadequacy of most of the statistics: a critique of Collier and Hoeffler on causes of civil war. Occasional Paper, vol. 12, No. 5 (December). The Centre for Conflict Resolution, University of Cape Town.

Ngo, E. (2001). When disasters and age collide: reviewing vulnerability of the elderly. *Natural Hazards Review*, vol. 2, No. 2 (May), pp. 80-89.

Obidegwu, C. (2003). Rwanda: the search for post-conflict socio-economic change, 1995-2001. Africa Region Working Paper, No. 59. Washington, D.C.: World Bank. October.

Ocampo, José Antonio (2003). Developing countries' anti-cyclical policies in a globalized world. In *Development Economics and Structuralist Macroeconomics: Essays in Honor of Lance Taylor*, Amitava Krishna Dutt and Jaime Ros, eds. Cheltenham, United Kingdom: Edward Elgar.

_____, and Rob Vos (coordinators) (2008). *Uneven Economic Development*. New York, London, Hyderabad, India, and Penang, Malaysia: Orient Longman, Zed Books and Third World Network.

_____, Shari Spiegel and Joseph Stiglitz, eds. (forthcoming). In *IPD Capital Markets Liberalization Companion Volume*. Oxford, United Kingdom: Oxford University Press.

Organization for Economic Cooperation and Development. (2005). *Employment Outlook 2005*. Paris: OECD.

_____ (2007a). *Agricultural Policies in OECD Countries: Monitoring and Evaluation 2007*. Paris: OECD.

_____ (2007b). Involuntary part time workers. *OECD Employment and Labour Market Statistics,* vol. 2007 (release 01). Paris: OECD.

_____ (2008). *Development Co-operation Report 2007. OECD Journal on Development*. Paris: OECD/Development Assistance Committee.

Orozco, Manuel (2003). Worker remittances in an international scope. Inter-American Dialogue. Research Series: Remittances Project. March. Paper originally presented on 28 February 2003 at the Inter-American Development Bank.

Osberg, Lars (1998). Economic Insecurity. *SPRC Discussion Paper*, No. 88. Sydney, Australia: University of New South Wales, Social Policy Research Centre. October.

Oxfam International (2007a). Climate alarm: disasters increase as climate change bites. Oxfam briefing paper, No. 108. Oxford, United Kingdom.

_____ (2007b). Africa's missing billions: international arms flows and the cost of conflict. Oxfam Briefing Paper, No.107. Oxford, United Kingdom.

Panić, M. (1992). *Managing Reforms in the East European Countries: Lessons from the Postwar Experience of Western Europe*: UN/ECE Discussion Paper No. 3. Geneva: United Nations.

_____ (2003). *Globalization and National Economic Welfare*. Basingstoke, United Kingdom: Palgrave Macmillan.

_____ (2005). Reconstruction, development and sustainable peace: a unified programme for post-conflict countries. In *Development Challenges in Sub-Saharan Africa and Post-conflict Countries: Report of the Committee for Development Policy on the Seventh Session (14-18 March 2005)*. Sales No. E.05.II.A.9. New York: United Nations.

_____ (2008). Aid effectiveness in post-conflict countries. Background paper for *World Economic and Social Survey 2008*.

Parandekar, Suhas, Rob Vos and Donald Winkler (2002). Ecuador: crisis, poverty and social protection. In *Crisis and Dollarization in Ecuador: Stability, Growth and Social Equity*, Paul Beckerman and Andres Solimano, eds. Washington D.C.: World Bank, pp. 127-176.

Paris, R. (2004). *At War's End: Building Peace After Civil Conflict*. New York, New York: Cambridge University Press.

Pastor, M., and J.K. Boyce (2000). El Salvador: economic disparities, external intervention, and civil conflict. In *War, Hunger, and Displacement: The Origins of Humanitarian Emergencies,* vol. 2, *Case Studies*, E. Wayne Nafziger, Frances Stewart and Raimo Vayrynen, eds. Oxford, United Kingdom: Oxford University Press, pp. 365-400.

Permanent Fund Dividend Division (2007). 2007 Annual Report. Juneau, State of Alaska: Department of Revenue.

Perry, Guillermo E., and others (2006). *Poverty Reduction and Growth: Virtuous and Vicious Circles.* Washington, D.C.: World Bank.

Persaud, Avinash (2000). Sending the herd off the cliff edge: the disturbing interaction between herding and market-sensitive risk management practices. First Prize Essay on Global Finance for the Year 2000, Institute of International Finance Competition in Honour of Jacques de Larosière. Washington, D.C.: Institute of International Finance.

Pierson, Christopher (2003). Late industrialisers and the development of the welfare State. *Social Policy and Development Working Paper,* No. 16. Geneva: United Nations Research Institute for Social Development.

Pinchotti, S., and P. Verwimp (2007). Social capital and the Rwandan genocide: a micro-level analysis. HiCN Working Paper, No. 30. Brighton, United Kingdom: Households in Conflict Network (HiCN), University of Sussex.

Pitt, Mark, and Shahidur Khandker (1998). Credit programs for the poor and seasonality in rural Bangladesh. Brown University, Providence, Rhode Island, and World Bank.

Polanyi, Karl (1944). *The Great Transformation: The Political and Economic Origins of Our Time.* Boston, Massachusetts: Beacon Press.

Powell, S., and others (2003). Post-traumatic growth after war: a study with former refugees and displaced people in Sarajevo. *Journal of Clinical Psychology*, vol. 59, No. 1, pp. 71-83.

Prasad, Eswar S., and others (2003). Effects of Financial Globalization on Developing Countries: Some Empirical Evidence. *IMF Occasional Paper*, No. 220. Washington, D.C.: International Monetary Fund.

Pritchett, Lant (2005). Who is *not* poor? dreaming of a world truly free of poverty. *The World Bank Research Observer,* vol. 21 No. 1, pp. 1-23.

Putzel, James (2004). The political impact of globalisation and liberalisation. *Crisis States Discussion Paper*, No. 7. London: Crisis States Development Research Centre, London School of Economics. November.

Ramey, Garey, and Valerie Ramey (1995). Cross-country evidence on the link between volatility and growth. *American Economic Review,* vol. 85, No. 5 (December), pp. 1138-1151.

Ranis, G., and F. Stewart (2007). Dynamic links between the economy and human development. In *Policy Matters: Economic and Social Policies to Sustain Equitable Development,* J.A. Ocampo, K.S. Jomo and Sarbuland Kahn, eds. London: Zed Books.

Rasmussen, T. (2004). Macroeconomic implications of natural disasters in the Caribbean. IMF Working Paper, No. WP/04/224. Washington, D.C.: International Monetary Fund. December.

Ratha, Dilip (2007). Leveraging remittances for development. Policy brief. World Bank: Migration Policy Institute, Program on Migrants, Migration, and Development. June.

_____, and others (2007). Migration and Development Brief 3: Remittance trends 2007. Washington, D.C.: World Bank. 29 November.

Ravallion, Martin (1991). Reaching the rural poor through public employment: arguments, evidence, lessons from South Asia. *The World Bank Research Observer*, vol. 6, No. 2 (July), pp. 153-175.

_____ (2003). Targeted transfers in poor countries: revisiting the tradeoffs and policy options. World Bank Policy Research Working Paper, No. 3048. Washington, D.C.: World Bank.

Ray, Debraj (1998). *Development Economics*. Princeton, New Jersey: Princeton University Press.

Reich, Robert (2007). *Supercapitalism: The Transformation of Business, Democracy and Everyday Life*. New York, New York: Borzoi Books.

Reinert, Eric (2007). *How Rich Countries Got Rich...and Why Poor Countries Stay Poor*. New York, New York: Carroll and Graf.

Roberts, J. Timmons, and Bradley Parks (2007). *A Climate of Injustice: Global Inequality, North-South Politics and Climate Policy*. Cambridge, Massachusetts: The MIT Press.

Rock, Michael (2007). Corruption and democracy. DESA Working Paper, No. 55. ST/ESA/2007/DWP/55. New York: Department of Economic and Social Affairs of the United Nations Secretariat. August.

Rodas-Martini, P. (2007). Building fiscal provisions into peace agreements: cautionary tales from Guatemala. In *Peace and the Public Purse: Economic Policies for Postwar Statebuilding*, James K. Boyce and Madalene O'Donnell, eds. Boulder, Colorado: Lynne Rienner.

Rodrik, Dani (2004). *Rethinking Economic Growth in Developing Countries*. Cambridge, Massachusetts: Harvard University Press.

_____ (2005). Policies for economic diversification. *Cepal Review* (Santiago), No. 87 (December), pp. 7-23.

_____ (2007). Industrial development: some stylized facts and policy directions. In Industrial development for the 21st century: sustainable development perspectives. New York: United Nations, Department of Economic and Social Affairs.

Rohde, D., and C. Gall (2005). Delays hurting U.S. rebuilding in Afghanistan. *The New York Times*, 7 November.

Ross, Michael L. (2004). What we know about natural resources and civil wars? *Journal of Peace Research*, vol. 41. No. 3. pp. 337-356.

Sandler, T., and W. Enders (2004). An economic perspective on transnational terrorism. *European Journal of Political Economy*, vol. 20, No. 2. pp. 301-316.

Sardesai, S., and P. Wam (2002). The conflict analysis framework (CAF): identifying conflict-related obstacles to development. Dissemination Notes, No. 5 (October). Washington D.C.: World Bank Social Development Department.

Scanteam (2005). Assessment: Afghanistan Reconstruction Trust Fund: final report. Oslo. March. Available from http://siteresources.worldbank.org/INTAFGHANISTAN/Resources/ARTFEvaluationFinalReport.pdf.

Schneider, Benu (2008). Clubbing in Paris: is debt sustainability an illusion? Paper presented at the Workshop on Debt, Finance and Emerging Issues in Financial Integration, organized by the Financing for Development Office (FFD), on 8 and 9 April, United Nations, New York.

Sedra, M., and P. Middlebrook (2005). Beyond Bonn: revisioning the International Compact for Afghanistan. *Foreign Policy in Focus,* vol. 9, No. 24 (November). Available from http://www.fpif.org/fpifzines/pr/2924.

Sen, Amartya (1995). The political economy of targeting. In *Public Spending and the Poor: Theory and Evidence,* D. van de Walle and K. Nead, eds. Baltimore, Maryland: Johns Hopkins University Press,

_____, and Jean Drèze (2006). *The Amartya Sen and Jean Drèze Omnibus: Poverty and Famines, Hunger and Public Action, India: Economic Development and Social Opportunity.* Reprint. New Delhi: Oxford University Press.

Sesman, S. (2004). The case for cash: Goma after the Nyiragongo eruption. HPN Humanitarian Exchange, No. 28. November. Cited in Clarke and Dercon (2008).

Sharma, Krishnan (2008). The impact of remittances on economic insecurity. Background paper prepared for *World Economic and Social Survey 2008.*

Shemyakina, O. (2006). The effect of armed conflict on accumulation of schooling: results from Tajikistan. HiCN Working Paper, No. 12. Brighton, United Kingdom: Households in Conflict Network (HiCN), University of Sussex. Available from www.hicn.org.

Skocpol, Theda (1991). Targeting within universalism: politically viable policies to combat poverty in the United States. In *The Urban Underclass,* Christopher Jencks and P.E Peterson, eds. Washington, D.C.: Brookings Institution Press.

Snyder, Richard, and Ravi Bhavnani (2005). Diamonds, blood and taxes: a revenue-centred framework for explaining political order. *Journal of Conflict Resolution*, vol. 49, No. 4, pp. 563-597.

Spiezia, Vincenzio (2004). Trade, foreign direct investment and employment: some empirical evidence. In *Understanding Globalization, Employment and Poverty Reduction,* E.Lee and M. Vivarelli, eds. London: Palgrave.

Stanton Elizabeth, and Frank Ackerman (2007). Florida and climate change: the costs of inaction. Medford, Massachusetts: Global Development and Environment Institute, Tufts University. November.

Steele, A. (2007). Massive civilian displacement in civil war: assessing variation in Colombia. HiCN Working Paper, No. 29. Brighton, United Kingdom: Households in Conflict Network (HiCN), University of Sussex.

Stephens, J., and D.B. Ottaway (2005). A rebuilding plan full of cracks. *Washington Post,* 19 November.

Stewart, F. (2002). Horizontal inequalities: a neglected dimension of development. CRISE Working Paper, No. 1. Oxford, United Kingdom: Centre for Research on Inequality, Human Security and Ethnicity, University of Oxford.

_____ (2004). Development and security. *Conflict, Security and Development*, vol. 4, No. 3, pp. 261-288.

_____, and Graham Brown (2007). Motivations for conflict: an overview and policy implications. CRISE Working Paper. Oxford, United Kingdom: Centre for Research on Inequality, Human Security and Ethnicity, Department of International Development, University of Oxford.

Stiglitz, Joseph, and others (2006). *Stability with Growth*. Oxford, United Kingdom: Oxford University Press.

Stockhammer, Englebert (2004). Financialisation and the slowdown of accumulation. *Cambridge Journal of Economics*, vol. 28, No. 5, pp. 719-741.

Streeten, Paul (1973). The multinational enterprise and theory of development policy. *World Development*, vol.1, No. 10 (October), pp.1-14.

Strömberg, D. (2007). Natural disasters, economic development and humanitarian aid, *Journal of Economic Perspectives*, vol. 21, No. 3, pp. 199-222.

Swiss Re (2007). World insurance in 2006: premiums came back to "life". *Sigma* 4 Study. Zurich.

Syroka, J. (2007). Overview of index-based insurance products for agriculture. Paper prepared for *World Economic and Social Survey 2008*.

Tanner, F. (1996). Consensual versus coercive disarmament. In *Disarmament and Conflict Resolution Project—Managing Arms in Peace Processes: The Issues*, E. Zawels and others, eds. Sales No. GV.E.96.0.33. Geneva: United Nations Institute for Disarmament Studies, pp. 169–204.

Tedeschi, R.G., and L.G. Calhoun (1996). The posttraumatic growth inventory. *Journal of Traumatic Stress*, vol. 9, pp. 455-471.

Teodosijeviæ, S.B. (2003). Armed conflicts and food security. ESA Working Paper, No. 03-11. Rome: Food and Agriculture Organization of the United Nations, Agricultural and Development Economics Division. June.

Tokman, Victor (2007). Modernizing the informal sector. DESA Working Paper, No. 42. ST/ESA/2007/DWP/42. New York: United Nations.

Toya, Hideki, and Mark Skidmore (2007). Economic development and the impacts of natural disasters, *Economic Letters*, vol. 94, No. 1 (January), pp. 20-25.

U.S. Committee for Refugees (2004). *World Refugee Survey 2004*. Washington, D.C.: USCR.

U.S. Committee for Refugees and Immigrants (2007). *World Refugee Survey 2007*. Washington, D.C.: USCRI.

United Nations (2003). *World Economic and Social Survey 2003*. Sales No. E.03.II.C.1.

_____ (2004). United Nations Expert Group Meeting on Conflict Prevention, Peacebuilding and Development, United Nations Headquarters, New York, 15 November 2004. Programme and documentation available from www.un.org/esa/peacebuilding.

_____ (2005a). *World Economic and Social Survey 2005: Financing for Development*. Sales No. E.05.II.C.1.

_____ (2005b). *Report on the World Social Situation 2005: The Inequality Predicament*. Sales No. E.05.IV.5.

_____ (2006). *World Economic and Social Survey 2006: Diverging Growth and Development*. Sales No. E.06.II.C.1.

_____ (2007a). *World Economic and Social Survey 2007*: Development in an Ageing World. Sales No. E.07.II.C.1.

_____ (2007b). *Report on the World Social Situation 2007: The Employment Imperative.* Sales No. E.07.IV.9.

_____ (2008a). *World Economic Situation and Prospects 2008.* Sales No. E.08.II.C.2.

_____ (2008b) Report of the Committee for Development Policy on its tenth session (17-20 March 2008). *Official Records of the Economic and Social Council, 2008, Supplement No. 33.* E/2008/13.

_____ (forthcoming). *Macroeconomic and Growth Policies.* National Development Strategies, Policy Notes. UN/DESA, New York.

United Nations, Economic and Social Commission for Asia and the Pacific (2008). *Economic and Social Survey of Asia and the Pacific 2008: Sustaining Growth and Sharing Prosperity.* Sales No. E.08.II.F.7.

_____, Economic Commission for Latin America and the Caribbean (2003). Handbook for estimating the socio-economic and environmental effects of disasters. LC/MEX/G.5-LC/L.1874.

_____ (2007a). *Statistical Yearbook for Latin America and the Caribbean 2006.* Sales No. E/S.07.II.G.1. LC/G.2332-P/B. March.

_____ (2007b). *Socioeconomic Vulnerability to Natural Disasters in Mexico: Rural Poor, Trade and Public Response.* Prepared by Sergio O. Saldaña-Zorrilla, Disaster Evaluation Unit, ECLAC/Mexico. *Serie Estudios y Perspectivas*, No. 92. Sales No. E.07.II.G.155.

United Nations Conference on Trade and Development (1991). *Trade and Development Report 1991.* Sales No. E.91.II.D.15.

_____ (1995). *Trade and Development Report 1995.* Sales No. E.95.II.D.16.

_____ (1996). *Trade and Development Report 1996.* Sales No. E.96.II.D.6.

_____ (1997). *Trade and Development Report, 1997: Globalization, Distribution and Growth.* Sales No. E.97.II.D.8.

_____ (1998). *Trade and Development Report 1998: Financial Instability; Growth in Africa.* Sales No. E.98.II.D.6.

_____ (2000). *Trade and Development Report 2000: Global Economic Growth and Imbalances.* Sales No. E.00.II.D.19.

_____ (2003). *Trade and Development Report 2003: Capital Accumulation, Growth and Structural Change.* Sales No. E.03.II.D.7.

_____ (2006). *Economic Development in Africa: Doubling Aid: Making the "Big Push" Work.* Sales No. E.06.II.D.10.

United Nations Development Programme (1994). *Human Development Report, 1994.* New York, New York: Oxford University Press.

_____ (2004). *United Nations Development Programme Annual Report 2004: 2015: Mobilizing Global Partnerships.* New York: UNDP.

_____ (2007). *Human Development Report 2007/2008: Fighting Climate Change: Human Solidarity in a Divided World.* Basingstoke, United Kingdom: Palgrave Macmillan.

United Nations Environment Programme (2007). Environment and vulnerability: emerging perspectives. Prepared on behalf of the United Nations International Strategy for Disaster Reduction. Environment and Disaster Working Group. Geneva: UNEP Post Conflict and Disaster Management Branch.

United Nations High Commissioner for Refugees (2007). UNHCR global report 2006. Geneva: Office of the United Nations High Commissioner for Refugees.

United Nations Human Settlements Programme (UN-Habitat) (2007). *Enhancing Urban Safety and Security: Global Report on Human Settlements 2007*. London: Earthscan.

United Nations Industrial Development Organization (2002). *Industrial Development Report. 2002/2003: Competing Through Innovation and Learning*. Vienna: UNIDO.

United Nations, International Strategy for Disaster Reduction (2006). Global survey of early warning systems: an assessment of capacities, gaps and opportunities towards building a comprehensive global early warning system for all natural hazards. Report prepared at the request of the Secretary-General of the United Nations. Final version. September. Available from http://www.unisdr.org/ppew/info_resources/ewc3/Global_Survey_of_Early_Warning_Systems.pdf.

_____ and International Recovery Platform (2007). Learning from disaster recovery: guidance for decision makers. Publication from the International Recovery Platform, supported by the Asian Disaster Reduction Center (ADRC), International Strategy for Disaster Reduction (ISDR) secretariat, and the United Nations Development Programme. Preliminary version for Consultation. Geneva and Hyogo, Japan. May.

_____, and World Bank (2007). Words into action: a guide for implementing the Hyogo Framework - Hyogo Framework for Action 2005-2015: building the resilience of nations and communities to disasters. April.

_____, Office for the Coordination of Humanitarian Affairs (2008). Consolidated and flash appeals 2007. Global requirements and funding per sector as of 27 March 2008. Available from http://ocha.unog.ch/fts/reports/daily/ocha_R21_Y2007_08030307.pdf.

van der Hoeven, R., and M. Lübker (2006). External openness and employment: the need for coherent international and national policies. Paper presented at the Twenty-second G-24 Technical Group Meeting, Geneva, 16 and 17 March.

Van Hear, N. (1998). *New Diasporas*. London: University College London Press.

_____ (2003). From durable solutions to transnational relations: home and exile among refugee diasporas. *New Issues in Refugee Research* Working Paper. No. 83. Geneva: UNHCR, Evaluation and Policy Analysis Unit.

Vartiainen, Juhana (1995). The State and structural change: what can be learnt from the successful late industrializers. In *The Role of the State in Economic Change*. Ha-Joon Chang and Robert Rowthorn, eds. *WIDER Studies in Development Economics*. New York, New York: Oxford University Press.

Velásquez, A.P. (2007). The formality in property rights: determinant in the military strategy of armed actors. HiCN Working Paper, No. 39. Brighton, United Kingdom: Households in Conflict Network (HiCN), University of Sussex.

Venkatachalam, V.B. (2006). Microfinance in post-conflict Tajikistan: issue and challenges. Paper prepared for the Conference on Poverty Reduction in Conflict and Fragile States: Perspectives from the Household Level, Washington, D.C., 8 and 9 November 2006, organized by the United States Agency for International Development, the Households in Conflict Network (HiCN) and the German Institute for Economic Research (DIW, Berlin).

Verpoorten, M. (2003). The determinants of income mobility in Rwanda, 1990-2002. Katholieke Universiteit Leuven, Belgium. Mimeo.

Verwimp, P. (2005). An economic profile of peasant perpetrators of genocide: micro-level evidence from Rwanda. *Journal of Development Economics,* vol. 77, No. 2 (August), pp. 297-323.

Vos, Rob (1994). *Debt and Adjustment in the World Economy.* London: Macmillan.

_____ (1999). How to measure the cost of natural disasters? The case of "El Nino" in Ecuador, 1997-8. *European Journal of Latin American and Caribbean Studies*, vol. 67 (December), pp. 21-34.

_____ (2007). What we do and don't know about trade liberalization and poverty reduction. DESA Working Paper, No. 50. ST/ESA/2007/DWP/50. New York: United Nations.

_____ (2008). The impact of the recent surge in food prices on global poverty. New York: United Nations, Development Policy and Analysis Division, Department of Economic and Social Affairs. Mimeo.

_____, and Mariangela Parra (2008). External shocks and economic development: plus ça change? Background paper prepared for *World Economic and Social Survey 2008.* Forthcoming as a DESA Working Paper.

_____, Margarita Velasco and Edgar de Labastida (1999). Economic and social effects of El Niño in Ecuador, 1997-1998. Technical Paper Series. Washington D.C.: Inter-American Development Bank, Sustainable Development Department.

Wade, Robert H. (1990). *Governing the Market.* Princeton, New Jersey: Princeton University Press.

Weiss, John (2004). Poverty targeting in Asia: experiences from India, Indonesia, the Philippines, Peoples' Republic of China and Thailand. Tokyo: Asian Development Bank.

White, W. (2006). Procyclicality in the financial system: do we need a new macrofinancial stabilization framework? *BIS Working Paper,* No. 193, Basel: Bank for International Settlements.

Willibald, S. (2006). Does money work? cash transfers to ex-combatants in disarmament, demobilisation and reintegration processes. *Disasters*, vol. 30, No. 3 (Special issue), pp. 316-339.

Wolf, Martin (2007). Fear makes a welcome return. *Financial Times*, 14 August.

Woodward, S.L. (1995). *Balkan Tragedy: Chaos and Dissolution After the Cold War.* Washington, D.C.: Brookings Institution Press.

World Bank (1998). The World Bank's experience with post-conflict reconstruction, vol. V, Desk reviews of Cambodia, Eritrea, Haiti, Lebanon, Rwanda, and Sri Lanka. Report No. 17769. Washington, D.C.: World Bank, Operations Evaluations Department. 4 May.

_____ (1999). *Global Economic Prospects 1998/99: Beyond Financial Crisis*. Washington, D.C.: World Bank.

_____ (2001). *World Development Report 2000/2001: Attacking Poverty*. New York, New York: Oxford University Press.

_____ (2005a). Afghanistan: Managing public finances for development, vol. V, Improving public finance management in the security sector. Report No. 34582-AF. Washington, D.C.: World Bank, Poverty Reduction and Economic Management Sector Unit South Asia Region. 22 December.

_____ (2005b). Afghanistan: managing public finances for development, vol. I, Main report. Report No. 34582-AF. Washington, D.C.: World Bank, Poverty Reduction and Economic Management Sector Unit South Asia Region. 22 December.

_____ (2007). *World Development Report 2008: Agriculture for Development*. Washington, D.C.: World Bank.

_____ (2008a). Rising food prices: policy options and World Bank response. Background note for the Development Committee. Washington, D.C., March.

_____ (2008b). Background note: catastrophe risk deferred drawdown option (DDO), or CAT DDO. Available from http://go.worldbank.org/G41ZXJZO30.

_____ (2008c). *Global Monitoring report 2008*. Washington, D.C.: World Bank.

_____ Independent Evaluation Group (2006). *The World Bank in Turkey: 1993-2004: An IEG Country Assistance Evaluation*. Washington, D.C.: World Bank.

World Health Organization (2002). *World Report on Violence and Health*. Geneva: World Health Organization.

Yang, Dean (2005). International migration, human capital and entrepreneurship: evidence ,from Philippine migrant's exchange rate shocks. World Bank Policy Research Working Paper, No. 3578. Washington, D.C.: World Bank, Research Program on International Migration and Development.

Yi, I., and B.-H. Lee (2003). Changing developmental characteristics in the Korean labour market policies. Paper presented at the United Nations Research Institute for Social Development workshop on social policy in a development context, Bangkok, 30 June-1 July 2003.

Zartman, W. (1995). *Collapsed States: The Disintegration and Restoration of Legitimate Authority*. Boulder, Colorado: Lynne Rienner.

كيفيــة الحصــول على منشــورات الأمــم المتحـدة

يمكـن الحصـول على منشـورات الأمـم المتحـدة من المكتبات ودور التوزيع في جميع أنحـاء العالـم . استعلـم عنهـا من المكتبة
التي تتعامـل معها أو اكتـب إلى : الأمـم المتحـدة ، قسـم البيـع في نيويـورك أو في جنيـف .

如何购取联合国出版物

联合国出版物在全世界各地的书店和经售处均有发售。请向书店询问或写信到纽约或日内瓦的
联合国销售组。

HOW TO OBTAIN UNITED NATIONS PUBLICATIONS

United Nations publications may be obtained from bookstores and distributors throughout the
world. Consult your bookstore or write to: United Nations, Sales Section, New York or Geneva.

COMMENT SE PROCURER LES PUBLICATIONS DES NATIONS UNIES

Les publications des Nations Unies sont en vente dans les librairies et les agences dépositaires
du monde entier. Informez-vous auprès de votre libraire ou adressez-vous à : Nations Unies,
Section des ventes, New York ou Genève.

КАК ПОЛУЧИТЬ ИЗДАНИЯ ОРГАНИЗАЦИИ ОБЪЕДИНЕННЫХ НАЦИЙ

Издания Организации Объединенных Наций можно купить в книжных магазинах
и агентствах во всех районах мира. Наводите справки об изданиях в вашем книжном
магазине или пишите по адресу: Организация Объединенных Наций, Секция по
продаже изданий, Нью-Йорк или Женева.

COMO CONSEGUIR PUBLICACIONES DE LAS NACIONES UNIDAS

Las publicaciones de las Naciones Unidas están en venta en librerías y casas distribuidoras en
todas partes del mundo. Consulte a su librero o diríjase a: Naciones Unidas, Sección de Ventas,
Nueva York o Ginebra.

Litho in United Nations, New York
08-27026—June 2008—5,110
ISBN 978-92-1-109157-1

United Nations publication
Sales No. E.08.II.C.1
E/2008/50/Rev. 1
Copyright © United Nations, 2008